Fathers&
DIVORCE

For Rob

Fathers & DIVORCE

Terry Arendell

SAGE Publications
International Educational and Professional Publisher
Thousand Oaks London New Delhi

For information address:

 SAGE Publications, Inc.
2455 Teller Road
Thousand Oaks, California 91320

SAGE Publications Ltd.
6 Bonhill Street
London EC2A 4PU
United Kingdom

SAGE Publications India Pvt. Ltd.
M-32 Market
Greater Kailash I
New Delhi 110 048 India

Printed in the United States of America

Library of Congress Cataloging-in-Publication Data

Arendell, Terry.
    Fathers and divorce / Terry Arendell.
        p.   cm.
    Includes bibliographical references and index.
    ISBN 0-8039-7188-5 (acid-free paper). — ISBN 0-8039-7189-3 (pbk.
    : acid-free paper).
    1. Divorced fathers—New York (State)   I. Title.
HQ756.A8   1995
306.89—dc20   94-42213

This book is printed on acid-free paper.

95 96 97 98 99 10 9 8 7 6 5 4 3 2 1

Sage Production Editor: Gillian Dickens
Ventura Typesetter: Janelle LeMaster

CONTENTS

Part IV. The Minority Story: Innovative Responses

ACKNOWLEDGMENTS

First and foremost, I thank the men who participated in this study. They generously made time in their busy lives to talk with me about their experiences of divorce and being a divorced father. Although the analysis and direction the work takes are mine alone and will surely meet with mixed reviews from those who were interviewed, the book is possible only because of these men's willingness to share how they view and respond to their social worlds. To protect the participants' anonymity, I can issue only this collective thank you. I also thank the family attorneys, therapists, mediators, and others who work with families and spoke with me for their input into this project.

Institutional support along the way assisted me in this project. Faculty research grants from Hobart and William Smith Colleges, City University of New York (PSC-CUNY 669492), and the University of Wisconsin–Madison helped defray some of the costs of the study. I am also grateful to the University of Wisconsin, School of Family Resources and Consumer Sciences, for course release time during 1992-93, which enabled me to concentrate more fully on writing.

Numerous colleagues and friends have offered advice, support, and encouragement over the course of this project. Special words of appreciation go to Dottie and Shan Mariner, who provided warm hospitality and friendship on various occasions when I interviewed in upstate New York.

Needing particular mention here among those who offered assistance and generous friendship, and who commented on material along the way, are Joseph Marino, Alan Berkowitz, Chip Capraro, Linda Barton, Barbara Owen, Robert Perinbanayagam, and Ruth Sidel. Special words of appreciation go to Bill Aquilino and Linda Thompson for friendship, hospitality, and overall generosity. To Arlie Hochschild for her unfailing friendship, support, and guidance, the latter especially at several crucial points during the evolution of this project, I extend my heartfelt thank you. To those at Sage Publications who offered support to and expedited the publication of this work, all with good humor and patience—especially, Mitch Allen, Executive Editor; Frances Borghi, Editorial Assistant; Gillian Dickens, Special Editor; and Kate Peterson, Copy Editor—I extend my gratitude. Last, but never least, appreciation goes to my brother Randy Pitstick and my son Rob Arendell for their love, good humor, unwavering support, and warmest of family ties.

PART I

Divorce in Contemporary America

1

MEN AND DIVORCE
Unanswered Questions

Men are relatively neglected in divorce research. A dearth of information on men's perceptions and actions persists even though divorce research increased dramatically over the past several decades, as the divorce rate remained strikingly high. This neglect of men, and particularly of divorced fathers, is not unique but is characteristic of fathers and fathering more generally. For example, Furstenberg (1988) observed: "Evidence on fatherhood, though far more abundant now than a few years ago, is still sparse" (p. 194; see also LaRossa 1988; Lewis and Salt 1986; Lamb 1987, 1986).[1] Much of what is known about divorced fathers comes from interviews with custodial mothers (e.g., Arendell 1986; Kurz 1995; Hetherington, Cox, and Cox 1976, 1978, 1982) and survey research, including the National Survey of Children (Furstenberg, Morgan, and Allison 1987; Furstenberg and Nord 1985; Furstenberg, Nord, and Zill 1983), the National Survey of the High School Class of 1972 (Teachman 1991a, 1991b), the National Survey of Child Health (Zill 1988), and the National Survey of Families and Households (Seltzer, Schaeffer, and Charng 1989; Seltzer and Bianchi 1988; Seltzer 1991a, 1991b). Neither mothers' reports nor survey findings, however, give expression to fathers' views or experiences.

Men are not mere understudies in the divorce dramas being played out nationally, as might be suggested by the limited research attention given them. Rather, they are key players in postdivorce families, whatever the nature of

3

their actions and level of parental involvement. The ways in which men draw from the culture, social institutions, and their personal histories and construct and direct their actions in the changed family tell us much about their attitudes, expectations, and relationships. Moreover, men's perceptions on and behaviors in divorce suggest a partial profile of contemporary American family life.

This Study

I previously had interviewed and written about divorced mothers (Arendell 1986, 1987). I also was interested in men's perspectives on and experiences in the family, an interest that was further piqued by the college and university courses I was teaching and by the various sociocultural and political developments regarding the family and relationships between men and women. Therefore, in the early 1990s I set out to study divorced men directly. Wanting to hear from men in their own words about their family and marital dissolution experiences, I interviewed 75 divorced fathers living in various parts of New York state. In my efforts to better situate the men's reports in the current social and legal context, I also spoke with numerous family attorneys, mediators, and mental health workers involved professionally with divorced families. This, then, is an exploratory study of fathers and divorce: It is an investigation of how 75 divorced men viewed and managed their situations and relationships, particularly the former spousal and parental ones, and handled their emotional lives and identities. Focused primarily on the accounts and actions of a small number of divorced fathers, the study is also about the changing American family. So, too, it is about gender—the sociocultural constructs and expectations of masculinity and femininity, assigned to the respective biological identities of male and female—and, more specifically, about the transitions in and challenges to gender roles, definitions, and identities. This book, then, confronts an array of contemporary issues and trends.

THE PARTICIPANTS

All participants in the study were volunteers who responded to notices placed in newsletters, magazines, and newspapers or to referrals from men who were interviewed. The sample, therefore, is one of convenience, recruited through a modified snowball technique (Rubin 1976; Wiseman 1979; Morse 1992). Because the sample is self-selected and, therefore, nonrepresentative, generalizations can be made only sparingly and with caution (Babbee 1992). McCracken (1988) addressed the matter of a lack of generalizability from interview data: "The issue is not one of generalizability. It is that of access.

The purpose of the qualitative interview is not to discover how many, and what kinds of, people share a certain characteristic. It is to gain access to the cultural categories and assumptions according to which one culture construes the world" (p. 17).[2] I try to exercise caution throughout the text not to generalize from these particular men's experiences to all divorced fathers even though most participants freely extrapolated from their own situations and perspectives, positing their experiences as ones universal to divorced fathers. Although often generalizing, over two thirds of the respondents also said at some point, usually in the initial contact with me when they indicated a willingness to participate in the study, and in varying ways, "Boy, do I have a story to tell you. This is one you haven't heard before." Most saw in their situations, then, both every man's and no other man's divorce, only theirs.

The respondents ranged in age from 23 to 59 years, with the median age being 38. Sixty-four interviewees were white, three were black, four Hispanic, two Asian American, and two Native American. Two respondents were northern European immigrants who had married and divorced in the United States as naturalized citizens. Additionally, five men stressed that their ethnic identity was Italian (Italian American) and another two that theirs was Greek (Greek American).

Nearly half of the respondents had some college education, with over one-third having completed college and approximately one-sixth having earned a graduate or professional degree. The group was largely middle class but included some stably employed working-class men. Occupationally, one-third of the employed participants worked in blue-collar and two-thirds in white-collar positions. Six men were unemployed at the time of the interview, three by choice.

The length of time the respondents had been divorced or legally separated ranged from 2 to 10 years; the median time since divorcing, *postdivorce* time, was 4¾ years. Only men divorced more than 2 years were included in the study. Called selective sampling (Schatzman and Strauss 1973), this strategy was used because persons whose divorces are more recent may have uniquely different perspectives than those divorced for longer periods: The first several years following a marital separation are especially tumultuous, and it takes a year or more for most divorcing persons to regain equilibrium and stability in their lives (Hetherington 1987; Chase-Lansdale and Hetherington 1990).[3]

At the time they were interviewed, 18 men were remarried, 5 were living with a woman in a marital-like relationship, and the others were unmarried. Nationally, the remarriage rate is declining: "Based on 1985 patterns, Norton and Moorman (1987) predicted that only seventy percent of currently divorced men and women will eventually remarry" (Chase-Lansdale and Hetherington 1990, p. 109). Nevertheless, the proportion of participants who were remarried was comparatively low, particularly given that the median postdivorce period was more than 4 years (Kitson and Holmes 1992). Additionally, with only several noticeable exceptions, the men who were remarried gave scant attention in their accounts to their remarriages or present wives.

Each participant was a parent to one or more minor children born to the marriage prior to its legal dissolution. As a group, the men were parents to 195 children, ranging in age from 2 to 25, with a median age of $9\frac{1}{2}$ years. The number of children per father was from one to six, with two children being the most common. Five men each had an additional child born to a subsequent and intact marriage.

Child custody arrangements differed among the men. Sixty-one fathers were nonresidential parents. Of these, 36 were regularly "visiting" fathers, 15 were "occasionally" visiting, and 11 were "absent" fathers, meaning that they had not seen their children in at least the past 12 months. Five fathers had primary physical custody, defined as a child spending more than 10 overnights in a 2-week period with a particular parent. (The terms *physical custody* and *residential custody* are used interchangeably in the study; so too are *noncustodial fathers* and *nonresidential fathers*.) These primary custodial fathers, then, had "responsibility and control for the child on a day-to-day basis" (Mnookin, Maccoby, Albiston, and Depner 1990, pp. 40-41; see also Ferreiro 1990; Chambers 1984; Patrician 1984). Nine men had co- or shared physical custody with their former wives. Of these, four had legally assigned joint custody arrangements and the other five had informally negotiated (de facto) shared parenting, with the court order being one of sole custody. Shared or joint custody is the situation in which "both parents have responsibility for the child for 'significant periods,' " with the child typically spending four or more overnights in a 2-week period with each parent (Mnookin et al. 1990, p. 40). Shared parenting, therefore, did not necessarily involve a fully equal division of childrearing responsibility and caretaking (see Fineman 1991; Ferreiro 1990; Wolchik, Braver, and Sandler 1985; Bowman and Ahrons 1985; Mnookin et al. 1990).

Other than asking a variety of questions aimed at assessing the consistency of the participants' accounts, for example, inquiring in several ways at various times during the interview as to how often they saw their children and what they typically did with them during those times, I had no way to verify fathers' reports of parental involvement. But researchers have found parents' responses to questions about children's living and custody arrangements to be consistent with each other. For example, in their ongoing study of over 1,000 divorced families in California, Mnookin and associates (1990) found parents' answers to inquiries about a child's living arrangements and the measure of de facto residence to correspond closely: "In a majority of cases in which the child was spending four or more overnights with each parent, the parents characterized the child as living with both of them, although many others were described as residing primarily with the mother" (p. 44). And Ambert (1988), in her exploratory study of 85 divorced couples, discovered parents giving comparable accounts with regard to their basic circumstances: "One key result of this study . . . is that ex-husbands and ex-wives *within* dyads gave nearly identical responses to these normative questions, as well as to the questions pertaining to frequency of contacts—in spite of the fact that they rarely saw each other. This result indicates that certain types of information can be as accurately obtained from one spouse or, in this case, one ex-spouse as from the other. This observation can be entered in the discussion on researchers' heavy reliance on one respondent in family studies" (p. 342, italics in original).

The participants in this study overrepresent involved divorced fathers. Approximately 15%, compared to the national figure of nearly 30% (Seltzer 1991b; Seltzer and Bianchi 1988), were absent fathers. Additionally, with very few exceptions, the nonresidential fathers wanted increased access to and involvement with their offspring. A majority of fathers desired more satisfying relations with their children. Further, irrespective of their levels or kinds of parental involvement, these were not indifferent divorced fathers: They voluntarily participated in a study that called for extensive disclosure about their personal lives, relationships, and actions.

THE METHOD

The research used qualitative research methodology, which involves "a direct concern with experience as it is 'lived' or 'felt' or 'undergone.' Qualitative research . . . has the aim of understanding experience as nearly as possible as its participants feel it or live it" (Sherman and Webb 1988, p. 7; see also Denzin and Lincoln 1994; Guba and Lincoln 1994; Lincoln and Guba 1985). More exactly, "in keeping with Weber's (1947) *verstehen* tradition, qualitative methods are suited to understanding the meanings, interpretations, and subjective experiences of family members" (Daly 1992, pp. 3-4). The overall research objective was "to develop and fill out as comprehensive and accurate a picture of the area of study as conditions allow" (Blumer 1969, p. 42), the area of study specifically being divorced fathers and their experiences, actions, and feelings. The goal was to obtain individuals' versions of their divorce and parenting experiences, to hear why it is they act as they do in their particular family circumstances, and to position these perspectives and behaviors in their broader social context (e.g., Ely, Anzul, Friedman, Garner, and Steinmetz 1991).

The specific research method, in-depth interviewing, was dictated by my research goal and the underlying methodological assumptions (see, e.g., Sherman and Webb 1988; McCracken 1988; Fontana and Frey 1994; Strauss and Corbin 1990, 1994). "Interviewing offers researchers access to people's ideas, thoughts, and memories in their own words rather than in the words of the researcher" (Reinharz 1992, pp. 18-19). I obtained personal accounts through face-to-face interviews (e.g., McCracken 1988; Fontana and Frey 1994; Morse 1992). Most interviews were one-on-one, but several involved two participants. The discussions were open ended and largely unstructured and tended to be long, lasting between 2 and 5 hours. Seven respondents participated in follow-up interviews. An instrument, initially developed and revised on the basis of 15 interviews (done in another state and then adapted, where necessary, with regard to domestic relations law in New York and in response to the preliminary interviews), was used as a reference to insure that certain areas were covered during the discussions (McCracken 1988).

Often emotionally intense, the sessions were "friendly conversations" (LaRossa, Bennett, and Gelles 1981) in which the participants were free to set and change the tack of the discussion. The men's engagement level was high; nearly all were notably talkative and reflective during the interviews. Numerous men remarked that they had seldom or, more commonly, *never* shared their experiences or feelings about divorce to the extent they did during our meeting even though the divorce experience inevitably involves an array of highly emotional and personal topics (see, e.g., Riessman 1990; Gove and Shin 1989). Most participants stressed that they especially exercised caution not to disclose their deeper feelings or even fully describe their divorce and afterdivorce experiences to other men. They talked to me with the detail and emotional depth that they did, many said explicitly, *because* I am a woman.[4] They expressed gratitude and appreciation "for having the chance" to share their experiences. A nonresidential father, for example, said, "Thank God, you're making the effort to talk to us [men] instead of always just asking our wives [*sic*] about us and what we think about divorce. It's about time we get to speak for ourselves." Another person, a custodial father of two, said, "This is the first opportunity [in over 6 years], talking to you, that I have had to talk about these things. As a matter of fact, thinking about calling you the other day, I tried to think what to say. I thought, 'How did this happen?' "[5] Researchers McKee and O'Brien (1983) were told similar things in their interviews with both married and divorced English fathers.

I conducted all research preparation, face-to-face interviews, transcriptions of the recorded sessions, and data analysis. Interviews were tape recorded, transcribed, and coded. I used the grounded theory approach in which "data collection, analysis, and theory stand in reciprocal relationship with each other" (Strauss and Corbin 1990, p. 23; see also Charmaz 1988, 1990; Glaser and Strauss 1967; Strauss 1987). That is, "data collection and analysis proceed simultaneously, and both the processes and products of research are shaped from the data rather than from preconceived logically deduced theoretical frameworks" (Charmaz 1988, p. 111).[6] I used the grounded theory method's coding paradigm, techniques of theoretical sampling, and the making of constant comparisons to ensure conceptual development and density (Strauss 1987). As Strauss (1987) specified, the method "'is a *detailed* grounding by systematically' and intensively 'analyzing data, often sentence by sentence, or phrase by phrase of the field note, interview, or other document'; by 'constant comparison' data are extensively collected and coded" (pp. 22-23, quoting Glaser 1978; italics in original). Coding was done first as initial coding and was followed by more focused coding (Glaser 1978; Charmaz 1988).[7]

THEORETICAL ASSUMPTIONS

The theoretical or conceptual premises underpinning the study were those of interpretive sociology or, more precisely, symbolic interactionism, from which qualitative methodology and the grounded theory method of data analysis are derived. This perspective was complemented and enhanced by feminist conceptual approaches.[8]

Interactionist theorists Thomas and Thomas, in an often-cited statement, observed that "if [people] define situations as real, they are real in their consequences" (1928, p. 572). And feminist theorists Stanley and Wise (1983), in a compatible statement, asserted that "feminism means accepting the essential validity of other people's experiences" (p. 8). Premises posited by interactionism, and to differing degrees, shared or assumed by feminist approaches, include: The self is social, language plays a central role in the emergence of self and in social group life, and a common set of symbols and understandings is at the core of group life (Blumer 1969). Human beings are reflexive. The nature of social group life and human action is emergent, dynamic, and processual. Meanings and actions are socially constructed, and action is an outcome of the meanings ascribed to situations; meanings, then, are both experientially derived and culturally based. To understand social agents' lived experiences, actions, and situations requires obtaining access to their definitions and understandings. People engage in role-taking: "The process whereby an individual imaginatively constructs the attitudes of the other, and thus anticipates the behavior of the other" (Lauer and Handel 1977, p. 60). All knowledge is socially situated as well as socially constructed (see Mead 1934; Blumer 1969; Perinbanayagam 1985, 1988; Collins 1985; Lauer and Handel 1977; Kollock and O'Brien 1994).

Committed, epistemologically and methodologically, to the premises of symbolic interactionism, more particularly the emergent or Blumerian wing of interactionist-social constructionist tradition (Denzin 1992, pp. 1-21; see also Olesen 1994), I entered into the research process sensitized to feminist conceptual contributions, influenced by my teaching, prior research and study, political orientation, community work, and private life. I viewed human group life as being socially constructed and maintained, and I regarded society as still ordered by gender ideologies and arrangements. Hence I believed that social interactions and actions are shaped inevitably, in this sociocultural milieu, by the interrelated (socially constructed and maintained) systems of gender beliefs and stratification. I was aware of a persistent (yet challenged) patriarchal tradition and its various effects on social processes and arrangements. Although I did not set out to study divorced fathers in these terms, I was influenced by feminist perspectives. My understandings of the feminist conceptual framework served as *sensitizing concepts* (Blumer 1969).

What are feminist theories? In brief, feminist theoretical perspectives—the fundamental purpose of which are "to analyze how we think, or do not think, or avoid thinking about gender" (Flax 1989, p. 57)—illumine and analyze the character of social group life *by attending consciously to gender* (e.g., Thompson 1992, 1993; Ferree 1990; Flax 1987, 1989; Olesen 1994; Harding 1991; Cook and Fonow 1990).[9] In so doing and thus extending the theoretical analysis of meaning construction and action, feminist approaches offer a means for relating subjective experience and perspectives to the larger societal context and its institutions and practices (see Kasper 1986; Wharton 1991). Gender is a recognized primary element in the situationally dependent presentation of self (Deaux and Kite 1987; Deaux and Major 1990).

Feminist theoretical contributions broke, or have begun to break, the silence that has enveloped, to a great extent, women's history as well as their present lived experiences. Feminist theories give voice to women. Among its numerous and rich contributions, feminism challenges the historical processes of denigrating and devaluing women and their experiences, and challenges the systems of gender stratification that have held women in a secondary status relative to men. Moreover, the perspective encourages women to be conscious of the common experience of subordination and oppression (Frye 1993) and helps account for men's general reticence or inability to accept that much of their status and privilege is unearned (Goode 1982). It helps also to account for many men's unwillingness or seemingly limited capacity to take the role of the other with respect to women. Likewise, feminism offers a framework for examining and explaining the varied general character of men's and women's social relations, that is, women typically being more connected and interdependent and men more autonomous and separate (see, e.g., Chodorow 1978, 1989; Gilligan 1982, 1983; Epstein 1991). Feminism, then, expands and further focuses the interactionist premise that all knowledge is socially situated (see Harding 1991).

As indicated by feminist theorist and researcher Reinharz (1992), among others, although its focus generally is on women's experiences, "feminist research is not limited to the study of women" (p. 142). Feminism can break through the silence surrounding men's subjective experiences and private lives: Men's personal lives are often kept hidden behind and subordinated to public lives (Filene 1986). The camouflaging of men's family lives can be uncovered and their contents and dynamics explored within a feminist framework.

When I initiated and pursued the research, then, I assumed a gender-structured society (Backett 1987, p. 76). As the primary research instrument, which is how qualitative methodology sees the field researcher (e.g., Emerson 1988; Taylor and Bogdan 1984; Ely et al. 1991; Denzin and Lincoln 1994), I was not a blank slate on which participants could inscribe their experiences and viewpoints. I was not a neutral investigator, but a *situated researcher* (Richardson 1994). Given my interpretist orientation and commitment to the underlying assumptions of qualitative research, I was not unduly concerned about the inevitable lack of objectivity: I did want, and sought, to be as open to the participants and their accounts as possible and to develop a trustworthy and credible study as free as possible of my biases (e.g., Guba and Lincoln 1994; Lincoln and Guba 1985; Brink 1991).[10] The analysis was neither objective nor subjective, it was interpretive. In grappling with how to both respect the men who participated in the study and their viewpoints and provide a contextual analysis, I was influenced by sociological theorist Schwandt's (1994) argument: To understand the world of meaning, we must interpret it. "The inquirer must elucidate the process of meaning construction and clarify what and how meanings are embodied in the language and actions of social actors. To prepare an interpretation is itself to construct a reading of those meanings; it is to offer the inquirer's construction of the constructions of the actor one studies" (Schwandt 1994, p. 118). Continuing, he noted: "The process of actors' interpretations is rendered intelligible not merely through the description of word and deed, but by taking that rich description as a point of departure for formulating an interpretation of what actors are up to" (Schwandt 1994, p. 124). And grounded theorist Strauss (1987) pointed out that the "focus of analysis is *not* merely on collecting or ordering a 'mass of data, but on *organizing many ideas* which have emerged from analysis of the data' " (p. 23, italics in original).

My theoretical perspective was consistent with the developing field of (pro-feminist) men's studies, which, according to Brod (1987b), has as its subject matter "the study of masculinities and male experiences as specific and varying social-historical-cultural formations" (p. 40).[11] Within men's studies, and consistent with feminism more generally, masculinity is seen to be a problematic construct (Kimmel 1987).

Feminist Contributions
to the Study of the Family

Much of the current scholarship and research on the family, including marriage and divorce, is based in feminist work (e.g., Thorne 1993; Flax 1987, 1989; Kimmel 1987; Thompson 1992, 1993; Thompson and Walker 1989; Zinn 1989): The study of the family has been transformed by feminist theorizing (Cheal 1991; Morgan 1975, 1985). Within the conceptual framework, a broad array of family issues are investigated, including the family as a social and ideological institution, dynamics of family life, variations in family experiences, and demographic trends and transitions in family arrangements and composition. Feminist family studies has propelled and clarified Burgess's (1926) earlier, influential interactionist assertion that the family is "a unity of interacting personalities [by which] is meant a living, changing, growing thing" (p. 5), showing that family experiences vary and, indeed, are often structured along the lines of gender. After stressing the value of interactionism's approach to family life, for example, in seeing family life and experiences as being dynamic, involving shifting patterns as behavior is negotiated and renegotiated, family theorist Cheal observed (1991), "From a feminist standpoint, the interactionist perspective has been criticized for obscuring asymmetry in relations between women and men, and for encouraging a benign view of family life that ignores the capacity of men to impose their definitions of reality upon women. . . . Prompted by emergent gender issues, symbolic interactionists have had to recognize that families are not always united" (p. 138). And feminist theorist Ferree (1990) argued that "the feminist perspective redefines families as arenas of gender and generational struggles, crucibles of caring and conflict, where claims for an identity are rooted, and separateness and solidarity are continually created and contested" (p. 880). Furthermore, "feminists agree that male dominance within families is part of a wider system of male power, is neither natural nor inevitable, and occurs at women's cost" (Ferree 1990, p. 866).

This research brought me more forcefully to a gender perspective. Gender as a central theme and category emerged from the data. It was the obtained accounts—more precisely, the predominant shared themes expressed and lines of action described by the respondents—that focused my attention on gender more definitively and led me to a feminist-interactionist perspective. Through this study of a group of New York divorced fathers, I came to take gender seriously, to paraphrase critical theorist Morgan (1981, 1990).

Although most participants in the study would not have phrased it as such, they were taking gender seriously, very seriously. Many talked repeatedly, in various ways, about "being a man" and "having to show that I wasn't a wimp," for example, and most spoke at length about the essential differences between men and women. As interpretist sociologists Denzin and Lincoln (1994) observed: "Subjects, or individuals, are seldom able to give full explanations of their actions or intentions: all they can offer are accounts, or stories, about what they did and why" (p. 12). How these men responded to divorce was entirely entwined with notions held about masculinity. "Being a man" was a master identity, a *master status* (Hughes 1945), which both overshadowed and dictated their responses to the divorce situation. And because they were involved in major life transitions, divorce and its aftermath, gender identities and gendered interactional dynamics became subject to explicit negotiation rather than remaining largely invisible and taken-for-granted social phenomena (Goffman 1975). As Foote (1981) explained, it is "unfamiliar situations" that call forth "taken as given identities" (p. 338). Divorce brought, or pulled more sharply, into question notions of their own manhood—assumptions about self and place in the family and world (Riessman 1990; Arendell 1992a, 1992b, 1994b). Thus, although when I began this research I expected to develop a study specifically about men's postdivorce parenting activities and relationships, the participants quickly made me aware that they were talking more broadly about their lives *as men*. To understand them as parents, divorced fathers, required examining their notions about manhood. Most, indeed, were far less concerned about fathering or the quality of their relationships with their children than they were with their identities as adult men. As Rocco Capraro (personal correspondence, 1993) observed, although the discourse was about divorce, the meta-discourse was about being a man.

The Findings in Brief

Remarkable similarities existed among the men's richly detailed accounts. These commonalities prevailed despite the variations in their circumstances. Overriding their differences, for the most part, was their shared membership as men in the masculine culture. Franklin (1988) described this culture: "Men in America share values, meanings and material items—in essence, a culture, a separate world. . . . Within certain boundaries, most men in America do many things in strikingly similar ways despite variations in income, race, ethnicity, political beliefs, educational levels, and so on. American men's penchant for violence, competitive sports, high status, viewing women as sex objects, and self-reliance, coupled with their disdain for identifying self with anything vaguely feminine, indicating physical or mental weaknesses, and passivity are all examples of perceptions, attitudes, and the like shared by most men in America" (p. 40). The men also shared, as employed men and irrespective of their occupational differences, the dominant middle-class culture with its focus on material consumption and the success ethic, both of which, as sociologist Halle (1987) argued, have greatly eroded the boundaries between the working and middle classes. Thus, although there was some racial, ethnic, and religious diversity within the group, the variations were overshadowed by the shared themes of masculinity, by the *masculine ethic* (Jaggar 1983).

Predominant in the men's accounts were several discursive themes. The majority of men perceived themselves to be victimized and their rights violated by divorce. Consequently, they were necessarily on the defensive in their actions and interpretations of events. Another common thesis, one on which their victimization was pinned, was a belief in gender (sex) differences and an underlying assumption of male superiority.[12] Related to both their victimization and belief in differences between men and women, divorce was understood as a battle—a "war between the sexes," in general, and with the former wife, in particular. Additionally, the family after divorce was understood to be a *broken* family from which they were actually or potentially marginalized. Men's, especially noncustodial fathers', place in the family altered by divorce was often unclear. Despite the high divorce rate and extensive public discussion about *changing men* and the *new father,* cultural signposts for fathering after divorce were scarce. Those that were located or established were often inconsistent, even contradictory. Fatherhood after divorce was, to appropriate Cherlin's (1978) description of remarriage, an "incomplete institution," as was the postdivorce family itself.

Impression management and emotional management were primary social processes evident in all of the participants' accounts, and the character expected of these processes was an additional shared and primary theme. That is, despite the situational ambiguity and stressful circumstances related to divorce, the men adhered to a definition of self that required a persistent demonstration, in action and comportment, of authority, confidence, and competency. They were not just *being* men, but were "doing gender" (West and Zimmerman 1987). But, importantly, they were not just role players in family dramas, specifically husbands and fathers, former husbands and divorced fathers, but were gendered persons. And because these identities had been brought into question by divorce in dramatic and far-reaching ways, they expended major efforts to reestablish and reassert their identities as men. Indeed, identity maintenance was typically at the core of their actions and perceptions. Despite feelings of dissatisfaction and even vulnerability, most gave the appearance that they were secure in their identities (Goffman 1959), convinced of the correctness of their actions. Such impression management did not come easily; it required extensive effort and exacted a high price in the quality of their family relationships.

A BIFURCATED STORY

This descriptive analysis, based on the narrative accounts of 75 divorced men who are fathers, contains two tales. Overlapping in many respects, the stories are quite distinctive in others. The stories are most similar in the portrayals of marital dissolution and divorce situations. The tales diverge along two rather distinctive trajectories with respect to the respondents' priorities and behaviors.

The participants, in response to divorce and the assorted changes it brought, pursued certain *strategies* of action. Strategies, consisting often of "consciously intended" lines of action, are "the techniques by means of which people manage the situations of their everyday lives" (Lofland 1978, p. 14). According to cultural theorist Swidler (1986), a strategy is an enduring way of organizing a life that makes sense given the structural and symbolic context in which people find themselves. Strategies allow for human agency while acknowledging other forces such as the influences of a society's organization (see also Mead 1934; Blumer 1969). More specifically, as these men sought "to sustain a certain gendered ego ideal" (Hochschild 1990), they responded to and maneuvered in the situation of divorce by employing *gender strategies*. Defined by Hochschild (1989), "a gender strategy is a plan of action through which a person tries to solve problems at hand, given the cultural notions of gender at play. To pursue a gender strategy, a man draws on beliefs about manhood and womanhood, beliefs that are forged in early childhood and thus anchored to deep emotions. He makes a connection between how he thinks about his manhood, what he feels about it, and what he does. The term 'strategy' refers to both his plan of action and to his emotional preparations for pursuing it" (p. 15). Preservation of identity is integral to gender strategies; they, then, are a composite of attitudes, meanings, feelings, and behaviors.

The respondents' strategies fell along a continuum that ranged from *traditionalist* to *innovative*, that is, from gender conformity to gender subversion (Bem 1993). There was far more gender conformity than subversion. Together, the discursive themes and strategies of action constituted a *masculinist discourse of divorce*. How these themes and strategies affected these participants' parenting activities and relationships after divorce is a primary subject of this book.[13]

The Majority Story: Traditionalization

Broadly outlined, the story shared by a large majority of these divorced fathers was one of perceived injustice and discrimination, resistance, and frustration and discontent. It was also, paradoxically, a story of self-confidence and certainty. Involving little role-taking or self-reflectiveness, the majority story was one of men preoccupied with identity maintenance and repair and self-assertion. These men sought answers, direction, and affirmation in divorce by looking to customary views and approaches. They acted in largely conventional ways, relying on the practices and tactics of the gender belief system. Not unlike fathers who respond to the stresses and uncertainty of new parenthood after the birth of a first child by assuming a more conventional division of labor (LaRossa and LaRossa 1989), they engaged primarily in the processes of *traditionalization.* To these divorced fathers, turning to that which was familiar entailed a search for definition and task assignment. But of equal or greater importance, traditionalization also involved efforts to restore a more accustomed sense of self.

Responding in traditional ways to unfamiliar and stressful situations is not, of course, unique to these divorced fathers (or to the new fathers in the LaRossa and LaRossa [1989] study). As Swidler (1986) explained, "People do not readily take advantage of new structural opportunities which would require them to abandon established ways of life. This is not because they cling to cultural values, but because they are reluctant to abandon familiar strategies of action for which they have the cultural equipment. Because cultural expertise underlies the ability of both individuals and groups to construct effective strategies of action, such matters as the style or ethos of action and related ways of organizing authority and cooperation are enduring aspects of individual and, especially, of collective life" (p. 281). Moreover, in addition to relying on the familiar culture of masculinity, these men were pushed toward conventional understandings and actions by prevailing social arrangements and practices. For instance, the only consistent legal or social expectation of them as divorced fathers was that they continue contributing economic support. Being a "good provider" remains a standard role for American men even as wives obtain and retain employment and as gender roles are challenged (Bernard 1981; Franklin 1988; May and Strikwerda 1992b).

Men engaging in the processes of traditionalization typically did not separate their children and the parental role from the former wife or the former spousal role. Relational boundaries were blurred. That is, in many instances, despite assorted rationalizations, antagonisms and resentments toward the former wife preceded or interfered with concern for children's well-being and the father-child relationship.

Men engaged in processes of traditionalization embraced two types of fathers: traditionalist and *neo-traditionalist*.[14] Importantly, these two types of fathers were more similar than different in their overall responses to divorce; it was in their consideration of their children where they sometimes diverged from each other in their actions. Their behaviors and attitudes constituted variations on a theme rather than being qualitatively and significantly different.

Traditionalist fathers, passionately committed to resisting perceived oppression, were generally inflexible in their conduct and views and had very limited, if any, relationships with their children. Thirty five fathers fell into this group. The other 31 (of the 66 total engaged in the processes of traditionalization) shifted some in their behaviors between active resistance and reluctant adjustment. Like the others, they felt victimized by divorce and were preoccupied with the former wife but, on occasion, they minimized their resistance. These neo-traditionalist fathers sometimes gave primary consideration to their parental relationships and children's well-being rather than to their determination to oppose the former wife. A further comparison is that, whereas the traditionalist fathers were relatively consistent in their actions and perspectives, the neotraditionalists vacillated: Tensions between the primacy of the former wife and concerns for parenting and their children led them to shift and waver.

The Minority Story: Innovation

The second divorce tale, not without elements of the first, was one of men caught up in both adaptation and creativity. In contrast to the others, these nine participants engaged in the processes of innovation. They actively rejected what they perceived to be men's standard behaviors in divorce and searched out and developed strategies more congruent with their objective to actively parent their children. Child-centeredness prevailed in their accounts and actions. Seeking to protect their offspring and enhance their development, and to ensure their own parental involvement, these men conscientiously and consistently collaborated with their former spouses. Cooperation rather than resistance was the ultimate goal, even if sometimes elusive. Each of these men had established, together with their former wives, some type of parenting partnership. They actively sought to create "best case scenarios" in divorce and were absorbed with family relationships and their maintenance, repair, and nurture. These fathers not only expressed affection for their offspring but actively engaged in parenting work (Tronto 1989). Unlike the majority of respondents, these men were satisfied, even pleased, with their parenting. At the same time, they saw themselves as defying the norms of masculinity that led them to question their identity as men. Traditionally, caring for others, including one's children, has been gendered, defined as women's work (Tronto 1989).[15] Thus self-confidence and uncertainty coexisted for these nine innovative fathers. Feeling fairly secure about their parenting, they were dubious about their identities as men.

Before turning to a more detailed consideration of these 75 men's narratives and behaviors, I review issues of contemporary divorce, family, gender, and fatherhood, setting the context for the respondents' accounts and actions in Chapter 2. In Part II, Chapters 3 and 4, I investigate, specifically, the masculinist discourse of divorce: the predominant discursive themes and related legal and financial experiences. Part III tells the story of the men engaged in conventional responses to divorce. Chapter 5 examines these men's relationships with their former wives. Accounts and analyses of traditionalist and neo-traditionalist fathers are given in Chapters 6 and 7, respectively. Then, in Part IV, I examine the narratives and situations of the nine men caught up in adaptation and innovation. In Chapter 8, the focus is these men's parenting associations with their former wives, and in Chapter 9 the focus is on their parenting activities and parent-child relationships. Last, Chapter 10 offers a brief synopsis of the study and then moves to a more in-depth treatment of divorce-related policy issues. Here attention shifts to the needs of dependent children who are part of families caught up in and affected by the ending of their parents' marriages and so to overall family functioning.

Notes

1. Reviewing the literature, Basow (1992) noted: "Although there is no mandate for fatherhood comparable to the Motherhood Mandate, gender roles and stereotypes still strongly affect father-child relationships. One effect is the paucity of research on paternal relationships, at least until recently, especially in comparison with research on maternal relationships" (p. 246).

2. Regarding family research specifically and the limitations of qualitative exploratory research, LaRossa and Wolf (1985) argued: "Exploratory, descriptive work generates more discoveries per hour expended than large scale quantitative verification or experimentally designed studies in lab" (p. 538).

3. Hetherington (1987), discussing the 6-year follow-up of a longitudinal study, observed: "Most studies, including this one, find that the first 2 to 3 years following divorce might be regarded as the crisis period during which most children and many parents experience emotional distress, psychological and behavior problems, disruptions in family functioning and problems in adjusting to new roles, relationships, and life changes associated with the altered family situation" (p. 185).

4. A challenging and necessary step to reaching full completion of this research project is the further ferreting out, from the tape recorded interviews and written field notes, of the cross-gender interactional dynamics and their effects on both the discussions and my interview probes, the obtained accounts, and analyses. But, based on my preliminary analyses, it is clear that certain benefits accrued to me because I was a woman interviewing men on this topic. Gender was an ever present component of the field research itself (see also, e.g., McKee and O'Brien 1983; Oakley 1981; Warren 1989; Fontana and Frey 1994). Through further study of both qualitative

and feminist methodologies, an undertaking prompted at least in part by the findings of this study, I came to realize that every facet of the research process was influenced by gender: the research topic and questions I brought to the study; personal as well as research biography; choice and interpretation of the theoretical perspectives and concepts used; character and timing of interview probes; interactional dynamics of the open-ended, unfolding interview conversation or discussion; data analysis; writing and rewriting of journal article and manuscript drafts; and public presentations of the research findings (Arendell 1994a). This awareness is compatible with recent intellectual developments, namely, poststructuralism, postmodernism, and cultural studies (e.g., Denzin and Lincoln 1994; Denzin 1992; Bordo 1990).

5. Sandelowski, Holditch-Davis, and Harris (1992), in their study of couples' infertility, had a similar finding: "The transformation of the interview situation into one resembling a friendly conversation can cause couples to forget the investigative parameters of the situation and reveal what they might not otherwise have revealed. . . . Couples expressed no detrimental effects, and, in many cases, stated that the interviews were beneficial and even therapeutic to them" (p. 306).

6. As described by Charmaz (1991), regarding her study of people living with chronic illness, and pertinent to my research analytical procedures: "In the grounded theory method, the researcher uses his or her emerging analysis to direct the data collection. Hence, my interview questions developed in theoretical scope and usefulness during the course of the study. The questions reflected my deepening knowledge of the area, as well as growing skill as an interviewer. Second, the grounded theory methods place emphasis on developing theoretical analyses of the collected materials rather than on statistical verification procedures" (p. 274).

7. For full discussions of grounded theory, see Glaser and Strauss (1967), Strauss (1987), Charmaz (1988, 1990, 1991). Sandelowski and associates' (1992) characterization of their use of grounded theory is pertinent: "Our interpretation of grounded theory had a phenomenological cast (Charmaz 1990, p. 1164); as the study progressed, it also acquired a narrative cast (Polkinghorne 1988); experiences were rendered in story form, and were embellished, revised, and (re)created" (p. 311).

8. Portions of this argument were presented at the American Sociological Association Meetings, August 1994, Los Angeles, California (Arendell 1994b). Other family researchers also have used a synthetic interactionist-feminist approach although the language used to identify the theoretical perspective sometimes differs. A list of such researchers includes but is not limited to Hochschild (1983, 1989), Backett (1982, 1987), Pestello and Voydanoff (1991), Risman and Schwartz (1989), Risman (1989), Cohen (1989), and Gerson (1993). Such approaches are advocated, in differing ways, by various theorists, including Ferree (1990), Thompson (1992, 1993), Kasper (1986), and Morgan (1975, 1981, 1985, 1990).

9. Cook and Fonow's (1990) analysis of feminist methodology identifies five central "feminist ways of knowing": (a) acknowledging the pervasive influence of gender, (b) uncovering the links between gender and other asymmetric systems, (c) focusing on consciousness raising, (d) rethinking the relationship between researcher and researched, and (e) emphasizing empowerment and transformation. See Richardson and Taylor (1993) for an overview of these assertions.

10. For criteria by which to assess qualitative research, see, for example, Brink (1991), Denzin and Lincoln (1994), Ely et al. (1991), Guba and Lincoln (1994), McCracken (1988), Schwandt (1994), and Strauss and Corbin (1990).

11. Franklin (1988) characterized the emerging discipline: "Major aspects of Men's Studies must be devoted to men's relationship to society, men's relationships with each other, and men's relationships with others. This means that our assumptions about the social order, social interaction, and social behavior are important considerations" (p. 19). For additional discussions of men's studies, see Brod (1987a, 1987b), Kimmel and Messner (1989), Kimmel (1987), and Clatterbaugh (1990, 1992).

12. Most participants used the language of sex differences and sex roles rather than gender differences and gender roles. Consistent with the social science usage of recent years, however, I use gender throughout the text except when individual men are being quoted directly. Gender refers to socially constructed and learned behaviors, traits, and expectations. Sex, in contrast, refers to physiological differences (Andersen 1993; Basow 1992).

13. Although unique because it involves divorced fathers specifically, this conceptualization of strategies of action ranging from traditional to innovative is not unlike others offered by various researchers studying men in domestic life or with respect to gender conformity. Hochschild (1989), in examining dual-career couples' division of domestic labor and rationales, characterized husbands' and wives' strategies of action as traditional, transitional, and egalitarian (see also Gilbert 1985). And, for example, Nordstrom (1986), investigating married men's attitudes and behaviors, characterized men as nontraditional and traditional.

14. The traditionalist and neo-traditionalist "types" of father roughly parallel those described by May and Strikwerda (1992a) as traditional and augmented traditional. The third type of divorced father in the study, the innovative, nurturing father, is similar to May and Strikwerda's nurturing father. According to them, the traditional father "promotes a conventional image of strength, the provider and arranger of all things in the public realm" (May and Strikwerda 1992a, p. 80). In modern society this father has become a "bureaucratic manager," whose primary responsibility "is that of disciplinarian, and secondarily one of role model for male children" (May and Strikwerda 1992a, p. 80). The augmented traditional father (or neo-traditional) is more complex, a transitional figure: "Here the central aspects of the traditional father are maintained but with an acknowledgment of the pressures of the dual career family. This father cooks dinner when his partner is working late, or at least takes the kids out to dinner. He also does the laundry occasionally, and a bit of light housekeeping when things get really bad. He consoles and cares for his children on occasion, but perhaps as much to help out his partner as for the sake of the children directly. She is the one who worries about the children's overall development, their clothes and the household. Even if the time commitment of such a father to nontraditional male parenting activities is considerable, it is not a commitment that is central to his self-conception" (May and Strikwerda 1992a, pp. 80-81). May and Strikwerda assessed each of these types as being inadequate and "quite anemic" models of fathering. The augmented traditional father is less open to criticism because he is more involved with the care of his children than is the traditional father. Nevertheless, the augmented traditional fathers also are deficient in that they do not "identify themselves as nurturers and they will have difficulty being motivated to be other than mere helpers, even though they may actually do as much child-rearing work as their partners" (1992a, p. 82). The ideal father type, in the May and Strikwerda schematic, is the nurturing father: "The ideal of fatherhood can be defined by reference to that dimension of nurturance which involves *caring* and *rearing toward maturity* involving nourishment, but also humane discipline and creative education into the public domain" (1992a, p. 90, italics in original). The nurturing father, who cares for as well as cares about his children, corresponds in type to Rotundo's (1985) androgynous father: "A good father is an active participant in the details of day-to-day child care. He involves himself in a more expressive and intimate way with his children, and he plays a larger part in the socialization process that his male forebears had long since abandoned to their wives" (p. 17). Referring to men in intact families, Rotundo noted that the androgynous father emerged especially since 1970 and is less a parenting activity than an advocacy, particularly by women. See also Lamb (1981, 1986, 1987). May and Strikwerda (1992a) identified a fourth type of father, the "sensitive new age guy." This father "seeks the kind of fulfillment in his children that he hasn't found in any of his other relationships" (May and Strikwerda 1992a, p. 81). Having a "hunger for intimacy" (Ehrensaft 1987), this father stresses intimacy and reciprocity in his relations, including parenting. Three men in the present study resembled the new-age father in their parenting, but their parenting behaviors were often

undermined by their largely conventional actions in other areas. Thus these men resemble the neo-traditionalist fathers in the study and are classified as such.

15. According to Tronto (1989), "If caring involves a commitment, then caring must have an object. Thus, caring is necessarily relational. We say that we care for or about something or someone. We can distinguish 'caring about' from 'caring for' based on the objects of caring. Caring about refers to less concrete objects; it is characterized by a more general form of commitment. Caring for implies a specific, particular object that is the focus of caring. The boundaries between caring about and caring for are not so neat as these statements imply. Nonetheless, this distinction is useful in revealing something about the way we think of caring in our society because this distinction fits with the engendered category of caring in our society. . . . Caring is engendered in both market and private life. Women's occupations are the caring occupations, and women do the disproportionate amount of caretaking in the private household. To put the point simply, traditional gender roles in our society imply that men care about but women care for" (pp. 173-74).

2

AT THE CROSSROADS
OF FAMILY AND GENDER
Divorce in Context

The particulars of these men's experiences and perspectives need to be positioned in social time and place to be fully meaningful and explicable. Their lives as divorced fathers unfolded in a specific social and historical context, a time of rapid and dramatic changes in family life and individual roles and activities.

Family

The assertion that the American family is being changed by divorce has become commonplace. Often viewed as a private trouble between couples, divorce is also a public issue (Mills 1959; Riessman 1990). Men and women ending their marriages are part of the continuing "divorce revolu-

AUTHOR'S NOTE: An earlier version of this chapter was given as a keynote address at the Association of American Family and Conciliation Courts annual meeting, May 1993. An abbreviated version of this chapter, specifically examining divorce as a gendered issue, appeared in Arendell, Terry, "Divorce: It's a Gender Issue" in the *Family Advocate,* August 1994. Reprinted by permission.

tion." Under way in its present form for some 30 years, the divorce revolution involves persistently high rates of marital dissolution; legal reforms, especially the shift to no-fault divorce statutes; and other social and demographic changes (Weitzman 1985; Jacob 1988; Kay 1990; Riley 1991). Subjected to sustained challenge and concern in this period of rapid and extensive change is the institution of family (e.g., Thorne 1993; Skolnick 1991). Additionally scrutinized are the conventions of gender. More specifically, the traditional notions and practices of masculinity and fathering are questioned (Kimmel 1987; Connell 1987; Seidler 1989, 1991, 1992; May and Strikwerda 1992a; Gerzon 1982). Various dominant cultural values, pertaining to both family and gender, are contested also (Bellah, Madsen, Sullivan, Swidler, and Tipton 1985; Hunter 1991).

THE DIVORCE RATE

The divorce rate more than doubled between the early 1960s and the mid-1970s (Cherlin 1981), and by 1975 over a million divorces took place annually. Although a leveling off occurred during the 1980s, the divorce rate remains high. In 1990, 1,175,000 marriages ended in divorce. If trends continue, three in five first marriages will be dissolved (Martin and Bumpass 1989); the divorce rate for second marriages is likely to be even higher, as it is now (U.S. Bureau of the Census 1992).

Divorce occurs disproportionately in shorter term marriages, among younger adults who are parents. Children are involved in approximately two-thirds of all divorces. In 1988, 1,044,000 dependent offspring experienced their parents' divorce; for each divorce decree in 1988, .89 minor children were involved (U.S. Bureau of the Census 1992). Divorcing women's and men's median ages, respectively, were 33 and 35 in 1988 (U.S. Bureau of the Census 1992), but the marital dissolution rate among older persons is increasing (Uhlenberg, Cooney, and Boyd 1990).

No-Fault Divorce Laws

In every state until 1969, a spouse seeking divorce had to sue the other. The primary grounds for divorce throughout the 20th century were adultery, cruelty, and desertion (Kay 1990; Glendon 1987; Riley 1991). Beginning in California, states implemented no-fault dissolution statutes and moved away from fault grounds. Within 5 years, nearly all states had some form of no-fault divorce (Freed and Walker 1989). "The transition from reform proposal to statutory orthodoxy was shorter for no-fault divorce than for any of the other law reform proposals of its era" (Zimring 1990,

p. vii). Reducing expense, acrimony, and fraud in resolving domestic matters were goals of the reforms (Rhode and Minow 1990, p. 195). Marriage is now "a contract terminable at will" (Kay 1990, p. 15), although specific criteria vary by state. For example, although in most states one spouse can obtain a divorce without the other's agreement, unilateral no-fault divorce is available in New York only when there is mutual consent between the spouses and voluntary adherence for a 1-year period to a separation agreement (Freed and Walker 1989; Sugarman 1990; *Family Law of the State of New York* 1990).

One certain outcome of no-fault divorce is the increased divorce rate; what its other effects are remains controversial. Specifically debated is whether no-fault divorce has worsened women's and their children's economic circumstances. Weitzman (1985), for example, concluded that divorce law reform adversely affects women, whereas others, including Mnookin et al. (1990) and Sugarman (1990), concluded otherwise. Contested also is the nature of the relationship between rules governing divorce and property settlements, spousal support, child support, and child custody (e.g., Glendon 1987; Sugarman 1990; Kay 1990; Garrison 1990; Riley 1991; Jacob 1988).

No-fault divorce statutes are only part of the changing divorce regime: "Even more broadly, discussion of no-fault comprehends not merely the formal law and its changes but also the judicial application and enforcement of the divorce regime. Most widely, some look at no-fault as part of the general environment in which the new system is functioning. That environment can include, for example, the roles of men and women in the labor force and in home life, the place of stepparents and biologic parents after second marriages, and the public commitment to the financial well-being of those involved in divorce" (Sugarman 1990, p. 3). Assessing the legal reforms associated with no-fault, Rhode and Minow (1990) posed concerns about the lack of attention to gender inequality and public responsibilities: "In our view, the most pressing problems stem from the inadequacy of public commitments both to equality between the sexes and to the quality of life, especially for children, following divorce. Addressing those concerns will require more fundamental reforms, not just in divorce law but in the broader family, work, and welfare policies with which it intersects" (p. 191).

FAMILY CHANGES

Numerous and multifaceted, family transitions include interrelated demographic, structural, and ideological shifts. Primary demographic trends, in addition to the high rate of divorce, include a decreasing birth-rate, closer spacing of births, a rising number and proportion of families headed by an unmarried woman, and an aging of the population (Cherlin 1988; Skolnick and Skolnick 1994). The conventional arrangement, formed on the basis of a heterosexual marital union and in which the husband is the income earner and the wife the caretaker, represents fewer than 15% of all American families (U.S. Bureau of the Census 1992). Assorted family arrangements exist, viable alternatives to the traditional nuclear family. Indeed, a "typical" family is likely "to be one of four other kinds: the two-earner family, the single-parent family, the 'binuclear family' of remarriage, or the 'empty nest' couple whose children have grown up and moved out" (Skolnick and Skolnick 1994, p. 1).

The Western family is the target of popular attention. For example, much rhetorical attention focused on the family in the 1992 U.S. political campaigns as various candidates, including presidential ones, claimed superior expertise for protecting and enhancing the well-being of American families. Entwined with the résumés offered were righteous claims to the moral high ground of family life. Much of the current welfare reform debate centers on definitions of and transitions in the family (Fraser and Gordon 1994; Fraser 1989).

Popular attitudes about marriage and the family are discordant. Social expectations for family behavior have eased, and an emphasis on individual freedom has expanded. With respect to marriage and both sexual activity and parenthood outside of marriage, the range of individual choices has grown (Thornton 1989, p. 887; Skolnick and Skolnick 1994). However, these trends and changes are not fully congruent: "Although prescriptive social norms concerning a significant number of issues have weakened while the norm of tolerance has expanded, these trends do not represent an endorsement of previously proscribed values and behavior. More specifically, in the family arena the normative and attitudinal shifts toward tolerance of a broad range of behavior does not mean that there has been an increased endorsement of remaining single, getting divorced, or reversing the roles of women and men" (Thornton 1989, p. 891). As rhetorical arguments wax and wane, and family and marital transitions continue, individuals struggle to reconcile conflicts between values. Marriage poses particular problems, especially as individuals anticipate and seek a modern, companionate relationship. As Kasper (1986) observed: "The idealized and unfulfilled cultural expectations of marriage which contrast so deeply with the dissatisfactions of marriage as a lived personal experience for both women and men may account for, in part, the proliferation of marriage counseling manuals and the high divorce rate in contemporary society" (p. 42). Examining the findings that parenthood may have negative consequences on the psychological well-being of adults, McLanahan and Adams (1987) concluded, "The flow of women into the labor market during the past two decades has meant a decline in the time available for childcare, and we expect that couples will continue to contest the division of parental responsibilities. Husbands will resist in part because of self interest and in part because norms are slow to change, even in the face of changing circumstances. Moreover, although some husbands are assuming a greater share of household responsibilities, it is doubtful that a satisfactory resolution to this struggle can be obtained simply through a readjustment of gender roles on an individual or couple, given the time demands on two working parents" (p. 254).

The family institution is the object of increased legislative and policy consideration. The growth of state intervention into the family is attributed by social theorist Morgan (1985, p. 5) to the interrelated crises in Western capitalism and the social welfare state (see also Abramovitz 1988; Gordon 1990b; Fraser 1989). The state, especially through its social welfare policies, attempts to minimize the adverse effects of the breakdown of traditional institutions and community. Family crises are entangled with the economic system: "Modern conservatism, which embraces both traditional gender roles and market capitalism, is at odds with itself. On the one hand, it seeks to hold onto the traditional family with its male breadwinner. On the other, it embraces a market capitalism that drives down real wages, makes many workers redundant, and refuses to pay a family wage, thus forcing more and more families to have multiple breadwinners. In other words, capitalism produces the very conditions that prevent the traditional family from surviving" (Clatterbaugh 1990, p. 152; see also Martin 1990; Bellah 1992).

The family also has been the subject of increased scholarly attention (e.g., Thomas and Wilcox 1987; Beutler, Burr, Bahr, and Herrin 1989; Sprey 1990; Cheal 1991; Morgan 1985): "The study of the family used to seem to many one of the dullest of endeavors. Now it appears as one of the most provocative and involving" (Giddens 1987, p. 23). Family theorizing has been energized especially by feminist theoretical developments (Morgan 1985; Cheal 1991; Thompson 1992). Feminist theory "attempts to situate the everyday events of women's and men's lives in an analysis that links our personal and collective experience to an understanding of the structure of gender relationships in society and culture. Feminists also claim that what we know, both intellectually and practically, is thoroughly infused with gendered assumptions about the character of the social world, its problems, its inhabitants, and its meaning" (Anderson 1993, p. 296). Feminist theoretical and political contributions have led to a "rethinking of the family" (Thorne 1982) and have had a "big bang" effect on family scholarship (Cheal 1991).

The Family Debate

The future of the family is hotly debated and disputed. On one side, calls are made for an undermining of the traditions of patriarchy (Jaggar 1983; Barrett and McIntosh 1982; Thorne 1993). For example, Okin (1989) argued that "family life as typically practiced in our society is not just, either to women or to children. Moreover, it is not conducive to the rearing of citizens with a strong sense of justice. . . . Any just and fair solution to the urgent problem of women's and children's vulnerability must encourage and facilitate the equal sharing by men and women of paid and unpaid work, of productive and reproductive labor. We must work toward a future in which all will be likely to choose this mode of life. A just future would be one without gender" (pp. 170-71), in that gender, as it now exists, inherently entails inequities.[1] A move away from a monolithic view of family is urged as is recognition of the viability of diverse family arrangements and experiences (e.g., Thorne 1982, 1993; Dill 1988).

On the other side, concerns are voiced that the family is in decline and its increasingly pluralist social character fatally flawed.[2] Whitehead (1993), for instance, contended that "these new families are not an improvement on the nuclear family, nor are they even just as good, whether you look at outcomes for children or outcomes for society as a whole. In short, far from representing social progress, family change represents a stunning example of social regress" (p. 80).[3] And similarly, Popenoe (1988) asserted that "in response to age-old concerns about family decline, many a family scholar of late has been fond of stating that families may have changed somewhat, but that these changes have few negative implications; the institution of the family is still strong and enduring, and there is little about which to be concerned. I do not take such an optimistic view. I see the family as a perishable social institution that is being quietly corroded by some of the social and cultural currents of our time" (p. 328).

A restoration of traditional family arrangements and dynamics—"traditional family values"—is sought by those believing the family is endangered (e.g., Popenoe 1988; Whitehead 1993; Blankenhorn, Bayme, and Elshtain 1992). "Nostalgia for a time when life was simpler is a common response to such disorienting change in family life and in professional life. One result is that people often find it comforting to think of a past when family values were strong, and when everyone knew the value of family living. The decade of the 1950s is a common reference point for such nostalgia" (Cheal 1991, p. 3). Feminists, in contrast, propose alternative visions of a just and equitable society and reject calls for a return to past family arrangements. For example, "the family that conservatives defend is an idealized, middle-class patriarchal family. Feminists have shown that many drawbacks of that family ideal, and its largely ideological nature is becoming ever more apparent in the present period of widely varying and fluid family forms. This variation is the result of demographic, economic, and social change, not of moral decline" (Thorne 1993, p. 24; see also Ferguson 1989; hooks 1984).[4] Critique, innovation, and uncertainty, on the one hand, and nostalgia and lamentation, on the other, surround the family cacophonously.

Gender

Increasingly over the course of the past three decades, as the family has been contested and family arrangements become more varied, gender too has been pulled into focus.[5] "Feminist scholarship has placed gender in the center of discourse on social organization" (Kimmel 1987, p. 10). Questioned and, in some areas, altered are gender roles and the gender hierarchy and belief system. Entwined with these processes of inquiry and change is marital dissolution. In the immediacy of intimate relationships, "divorce is a solution. It 'solves' the problems of masculinity and femininity" (Gerzon 1982, p. 186).

GENDER CONSTRUCTS

Assumptions about what it means to be a woman or man have been analyzed and evidence amassed that gender is a cultural construct: learned, the result of socially created notions and not of innate, biological imperatives. Thus meanings attached to gender are shaped by and vary across human history and culture (Watzlawick 1984; Kimmel 1987; Kimmel and Messner 1992; Seidler 1991; Thorne 1993). "Gender is accomplished through everyday interaction. We create ourselves as gendered persons through our relations with others. Moment-by-moment, day-by-day, people negotiate gender with each other" (Thompson 1993, p. 15).

Gender is relational (Flax 1987; Wharton 1991; Kimmel and Messner 1992; Glenn 1987).[6] That is, the dichotomous categories of masculinity and femininity are meaningful only when considered in relationship to each other: "It is impossible to understand the roles of men and women in society without seeing them in relation to one another" (Pestello and Voydanoff 1991, p. 106).

It is in the family where gender identity is initially acquired through socialization processes and maintained, repaired, and altered through interactions. Interrelated cultural ideologies about family and gender shape family dynamics and family transitions (Barrett and McIntosh 1982; Morgan 1985; Thorne 1993).

Although challenged, the gender belief system—attitudes about men and women and "the purported qualities of masculinity and femininity"—persists. "Many aspects of the gender belief system are shared by substantial numbers of individuals within a society, so one can speak of consensual categories and normative beliefs" (Deaux and Kite 1987, p. 97). "Worldliness, dominance, aggressiveness, and nonemotionalism are considered to be components of masculinity in America, while talkativeness, gentleness, dependence, and expressiveness are perceived by many as feminine traits" (Franklin 1988, p. 9). Masculinity remains valued more highly than femininity: "Masculine traits are culturally supported more than feminine traits and are associated with power and control. In contrast, feminine traits are associated with powerlessness and being controlled" (Basow 1992, pp. 6-7; see also Canter and Meyerowitz 1984; Lewin and Tragos 1987; Eagley and Mladinic 1989). Gender expectations and beliefs are not inevitably consistent internally (Ferree 1990), and individuals may well experience intragender conflict (Rosenblum 1990; Cancian 1987).

Gender is a, perhaps *the,* primary factor in social organization (Thorne 1993; Hess and Ferre 1987; Hare-Mustin 1988). Serving as the basis for a hierarchical system of male dominance and female subordination, gender then is also about power. "The imposition of an ideology of two genders and the differential evaluation of these differences have one universal outcome: systems of gender stratification in which males have greater claims on and access to the scarce resources—power, prestige, and property—of a society than do females" (Ferree and Hess 1987, p. 22).

Gender stratification is evident throughout social life and arrangements; for instance, occupational segregation, wage differentials, and political underrepresentation of women attest to the persistence of gender hierarchy in American society (e.g., Richardson and Taylor 1993; U.S. Bureau of the Census 1992). Recognizing an unease about explicitly labeling and confronting patriarchy, as feminists demand, Morgan (1985) noted: "Indeed the very fact that it was and still is difficult for many people to think or talk of male dominance or male interests shows the pervasiveness of this domination for it derives its daily legitimation through its identification with the natural order of things" (p. 219).

GENDER CHANGES

Despite its deep ideological and institutional entrenchment, gender is being challenged and changed. Specifically, the conventions of masculinity—"those sets of signs indicating that a person is a 'man,' or 'not a woman' or 'not a child' " (Hearn 1987, p. 137) and that are "the social reality for men in modern society" (Clatterbaugh 1990, p. 3)—are questioned (Hearn 1987; Clatterbaugh 1990; Kimmel 1987). Indeed, Kimmel (1987) concluded that contemporary men, like men in other periods characterized by dramatic social and economic change, "confront a crisis in masculinity" (p. 153; see also Seidler 1989, 1991).

Sociocultural transitions in gender have occurred at discrepant rates, with women having expanded the scope of their activities and gender definitions more than men. Having entered the labor force in unprecedented numbers over the past several decades, women couple their traditional domestic and parenting roles with those of income earning. In contrast, few men have increased their household efforts significantly; they remain preoccupied predominantly with activities outside the home (Hochschild 1989; Pleck 1985; Douthitt 1988; Seidler 1992).

The "stalled revolution" in gender, however, in which women work a "second shift" (Hochschild 1989), is not a result solely of individual men's resistance to change. Social institutions continue to support and even require the traditional practices and arrangements of gender and the related nuclear family, with its ideologies of women's motherhood and men's provider roles (see Cohen 1989; Coltrane 1989; Pestello and Voyandoff 1991; Sidel 1992). "If we are right, that gender is created by everyday life and everyday institutions, then escaping gender constraints is a matter of redesigning the social structure" (Risman and Schwartz 1989, p. 8). Likewise, "women cannot win an equal place in democratic productive life and citizenship if they are deemed to be destined for one ascribed task, but nor can fathers take an equal share in reproductive activities without a transformation in our conception of 'work' and of the structure of economic life" (Pateman 1989, pp. 222-23).

Although some men resist change, others participate in the questioning of conventional gender stereotypes and arrangements (Brod 1987a; Clatterbaugh 1990, 1992; Pleck 1985, 1987; May and Strikwerda 1992a). Caution is warranted here: "If men are changing at all, however, it is not because they have stumbled upon the limits of traditional masculinity all by themselves. For at least two decades, the women's movement (and also, since 1969, the gay liberation movement) has suggested that the traditional enactments of masculinity were in desperate need of overhaul. For some men, these critiques have prompted a terrified retreat to traditional constructions; to others it has inspired a serious reevaluation of traditional worldviews, and offers of support for the social, political, and economic struggles of women and gays" (Kimmel 1987, pp. 9-10).

The gender revolution, under way for more than two decades, remains unfinished. Divorce exemplifies and prompts a crisis in gender identity and arrangements (Riessman 1990; Vaughan 1986; Finlay, Starnes, and Alvarez 1985) and illumines both the continuities and discontinuities in men's relationships and circumstances.

FATHERHOOD

Located in the nexus between the overlapping transitions in family and gender, fatherhood is also in a state of flux (Rotundo 1985; Griswold 1993). The *culture of fatherhood*—"the shared norms, values, and beliefs surrounding men's parenting"—has changed more dramatically than have the behaviors of fathers, which "seem minimal at best" (LaRossa 1988, p. 451). Moreover, although women's identities remain synonymous in many ways with mothering and family activities, even as women increasingly participate in spheres outside of the home (Flax 1987; Chodorow 1978), the relation of men's identities to fathering and family is less clear (see also Backett 1987). As observed by Chodorow (1978): "Though men are interested in being husbands and fathers, and most men do occupy these roles during their lifetime, ideologies about men and definitions of what is masculine come predominantly from men's nonfamilial roles" (p. 178). What is clear is that men's role as family providers persists, with masculine identity being inextricably linked to success as an income earner.

A sizable discrepancy exists between "the rate of change in men and the profusion of profathering imagery." Although the father-breadwinner role remains dominant in American society, competing images exist alongside it. These include the moral overseer, sex role model, and "new father." "In the future, tensions between the breadwinner model and more involved conceptions of fatherhood will continue, if not increase" (Pleck 1987, pp. 93-95). And, despite much rhetorical attention to men's changing family roles, many fathers remain on the periphery of family interactional life, suspended in time (Cowan and Cowan 1988). Others attempt to forge new pathways, whereas others equivocate, bewildered. "Not only are there distant, silent, tyrannical, demanding fathers but there are also liberal, affectionate, eccentric, bizarre fathers. . . . Perhaps above all there are confused fathers" (Hearn 1987, p. 154).

The proposition that a sizable proportion of fathers, irrespective of class status, are only "weakly attached" to their children is supported by an array of findings (Furstenberg 1988, p. 202); for example, the limited parental involvement of married fathers (Backett 1987; Lamb, Pleck, and Levine 1986); the absence or near absence of one-third or more of unmarried or no-longer-married, nonresidential fathers (Seltzer 1991b; Seltzer and Bianchi 1988); and the restricted or total absence of economic and other kinds of parental support for children not residing with them (U.S. Bureau of the Census 1992; Teachman 1991a, 1991b; Seltzer 1991a, 1991b). Ehrenreich (1983) observed more than a decade ago that men have been leaving families for decades. And Furstenberg (1988) noted that, although more men deny paternity and fail to meet their parental responsibilities, "what may be new is the number of middle-class men who are reneging on their paternal obligations—men who presumably have the resources but not the commitment to perform their fatherly responsibilities" (pp. 204-5).

In general, American men have not much increased their participation in direct parental and daily child care when they are present in families (Marsiglio 1991; Douthitt 1988). Reviewing the literature on men's parenting involvement and concluding that little has changed, LaRossa (1988) referred to the pattern of paternal participation as "technically present but functionally absent" (p. 5). "One recent study found that mothers of young children spent an average of 44.45 hours per week in total child-interaction time (which goes beyond engagement), while fathers spent an average of 29.48 per week, an 1.5 to 1 difference. If one looked, however, at time spent alone with children, one discovered that 19.56 hours of mother's child-interaction time, compared with 5.48 hours of father's child-interaction time, was solo time, a 3.6 to 1 difference. Moreover, although fathers' total interaction time was positively affected by the number of hours their wives worked, father's solo time was not affected at all" (LaRossa 1988, p. 5).

When men have increased their parental activity, it is mostly in the area of play (Marsiglio 1991; Backett 1987); further, many men restrict their child care activities mostly to the weekends (Douthitt 1988). Among couples in which both parents have jobs, only a minority of men share parenting responsibility and caregiving fairly equally (Hochschild 1989; Blair and Lichter 1991; Weiss 1990). Additionally, unemployed fathers are no more active in parenting than employed fathers (Marsiglio 1991). And even married parents committed to shared parenting encounter some difficulties and tensions in achieving an egalitarian division of labor (Ehrensaft 1987; Coltrane 1990). "Couples find it easier to split housework than childcare" (Pestello and Voyandoff 1991, p. 110).

Mothers typically mediate the father-child relationship (Parke 1985; Fox 1985), consistent with women's marital role as emotional worker (Hochschild 1983, 1989). Commenting on men's parental involvement in two-parent middle-class families, Backett (1987) concluded that "even when he *was* directly involved with the child, such interaction tended in any case to be mediated through the indirect understandings provided by the mother" (p. 84, italics in original).

Women and men obscure the inequities in parenting labor. Among middle-class families, Backett (1987) found that both parents use different standards to measure and explain away fathers' limited involvement, thus sustaining the myth of egalitarianism: "Both parents participated in the construction and sustaining of a belief that the father was 'involved' even though substantial inequities in parental involvement and responsibility were evident" (p. 85). One consequence of men's actual limited parental involvement was that "the father had the problem of making time to 'get to know the child' in a way in which the mother did not" (Backett 1987, p. 85; see also Hochschild 1989).[7]

Men are being pushed from different directions to become more involved parents. Wives especially are demanding change from their husbands. But men also are urging increased paternal participation and recognition. For example, each of the six sociopolitical perspectives that dominate contemporary discussions of men and masculinity—conservative, pro-feminist, men's rights, spiritual, socialist, and group specific—attends to issues of fathering (Clatterbaugh 1992, p. 2). Part of the men's rights movement, "the fathers' rights movement is also a significant force on the cultural scene. This movement reflects a complex amalgam of fathers driven by antifeminist backlash (echoing the critics of maternal influence earlier in this century) with other fathers motivated by an actual denial of their genuine desire to remain involved as fathers after divorce. The 'new father' coexists somewhat uneasily with this as well as the other profathering ideologies having an impact today" (Pleck 1987, p. 94; see also Fineman 1991). Divorce often confounds, impeding as well as magnifying, the summons to fathers to transform their parental involvement.

Cultural Tensions

Family and gender transitions are facets of a culture riddled with contradictions and inconsistencies (Bellah et al. 1985; Dizard and Gadlin 1990; Wolfe 1989). Flax (1987), for example, observed that Western culture appears to be in the middle of a fundamental transformation: "a 'shape of life' is growing old," involving a shift that "may be as radical as the shift from medieval to a modern society" (p. 51) and yet is little understood. Tensions persist between the values of separation and commitment, competition and cooperation, autonomy and intimacy, utilitarian individualism and love, and obligation and freedom (Swidler 1980; Berger and Berger 1983). "Most Americans are, in fact, caught between ideals of obligation and freedom" (Bellah et al. 1985, p. 102).[8] "With the rise of what is sometimes called 'late modernization,' self-fulfillment has become one of the paramount cultural values. This means that familism and the family today face what can reasonably be described as an unprecedented, adverse cultural climate" (Popenoe 1988, p. 329).

Intertwined with the cultural confusions, and bearing down on many families directly, is economic anxiety and uncertainty (see, e.g., Dizard and Gadlin 1990; Bellah 1992; Schor 1992). A national economic malaise, fostering a crisis in confidence, persists even as individual assessments cycle between relatively lesser and greater pessimism (Uchitelle 1993). The "family wage" is available to fewer and fewer adult wage earners, the poverty rate for households with children continues to rise, and public assistance benefit levels are woefully inadequate (Martin 1990; Cheal 1991; Abramovitz 1988; U.S. Bureau of the Census 1992).

Cultural and economic tensions impacting on the family generally are especially evident and significant in divorce. Thus the personal experiences contributing to and inherent in divorce are positioned in a context of contradictions and uncertainty.

BACKLASH AGAINST CHANGE AND AMBIGUITY

Transitions in family and gender do not proceed unimpeded: A backlash, often highly organized, perseveres (Faludi 1991). Clatterbaugh (1992) observed that "in our present world the standards are changing. The norms by which people are judged to be worthy are no longer so uniformly (white) male. It is this change that men fear and it is this changing standard that leaves some men less prepared for this world. Instead of welcoming a new and more humane conception of what is truly human, these men resist that change. They attack the revolutionaries as oppressors" (pp. 187-88). Men especially resist, according to Morgan (1985), because the family is "an important location of a whole set of privileges that men enjoy and which they would be reluctant to relinquish; this may be especially the case for men workers with relatively few alternative sources of privilege in society. It provides, just as it is shaped by, a set of powerful and pervasive images through which we come to understand our society and the place of the gender order within it" (p. 253; see also Clatterbaugh 1990; Kimmel 1987; Seidler 1991). Moreover, remarked Kimmel (1987), "masculine 'reactivity' has a political component . . . ; in a society based upon the institutional power of men over women, men benefit from inherited definitions of masculinity and femininity and would be unlikely to change them—indeed, unlikely to even call them into question. Men, as a group, have historically exhibited a smug satisfaction with existing gender relations" (p. 14).

Numerous men thus invest their energies not in accommodation and change but in resistance and retrenchment. Expressed attitudes often contradict actions. For example, in his study of married men, Nordstrom (1986) found that "behavior and attitudes were usually roughly similar, but when they were 'out of sync' men were nearly always more liberal in their attitudes than in their personal lifestyles" (p. 50, footnote 1). And in her research with dual-career couples, Hochschild (1989) concluded that "most men were 'transitional' in gender ideology, and resistant in strategy," and "many men seemed to alternate between periods of cooperation and resistance" (pp. 200-1).

A gender gap exists in which, generally, women perceive inequity "in the race of life" and want redress and change, and men drag their feet. "We should expect that the recognition of the need for value changes will come first to those in whose interests the changes are occurring (the subordinate class), while resistance to such changes should be greatest in those with the most to lose by the challenges to the old system—the most powerful members of the dominant group" (Finlay et al. 1985, p. 651). The contesting of values involves not only status but identity issues. "Because personal identity (and all its concomitant social, political, religious, psychological, biological, and economic relations) is so heavily gendered, any threat to sex/ gender categories is derivatively (though primarily non-consciously) interpreted as a threat to personal identity—a threat to what it means to *be* and especially what it means to *be me*. A threat to manhood (masculinity) is a threat to personhood (personal identity). Not surprisingly then, a threat to established gender categories, like most other serious threats, is often met with grave resistance" (Hopkins 1992, p. 114; italics in original).

Documenting perceptions about gender inequality, journalist Faludi (1991) concluded that the "gulf between the sexes" widened during the 1980s. "By the '80s, as the poll results made evident, men were interpreting small advances in women's rights as big, and complete ones; they believed women had made major progress toward equality—while women believed the struggle was just beginning. . . . The American Male Opinion Index found that the proportion of men who fell into the group opposing changes in sex roles and other feminist objectives had risen from 48 percent in 1988 to 60 percent in 1990—and the group willing to adapt to these changes had shrunk from 52 percent to 40 percent" (p. 60). She continued: "In 1989, while a majority of women in [a] *New York Times* poll

believed American society had not changed enough to grant women equality, only a minority of men agreed. A majority of men *were* saying,
however, that the women's movement had 'made things harder for men at
home' " (Faludi 1991, p. 61, italics in original). Similarly, Astrachan
(1985) found that no more than 5% to 10% of the American men he
surveyed over a 7-year period "genuinely support women's demands for
independence and equality" (p. 27). Goode's (1982) assertion of a decade
ago still resounds: "Men view even small losses of deference, advantages,
or opportunities as large threats" (p. 137; see also Blumstein and Schwartz
1983).

Raising the question of what it is about women's equality that threatens
"to erase male identity," Faludi (1991) probed survey data: "A little-noted
finding by the Yankelovich Monitor survey, a large nationwide poll that
has tracked social attitudes for the last two decades, takes us a good way
toward a possible answer. For twenty years, the Monitor's pollsters have
asked its subjects to define masculinity. And for twenty years, the leading
definition, ahead by a huge margin, has never changed. It isn't being a
leader, athlete, lothario, decision maker, or even just being 'born male.' It
is simply this: being a good provider for his family' " (p. 65). Men are not
alone in adhering to the good-provider definition of masculinity: "To a
great extent so many men have clung to sole-provider status as proof of
their manhood because so many women have expected it of them. In the
Yankelovich poll, it's not just men who have consistently identified the
breadwinner role as the leading masculine trait; it has also consistently
been women's first choice" (Faludi 1991, p. 457). Thus, even as men are
challenged to reform the norms of conventional masculinity and allow
women to be equal partners in all spheres of social life, both sexes continue
to emphasize men's provider role.

The gender gap in attitudes and expectations is not exclusive to older
Americans but exists also among young adults. A recent annual survey of
first-year university and college students reveals that less than one-fifth of
first-year women students anticipate that they will marry and stay home
with their children ("Attitudes of College Freshmen" 1993). Many women
expect they will successfully coordinate careers and children and sometimes marriage. Yet numerous young women believe they will manage
largely "on their own" (Sidel 1990). In contrast, over one-third of first-year
men students anticipate a traditional marriage in which they provide
income while their wives remain at home ("Attitudes of College Freshmen" 1993). Who will these young men be marrying? How do they expect
to defy the major social trends?

Although traditional gender attitudes are not uncommon among men in
the general population, such attitudes may be more prevalent among the

population of divorced men. Identifying four types of gender role behavior, one research team suggested that marriages ending in divorce increasingly involve "ideologically dissonant" couples: "It seems reasonable to expect that most of these cases would involve the husband traditional and wife nontraditional category, rather than the reverse, since nontraditional husbands still receive many benefits from their marriages to traditional wives. Nontraditional wives, on the other hand, would tend to perceive the traditional role demands of their husbands as unfair, and especially if they were working, they would be in a better position than other wives to opt for divorce" (Finlay et al. 1985, pp. 639-40). The growing gender gap among the divorced population is further extended by their postdivorce experiences; divorced women push for greater egalitarianism, but it is doubtful that men do (Finlay et al. 1985).

The efforts to resist or even reverse change are not likely to prevail, given the dynamics of social movement (e.g., Zimmerman 1988; Smelser 1963; Zald and McCarthy 1979). Rather, changing gender constructs and roles are on a collision course with private patriarchy and its legions. Men's traditional family authority and prerogatives are being eroded, albeit slowly in some quarters (e.g., Brod 1987a; Jaggar 1983; Goode 1982; Pateman 1989). But the struggle for family democracy and gender equity is far from over (e.g., Okin 1989; Fraser and Gordon 1994). Evidence of the unfinished, interrelated revolutions is evidenced in the systematic character of divorce outcomes.

The *His* and *Hers* of Divorce

As first identified by Bernard (1981), there are *his* and *hers* experiences of marriage (see also Lewis 1986). Marital roles vary, and her marriage is typically less satisfactory and more taxing than is his (see Thompson and Walker 1989; Hochschild 1989; Bernard 1981; Cancian 1987). "Research consistently shows that men are more satisfied with their marriage than women are" (Riessman 1990, p. 206; see also Chiriboga, Roberts, and Stein 1978; Wallerstein and Blakeslee 1989; Kelly, Gigy, and Hausman 1988). The ending of a marriage does not occur in a cultural or institutional vacuum, and thus there are also his and hers experiences and perceptions of divorce (Riessman 1990; Arendell 1986; Kurz 1995). Various measures indicate clearly that divorce consequences occur along the paths of gender (Chiriboga and Catron 1991). Gender differences in divorce outcomes are unmistakable in child custody, parental involvement, economic consequences and support of dependent children, emotional well-being, and remarriage.

Maternal custody remains the national pattern, as it has been for most of the century (U.S. Bureau of the Census 1992). More than 85% of children whose parents are divorced are in the custody of their mothers. The proportion of children living with their fathers increased from 8.8% in 1980 to 11.4% in 1986 (Furstenberg and Cherlin 1991, p. 32). As was the case during marriage, women perform most parenting tasks after divorce.

Noncustodial fathers' involvement with children declines over time (Furstenberg, Morgan, and Allison 1987; Seltzer 1991b). According to recent analyses of data from National Survey of Families and Households, nearly 30% of children whose parents are divorced did not see their fathers at all during the past year. Almost 60% see their fathers several times or less during the year, and only about 25% of the children see theirs at least weekly (Seltzer 1991b). These figures are somewhat higher than those of earlier analyses of the National Survey of Children done in the 1980s (Furstenberg et al. 1987; Furstenberg and Nord 1985). Nonetheless, "the pattern of modest initial contact and a sharp drop-off over time is strikingly similar across studies" (Furstenberg and Cherlin 1991, p. 36). Less than one-third of children who see their fathers have extended periods of time with them; just under one-third who live with their mothers visit at least once a week or spend at least 3 weeks a year with their fathers (Seltzer 1991b).

Fewer than one third of divorced parents discuss their children with each other during a 12-month period, and just over 20% talk with each other about their children at least weekly. Even among those parents, the level of fathers' participation in decision making is limited: Only 17% have a great deal of influence on decisions about important aspects of children's rearing, such as health care matters, education, or religious teaching (Seltzer 1991a, 1991b; see also Furstenberg and Cherlin 1991).

Women often experience a dramatic decline in economic status as a result of divorce (Weitzman 1985; Holden and Smock 1991). About 40% of divorcing women lose more than half of their family income, whereas fewer than 17% of men experience this large a drop. Overall, as a group, women's income drops about 30% following divorce. Men, in general, experience an increase in their income, partially because they share less of their income with their children (Duncan and Hoffman 1985; Furstenberg and Cherlin 1991). "Divorce or separation leads to a dramatic decline in well-being for nearly one-quarter of the women who experience it between ages 26 and 35. This is almost six times the risk for men. The incidence of divorce-induced income loss falls at older ages, but divorce remains the single most devastating event for young and middle-aged women" (Burk-hauser and Duncan 1989, p. 15). Divorce may be the most ruinous economic experience for older women as well (Burkhauser and Duncan 1989; Arendell and Estes 1991; Kitson and Morgan 1990; Morgan 1991).

For many women, the financial hardships accompanying divorce become the overriding experience, affecting psychological well-being and parenting and dictating such decisions as where to live, type of child care to use, and whether to obtain health care (Arendell 1986; Weitzman 1985; Kurz 1995). Women's decisions to remarry often involve economic considerations: The surest route to economic well-being for many women is remarriage (Arendell 1986, 1987; Weitzman 1985; Furstenberg and Cherlin 1991; Kitson and Morgan 1990).

Children's economic well-being after divorce is directly related to their mothers' economic status. As primary custodial parents, women disproportionately carry the financial burdens of childrearing. Children living with a single mother are far more likely to be poor than are children in other living arrangements: Families headed by a single mother are six times more likely to be impoverished than are families having both parents present (U.S. Bureau of the Census 1992). Divorced women and their children do not regain their predivorce standard of living until 5 years after the marital breakup.

Child support does not ameliorate the divorce-induced economic decline. Child support payments amounted to only about 17% of the income of divorced mothers and their children in 1989 (U.S. Bureau of the Census 1992). That same year, of the three-fourths of divorced mothers who had a child support agreement, roughly three-fourths received some support and one-fourth received no payment whatsoever. Only about half received the full amount ordered. This pattern of compliance and noncompliance remained basically stable across the 1980s. The average monthly child support paid by the three-fifths of divorced fathers contributing any economic support in 1989 was $277 (U.S. Bureau of the Census 1992).

Spousal support or maintenance is of little significance for the large majority of divorced women. Fewer than 15% of divorcing women were awarded any such support in 1985 (Furstenberg and Cherlin 1991). The dominant trend has been the granting of only short-term, "rehabilitative" support to a spouse who was economically dependent in marriage (Kay 1990; Weitzman 1985). Moreover, noncompliance with alimony or spousal payment orders is vast: By 1985 only 10.7% of women awarded such payment received any payment (Furstenberg and Cherlin 1991, p. 57).

PROPERTY

Property settlements do not offset income inequities. Most divorcing couples have assets of only relatively modest value. A husband's career assets and earning capacity are typically worth more than the tangible assets of the marriage (Weitzman 1985, p. 53), and about 40% of divorcing couples make no property settlement because there is nothing of value to divide (Seltzer and Garfinkel 1990; Furstenberg and Cherlin 1991). When there is property, it usually involves cars or household furnishings and goods of relatively low value (Weitzman 1985, p. 53; McLindon 1987; Seltzer and Garfinkel 1990). "Even if women received all joint assets at divorce, they would still be severely disadvantaged compared to men" (Seltzer and Garfinkel 1990, p. 107). The transition to equitable property statutes has not equalized divorce outcomes, and property settlements continue to favor men (Weitzman 1985; Seltzer and Garfinkel 1990; Garrison 1990).

EMOTIONAL WELL-BEING

Divorce constitutes a major life transition, evoking for most women and men a questioning of identity. But these emotional experiences tend to vary by gender (e.g., Riessman and Gerstel 1985; Kitson and Holmes 1992; Riessman 1990; Kitson and Morgan 1990; Morgan 1991). Women, consistent with their family roles as emotional caretakers and their greater awareness of marital problems (Weiss 1990; Hochschild 1989), are not as surprised by the experiences of separation and divorce, having more fully anticipated them. Men often are more distressed initially, being less prepared for the feelings of loss, grief, and disruption that typically accompany separation (e.g., Riessman 1990; Chase-Lansdale and Hetherington 1990). Additionally, whereas husbands depend primarily on wives for support and nurture, wives generally have other close relationships, especially with female relatives and friends, to which to turn (Rubin 1983; Cancian 1987; Belle 1987).

But the findings on longer term divorce adjustment are inconclusive. Using a multidimensional approach to examine divorce adjustment, Kitson and Holmes (1992) concluded that "women and whites have greater difficulty adjusting than do men and nonwhites" (p. 175). Moreover, "a greater variety of variables were associated with adjustment outcomes for women; often, more variance was accounted for than was true for men or for either racial group (Kitson and Holmes 1992, p. 336; see also Kitson and Morgan 1991). In contrast, other researchers suggest gender differences are insignificant. For example, results show that "among the divorced the differences in the psychological well-being of males and females are modest and that neither sex is consistently favored. . . . There are no significant gender differences in psychological well-being among the divorced" (Gove and Shin 1989, pp. 133, 142).

REMARRIAGE

Remarriage patterns also occur along gender lines. Men remarry sooner and at higher rates than do women (National Center for Health Statistics 1992; U.S. Bureau of the Census 1992), presumably in part because men find marriage more satisfactory. Younger persons are more likely to remarry. Two to 3 years after divorce, "men with higher incomes, and those of both sexes who were younger and had no or fewer children were more likely to be re-affiliated" (Kitson and Holmes 1992, p. 289).

In sum, the divorced fathers in the present study lived, and recounted their experiences and shared their feelings, in a particular cultural milieu. They were constituents of the uneven and demanding social revolutions in gender, marriage, family, and divorce.

Notes

1. Analyzing the relationship between the family and the discursive battle over the naturalness of gender and the matter of gender subjectivity, Weedon (1987) noted: "This battle over family life is not confined to the domestic sphere. It is found in all the social institutions and practices which help to define the family, for example, the law, social welfare provision, marriage guidance, the media and the churches. Yet it is on the terrain of the family that the effects of this discursive battle are realized" (p. 100).

2. "Those who claim that the family is in crisis cite as evidence the high divorce rate, the increase in single-parent families, which some see as a major cause of expanding welfare rolls; the increase in people living alone; the growing visibility of lesbian and gay couples; the rising employment rates of married women, especially mothers of young children; and a general undermining of parental authority" (Thorne 1993, p. 3).

3. Copyright © 1993, as first published in *The Atlantic Monthly.*

4. "Feminist thinking about families continually returns to questions of social change. . . . From a visionary profeminist perspective, this period of rapid social change opens up dramatically new possibilities. . . . There is strong resistance to that vision because it threatens vested class, race, and gender interests, as well as deeply held notions of social order" (Thorne 1993, pp. 23-25).

5. Gender consists of interrelated components: (a) "culturally available symbols that evoke multiple (and often contradictory) representations"; (b) "normative concepts that set forth interpretations of the meanings of the symbols that attempt to limit and contain their metaphoric possibilities" and that "are expressed in religious, educational, scientific, legal, and political doctrines and typically take the form of a fixed binary opposition, categorically and unequivocally

asserting the meaning of male and female, masculine and feminine"; (c) a notion of politics as well as reference to social institutions and organizations; and (d) subjective or individual identity (Scott 1988, p. 43).

6. " 'Gender relations' is a category meant to capture a complex set of social relations to refer to a changing set of historically variable social processes . . . complex and unstable processes (or temporary 'totalities' in the language of dialectics) constituted by and through interrelated parts. These parts are interdependent, that is, each part can have no meaning or existence without the others" (Flax 1987, p. 58).

7. Backett (1987) continued: "Popular belief in the more 'involved' father must therefore be seen as something of an illusion. My respondents, by invoking notions of 'fairness' and 'sharing,' were attempting to take only small strides towards 'equity' (and on the way towards equality). Even such limited change appeared constantly thwarted, however, as long as the men were still given and took the very special freedom of 'opting in' to childrearing and the women continued to tolerate their minimal opportunities to 'opt out.' Until the existence of these fundamental inequalities is fully appreciated, and the processes revealed, proper understanding of the nature of fatherhood in our society and its true potential for change will not be achieved" (p. 88).

8. Affecting the family directly, according to Dahlstrom (1989) in his analysis of Western, modern society, are four major sociocultural contradictions. They are between (a) the patriarchal heritage of traditional family structures and reformist ideas for improving the possibilities for personal development; (b) security and experimentation; (c) the private and public spheres of action, or the bureaucratic culture and primary-group culture; and (d) the idealization of one family type and the reality of numerous family types (cited in Cheal 1991, pp. 20-22).

PART II

Divorce Injustice

3

A MASCULINIST
DISCOURSE OF DIVORCE

Even though the particulars of their situations varied, the men offered narratives that were remarkably similar. In like ways, the 75 participants accounted for past and present actions and described and implied intended future courses of action and their meanings. Responses to divorce were formed and enacted on the basis of a core of shared themes and definitions. Situated in a cultural milieu to which they contributed and from which they actively drew as they shaped behavior and sought meaning, these men shared a *discourse*—a particular "matrix of perceptions, appreciations, and actions" (Bourdieu 1987, p. 83). More specifically, they shared a *masculinist discourse of divorce* (Arendell 1992a, 1992b). Three interrelated discursive themes dominated the respondents' narratives: a rhetoric of rights and victimization, a belief in sex differences and male superiority, and a definition of the afterdivorce family as a broken family.

A Rhetoric of Rights

More than three-fourths of the participants insisted that divorce had meant their victimization: "Men are discriminated against in divorce, plain and simple." Further, no one, not even men who managed to avoid being mistreated during the dissolution process, was immune from future victimization. "As long as children are minors," many insisted in various ways, "fathers risk disenfranchisement as parents" and can be reduced to being "only faceless money machines" for former wives. Lost in divorce, they claimed, were their rights to fatherhood, discretionary control of their earnings, exercise of familial authority, and autonomy to plan and handle their futures.

Integral to the men's accounts of being cheated, and so also to their family experiences and understandings, was a *rhetoric of rights.*[1] The rights framework provided responses to changing conditions; it endorsed resistance and a reluctance to search out alternatives. Rights-talk, then, was used most extensively by those relying on conventional divorce responses. It was not firmly tied to type of custody, visitation arrangement, or extent of dissatisfaction with their situations.

The rhetoric of rights encompassed abstract philosophical principles, especially the overlapping ones of liberalism and market capitalism (e.g., Rawls 1971; Walzer 1983; Richards 1980; Tushnet 1984). As one participant said, "When it came to my divorce, there was no Bill of Rights. Forget the Constitution, there is no due process. Men lose their rights. They take a beating. It's as simple as that." Involved also in the talk of rights, and linked to political and economic premises, was the *masculinist ethic,* with its prescriptive norms of male independence, dominance, and achievement (Jaggar 1983; Chodorow 1978; Pateman 1989; Okin 1989; Stoltenberg 1989). Thus the individualist ethic and beliefs about choice, control, and authority were core aspects of the rhetoric.

Rights-talk was about gender. Despite being couched in the abstract principles of justice and equity, the language of rights was a euphemism for prerogatives, expected if not actually held, within the stratified gender system.[2] Divorce unseated men, especially noncustodial fathers, from their positions of privilege in the family. As divorce researcher Riessman (1990) commented: "With divorce, men experience a decline in their spheres of control and women experience an increase in theirs" (p. 208; see also Furstenberg and Cherlin 1991). That rights were to be secured in relation to another, primarily the former wife, demystified these men's various rhetorical assertions. For example, this person insisted repeatedly throughout much of his account that he had been victimized in divorce and was vulnerable yet to further mistreatment. He had obtained primary custody of their children after "forcing my wife out of the house" and claiming "she deserted us" in response to her request for a divorce.[3] Yet he declared, you have to stop believing in the American way: truth and justice and all of that, that's not what happens. That only happens in books and TV shows. None of my rights were protected, but had I been a woman, you can bet that if I were a female, I'd have had these things automatically, without any fight at all.

He continued on with the theme that divorced men are a persecuted minority:

You pull your hair and spend thousands of dollars and say, "Aren't I a human being?" I mean I saw on TV: gay rights, pink rights, blue rights; everybody has rights and they're all demonstrating. I said, "Don't men have rights too? Aren't these my children? Isn't this my house? Don't they bear my name?" I mean I was the first one to hold each of them when they were just born. I was there for it all. I mean, did I have this thing backwards or something?

Having achieved what he most wanted, "beating" his former wife "at this game" by obtaining primary custody of their children and retaining the family home, he nevertheless felt violated, "raped," he said. Rather than being contested, his rights "should have been" automatically assured, as befits rights. That the former spouse also might have such claims was simply unrecognized, lost in a myopic fog of self-interest.

Similarly, for a majority of the participants, when children's rights were recognized, albeit rarely, they involved their "rights of access to their fathers." Children's rights were synonymous with fathers' rights (see also Fineman 1991, p. 89). For instance, this father of two explained why he "fought" for custody: "They needed to be with me. They were my kids. I was their father. Who would they be without me? They needed a father's hand, the father's presence, especially boys, they need that. It's their basic right."

SOURCES

"The idea that legal rights have some intrinsic value is widespread in our culture" (Schneider 1991, p. 318). The concept of rights with regard to divorce specifically had several sources. Attorneys often used a language of rights, sometimes explicitly announcing that men are at risk in divorce. This respondent energetically and persistently resisted his former wife's efforts "to keep me out of my kids' lives." He had been warned that men are handicapped in divorce. "My lawyer told me, 'Fathers in this system are like batters going up to base without balls. Even the umpire is unable to do his job.' " And another, also engaged in ongoing conflicts with his former spouse, said, "I guess if you want to take and know the game, know your opponent well. I think Rommel used to do that. Basically, what we have here is a war, that's what my attorney told me. He warned me. But I had to experience it to realize how vicious it is."

In their use of the language of rights, attorneys borrowed not only from the political culture but from family law codes: The statutory approach to family relations is one of rights *and* obligations (e.g., *Family Law of the State of New York* 1990; see Chambers 1984; Novinson 1983). But the legal counterpart to rights, obligations, was rarely mentioned by the respondents. Those few men who did incorporate this side of the dualism— parental obligations, and so too then, children's needs—used the language of rights far less than did the majority. These exceptions were, for the most part, the men engaged in innovative strategies of action.

Another source of the rhetoric of rights was television and newspaper coverage of divorce-related controversies and legal developments. Covered routinely by the local New York media were the fathers' rights movement and its various activities. "Having proliferated in the 1980s," every state has roughly 200 men's and fathers' rights organizations, which consist largely "of men and some women who are concerned with a legal system that they believe discriminates against men, particularly in the areas of divorce and child custody" (Clatterbaugh 1990, p. 61). Media coverage extended the rights discourse beyond group membership rolls and contacts (see also Coltrane and Hickman 1992) and contributed to the shaping of a public discourse about divorce and men and women.

A majority of the participants were familiar with the fathers' rights movement. Nearly one-third had direct experience with an organization or knew well someone who was active in an organization. Seventeen of the 75 participants had some sustained group involvement (defined loosely here as extending beyond a 2-month exploratory and informational period). Men active in fathers' rights organizations typically, although not universally, responded to divorce in conventional ways. These men especially drew parallels between their oppression and resistance in divorce and other social movements, such as the civil rights and women's movements. Three likened their personal situations as divorced fathers to American slaves in earlier centuries: "As a divorced father, I'm in the same situation black slaves were in 100 [and 30 plus] years ago. In this system, I'm told what to do. I'm given no rights." And another, for example, compared his resistance to injustice to racial integration efforts of several decades ago: "It's the equality, one's rights. It's the black person who stands up and says, 'Don't give me separate but equal, don't give me a beautiful facility but keep it over there.' "

According to several respondents, among the members in their particular fathers' rights organizations were prominent state legislators, judges, or family law attorneys who, because of their professional activities, had to remain "invisible," off the official rolls. Their very involvement served as further testimony to the "corruptness of the law in its antimale stance," as one father, who shared childrearing with his former wife, put it.

Used to explain the injustice done to them as men, the rhetoric of rights was idiosyncratic in that women do not use rights-talk in discussing their divorces (Arendell 1986). Coltrane and Hickman (1992), examining the rhetoric of rights and needs in custody and child support reform movements, in which "unfair treatment based on gender was the rallying cry for both [men's and women's] groups," concluded similarly: "Fathers' and mothers' groups offered compelling stories about the injustices suffered by their constituents, but only the fathers' rights groups repeatedly advanced claims based on the language of entitlement" (p. 403). That women typically take custody, and so do not lose their "mothering rights," as several respondents stated, partially may explain the gender difference in the use of rights-talk. But more is involved. For example, several custodial and co-custodial fathers used rights-talk extensively. Nor does being "on the losing end, always waiting to be slam-dunked," as one man complained in a representative comment, adequately account for the difference because many women live with continuous fears that they will lose custody, their parenting dismissed or discounted in a legal challenge (Arendell 1986; Weitzman 1985; Kurz 1995). And many live in economically depressed conditions, supporting their children alone. Nonetheless, they do not couch these issues in the terms of rights or their infringement.

That they do not use rights-talk to discuss their divorce experiences does not mean, of course, that women never use such language or notions. The women's movement itself is about rights: citizenship, legal and economic autonomy, reproductive control, and personal safety, among others (Jaggar 1983; Andersen 1993; Schneider 1990; Rhode 1990). But women's claims to rights are, for the most part, about full access and protection; they are issued from subordinate positions in a gender-stratified society. In contrast, men's demands are made from positions of relative dominance and focus on matters of perceived losses, especially in the domestic sphere. It is the decline of familial power and authority in divorce that especially elicits from men the talk of fathers' rights (Clatterbaugh 1988). Additionally, the concepts of women's rights and mothers' rights are not typically used synonymously, whereas fathers' rights and men's rights are (e.g., Doyle 1985; Bauer and Bauer 1985; see also Clatterbaugh 1990).[4]

Rights violations extended beyond their individual marital histories and divorce experiences; they were representations of a cultural phenomenon: the war between the sexes. This language was used explicitly by one-third of the men and implied by many others. Divorce attorneys contributed to the discourse. On being advised such things as "You have little or no chance of getting custody as a father," "This is what you'll be required to pay in child support," and "This is how the property is likely to be divided," the private ending of a marriage expanded to encompass the political. For some men, these unfavorable messages were a call to arms, galvanizing them "for battle." Divorce became a fight "for survival" in which, although both became "bloodied," as one man characterized it, one spouse won and the other lost. Thus rights-talk in divorce spoke to broader grievances: the challenges to men's status more generally. Women were given preferential treatment, at least in part, to remedy a history of "alleged injustice."[5] One person explained it this way: "It's like the race thing, all the women's stuff, the women's thing. After about '76 it began to turn around and turn into its opposite so that women have a double standard, so that they want to be given all the fruits of fair competition [and] at the same time be given advantages in the competition. And they also want the results without the effort. I think it's very true." Ignored, they argued, were men's sacrifices and suffering: Women's experiences dominated social and legal discussion and action. This next respondent linked women's complaints about inequality to perceived differences in sexuality and sexual activity (see also Riessman 1990; Rubin 1975):

> The problem is that this generation of women bitch and complain about men, they say they're fed up and not going to take it anymore. But the real problem is that men continue to be men and they refuse to become women. That's what the problem is. Little do these women know. Do you know what men complain about women? Men complain that women aren't sexually adequate for them, that they're too passive sexually or there's something else about the sexual activity they engage in which is not satisfying. But they're not allowed to bring that up in court. "That's irrelevant," we're told. Irrelevant! Yeah, right. To whom?

Various men, and especially those adhering to more conventional views, attributed the politicization of divorce to the women's movement or "those feminists." An opinion not limited to those in men's or fathers' organizations was that contemporary divorce law was shaped specifically by the demands of the women's movement. Accordingly, feminists acted, and act, in either deliberate disregard or ignorance of the institutional biases operating against men. Contemporary feminist actions, issues, and achievements working against men included, for example, "hiring quotas," "abortion on demand" and "abortion without a husband's consent," "illegitimate babies," "radical lesbians," and "welfare fraud," as well as divorce-related matters. Also victimized by feminists were other women, who were unsuspecting and naive. These included especially their former wives. "I feel sorry for women, I really do. They have to deal with this women's liberation and everything. They have to deal with all kinds of things, all kinds of pressures from these other women about what they *should* do, how they *should* oppose men. They aren't allowed to be free thinkers. That's what happened to my wife [*sic*]. The feminists got ahold of her." That he wanted to influence women's thinking was not seen by this participant as a possible impediment to their "free thinking."

In contrast to these assertions, scholars have demonstrated that the divorce revolution was based in a complex array of developments, not the direct effect of the women's movement (e.g., Weitzman 1985; Riley 1991). Jacob (1988), for example, refuted the argument that the women's movement brought about divorce law reforms:

> It may have surprised many readers that feminists were not responsible for the transformation of American divorce law. Many simply assume that divorce is a woman's issue and that, since the change in divorce laws coincided with the rise to prominence of feminist organizations, the new divorce laws would be the product of their agitation. As we have repeatedly shown, however, feminists stood on the sidelines during most of the activities that led to the adoption of these laws, and the interests of women in general were poorly represented during their consideration. (p. 172)

Numerous men agreed with the claims, attributed to various male relatives, friends, and work associates, that women are increasingly less committed to marriage than men. Because women "make out better in divorce" and are relatively assured of obtaining child custody, they are more inclined to initiate divorce. This person placed the entire dramatic increase in divorce over the past several decades clearly in the hands of women:

> In California it goes like this: You love this woman, you marry this woman, you take care of these children she has that you don't even really know, and she wakes up one day and says, "You know, Harry, I don't really think this is working out. Now I've made all of these arrangements and this is what's going to happen." The guy has just woken up, he hasn't even had his coffee

yet and he finds out his marriage is over: "It just doesn't feel right anymore so we go and we turn a new leaf."

Without pausing, he continued, shifting from the topic of marriage to changing gender rules: "I mean, what's wrong with holding a door for a woman. I always let a woman get off an elevator first. Oh, no, they don't want that. 'Oh, I didn't know that.' So I have to learn to do it right. But I'd say, 'That's bullshit,' and they'd say, 'Of course it's bullshit.' But that's the way they want it. But what I've decided is that at least in the last 20 years, and maybe longer, men are fugitives in a way." Another complaint was that women are less willing to compromise than were women in the past. Numerous men, including the next one, cited their own mothers as comparisons: "My mother never walked out. She put up with a lot of shit, too, and once in a while, she'd just let him have it. But she never walked out."

A Belief in Gender Differences

Rights violations were defined, framed, and magnified by the participants' beliefs about men and women and differences between the sexes. These assumptions were independent of present marital status and were carried over from marriage to divorce. In most cases, divorce experiences were used to reaffirm rather than to reevaluate these beliefs (see also Finlay et al. 1985); resentments about the specifics of their circumstances were entwined with the premises of the gender belief system (see Deaux and Kite 1987).

Differences between the sexes were assumed to be self-evident, universal, and largely immutable. Consequently, men's and women's respective standings and activities in marriage and family varied "naturally." No matter how problematic or prominent in marriage, such differences were highlighted in divorce. "I'll never remarry. I just can't trust women after all I've been through. The sexes just can't get along, they're too different. It's true." And this next person, who had been divorced nearly 8 years, described his continued emotional response to his former wife as being based in his being male: "If I ever see her on the street or anything, I go into a kind of shock, even now, all these years later. I think if I ever saw her on the street with another man, I probably would really commit violence, I probably would kill them. It's instinct. But we deny that men are governed by instincts, we only allow that women have a maternal instinct." As did nearly all the others, two-thirds of the men pursuing nonconventional responses to divorce assumed psychological, temperamental, and intellectual differences between the sexes. One of the minority group said,

> Some of my best friends are women. I really like women. But, I don't know what it is, but women just too often depend on someone else to make them happy. Me, I can sit and read a book and be happy. It all comes down to being happy with yourself. Your mind controls your emotions. You can't depend on someone else for it. You have to depend on yourself. Men can do that. I see the difference in my son and daughter already.

MALE SUPERIORITY

Nearly all the respondents were fully confident that their own experiences and perceptions were, and during marriage had been, the more "valid," "logical," "reliable," or "objective" ones. Men are "naturally" superior to women. Dismissing "women's logic as [being] so mysterious as to be incomprehensible," one respondent noted that "women speak a different language." Another said, "I just mostly stayed rational and reasonable during the months we considered separation but she just got crazier and crazier through the whole thing, and she's stayed crazy, impossible to deal with. I should have been prepared for that; I always knew during the marriage not to take her too seriously because she could be so illogical. I mean, you know, it's men's rationality that keeps a marriage together to begin with."

Pro-feminist men's studies scholar Franklin (1988) addressed the pervasiveness of continued sexist beliefs: "Perhaps because male dominance is so much a part of American society, it has been axiomatic that an ideology would develop to support the ensuing sex and gender ideology. Many who support such an ideology justify their position by referring to biological differences between the sexes which make men superior to women. Never mind the fact that little evidence exists to support such a pernicious ideology. Male sexism has three major aspects: a belief that males are superior to females; an ideology that supports relegating females to a lower position than males; and behaviors by males and females based on the beliefs and ideology. The latter frequently entails sexism being a part of the norms and standards of society" (p. 11).

Holding the assumptions that their own perspectives were the correct ones and competing viewpoints invalid was independent of the varied particulars of the participants' situations: Such beliefs were consistent with their positions in the gender hierarchy. They assessed their marriages as being free of gender (or sexual) politics. These assertions were consistent with the social psychology of power relations and men's status as husbands in families (Riessman 1990; Rubin 1976; Blumenberg and Coleman 1989); men typically are less aware than women of the dynamics of power in their marital relations (Thompson and Walker 1989; Komter 1989). That men are the relatively dominant spouse in marriage is empirically supported: "Remember that, although a growing number of women are attaining money and position through employment outside the home, even the most recent reports indicate that the average man still earns more than his wife and is likely to advance farther in his career than she does. . . . Although it may be somewhat distasteful, it is widely accepted by scholars that if power is defined as the access to tangible resources obtained outside the relationship, women continue to occupy subordinate positions" (Arliss 1991, p. 208; see also U.S. Department of Labor, Bureau of Labor Statistics 1991; U.S. Bureau of the Census 1992).[6] These men, like others in the upper levels of stratified rankings, could minimize their role-taking, as noted by theorist Glenn (1987): "It can be readily observed in a variety of situations that subordinates (women, servants, racial minorities) must be more sensitive to and responsive to the point of view of superordinates (men, masters, dominant racial groups) than the other way around" (p. 356). The benefits of occupying the dominant position in the gender hierarchy were taken for granted, largely unseen, as are gender assumptions typically (Deaux and Kite 1987; Goffman 1975). Previously held to the margins, the politics of marriage and family were pulled into focus by marital dissolution.

Views on gender differences were often inconsistent. Many respondents insisted that their marriages had been basically egalitarian because "difference does not mean inequality." From this angle, they entered divorce on an equal footing only to be pushed aside as the former wife received preferential treatment. She gained at his expense. From another perspective, often also argued by the same persons making the other one, they came into divorce with a higher status as men and heads of household, and so were deserving of certain privileges that they were then denied. Both perspectives—that inequality did not exist in marriage and that it did— were endorsed by cultural traditions and social arrangements.

These men assumed and expected a degree of dominance, even if only benign, in marriage. This co-custodial parent, for example, one of the nonconventional men in his overall postdivorce actions, had opted out of his marriage 2 years earlier but was seeking a reconciliation. He believed some of their marital problems were a result of his "not being in charge."

I'm not talking about [wanting] a marriage and family with a patriarchal model but the priority of the relationship between a man and a woman as a husband and wife. I want an equal relationship, a partnership. But let me word it this way, I would like her to be able to trust me to be the leader of the family. When there are times we can't sit down at the table and make decisions cooperatively, then I will make the decisions and she will trust me. I want to be able to do that in a marriage, to have that trust from her. I want her to be the first one to say, "We've talked about it and I'll let you decide." I guess I expect her to relinquish the control of the situation first.

Wanting facets of both the traditional and companionate marriages —both dominance and equality (Dizard and Gadlin 1990; Cancian 1987; Bellah et al. 1985)—this participant, like many, overlooked the contradictions between relational hierarchy and parity. Noting such inconsistencies, Riessman (1990) explained: "The realization of the core ingredients of the companionate marriage—emotional intimacy, primacy and companion-ship, and mutual sexual fulfillment— depends on equality between husbands and wives. Yet institutionalized roles call for differentiation: neither husbands nor wives have been socialized to be equals" (p. 73).

Devaluing

Derogatory remarks about former wives were commonplace in the majority of participants' reports, and such comments were more extensive than overt claims of male superiority. Men's denigrating of women is an element of the traditional masculine culture, as Franklin (1988) explained: "Evidence for the devaluation of femininity rests on the existence of pronounced social and economic inequality of the sexes; widespread categorical perception and objectification of women; pervasive devalu-ation of women in cultural symbolism; and multitudes of specific deviance imputed to women under a gender system signifying that femininity by its very nature is deviance" (pp. 124-25; see also Basow 1992; Riessman 1990; Hochschild 1989; Gilligan 1982).[7] Additionally, the discrediting of an estranged spouse, man or woman, is often part of the "uncoupling" process (Vaughan 1986; Riessman 1990). But it was the extent and char-acter of the derision that stood out in these men's accounts, especially given the length of time since the divorce. For instance, divorced for 8 years after an 8-year marriage, this next person believed he had been grievously wronged by both not receiving primary custody and having to pay child support. He focused extensively on his former wife throughout his description:

I mean, she had a brain but did not use it and did not think before she talked and said things that were really kind of silly and easily rebuttable. . . . She was a spiteful bitch when she was upset and when I said it, which was rarely, it was like it was incredible. She acted like she found me in bed with her sister on the basis of my maybe calling her a whore, or some other nasty name. It was incredible. She's still that way, of course.

And divorced 2 years, this father of three discussed his former spouse: "That bitch. That bitch! Actually I never refer her to that way. I don't like it when I hear people say that. I never liked that; I'll never understand the way men talk about their wives. I mean give me a break. It's [sic] your wife. Isn't anything sacred? And they're still married. But she's been such a bitch." Especially targeted for criticism were women's mothering abilities and activities. Another respondent declared: "She tried to breastfeed them but failed at that too. All three times she was too nervous and dried up; there wasn't enough milk. Once a night I was always up, warming the bottle and feeding the baby. She was less informed than I about parenting. . . . She over-hovered. She couldn't manage her time at all. She couldn't manage being a mother. That's all she had to do, and she couldn't manage it." And this noncustodial father of two, whose career development had demanded exceptionally long work weeks, insisted, in a representative remark, that "after all, I was able to do *it* [work and family] all while she did next to nothing—*nothing,* I mean *nothing.* I don't see what these women are complaining about, how can they say they're overworked?"

Traditionally defined as "women's work" and unpaid, an especially significant factor in capitalist industrial society where individual worth is tied to earnings or wealth (Zaretsky 1976; Hartmann 1981a, 1981b; Jaggar 1983; Ruddick 1983), a wife's domestic activities were easily derided or rendered invisible. This person, for example, engaged in innovative strategies of action, had an unusually cooperative postdivorce parenting relationship with his former wife. He was also atypical in that the issue of gender difference was not especially significant for him. Moreover, he consistently expressed great admiration and respect for his former wife's parenting and observed that their experiences of marriage and divorce might differ. Yet he too relied on the conventional standards of employment sector participation to describe her choices and, by implication, her character. "I'm not saying that the wife has to be a happy housewife. It's just that in our situation that's how we did it, that's what we chose. She could have gone out and done something on her own; I never put pressure on her to stay at home full-time. She may have thought I did but I don't think I really truly did. I don't think she was opposed to be a working mother, she just never liked to work. She still doesn't and so just works [for pay] part-time; I'm not surprised."

Over one-third of the men contended that they were "exceptional" men in their marriages, carrying the major share of both income-earning and caretaking activities. Several fathers quipped that they were "supermen," in contrast to the popularized notion of "superwomen." Defining themselves as extraordinary family men was self-congratulatory and served to denigrate further the former spouse: *Her* inadequacies had made it necessary for *him* to assume multiple roles and responsibilities. For this, rather than being treated shabbily in divorce, as they had been, they insisted, they deserved special recognition and protection. Their unique family participation should have been rewarded: They should have had more say in the divorce outcome.

Suggesting the possibility that assessments of their family caretaking activities were sometimes exaggerated, numerous men supported their claims by referring to particular caretaking episodes, such as a child's or wife's specific bout with the flu. Assertions such as "I was there at the birth" and "I changed diapers, too" were used also to buttress their claims. When a list of caregiving tasks was reviewed with the participants (Chambers 1984), however, only a small minority acknowledged having performed them regularly while married and even fewer had been principally responsible for them (Lamb 1986, 1987; see also DeVault 1991).

Another way of devaluing the former wife involved acknowledging that she had done most of the parenting during the marriage but qualifying the merit of her efforts. Their own parenting involvement, even though limited in scope because of employment and other demands, had been the more vital to their children's well-being. Said several men, "She couldn't have done it without me." "Quality and not quantity is what matters," argued another.

Irrespective of the accuracy of their representations of their domestic contributions, these men felt unappreciated in divorce. They felt shortchanged in the "economy of gratitude" (Hochschild 1989). They were "not like most other men" in their judgments; they had helped out with children and housekeeping, and their income-earning efforts involved some sacrifice that went unrewarded.

I mean, life is tough: buying a house, having kids at the same time, [and her] keeping the kids, doing the care for them, while I would go off to work. I was working late—long hours for a month or 6 weeks at a time. But there are some wives I've talked to, of my friends, who say sure they're exhausted, they're tired, they're mad at their husbands for doing it, but they understand

that that's the husband's role: You've got to be the breadwinner when you've
got children and the wife doesn't have a profession.

Additionally, they felt betrayed. The former wife who, "of all people,"
was in a unique position to value and publicly legitimate their family
efforts, joined forces instead with the legal system. She allowed him to be
"emasculated." Hurt feelings were compounded by resentments about a
former wife's evident discretionary authority in divorce; much of women's
power is kept hidden in marriage (Backett 1987; Pestello and Voyandoff
1991). The shift, in which she apparently gained authority, was a direct affront to assumptions about the sexes and their relationships. Furthermore,
both hurt feelings and resentments were exacerbated by a former wife's
retraction of support. Prior to divorce, at least in many cases, a wife collaborated with her husband in his assessment of his family labor (Backett
1987; Hochschild 1989). Several phenomena were likely at play in the
former spouse's collusion. First, wives generally compare their own husbands' efforts to those of other men's (Hochschild 1989; Rubin 1976).
Second, they deliberately try to provide positive reinforcement to increase
the likelihood of repeated helping activities. And some wives probably
cooperate in maintaining marital fictions about domestic work out of their
own ambivalence about how extensive a husband's participation should be
in the home (Ehrensaft 1987; Coltrane 1989; Hiller and Philliber 1986);
women too are socialized to expect a gendered division of labor. With
separation and divorce, however, the incentives to embellish a husband's
direct family contributions were lost. But an estranged wife's reconstruc-
tion of the domestic division of labor was not a shared one.

Degrading the former wife served several functions. It lent support to
assertions about a miscarriage of justice, including that they had been
badly mistreated in the divorce settlement and illegitimately stripped of
authority in the family. Denigrating the former spouse buttressed self-esteem: The person "who came out ahead" in divorce was undeserving and
unworthy, especially in comparison to him. And presenting the former wife
in a negative light served also as a rationalization for her extensive
presence in their accounts and strategies: Because of *her* actions and
attitudes, they were "divorced, but [he will be] never, never, never free of
her," as one participant declared.

"Maternal Nature"

Belittling a former spouse did not exclude also commending her; similarly, denigrating women as a group did not exclude extolling them (see

also Chodorow and Contratto 1982). In tandem with criticizing women's natures and activities, over half of the men asserted that women have particular and distinctive abilities for nurturing and mothering. Most criticized their former wife's parenting and, at other points in the interview, described her as a "good mother." The contradictory assessments created a dilemma. Accepting the notion of maternal superiority undermined their grievances about maternal custody. For example, one respondent, who had several postgraduate degrees in the humanities and social sciences, believed he should be the custodial parent because his former wife "though beautiful, isn't very bright." He vigorously defended his position that men and women are "naturally" different and argued that women are to blame for an array of social problems and are the appropriate caretakers of children and gatekeepers of the family.

> What gets lost in the judges' decisions [granting maternal custody] is the determinative voice of the father. That's the problem with the American family: There's never been such a weak family in all of history. Take the Greek family. In Greek times, boys were taken out of the hands of women at a certain age and placed in the hands of men, that's how they became men. We have to reclaim all that; men have to be allowed to be men. Otherwise the society will just continue to disintegrate. But the Greeks understood that women had special instincts for nurturing the young. They divided child-rearing up into stages and all women were expected to do was nurture the young.

Another person "fought like the devil" several years after divorcing to obtain custody of his son (although not of his daughter). After securing custody temporarily as a result of "child snatching" (his term), he let his son return to his mother's prior to court rulings on the custody challenge and abduction charges. Leaving the marriage had been "the best action" for himself, but it had left both children "screwed up."

> This is what people have to get straight: Women are superior emotionally to men. Men are superior physically. It's from the centuries of survival games. We are different. Women are the healers, the spiritual teachers. Women have the nurturing powers. Men will never have that. I see it with my own kids. Boys take divorce harder than girls. They need a mother's love and they need the father's discipline. It was impossible for me to both love them and discipline them. There's a role differentiation and I couldn't be both to them.

One way participants tried to work themselves out of the contradiction between denigrating a former wife's mothering and believing in "maternal instinct," when they recognized the paradox, was to argue that wives had been able to fulfill their maternal nature only because they, as husbands, provided economic support. Although most of the participants' wives had been employed during some periods of the marital years, the men's own earnings had been the predominant source of family income, as is the case nationally (U.S. Department of Labor, Bureau of Labor Statistics 1991; U.S. Bureau of the Census 1992). As married couples, then, with only several exceptions, they had followed a relatively conventional division of labor. Therefore, as the primary income earners, they should have automatically been granted custody, argued nearly one third of the participants.

In retrospect, the participants concluded that the former wife's economic dependency during marriage was unjust. For instance, this man's wife, a secretary, "had not worked" for 4 years after the birth of their first and then, 18 months later, their second child. At the time, the two agreed that she should care for their young children full-time. But divorce changed his perspective: "She was a parasite, a money-sucking parasite and she still is. That's what the law [in awarding a custodial mother child support] does, rewards parasitic women." The implicit marriage contract operative during marriage, involving a culturally defined and socially structured gender-based division of labor and exchange (Weitzman 1985), was independent of their shared parenthood and was subject to both redefinition and termination on divorce.

Double standards for behavior were operative in the men's assessments of both marriage and divorce: Women and men carry particular and distinctive responsibilities. Describing his resentment about the divorce and maternal custody outcome, this father of two young daughters reflected on the marriage breakdown. Besides being employed full-time, as was his wife, he typically "was out six out of seven evenings," involved in local politics.

I would get home, tired from work, have meetings to go to, and ask her what was wrong. She'd say, "Nothing." Once she said, "You don't know me at all. You don't know who I am." "I don't know who you are?" I looked at her and I said, "You know, this is one hell of a damned time for you to be telling me all of these things because we're into the big time, *big time,* big league." Once she said, "Well, if you loved me, you would've known something was wrong." I looked at her and said, "I want to ask you something." She said, "What's that?" "Do you think that I should take it in through osmosis? Women need to talk to men. If you don't tell me, I don't know. If I'm busy in my particular life and I don't see what's going on, let me know."

Seemingly unaware of his dual marital expectations—that his wife alone should be responsible for their children outside of the hours spent in paid work—he did incorporate into his personal assessment an awareness of cultural shifts. He continued:

> I said [to her], "It's kind of crazy. When we grow up, you've [men have] got to ask for the dates, you've got to pay for this, you've got to do all of this initiating. We're told all of this. Now all of a sudden we get to this point in life when the women want to initiate something or they want to be more aggressive. That's great. But how's about telling us what's going on? You know, we're in this changing of the gears in society or whatever, but you [as a woman] know, you've [women have] got to talk."

A Broken Family

How these men understood the family was a major factor in their reliance on conventional approaches in divorce and their unwillingness or inability to locate alternative lines of action. A family was the "normal," nuclear family, headed by a legally married heterosexual couple, and their offspring (see Cheal 1991; Morgan 1985; Thorne 1993). Any other arrangement was a deficit family (Marotz-Baden, Adams, Bueche, Munro, and Munro 1979). Left in the wake of divorce was a broken family, consisting of two parts: himself and the former wife and children or, as commonly referred to, "me and them." Even men who had sought the divorce, about one-third of the group, and several of those who had primary or shared custody of children understood the postdivorce family to be a broken one. Altered residential arrangements and changes in interactional dynamics reinforced the view that the family was fractured, damaged irreparably by divorce. Other people, including attorneys and judges, relatives, school principals and teachers, and health care and social service workers, took and endorsed the perception that the postdivorce family was a broken family.

Subscribing to the predominant cultural definition of the family, the prevalent *family discourse* (Gubrium and Holstein 1990), these men perceived only a restricted range of options for after-divorce associations with the former spouse. Alternatives to tension-filled relationships were largely unimaginable.[8] Although most insisted that they "would have liked" the "ideal" former spousal relationship— cooperative, mutually supportive, and friendly—they neither knew how to attain it (see also Ahrons and Wallisch 1987b; Ambert 1988) nor believed such a relationship was truly possible. Family was predicated on marriage: Termination of marriage meant a breach in family, not just in the marital relationship. Marriage and parenthood went hand in hand, a package deal; the men's understandings of themselves as fathers assumed a marital relationship to the mothers of their children. As researchers Furstenberg and Cherlin (1991) noted: "Men's ties to their children, and their feelings of responsibility for their children, depend on their ties to their wives" (p. 118; see also Backett 1982, 1987; Fox 1985). Because spousal relations proved to be transitory, so too parental relations could be, as this father suggested: "Every time I see those children, I am overwhelmed by memories. They are a living reminder of *my* marriage, *my* wife, and the years of pointless effort. Being a father is all tied up with being a husband. That's ended." Further, the behavioral prescriptions and meanings offered by the institution of marriage (e.g., Berger and Kellner 1964; Riessman 1990) were thrown into disarray by marital dissolution. The *negotiated order* of family was disrupted (Strauss 1978).

Another factor in the notion of a fractured family was the participants' understanding that men's and women's relationships with their offspring differ. Mother-child relations were distinctive and separate from father-child ones, a view held by most men, irrespective of their children's ages. In stark contrast to the independent mother-child relationship was the father-mother-child interactional triad, as was the case for them. This view was not unique to these men; in other studies, divorced mothers as well believed that parental bonds differ for men and women (Arendell 1986; Hetherington et al. 1976).[9] Nor was the perspective idiosyncratic to the situation of divorce. For instance, Backett (1987) found that "the development of the mother role is much less problematic than the father role. *Motherhood* was described by the participants as having special features: the overall responsibility for organization of children and the home; having greater knowledge of the child and its needs as a result of having greater direct involvement with children; being potentially more readily available to the child than was the father. . . . For the majority of the men, time limitations and personal choice lead them *in practice* only to be minimally involved" (p. 79, italics in original) in the development of a direct relationship with the child. Additionally, when a father "*was* directly involved with the child, such interaction tended in any case to be mediated through the indirect understandings provided by the mother" (Backett 1987, p. 84; see also Rossi and Rossi 1990). A wife's mediation of the father-child relationship was consistent with her family role as emotional worker (Hochschild 1983, 1989; Liljestrom 1986)[10] and reinforced by the dominant sociocultural ethos linking children to their mothers (Chodorow 1978; Coltrane 1989). One father, who had read extensively about the psychological effects of divorce on children, compared the outcomes of his two divorces:

> I would have to say that my children's primary attachment really was with their mother. I think that's typical in families: Mothers are just better trained —maybe it's an instinct—for parenting. Maybe fathers just don't make the effort. Anyway, even after my first divorce, I found that my ex-wife was vital to my relationship with the child of our marriage: She thought it was important that he maintain contact with me and that I be a part of his life. So she really encouraged him to do this and so it continued to be a relationship. She ran a kind of interference between us. He's 21 now and we have a good, solid relationship, but my children of this last marriage are essentially withdrawn from me. Their mother, my second wife, never really facilitated our relationship.

Having relied on their wife to mediate relations with their children during marriage proved problematic after divorce, for these men, affecting and entangling in complicated ways the former spousal and parental relations. On the one hand, most of the participants actively devalued and denigrated the former wife's family activities. On the other, they depended on them. No ready substitute was available when the children's mother ceased participating directly in the triad. Moreover, both dependency on the former wife and her withdrawal from the role of intermediary were deeply resented, seen as abuses of power on her part.

That most participants understood the postdivorce family as broken and that this understanding inherently involved the former wife in varying ways is consistent with the dynamics of the contemporary family and its gendered character (e.g., Thorne 1993; Skolnick and Skolnick 1994). Family theorist Liljestrom (1986) described the modern family and women's pivotal roles: "The core [of the family] has been formed around the woman. Regardless of whether she has chosen it herself or been forced into 'exile,' she has made the family's interests her own. She has lived her life vicariously, and shared other family members' triumphs and failures. She has held everything together. The bond between mother and child is the last to be broken. She has held together a shared daily life for the family members; she has joined father and children together. She has been the glue that has bonded the first and third generations. She has maintained contact with kin and other supporting networks" (p. 146). Women as wives and mothers have been the primary interactional and emotional laborers of the family. Liljestrom (1986) continued, noting that as the family has adapted in response to the processes of modernization, the "core [of the family] bursts and is divided into two distinct institutions: marriage and parenthood. Thus, the social disclosed asymmetry between motherhood and fatherhood is also exposed" (p. 146). For numerous divorced men in this study, that asymmetry became acutely evident after the ending of their marriages.

The understanding that the postdivorce family was broken contained a profound dissatisfaction with legally allocated responsibilities and entitlements. Especially the fathers without primary custody were faced with an incongruous situation. They were granted little, if any, authority over child-related decisions or the former wife's expenditures. Yet they were expected to continue contributing to the economic support of their children. The two facets of the good-provider role—head-of-household and income earner—were severed, separated out, in the family changed by divorce. The few men who retained some discretionary jurisdiction in their children's lives believed they too were vulnerable, at risk of being displaced and disregarded. The fractured family still could be shattered— themselves the expendable pieces.

Tied to the broken family were twin conditions for most men: stigma and marginality. This person explained: "You're not part of the family, part of the society anymore. You really don't have a proper place, a place where you have input into what goes on in your life. You're treated as if you're just scum, that's what you are really." And this one said, "The whole society stigmatizes the noncustodial father. Absolutely. It's thrown at you in all different ways. We're damaged goods, plain and simple, damaged goods." Being "branded" undermined a sense of self, countered assertions of rights, and reinforced the belief that resistance was necessary.

Backett's (1982, 1987) analyses offer further insights into these men's perceptions that they were marginalized from family by divorce. Characterizing men's dependence on a wife for information about their children, she reported: "The father relied heavily on the mother's information about herself and the children for cues to his own behavior. He was vulnerable in his personal evaluations of everyday family events since he was, in fact, absent from a great deal of the child-rearing activity. The mother's account was his prime source of information but he could never be certain that he had grasped the 'total picture' since, inadvertently or deliberately, her account was bound to be selective" (1987, pp. 81-82). Divorced, these fathers were cut off, for the most part, from their prior source of information, their children's mother. Thus they were even more vulnerable in their assessments of and sense of involvement in family events than the married fathers in Backett's study. Particularly noncustodial fathers were disadvantaged because their lack of direct experience was much more extensive than the typical residential father's described by Backett.

Feeling marginalized, pushed to the periphery of family life, countered the men's expectation that they would feel liberated, freed of the responsibilities and burdens of marriage and family. In divorcing, they expected to be the beneficiaries of increased freedom and autonomy, irrespective of whether they had wanted to maintain the marriage (see also Riessman 1990). One man, using the language of broken family explicitly, summed up his dilemma: "I guess I'm sort of at a loss in all of this; I just don't know what to do to fix a broken family. I can't say I didn't want the divorce; it was a mutual decision. I wanted my freedom and I like having it, really like having it. The freedom is a great benefit, *great.* But I just hadn't understood before what it [divorce] would do. It's really become them and me, and I don't know what to do."

Aggravating the sense of marginalization was their isolation. Marriage and family were viewed as intensely private matters, and divorce a failure made all too public.[11] Although they believed they were members of a class—divorced fathers—the group was an amorphous one. Family experiences were understood to be personal and discrete, consistent with the dominant norms regarding family and masculinity—privacy and self-determination (e.g., Dizard and Gadlin 1990; Bernardes 1985) and autonomy and independence (Jaggar 1983), respectively. Actions taken in response to divorce by the majority of participants were almost entirely individualized ones, limited to their particular circumstances and cast of players. Some men did seek support and guidance from professionals, especially attorneys and counselors, and a few relied on family members, but most, especially those engaged in the more conventional responses, "went it largely alone."

Even participants involved in fathers' or men's groups felt isolated within their particular circumstances. Although nearly one-quarter of the men had some contact with a fathers' organization, only three men allowed their personal situations and social activism to touch openly by telling others details of their lives. Two of these men complained that local fathers' organizations flounder because individuals approach them usually only briefly, on the basis of their own narrowly defined needs and interests, which they typically keep hidden. One explained:

Men are conditioned to not be involved in these kinds of issues, to not be public. Besides, who wants to put on their résumé that they worked for men's rights? Who wants to go out there in the streets and expose themselves to scrutiny when "that judge is going to be in the window seeing me specifically in that crowd? I've never met Judge So-and-So, but when he sees me and picks me out of that crowd of hundreds of people, he's going to do a job on me in the courtroom," this kind of thinking. And it's a masculine kind of thing, problems with intimacy, relating with other men, relating on emotional issues, stuff like that. You get men together on certain issues related to business, you know, traditional issues where men are supposed to be. But don't get a father out there and try to say, "I love my children and will be damned if you're going to keep me away from them." It's almost impossible to get a man to do that. He loves his kids, but to have to say it out in public, no way.

Organized efforts also were hampered, participants argued, by the public neglect of men and the widely held, "erroneous" view that men are the perpetrators and women and children the victims in divorce. Furthermore, beyond denouncing particular attorneys, publicly complaining about divorce injustice, and seeking the support of elected officials, what constituted appropriate lines of collective action was unclear.

Exceptions

The men responding in unconventional and innovative ways diverged noticeably from the others even though most also subscribed to beliefs in differences and increasing tensions between men and women. They also held women responsible for the quality of marriage and divorce, but their assessments were more ambivalent:

> I think many of us [men] suspect that there's something wrong where so many women do want to sue for divorce, and so there may be an element of unfairness to women in marriage somehow. But does that mean that the whole thing should be turned into a revenge-type thing in the divorce? I don't think so. I don't think kids benefit from divorce if it becomes a revenge for all of the inequities of the marriage.

Also, whereas most of the respondents claimed to have become more fully aware through divorce of the significance of the differences between the sexes, each of these nine men observed that he had come to realize how much he shared with his former wife specifically, and women generally, especially divorced mothers. One noted, for example, "The only difference between most guys I know and me is that they look at divorce from a kind of sexist view, men being the victim and women the, you know, perpetrator. I see it being about even. I see a lot of women going through the same kind of thing I have. It's tough all around." Furthermore, these men tended to attribute their marital difficulties not to innate differences between the sexes but to the particulars of their relationship, respective personalities, and family histories. References to differences in values, often attributed to variations in religious upbringing, were typical. Sex differences were a factor in these differences, not determinants. These men did much less generalizing from their personal situations to divorced men's overall, and when they evaluated the former spouse negatively, they qualified or tempered their remarks. This person, a father of two, for instance, said, "I keep saying 'her,' 'her,' 'her.' I mean the problem was both of ours, not hers, so I'm giving the wrong impression saying 'her,' 'her,' 'her,' all the time."

Held in common by nearly all of the participants, and both a part and a reinforcer of the masculinist discourse of divorce, was a general disdain for divorce law and legal practitioners. Although levels of legal engagement varied, the generally shared viewpoint was that divorce law disadvantages men and favors women.

Notes

1. The issue of rights is a lively one not only in legal scholarship but in the social sciences and philosophy. For discussions of the effects of individual rights doctrine on social life and interpersonal relations particularly, see, for example, Bellah et al. (1985), Dizard and Gadlin (1990), and Wolfe (1989). For feminist critical analyses of rights, see, for example, Pateman (1989), Fineman (1991), and Jaggar (1983). See generally Gordon (1990a, 1990b).

2. "It does not advance understanding to speak of rights in the abstract. It matters only that some specific right is or is not recognized in some specific social setting . . . rights-talk often conceals a claim that things ought to be different within an argument that things are as the claimant contends. That masquerade is sometimes successful, at least until the claim is rejected by the courts or by the wider audience for the claim. It is successful because the language of rights is so open and indeterminate that opposing parties can use the same language to express their positions. Because rights-talk is indeterminate, it can provide only momentary advantages in ongoing political struggles" (Tushnet 1984, pp. 1364, 1371).

3. Presumably the actual threatened grounds for action for divorce in this situation was cruel and inhuman treatment because the period of abandonment as grounds for divorce in New York state was 1 or more years (*Family Law of the State of New York* 1990, p. 284).

4. A prominent exception to the argument that women's and mothers' rights are not used interchangeably is Chesler (1991).

5. The men's claims about reverse sexism parallel the white backlash against affirmative action and other programs aimed at redressing a history of racism. See, for example, Blauner (1989) and Terkel (1992).

6. See also Thompson and Walker (1989) for a succinct overview of the research on power relations between women and men in marriage. For other discussions of differential power in marriage, see Riessman (1990), Hochschild (1989), Rubin (1976), and Weiss (1987, 1990). For theoretical discussions of men's power in heterosexual relations more generally, see, among numerous possibilities, Pleck (1992a), Sattel (1976), Brod (1987a, 1987b), Rhode (1990), Astrachan (1985), Kaufman (1987), Blumstein and Schwartz (1983), Scanzoni (1982), Goode (1982), Glenn (1987), and Blumenberg and Coleman (1989).

7. For a neo-psychoanalytic perspective on men's devaluation of women or anything perceived to be female or feminine, see Chodorow (1980, 1989). See also Cancian (1987), Hochschild (1989), Basow (1992), and Gilligan (1982).

8. "If discourse assigns meaning to everyday life and thereby instructs our actions, life's potential meanings are limited to the discourses available" (Gubrium and Holstein 1990, p. 16). Within a discursive field, not all discourses carry equal weight and power (Weedon 1987): Discursive choices "exist in a hierarchical network of antagonistic relations in which certain versions . . . [hold] more social and institutional power than others" (p. 126).

9. See Aquilino (1993) for a thorough review of the literature and analysis of recent data indicating that adult child and parent relationships vary by parent also, especially by parent custodial status: "Becoming a *noncustodial father* has a large negative impact on adult children's relations with their fathers" (p. 25, italics in original).

10. Reviewing the literature, Basow (1992) noted: "Given the small amount of time fathers generally spend engaged with their children, it is not surprising that most children and teenagers report a closer and better relationship with their mother than with their father" (p. 252).

11. For a theoretical discussion of the spheres labeled private and public and the family, see Cheal (1991) and Zaretsky (1976).

4

THE LAW AND
"MISCARRIAGES OF JUSTICE"

Oppression in divorce is rooted in the laws governing marital dissolution: Not only does the law favor women through an intrinsic maternal bias, according to the respondents, it penalizes men for their family role, which necessitates investment in employment rather than direct child care. Together, the legal system and former wives exploit men's income-earning history and abilities and disregard the significance of their provider activity. One person explained: "You know, as a man you have no rights. That is, you're treated as a nonperson or as a second, third, fourth, or fifth class citizen. They look at us: You know, 'Who's that guy with the mother?' Suddenly we're just sperm donors or something. We're a paycheck and sperm donors and that's our total function in society. The legal bias for the mother is incredible." And another man noted: "They use us up, drain us dry like a can of oil, and then throw us aside." Negative cultural stereotypes about fathers fueled and even legitimated the divorce inequities. "They all just think we're all 'deadbeat dads,' you know, do-nothings."

State Intrusion

Involved in divorce injustice was the public, that is, state, intrusion into matters deemed sacrosanct, insisted these men. Just as marriage and family are private affairs, at least ostensibly, so too then, should be divorce.[1] What began as a personal matter, marital troubles, came to be publicly announced and regulated, and scrutinized by attorneys and sometimes judges and caseworkers. The argument that divorce is handled differently than marriage and family is not restricted to the respondents. For example, social historian Jacob (1988) observed: "Family life is generally considered to be private; American homes are private castles. That remains true for those families whose lives have not been disrupted by divorce. Divorced men and women and their children, however, operate under an entirely different set of rules" (p. 172). Although procedures are particular to each state (Freed and Walker 1989; Fineman 1991), regulation of domestic life has increased everywhere (Jacob 1988).[2] More specifically, "the issues [between couples in divorce] are defined legally as the grounds for divorce, the division of property, spousal maintenance, child support, and custody and visitation" (Girdner 1988, p. 51).

"Unjustified" in the first place, state intervention, according to the men, was also unbalanced: Maternal bias prevailed despite the "alleged gender neutrality of the law." In addition to the national preponderance of mother custody, systematic discrimination was evidenced especially in the absence of joint physical custody mandates and the recent passage of the New York State Child Support Guidelines, of which all respondents except for several of the sole custodial fathers were aware. Had they been able to negotiate privately, a majority claimed—"without the involvement of the law"—they would "have been able to resist its maternal biases." In contrast to their claims, however, divorce settlements reached entirely without legal representation are not inevitably more fair. Rather, they typically advantage men and disadvantage women (Fineman 1991; Rhode and Minow 1990; Weitzman 1985; Erlanger, Chambliss, and Melli 1987). Making this point, researchers Seltzer and Garfinkel (1990) stated: "The picture of relatively equal parents bargaining and trading until they reach agreement is inaccurate. Inequality characterizes most divorce negotiations" (p. 107).[3]

Specifically usurped by the state in its divorce law and practices, claimed these men, was the right to autonomy and self-determination. The ability of the other spouse to attain divorce without their full agreement was an especially galling violation: Preserving the marriage was not a prerogative but was conditional. The other spouse could sue for divorce.[4] Despite the lack of a unilateral no-fault divorce option (in New York state), preventing divorce in practice was nearly impossible. A spouse could initiate a lawsuit and present a fabricated case, "mocking justice," as one respondent said. The threat of being sued for divorce was "a kind of blackmail" because "proving" one's innocence against the charges of marital violations was a precarious process, having uncertain outcomes. The "facts" were not inevitably recognized by those ruling in divorce cases. Moreover, attempting to refute false charges "upped the ante" and pushed them and their attorneys to even higher levels of aggressiveness and confrontation.

The men's arguments that the court sometimes finds it difficult to determine marital facts and that the judicial process can intensify conflict both are recognized by scholars. For example, "the use of grounds [as cause for divorce] requires substantiation or proof. The offering of proof typically escalates the conflict, as parties exchange accusations and denials" (Milne 1988, p. 42). Indeed, a primary consideration in the displacement of fault-based divorce throughout most of the nation was the frequency with which fraud was committed by persons seeking to end their marriages (Weitzman 1985; Fineman 1991; Halem 1980; Jacob 1988).

"The major criticisms [by the 1960s] leveled at the fault system were that it tended to aggravate and perpetuate bitterness between the spouses, and that the widespread practice of using perjured testimony in collusive divorces promoted disrespect for the legal system" (Glendon 1987, p. 65).

Most respondents discussed their divorces in terms of fault, consistent with New York state's legal criteria. The few who did little blaming for the dissolution either assigned joint or took sole responsibility for the marital troubles or discontent; those in the latter case had initiated divorce themselves without the wife's early consent. But over two-thirds of the men held their former wives culpable for the disintegration of their marriages, a phenomenon they saw as distinct and separate from who actually filed for divorce. Three explanations dominated. The former wife had demanded divorce outright. This usually raised the suspicion of marital infidelity: Fully one-third of the men in the study believed that their former wives were having extramarital affairs, although only three former wives "had admitted" as much. Second, the former wife had allowed the marriage to deteriorate to the point at which both agreed that dissolution was the appropriate, even "sane," course of action. Or, third, she had "abandoned" the marriage, leaving him to eventually seek divorce.

Attributing divorce to the former wife was not unique to men (Kitson and Holmes 1992; Kruk 1991) living in a fault-based state. According to a May 1989 Gallup Poll that examined attitudes of Americans: "Thirty-one percent of men said they were the spouse who wanted the divorce versus 55 percent of women. In only 20 percent of the cases did both spouses want the divorce. [Furthermore,] the 1985 *Cosmopolitan/Battelle* report also found that women were more approving than men of divorce for unhappily married couples with young children: 43 percent versus 31 percent" (Faludi 1991, p. 470). Additionally, the belief that women are overwhelmingly responsible for divorce predominates in other Western countries (Kruk 1991).

Legal Encounters

A large majority of the 75 participants settled their divorces without actually going to trial, as is the case nationally (Emery 1988; Erlanger et al. 1987; Seltzer and Garfinkel 1990). Settlement discussions, however, usually involved the assistance of attorneys. But whether using legal counsel or not, the divorcing couples bargained in the "shadow of the law" in that agreements had to meet certain legal criteria (Mnookin and Kornhauser 1979; Mnookin et al. 1990).

Participation in the legal process, even when the courts were circumvented, was a constant reminder of the public intrusion into their family lives and the consequent loss of privacy, power, and authority (see also Folberg and Milne 1988). Made known and sometimes investigated were such matters as marital, including sexual, relations; childrearing practices and parental involvement; and financial status and management. Moreover, the public airing of domestic life issues was subject to distortion:

> When I went to court [seeking to deny the divorce petition], my wife had gotten one of the best lawyers. I sat there and felt like I was being raped. I couldn't understand how they could say things like that about me. I was humiliated, degraded. One of my problems was being overly generous, too generous. They would hit at things like, "he never bought anything," "he was stingy."

Three respondents had cursory contact with the legal system, encountering it directly only to file the requisite paperwork. They and their spouses reached agreement about child custody and the disposition of property, of which there was little, through informal conversations. Two of these men acquired sole responsibility of their children when their wives left the family, and the other explicitly waived any rights to custody when he left. Child support agreements were eventually written, but none was followed and no formal efforts were taken to enforce them.

The others' experiences and levels of involvement with the legal system ranged from minimal and short-term association with attorneys to intense and repeated involvement with both legal counselors and the courts. Just seeking advice from an attorney was described by many participants as involvement with the courts (Emery and Wyer 1987a; Mnookin et al. 1990; Kelly et al. 1988; Ahrons 1983). (Probes were used during the interviews to clarify the actual nature of participants' legal involvement). At the extremes of legal entanglement, several men had spent in excess of $100,000 on fees and numbered their court appearances at more than 40 over a period of years. Because individuals can avoid incurring attorney costs by representing themselves in family court,[5] repeat court appearances in New York may be higher than in other states even though they are not uncommon elsewhere either.

The legal system was the object of intense bitterness and scorn. According to one respondent, "If you're a man, you're guilty; you're automatically a criminal," and another, "The system simply doesn't give a shit about fathers, it doesn't and never did give a shit about me." Family law attorneys were particular targets of anger and disdain: "Lawyers are the new carpetbaggers. In divorce they too often accelerate people's crap with each other; they expand upon it, and get rich themselves. Lawyers have a good business off our problems, that's it. They just fan the flames. They know nothing about human emotions."

Adding to their resentments about divorce and the role of attorneys was the cost of legal representation, which most believed was too high, "exorbitant, in fact." Being required to pay an estranged wife's legal costs as well as their own, as some were, was particularly infuriating and unfair. "Later, I got a bill from her lawyer. That's the worst insult. Here's a guy who has insulted me, struck at my character, emasculated me, and actually believed everything that was said about me, which were lies; believed everything, is charging me, wants me to pay him. Like he wants me to pay him to kill me." Ten men, all of whom earned significantly more than their former wives, reported having to cover all the legal fees.

Direct experience with judges was less common than with attorneys, but was also assessed negatively. "They're attorneys too, only more consumed by ambition." Judges were indicted especially with regard to custody issues.

Aside from whatever legitimate grievances the respondents had as clients, legal practitioners were in "no-win" situations: Marital dissolution was an intensely emotional matter involving conflicts of interest. Attorneys and judges were easy targets, ready scapegoats for divorce-related frustrations and disappointments. As mediation expert Milne (1988) wrote, "Designed to resolve conflict, the legal system is handicapped when presented with disputes of an interpersonal nature such as divorce. Well-intentioned players, such as lawyers, judges, and family members, often become pawns in a system that, as it attempts to promote peace, precipitates pernicious conflict" (p. 43). Gender identity may have contributed to the men's vehement blaming of attorneys and judges because, as a result of gender socialization, men typically attribute success to ability and failure to external factors (see Basow 1992, pp. 175-78; Epstein 1988). Divorce was viewed as a failure made public. But women, who more typically attribute failure to themselves, also have harsh complaints about the legal system (Arendell 1986).

THE LEGAL GAME

How state intrusion and attorneys were evaluated had a fickle character. Attorneys who were perceived to be insufficiently aggressive were replaced with ones having reputations as "bulldogs" or "hot shots." And, despite the general hostility toward the legal profession, select attorneys were viewed as being strong allies or, as one described his lawyer, "my golden boy." In these instances, when a settlement was disappointing, it was attributed to the inherent biases operating against them as male clients, not to the favored attorney's competency.

Several men continued to associate with their attorneys after the divorce was finalized because "the rapport was so good" (see Arendell 1986). For example, this man succeeded in obtaining shared residential custody of their young child despite his estranged wife's opposition. He had threatened to seek sole custody if she did not agree to his proposed joint physical custody arrangement. Annual earnings of more than $200,000 made the threats of further legal challenge, to be handled by well-qualified and experienced legal representa-tives, realistic.

> I went to an attorney who was reputed to be the best matrimonial attorney, at least in the county and probably in New York state, and possibly one of the best anywhere. He and I had a real good relationship and still do. He had respect for my intelligence and respect for my basic knowledge for certain things, so we didn't have to spend hours going over trivial legalities. I had enough respect for his professionalism to say, "This is what I want, you do it. You don't have to explain to me the whys and wherefores; if I have a question, I'll ask you." And he treated me like an equal. Plus, I didn't go running to him every time I had a problem. We had a real respect for each other. We still play tennis every Sunday.

The use of greater resources to exert leverage in the custody and support bargaining was not uncommon. Although no others had such financial means as the person cited above, nearly one-half of the participants claimed they had threatened to "win by outspending" their estranged wife. That men use superior incomes to attain more favorable divorce outcomes is an argument commonly made by former wives (Arendell 1986; Weitzman 1985; Kurz 1995) and is supported by other research (e.g., Furstenberg and Cherlin 1991; Mnookin et al. 1990; Seltzer 1991a).

Complaining vociferously about the legal order, and its failure to be "objective," "neutral," and "fair," what many men in the study wanted from the system was the endorsement and protection of their individual rights, as they defined them. The stakes were high. Thus those who succeeded in their legal battles and achieved their desired outcomes, although angered that their rights were not automatically secured, were nonetheless satisfied overall. This small minority "had made the system work." And those who had successfully circumvented a legal struggle, although insisting that it always remained a possibility, credited their avoidance thus far to their own actions and choices: "I stayed logical and reasonable and made the right moves, and she couldn't fight that."

Most, however, were resentful and frustrated. They bemoaned the necessity of their participation in the legal system even as they defined it as a "battleground" on which the "divorce war" was fought. For instance, angered by seeing his estranged wife out to lunch with her boss, with whom he suspected she had an affair before leaving the marriage, this person initiated legal action: "I just called up my attorney and told him to get on her butt. That's what I do when she crosses me." And, when asked by his former wife about child support owed, this father of three also called on his attorney: "I get my buddy [attorney] to phone her attorney and make threats about custody. It keeps her off balance, respectful. And it costs her money. I figure the child support just about covers her legal costs." For most, to not engage intensely in the system was to allow the possibility of defeat without resistance. The alternative was to depend on negotiation and compromise with the former spouse directly, a risk few believed they safely could take.

MEDIATION

Mediation in divorce receives mixed assessments (e.g., Emery 1988; Kelly et al. 1988; Dingwall and Greatbatch 1991). For example, Emery (1988) concluded that mediation has numerous positive effects, including a reduction in custody hearings; agreements comparable to those reached through litigation except for more joint legal custody assignments; higher compliance with agreements; and greater parental, especially paternal, satisfaction (p. 134; see also Kelly 1988). Advocating mediation, Milne and Folberg (1988) observed that "divorce mediation facilitates private ordering and recognizes both the emotional and legal dimensions of marital dissolution" (p. 3). But Kelly and associates (1988) concluded that "mediation may not be an appropriate alternative for as many as 60 percent of the couples who attempt to reach agreements through the mediation process" (p. 466). Yet for couples who benefited from mediation, its value "lies in its ability to affect the quality and future direction of the spousal relationship, particularly with regard to the ability to cooperate after divorce and the more realistic perception of each other's anger" not in short-term psychological benefits (p. 472).

In this study, four of the five men most satisfied with the divorcing process and outcome went the mediation route. The spouses agreed about the desired outcomes in each case, cooperated during the divorcing process, and continued to collaborate in parenting subsequent to divorce. Another participant who had used mediation to reach a divorce settlement disliked the outcome and was using the conventional legal system in his efforts to alter the results.

Others unsuccessfully sought alternatives to the legal system.[6] Two men had wanted to establish a divorce settlement through a *get,* a bill of contract for divorce under Jewish law in which the husband has authority over the decision to divorce. Both men remained convinced that the religiously based divorce system would have resulted in more fair outcomes than did the secular legal process. But "fair" here may well have been self-serving because the *get* typically benefits men, granting them far more authority in the divorcing process (*Encyclopedia Judicia* 1971).[7]

Six of the numerous men indicating they would have preferred mediation were especially bitter that the standard legal procedures instead had been used. But these men's objectives were contrary to those of mediation. Defining divorce and its outcomes as matters of winning or losing, the safeguarding of self-interest was their overriding priority, whereas the goal of mediation is to assist participants in locating common ground (Folberg and Milne 1988). Not mentioned at all by these men in their arguments as to why mediation would have been a better process or achieved more satisfactory results were children's needs (see also Dingwall and Greatbatch 1991).

The incongruent goals of prioritizing personal interests and desiring mediation had cultural roots. Mediation researcher Girdner (1988) argued, "In any societies where mediation is practiced, resolving the dispute amicably is more important than victory or establishing right or wrong. In United States culture, competition, winning and individual gain are domi-

nant cultural values. Compromise and accommodation are seen as weaknesses and are not positively valued, except in terms of the traditional view
of women's role in the family" (p. 51). And, she continued, "the cross-cultural literature indicates that mediation between people of unequal power
tends to lead to agreements that reflect that inequality" (Girdner 1988,
p. 56). Because wives are typically the less powerful spouse (Blumstein
and Schwartz 1983; Scanzoni 1982; Goode 1982; Glenn 1987; Blumenberg and Coleman 1989), it is husbands who stand to benefit most if
inequities are not handled adequately.[8] Legal scholar Fineman (1991), for
example, argued that mediators discriminate against women and favor men
because of their attachment to symbolic equality and favoring of joint
custody. The presumption of joint custody disregards women's family
activities and commitments, especially their primary parenting.[9]

Believing men are systematically disadvantaged in divorce and recognizing that the mediation process can be manipulated to advantage, two
respondents were being trained to become family mediators, intending to
work with divorcing couples. Both men were active in fathers' rights
groups. One noted: "It's time someone gets in there to fight for men. The
decks need leveling." The other said, similarly: "It's high time men
infiltrate this mediation business. Who else is going to protect fathers'
rights if we don't?" Mediation practice and the profession, just as the legal
one, are not immune from gender struggles and politics.

Primary Injustices

The most prevalent and gravest injustice in divorce, according to nearly
all of the respondents, is the mandating of children into custody.[10] Assigning custody to one and visitation to the other parent was held to be, as one
father described it, an "abomination."[11] More exactly, most men's outrage
was over maternal custody, which was the arrangement for the children of
61 men.[12] The "best interests of the child" standard was a deceit for
maternal custody (see also Thompson 1986).

MATERNAL CUSTODY

The men's insistence that the legal standard of the best interests of the
child is a ruse for maternal bias is contested by scholarly analyses. Legal
scholar Chambers (1984), for example, challenged the common claim of
sexist bias in the current custody standard of the best interests of the child:
"Many people criticize judges who decide custody cases for giving inap-

propriate expression to personal or sexist biases. In our peculiarly American tradition, the decisions are regarded not merely as arbitrary but as discriminatory as well. The father, if he loses, will believe that the judge was prejudiced in the mother's favor just because she is a woman. [In turn,] the mother, if she loses, will believe that the judge gave inappropriate weight to the father's better financial circumstances. These criticisms have some merit but reflect deeper, more fundamental problems in the best-interests standard" (p. 481). Additionally, arguments about the outcomes of custody contests are contentious and conflicting. Some researchers have concluded that fathers disproportionately obtain custody: "Nationally, of the 17% of divorcing fathers who seek custody, 65% are awarded it" (Chase-Lansdale and Hetherington 1990, p. 110; see also Chesler 1991; Polikoff 1983; Weitzman 1985). In contrast, Mnookin et al. (1990) concluded that no paternal bias exists in custody disputes: "Our findings contradict the claims of those who suggest that mothers are losing custody in a high proportion of cases" (p. 71). A respondent in the present study who had repeatedly gone to court seeking a custody change said, "I'm here to tell you that no father has ever, *not ever,* won a custody fight in the state of New York. I looked it up." But even just among this group, two fathers had "won custody" through court challenges. And several others were able to secure a shared custody arrangement by threatening a custody fight.

Many participants rejected the argument that maternal custody is a logical outcome in divorce because women typically perform the bulk of child care and parenting activities. Even if that were the case, they contended, "rewarding" women with custody because they do most caretaking during marriage "penalizes" men in divorce for having been income providers. One representative assertion was, "And who do they think made it possible for her to be a mother?" Another complained, "You must prove your commitment as a father, whereas it is automatically assumed the mother is the better parent. No one asked me if I loved my children, they only asked to see my paycheck." Additionally, they argued, maternal custody ignores fathers' attachments as well as their unique contributions to children. These views were supported by their ardent devaluing of women's family activities.

Although a few men wanted sole physical custody and several had initiated a custody challenge, a large majority of fathers wanted shared or joint physical custody.[13] Yet over half indicated that they had engaged in few, if any, substantive planning discussions with their former wives regarding these preferences. Children went into mothers' custody largely by default (see also Arendell 1986). The inconsistency between these participants' expressed desires and the actions they took earlier during the divorce process was not unique. For example, many fathers in the Stanford

Custody Project,[14] involving a sample of more than 1,000 families, indicated that they would have preferred an arrangement other than mother physical custody. But most never requested or sought an alternative (Mnookin et al. 1990). "Why did so many fathers in our study not request the form of physical custody they said they wanted? It is possible that fathers who told us they wanted custody meant it less passionately than mothers who told us the same. . . . Fathers might also have been responding to what they believed was the social expectation that women are 'supposed' to have custody and that fathers should not request it except in unusual circumstances. Another possibility is that the custodial desires of the mothers and fathers were almost equally strong but that many fathers realized their wishes were not realistic either because they were less experienced in the day-to-day management of the children's lives or because they expected to find it too difficult to coordinate the demands of their jobs with the demands of child care" (Mnookin et al. 1990, p. 72).[15]

Several of the New York fathers did not pursue custody because their work schedules were insufficiently flexible for them to parent full-time. Six others decided "to go along" with maternal custody out of concern for their children. One father believed that his estranged wife would fight him in court if he sought custody, so "I let it [custody] go because I was determined not to put my child in the crossfire between his parents." His perception that challenging custody exacerbates conflict between divorcing parents is supported by other research (e.g., Mnookin et al. 1990).[16] And another respondent concluded that his children were best served by living primarily with their mother. Such mention of children's needs with respect to custody was rare, confined mostly to the nine primary-parent, nurturing fathers: "I would take custody in a minute, if she'd give them to me. But what was I supposed to do? They were young, just 3 and 5. It wasn't fair to them. She's stayed home with them. I couldn't just pull them away and say, 'Here, now you're living with me. You can visit your mother.' "

Most men did not pursue sole or shared custody because they were certain they would fail, given the national pattern in which over 85% of children whose parents divorce go into their mother's custody.[17] Also, with rare exceptions, shared residential custody is granted in New York *only* when both parents voluntarily agree to it.[18] Wives have "veto power," the men insisted, and little incentive for agreeing to anything other than maternal custody. "Why should she have compromised when she knew she'd probably get it all, anyway?" This father who, like the majority, reached a divorce settlement, including custody determination, through the involvement of attorneys and informal discussions but not a court trial summarized his acquired perspective: "I learned that the court views a father as someone who takes the kids to dinner one evening a week and every other weekend takes them out to play somewhere. Fathers are reduced to visiting uncles. And if my ex-wife allows that, I'm to be grateful." And this person, an attorney himself, explained:

> The biases are in the system. There are some judges who say there's no bigger pain in the ass in the world than a father who wants to be involved in his child's life, wants to pick him up at school: "These fathers are sickening, they're disgusting." Especially judges in older generations have those attitudes. But most attorneys are workaholics and achievement oriented and they delegate parenting responsibilities to their wives. Most judges are greater workaholics who delegated parenting responsibilities to their wives and moved up. So they think the purpose of fathers is to raise money and the purpose of mothers is to raise children. Fathers are not supposed to raise children any more than mothers are supposed to make money. This is blatant sexist discrimination.

Most of the men who insisted that they should have been granted shared residential custody because of their unusually high levels of involvement in day-to-day parenting while married were unable to detail their parental involvement. They typically shifted their argument from logical cause to moral superiority. For instance, this father worked more than 70 hours a week during his marriage (and subsequently), trying to establish a small business while his wife was a full-time homemaker and mother. As did others, he claimed a unique, altruistic spirit: "I was willing to share, I was the more generous of the two of us. I was willing to have shared custody. She wasn't. She wanted it all, all for herself." But the context of these men's generosity of spirit, as evidenced in their "willingness to share," as they put it, differed from that of their former wives. Moving to half-time parenting would have constituted a significant increase in parent-child contact and parental responsibility for a majority of men, whereas it would have involved a considerable reduction for their former wives. This differential effect was ignored, obscured by self-interested arguments. Moreover, the underlying assumption that their children would benefit from split living arrangements is not entirely supported by research findings. Although some scholars endorse the push for shared residential custody (e.g., Williams 1988; Roman and Haddad 1978), others vigorously argue against it (e.g., Fineman 1991; Goldstein, Freud, and Solnit 1979).

Resentments about maternal custody were more complicated than the complaints about constraints on their parental involvement, however. In desiring shared custody, what the men wanted was not only greater and more meaningful involvement with their children; they wanted acknowledgment of their parental status and importance. So too, they wanted to "balance out" the power of their former wives by prohibiting maternal custody because it was the prime example of their losses. Women's disproportionate authority in divorce was gained at their expense. As one participant noted: "She has it all now, that's what custody does. I'm left with whatever crumbs she wants to toss me. I'm the dog waiting for a bone." Reviewing the literature, Patrician (1984) linked together these various issues: "Pearson (1982) found that many custody disputes are about custody labels, not the concrete child custody arrangements themselves. Folberg and Graham (1979) point out that parents, especially fathers, want legal definition of their rights to participate in their children's lives. They also want assurances that the other parent does not have more power. Thus, these authors state . . . that the resistance against sole custody, which provides for unequal custody rights, and the agitation for joint custody, which provides for equal custody rights, involves a 'search for status as a legal custodian as much as a search for a new or different living pattern' " (p. 42).

Pointing to the greater complexity of some of their resentments, three men who complained passionately about the injustice of maternal custody had relinquished custody voluntary after having obtained it subsequent to divorce. Other researchers have found that even in many joint custody situations, mothers continue to be the primary parent. For example, "the increase in joint custody does not necessarily mean that children are more likely to live with both of their parents. In this research we have shown that most children still live with their mothers after their parents separate" (Seltzer and Bianchi 1988, p. 675; see also Weitzman 1985; Furstenberg and Cherlin 1991; Seltzer 1991b). Initially denied it despite a custody challenge, this father had assumed custody of their four children when his former wife fell ill. He saw mother custody as being unfair in numerous and profound ways:

> When you go into court as a father, you love your kids, you want a relationship with your kids, you want to be with them as much as you can; then you go into a courtroom situation and you're in a battle, a battle they call it, and somebody is going to win and somebody is going to lose. It's so ridiculous. And what is it that they're going to win or lose? Your kids. Your flesh and blood, part of your dreams and hope about life, this that you fathered. And this is what the state has set up for a man. Men are told by society—like the Vietnam vets who came home, "Well, you know it wasn't a good war, we're sorry"—it's like that for fathers: "Well, we know you fathered these kids but now we're in this battle here and you might lose your children." That's getting at the basic nature of your manhood—lose your children; if you lose

this battle, you might lose your children, you might lose your house, all of these things. And women usually win this, you see, there's a winner.

Yet, after the children returned to live with their mother, at their insistence, this father withdrew completely from their lives. He neither contacted them nor contributed to their economic support. Explaining, he said, "I just checked out after they left me." Similarly, over one-third of the men complaining about the limitations of parental involvement resulting from maternal custody and paternal visitation had much less contact with their offspring than that specified in the custody and visitation agreement.

Custody assignments were emblematic also of inappropriate state intrusiveness. Paradoxically, some men who complained about public interference in their "private lives" initiated legal procedures, thus instigating state intrusiveness, in efforts to alter their children's custody arrangements. And many who complained about the state's reach into the privacy of family life also objected to the irrelevancy of spousal fault in custody determinations (see Kay 1990; Glendon 1987; Fineman 1991; Jacob 1988). What they especially wanted considered were their allegations about the former wife's marital unfitness. Wives who are "unfaithful," "unnecessarily vindictive about the marriage and demand divorce," or as another phrased it, "wanting to go and find themselves, husbands be damned" should have their divorce actions met with a loss of child custody. In turn, husbands "willing to work on the marriage" should be rewarded with custody. As some two-thirds of the men held their former spouses responsible for the deterioration of the marriage, these were highly self-serving arguments. Two men making the case for blackmailing wives into remaining married by linking initiation of divorce with the automatic loss of child custody did offer a qualification: If there had been "serious" wife or child sexual abuse during the marriage, then "of course, it shouldn't be automatic that the husband gets custody if he doesn't want the divorce." Most who raised the issue of abuse allegations, though, argued against any consideration of it in custody discussions. Especially violence between spouses, they insisted, was irrelevant, a "private matter." This perspective dominates nationally: "In the vast majority of cases, domestic violence is either deemed irrelevant to custody decisions or is not taken seriously [by the courts]" (Cahn 1991, p. 1072).[19]

There was a flip side to the men's complaints about sole physical custody. Not one of the primary custodial fathers critiqued the sole custody situation in terms of its effects on the mother's access to or involvement with their children. Each of these fathers argued that he encouraged the other parent's involvement and allowed her to establish the level and frequency of her contact with their children. At the same time, because of the complications her involvement entailed in his family life, each expressed having occasional desires to "have her just disappear." These remarks were similar to those made by several custodial mothers about their former husbands as visiting fathers (Arendell 1986). Noncustodial fathers in the present study strongly rejected the sole custody condition; custodial fathers, in contrast and with one dramatic exception, looked on their sole custody situations with enthusiastic approval.

ACCESS

Except under unusual situations, a noncustodial parent has legally protected access to the children of the marriage after divorce (Novinson 1983; *Family Law of the State of New York* 1990). Varying by state, visitation schedules are shaped by both family law statutes and customary practice. In New York, the "standard visitation arrangement," language used by most participants and attributed to their attorneys, was every other weekend with an overnight stay and one evening a week. Usually, additional time was specified in the visitation agreement for certain holidays and summer vacations.

Visitation undermined "any possibility" of meaningful postdivorce parenting and was deeply resented. "I cannot describe the grief [being a noncustodial parent limited to a standard visitation arrangement]. You can't imagine how bitter I've become." Pushing them to the margins of their children's lives, visitation disenfranchised them from parenting and demeaned them as parents: " 'Visitation' is one of the sorest words in the vocabulary as far as fathers are concerned. It's an awful word, a god-awful word: It puts you in the position that you're a visitor to your child." As this father continued, he touched on the ambiguity of postdivorce fathering that is worsened by the visitation status. "They ask fathers why they don't stay more involved? Well the system, the whole system, says to them, 'All we need is your money, we don't need you as a person, all we need is your money.' They drive you away. 'We drop you away as a person.' So you go to see your kids and they are strangers." The men's arguments about the injustice of the sole custody-visitation arrangement, more precisely, maternal custody and paternal visitation, were not unique. Such claims of injustice form the core of the fathers' rights movement (see Ferreiro 1990; Chambers 1984; Jacob 1988; Fineman 1991; Coltrane and Hickman 1992).

Joint Legal Custody

Twelve men had joint legal custody, which meant both that the parents were to be involved in major decision making and, when specified, that the parent having physical custody was not to move the children out of the area without the other's permission. These men's parenting circumstances were similar to those of the other nonresidential parents. So too were their assessments. Thus joint legal custody was not a panacea for maternal residential custody; rather, it was largely "irrelevant," "imprecise," and even "unworkable," descriptors used by various respondents. Other research supports these men's contentions: "Joint legal custody, which was supposed to increase fathers' visits, boost child-support payments, and reduce conflict between the parents seems to have done none of the above. Moreover, joint legal custody doesn't seem to increase fathers' involvement after divorce" (Furstenberg and Cherlin 1991, p. 107).

ALLEGATIONS OF CHILD ABUSE

Related to custody and visitation was the issue of child abuse allegations. In comparison to matters of custody, and even child support and property settlements, however, relatively few of these participants had been directly affected by accusations of abuse. Nonetheless, numerous men expressed the belief that they indiscriminately could be charged with abusing their children, especially abusing them sexually, given the "social hysteria in today's society," as one characterized it. Charges could undermine claims to joint or sole physical custody and result in a denial of visitation. They could lead to criminal investigations.

Seven men had been subjected to at least preliminary inquiries by social service or child protective agencies for alleged abuse. Three fathers were accused of molestation during the divorcing process, two of whom were allowed only supervised visitation while their cases were considered. One father, who had been involved extensively with his child's care during marriage, initially sought shared, or, in lieu of that, sole, custody. During the investigation of abuse allegations, he was allowed only limited visitation, observed by a court-appointed officer. The charges eventually were dismissed. His former wife and her attorney, he reported, were warned by the judge not to attempt "such a manipulation" of the custody review process again.

Not in my wildest imagination did I think she [former wife] would stoop so low. But I think that's what our adversarial system does to people. I think she realized I had a legitimate argument for joint or sole custody. She realized that in order to achieve her goal of sole custody she and her attorney had a job to do. She was threatened. She didn't want to lose her child, and she perceived that if she didn't have sole custody that's what would happen. So she and her attorney did what they had to do. He gave her the options. And they did the work as best they could within the system, the system that values mothers and not fathers. I was devastated. They victimized me. They victimized my child. And they victimized the system. You know, it was "the end justifies the means." The goal was to get sole custody and if the way to get sole custody was to bring false allegations, well, "What the hell?"

He was convinced, as were many other participants, that false charges of abuse during the legal dissolution process commonly are levied against fathers.

Four other men had been charged and investigated several times for physical or sexual abuse long after their divorces were final. Another three had been investigated for allegations of child neglect. All accused reported having been vindicated. One father, who repeatedly proclaimed his innocence, had lost shared custody of his two teenaged daughters. Both refused to recant their accusations, and so he terminated all contact with them.

I know of many cases of false charges of abuse; I am the victim of one. To eliminate me totally [from their lives], she [the former wife] went this avenue and has brainwashed one of the children. This tactic was used so that I now have no parenting at all. I cannot come near my children for fear that I'll be brought back into court because this situation could arise at any time. The judge told them in essence that, "You just lynched this guy; you brought him in here without a case." Fathers are treated like criminals: Just say "abuse" and we're considered guilty. They didn't have a bit of evidence against me, not one bit. Yet look what they put me through. Because a few fathers out there do these scummy things, all fathers are treated like criminals.

Two other fathers also ended all parental involvement subsequent to the charges of abuse.

According to various studies, false allegations of sexual abuse are rare (e.g., Thoennes and Pearson 1988; Jones and Seig 1988; Paradise, Rostain, and Nathanson 1988; Benedek and Schetky 1985; Schuman 1986; Faller 1991).[20] And, contrary to the rhetoric of some men's rights groups and the claims of some participants, indiscriminate denial of visitation rights due to allegations of abuse appear to be unusual: "Our review of [California] court records indicated many disputes over visitation, including allegations of sexual misconduct (by the father or by the mother's male companions) toward the children. Nevertheless, visitation privileges were almost never denied or revoked by the court" (Weitzman 1985, pp. 229-30). Such findings challenge the claims that a "witch-hunt against men" is occurring with regard to both physical and sexual abuse (e.g., Doyle 1976,

1985). Although researchers conclude that only a fraction of such actions are reported (Gomes-Schwartz, Horowitz, and Cardarelli 1990; see also Gelles and Conte 1990), no solid information is available as to what proportion of divorces involve child sexual abuse. But because sexual abuse of a child may be a factor in the decision to end a marriage, the percentages may be higher among the divorcing population than among others (Faller 1991). "Finkelhor (1984) estimates that 75 percent to 90 percent of the incidents in the general population are never reported" (Sheffield 1987).[21]

The high estimated incidence of child sexual abuse generally and the findings thus far that most allegations in divorce situations are not fabricated offer no consolation to those falsely accused. Nor do they compensate parents wrongly charged for the damage done to their parental relations or reputations, more generally. For example, the father whose parental involvement before divorce was high and who had been cleared of abuse charges lost months of parenting while the investigation dragged out. The absence from primary parenting, in turn, weakened his argument for shared residential custody because maternal custody had become the precedent. He was certain his child had been affected adversely, and he was publicly humiliated.

Child abuse allegations were not made only against them by the former or estranged wife.[22] Four men reported that they were convinced that the boyfriends of their former wives had molested their children. Attempts to alter custody on the basis of these accusations had been denied although two fathers were in the process of refiling charges. Two others had attained custody because of police-documented physical abuse of their children while in the mother's care. The children of one of these men, at their insistence, returned to live with their mother. Five fathers had unsuccessfully sought investigations into maternal child neglect. The failure of social services' personnel to heed their charges was due to pervasive maternal bias: "No one wants to believe mothers do these things." Or, "It's part of the same old crap: 'mother of the ages' kind of nonsense."

Beyond these cases, the particulars and validity of which the social service agencies and courts were required to ascertain, abuse allegations encompassed other issues and was tied to the general persecution of men, the flames of which were fanned by "feminists." Attorneys and judges were zealously indicted for making available to women "intent on restricting or reducing a father's involvement" the weapon of child abuse allegations. The legal system, they argued, was incompetent in not stopping false allegations, and women generally biased in their willingness to believe unsubstantiated charges.

Numerous men claimed their children were being emotionally abused by their mothers. A majority of these charges had to do with sole physical custody: The custodial mother was "tacitly allowed," for example, to interfere with visitation or determine independently child care and supervision, and so "abused" their children. Most of these charges were extensions of an array of grievances levied against their former wives. But several fathers reported that judges and court-appointed counselors had characterized their children as being psychologically manipulated by their custodial mothers. This person, for instance, had been searching for his daughters for over 2 years, ever since his former wife had taken them out of state in violation of the joint legal custody arrangement.

> The judge used that language: "She is an unfit mother." That was the language, the statement, they expressed. She violated every aspect of the agreement. She obstructed. She yanked them from one place to another: out of the church, out of their neighborhood, then out of town and to some new place. They had too many changes in their lives. The closest thing I could compare with is that for me it was a Patty Hearst kind of thing. The circumstances are different but their environment is being managed. The lack of communication, the control of the phone, is part of that management. I kept saying that my daughters are being treated like hostages. It was in that context that the judge used the language. The reason, at the time, that he did nothing about changing custody was because he and the child law guardian had images or fears of them screaming and yelling and crying and being pulled away from their mother. And they didn't want to see that. It just didn't make any sense. The judge said in the long run the children would be much better off with me, but in the short run it would be upsetting to them. Those were his words.

Having to cope with the sorrow that accompanied the unwanted absence from, and thus loss of, his children, this father was one of the more moderate voices among the group. He explained: "Anything having to do with men and custody is unusual. I'm not surprised by anything. There are extremes at both ends."

CHILD SUPPORT

Child support was inextricably entangled with issues of child custody for most men and contributed to the view that men are dealt injustices in divorce. "Mother custody is part of the old double standard bullshit: It's called 'the divorced father two-step.' Custody is profitable for my former wife, she benefits economically. I'm reduced to being an ATM [automatic teller machine]." Nearly two-thirds of the noncustodial and co-custodial fathers in the study paid child support regularly and fully. Thus the reported overall payment pattern of this group was higher than the national one as only about half of all divorced, custodial mothers receive payments as established in child support agreements (U.S. Bureau of the Census 1992; see also Burkhauser and Duncan 1989; Holden and Smock 1991). Support ranged from $25 a month total for three children to $500 a month for one child; the father paying the latter amount also covered the private school tuition for his child. The average monthly child support paid per child by the fathers making payments was $283.

These men's general compliance with support did not mean that they assessed the system as being fair. Only a few considered their child support obligations just and appropriate. Instead, most saw the support levels as excessively high and were deeply resentful about them. At the same time, many also asserted that parents have moral, social, and legal responsibilities to support their children, as a general matter. Most even insisted that the national abuses of support compliance are grievous. Nationally, as well, most men believe divorced fathers should pay child support (Weitzman 1988; Chambers 1979; Haskins 1988); nonetheless, the rate of noncompliance is higher than that of compliance. But, of the few circumstances in which child support noncompliance is seen to be acceptable by noncustodial fathers, two—a mother's failure to spend money on children (Haskins 1988) and a belief that the child support level is set at an unreasonably high amount (Greif 1982)—are entirely subjective interpretations. Both allegations were made by numerous respondents. By using these charges, they established a possible context for future support noncompliance and kept the former wife at the center of the child support issue.

Myths about child support abound. Weitzman (1988, pp. 253-61) listed the primary fictions. They include that child support obligations exceed childrearing costs, place too great a burden on the payer's income, prevent the men making payments from maintaining their standards of living, are paid by all but lower income men, point to unfair and unjust laws, and are violated in response to visitation interference. Weitzman systematically refuted each myth; in one way or another, each was stated as fact by various participants in the study.

"A Monthly Injustice"

For those for whom child support represented one of the primary injustices of divorce—well over half of the participants—various issues were involved. Child support agreements, in effect until a minor reaches legal majority, were a continual reminder of state intervention into "private lives": "Believe me, I'd pay if they'd leave me alone. It's that I'm 'ordered to pay' that I resent." Yet the national record shows that many nonresidential divorced parents do not contribute regularly, let alone generously, to their children's support (Garfinkel 1992; Weitzman 1988; Haskins 1988; Robins 1989). Payment is even more irregular in the absence of formal child support agreements (U.S. Bureau of the Census 1992). Moreover, when child support is withheld automatically from wages, higher amounts are paid (e.g., Seltzer 1991b; Garfinkel 1986, 1988, 1992). One study, for example, showed routine withholding increased payments between 11% and 30% (Garfinkel and Klawiter 1990).

Earnings were viewed as private property by most of the participants, rightfully subject only to personal discretionary authority. Money matters were entangled with basic identity issues. Resentful on the one hand for being pegged principally as the family income provider, most men defined themselves, their autonomy and independence, in relation to the sole control of their finances. Being directed to contribute support was symbolic of the legal and social disregard of men in families and of their loss of power in divorce (see also Riessman 1990; Furstenberg and Cherlin 1991).

The most contentious aspect of child support obligations for all but a few of the respondents was the fact that the former wife was the direct recipient and handler of support monies. As the custodial parent, she was inevitably involved in child support issues. Furthermore, their "hard-earned money," as numerous men put it, although labeled "child support," contributed to the former wife's support, "to her standard of living." Child support levels were "so high," according to the informants, that "nearly all of the money" goes to the former spouse rather than to meeting children's expenses. Even men paying less than $100 a month argued that their support payments exceeded children's needs.[23] Men argued that what was really at issue in the child support system was a "private welfare scheme" or "an unearned subsidy," a substitute for the "old alimony system." This father, a health care professional, explained: "A year and a half after she left, while sending my children out in ragged clothing, she bought a gorgeous home. She paid 66 [thousand] for it; it's now worth $185,000. Tax-free money from me paid the mortgage—this is called child support. She's living on my money, buying a new house, and not even taxed." Continuing, he explained how child support levels should be formulated. "A woman who lives alone needs an apartment for $500 a month, if she has a child she needs an extra bedroom, needs $600 a month. What I'm saying is that the argument that she needs it to keep up a household for a child is a false issue." Others insisted that their former wives wanted and retained custody only because of the child support received. One argued, for instance, "If I said to her that she could still have the same amount of money, I guarantee if I gave her the house and the money, then I'd have the kids. That's all it is, she wants the money."

The men's claims that their child support obligations were excessively high were mostly exaggerations (see Weitzman 1988). For the most part, these men's payment levels were comparable to the national median, and child support payments comprise less than one-fifth of divorced women's and their children's total incomes (U.S. Bureau of the Census 1992). Noncustodial fathers, as Furstenberg and Cherlin (1991) noted, "may believe that they are making economic sacrifices equivalent to their former wives'. But the facts don't generally support their contention" (p. 49).

Underestimating the costs of childrearing was a common phenomenon. For instance, a father of three declared: "My 29% of my income [$32,000 annually] does not support my children. It meets 100% of their financial need and also meets a percentage of my former wife's financial need. It is superfluous to my children." The assertion that his contribution, just under $9,300 a year, exceeded the costs of supporting three children countered all official estimates of the costs of childrearing (Douthitt 1990; Leehy 1991; Garfinkel 1992; Cassetty and Douthitt 1984). More probably, his contribution did not meet even one-half the costs of supporting the three children, and his former wife's earnings were less than his.

A misconstruing or lack of understanding of childrearing costs was evident also in other ways. A school administrator and father of two, this respondent earned more than $75,000 annually. Divorced nearly 10 years, he was proud of his steady record of compliance: "Seventy-five dollars a month [is what I pay]. That's what the court ordered. That's the level it's stayed at. In all of these years, I've never missed a child support payment, not one." His agreement contained no provisions for cost-of-living adjustments or increased expenses as the children became older. He had not considered voluntarily increasing his support contributions. And this noncustodial father of three, earning nearly $40,000 annually, paid no child support whatsoever:

> I refuse to contribute one cent to her [the former wife], not one cent. . . . I don't know how they [former wife and children] manage. But they can't be in poverty like she claims. The kids always have the latest, state-of-the-art clothes and equipment, stereos and all of that. Besides, poverty today is

exaggerated. There was real poverty during the Depression, not like today. My parents knew poverty. Besides, I'm not Donald Trump; I've had to work for every penny that's come my way. What's she done? Soaked me, that's all.

He knew that his former wife supported the children with public assistance from the Aid for Dependent Children program. He also suspected that she received additional money from her parents; nearly half of the men believed their former wives were receiving some economic assistance from parents.[24] This possibility was used to justify their lack of or limited levels of support. Yet, despite some men's claims that their children were not harmed by the absence or low levels of child support payments, such contributions can be a crucial source of income. Nationally, "the lack of financial support from the absent parent, usually the father, is a major factor in child poverty" (Kahn and Kamerman 1988, p. 10; see also Arendell 1986; Weitzman 1985; Kurz 1995). Mother-only families have much higher rates of poverty than two-parent families. And "income is the single most important factor in accounting for differences in the attainment of children in one-parent and two-parent homes. Differences in family income account for between 25 and 50 percent of the differential risk of dropping out of high school and for about 25 percent of the differential risk of premarital birth" (Garfinkel and McLanahan 1990, p. 14).

Although a majority of the participants met their support responsibilities, few were critical of men who refuse to comply. Child support represented the collective oppression of men in divorce and resistance was, therefore, understandable.

There are men who are indifferent. There are men who hate women. I think it's a small proportion though, it's a small number of men. There are deadbeat fathers out there. Say there are 50% of the guys who aren't paying child support. Ask why. Out of that 50% who aren't paying child support, I would say the percentage who just don't give a damn about their kids is very, very low. A lot of fathers who aren't paying, they can't pay, they have no other way of protesting for the treatment they've been given, they've been forced out of their children's lives. You know, a lot of other reasons, not that they don't care or don't want to. They just can't, can't bring themselves to do it.

And many participants noted that, under certain circumstances, they too would refuse to pay.

One factor in the acceptance, and sometimes outright endorsement, of other men's noncompliance was the knowledge of extensive variations in child support orders (see also Weitzman 1985; Glendon 1987). As legal scholar Glendon (1987) observed: "Even though it is not uncommon for a noncustodial parent's child support payments to be lower than his car payments, every support debtor knows someone whose economic circumstances are similar to his, but whose child support payments are lower. Discontent and a sense of the essential unfairness of the system are widespread" (p. 92). On the other hand, nearly every person in the study described someone who was hamstrung by excessively high payments. One of the informants who was sympathetic to noncompliant fathers explained: "I've seen men who are totally devastated by the court orders. I have a friend who has to give his wife $585 a week after taxes and pay all sorts of bills for her. The woman gets a paycheck. He winds up some weeks with $25 and nobody gives a damn if he can live on that. They just say he's got a wife and four kids and this is what she's got to get. . . . So a guy makes a real lot of money and on occasion gets $25 a week. Loves his kids so hasn't taken off." And another person said, "Hey, I know a guy who is on the streets. He's homeless, lost everything. What he had to pay her busted him. No one paid any attention to him or *his* needs." The variability in support levels has had two principal sources: the extensive degree of judicial discretion legislatively allowed in the establishing of support orders and the wide latitude divorcing spouses and their attorneys have in negotiating settlements outside of the judicial system (Weitzman 1985; Glendon 1987). This variability in award levels should be reduced by the child support reforms being implemented nationally in accordance with congressional mandate.

Another element in the acceptability of other men's support noncompliance and that was based on more than hearsay were feelings of resentment about former wives' lack of accountability for child support use: "It's a sharecropper system: I work and she gets the profits. No checks. No balances." "Good Lord," said another respondent, "even the Pentagon has to show how it uses our money. Why can't we have a system where she has to show me how she used the money before I have to give her the next month's?" Discomfort about this facet of the child support system reached across the group and included men who paid fully and regularly without resentment as well as those who refused to pay. Assessments ranged from concern that the former wife was being "economically reckless" to the assertion that "not one cent of the child support has ever gone to the kids. She squanders it all on herself and her boyfriends." Exacerbating the injustice, they argued, was the fact that they had been the fiscal managers and the more financially responsible spouse during marriage. Adding to the men's unease about the lack of accountability was the disregard of contributions other than child support. Even fathers seeing their children only occasionally felt misused because the expenses involved in visits went unacknowledged. This neglect reinforced the view that divorced fathers are recognized primarily or only as income providers, not as participating parents. This father recalled an earlier experience:

> When I was seeing them and paying child support, I'd take them shopping and buy them school clothes and sneakers and things like that. At the beginning of one school year, she wasn't going to buy them clothes at all. So I went up there and charged up all my charge cards [being unemployed at the time]. I bought them what they needed. I got into some trouble with the bills. The courts didn't want to hear about that. They said, "That's just gifts. You're responsible for your bills, we don't want to hear about that. Pay the child support as ordered."

Like others, the complaints that child support levels did not take their other expenditures into account illustrated these fathers' lack of awareness about the high costs of childrearing.

The few fathers in the study who contributed liberally to their children, in child support or combinations of support and the direct covering of expenses, such as clothes and music or sports lessons, were dissimilar from most divorced fathers nationally. For example, Teachman (1991a), in his examination of eight types of assistance besides child support—clothes, gifts, vacations, dental care, medical insurance, uninsured medical expenses, help with homework, and attending school events—found that other kinds of assistance are not typically substituted for child support. "Excluding child support, the results indicate that fathers seldom provide any given assistance. For only one item, purchasing gifts, have more than 50% of the fathers ever provided assistance. Except for the provision of medical insurance, which is likely to be included in divorce settlements, fewer than 1 out of 7 fathers provides assistance on a very regular basis" (Teachman 1991a, p. 360).

Only one of the residential fathers was receiving child support from his former spouse and that was a recent development. A building contractor, he had finally requested support assistance when his income fell sharply and remained down as the economic recession in home building persisted. Because of her own low earnings, the former wife was paying only $125 a month total for their two children. Two other custodial fathers had received contributions sporadically from their children's mothers when, as one described it, "She's had any money herself; mostly she's struggled to stay alive, just like we [the children and I] have." But disdain was expressed by an array of fathers, irrespective of their particular situations, about the supposed gender neutrality of the child support system. "How many [noncustodial] mothers do you know who pay support or are even

ordered to?" The New York Child Support Standards Act is gender neutral
(*Family Law of the State of New York* 1990). But noncustodial mothers will
typically pay less in child support than noncustodial fathers simply because of the gender differential in earnings (U.S. Bureau of the Census
1992; U.S. Department of Labor, Bureau of Labor Statistics 1991).

REFORM IN THE CHILD SUPPORT SYSTEM

Noncustodial parents' noncompliance with legally contracted child support agreements has received extensive attention over the past decade. In
recent years, federal and state legislatures have sought to better enforce
the payment of child support by nonresidential parents and to increase the
average award levels (e.g., Kahn and Kamerman 1988; Garfinkel 1992;
Cassetty 1983). Both the Child Support Standards Act of 1989 and the
Family Support Act of 1988 were intended by Congress to strengthen and
extend the reforms instituted by the 1984 Child Support Act and Child
Support Enforcement Amendments of 1988.[25] These reforms have met with
only limited success to date (U.S. Bureau of the Census 1992).

New York is a laggard state with regard to divorce law reform generally
(e.g., Freed and Walker 1989; Jacob 1988; Wadlington 1990; Fineman
1991; Marcus 1988/89) and was slow to develop and implement the
federally required reforms. The New York State Child Support Guidelines,
passed into law in 1989, drew particularly negative assessments from many
participants because of both its formula for establishing child support
levels and its administrative collection mechanism. According to the new
statutes, support amounts are to be 17% of gross income for one child, 25%
for two children, 29% for three children, 31% for four children, and 35%
and more for five or more children (*Family Law of the State of New York*
1990; Garfinkel 1988). These percentages are being instituted incrementally for past divorces; all previously determined child support orders are
to be reviewed and updated by 1994, according to the new formula (*Family
Law of the State of New York* 1990; Garfinkel and McLanahan 1990). Most
of the respondents, therefore, had not had their support levels reviewed
and revised at the time of the interviews, and so were paying less than they
will in the future as they become subject to the guidelines. Their resentments about child support levels, therefore, can be expected to increase.

Over two-thirds of the participants freely expressed opposition to the
allocation scheme in the guidelines. They insisted that the formula was
gender discriminatory and set unfairly high levels of support (see also
Furstenberg and Cherlin 1991), especially because the percentage was
applied against the gross rather than net income. Numerous men held

Governor Cuomo, the New York State Division of Women, and/or "those feminists" directly responsible for the guidelines (see also Kay 1990; Fineman 1991). These assessments were based on information (or misinformation) reportedly made available by men's groups, including fathers' rights organizations, newspaper articles, television news reports, union newsletters, and attorneys. These various sources, the men reported, reinforced their perceptions that the guidelines deal with fathers, specifying their responsibilities, but ignore mothers. "It would be different if it were gender neutral as it claims, but it's not. What it does is it states 'custodial versus noncustodial' parents. Everybody supposedly contributes, but the person who actually contributes is the noncustodial parent who, as we all know, 90% of the time is the male. So, given that issue, you cannot tell me that child support, and so custody too, is not a gender biased decision [favoring mothers]."

Legal scholar Leehy, among others (e.g., Douthitt 1990; Garfinkel 1992), rejected the argument that noncustodial parents are contributing disproportionately high levels of support to their children under the New York reforms. Evaluating the state's legislation specifically, Leehy (1991), argued: "A closer look at the guidelines . . . reveals that the guidelines percentages are not 'onerous,' as their critics suggest" (p. 1314). He continued: "The support percentage levels adopted by the legislature for raising children have failed to achieve consistent acceptance by economists and social scientists alike and by the state's own Commission on Child Support" (Leehy 1991, p. 1316). Noncustodial parents pay a disproportionately high share of the costs of childrearing. The legislative reform misrepresents the problem and, in so doing, is gender biased against custodial mothers: "The history of child support abuse in New York, the plain language of the Act, and the explicit legislative declarations accompanying its passage all point to the Act's underlying, somewhat one-sided, mission: forcing divorced parents to fairly contribute toward the support of their children following divorce. This mission is one-sided because inadequate child support as a rule has not resulted from the custodial parent's unwillingness to share her resources. In the vast majority of cases, insufficient support has been the product of a system that permitted noncustodial parents alone to benefit by requiring unrealistically low support payments" (Leehy 1991, p. 1350).

The exceptional assessments offered by several respondents gave serendipitous support to the scholarly evaluations. This next respondent, for example, was one of the nurturing fathers, engaged in innovative responses to divorce. "Obviously, she [the former wife] wanted more child support and I would have paid less. But it's what we ended up with. It's a reasonable amount. The point is that the state guidelines were the exact amount I'd been paying for two and a half years without even knowing what the formula would be. It just hit it right on the head. We sat down and worked out what seemed right. So it was just what I could afford to pay her."

Nationally, child support reforms appear to have mixed consequences. Some studies have found that paying child support is positively related to paternal involvement. Increased paternal satisfaction may further enhance fathers' desires to spend time with their children (Seltzer et al. 1989). At the same time, increased association by the nonresidential parent increases the contact between the divorced spouses, which may lead to greater conflict (Garfinkel and McLanahan 1990). Further, the reforms may elicit an unexpected response: Nearly half of the respondents insisted that many more divorcing fathers will demand and fight for custody in the future as a result of the new child support mandates. Their argument clearly reflected the position that, irrespective of the disaggregation within the law, issues of support and custody are entwined. "With sole custody, fathers will keep control of their incomes." Or, as another father stated, "Shoot, under this arrangement, I might as well fight for custody. At least then I'd have control of my investments [children]!"

Because the standards were just being implemented in New York, confusion and inaccuracy characterized much of the men's criticisms. Most believed, for example, that the percentage of income prescribed as child support was fixed and took no account of his other contributions, the custodial mother's income, or children's needs.[26] Some men also insisted that the Child Support Guidelines essentially precluded remarriage because any assets or earned income of a wife would be included automatically and fully in the support calculations. Attorneys were also sometimes unclear, apparently, about the details of the new standards. For example, in two cases, the paternal financial obligation had not been determined because the spouses' attorneys disagreed on how to assess support levels when some children were minors, living with their mothers, and others were in college, living mostly away with educational costs assigned to the parents.

These divorced fathers were positioned in an expanding national discussion about noncustodial fathers' child support responsibilities. The historical pattern of juridical benign neglect, in which child support obligations were legally assigned and then often ignored (Leehy 1991), was being challenged and reform efforts were extensive. Many participants were uncertain about how the new legislation was going to affect them, thus impeding future planning. Yet, although many complained about the child support system and its burden, none argued for a greater societal role in providing for children. Policy recommendations beyond making the child support system more "father friendly" were limited to tax reforms: Numerous men contended that child support payers should be granted dependent deductions for the children not living with them. In this limited social critique, the participants not only again indicated a lack of awareness of the costs of primary parenting. They demonstrated an adherence to the dominant cultural ideologies emphasizing the individualist ethic and familial self-sufficiency (Dizard and Gadlin 1990; Skolnick 1991).

PROPERTY SETTLEMENTS AND EARNINGS

"A woman gets the gold mine, a man gets the shaft." Have you heard that song? It's right on.

Believing that most of what had been acquired during marriage was a result of their own income-earning efforts, not theirs combined or those of the former wife, a majority of men were displeased with the divorce property settlement. Entwined with issues of child custody, like child support, property settlements were deemed unjust: "With the kids, went the house and money. Simple as that. She got it all." Another said, "Everything that was ours became hers, and everything that was mine became hers also." One participant bluntly expressed what many others intimated: "The fact is the so-called marital property never really was shared to begin with. I earned the money. I bought and paid for everything *we* owned. What we had was a result of *my* work, my efforts. My mistake was in ever letting her think she had a claim to any of it."[27]

Two groups of men had minimal complaints about the property outcome: the few who had assumed custody when their wives left and the several who had wanted to end their marriages because they were in love with someone else. But the general consensus was that wives "make out" in divorce.

Looking at the larger context of divorce in New York state, however, either these men's experiences were atypical or their assessments somewhat distorted. With respect to property, New York is a common law state, as are 41 others. The Equitable Distribution of Property Law was implemented in 1986 (Garrison 1990, p. 81), making equity the dominating principle for property division (New York Domestic Relations Law, section 236[B(6)], *Family Law of the State of New York* 1990). Despite the shift away from the common law tradition, in which men were typically advantaged (e.g., Weitzman 1985; Marcus 1988/89; Garrison 1990; Fineman 1991), settlement outcomes under equitable property rules still favor men: "Two observers of judicial practice under the New York Equitable Distribution Law concluded in 1984 that 'with few exceptions the courts are not treating the wife as an equal partner' " (Kay 1990, p. 12; see also Garrison 1990). Nationally, in general, property settlements in divorce do not "alter the disparity between men's and women's postdivorce economic welfare" (Seltzer and Garfinkel 1990, p. 107).

Marital possessions at the time of these men's divorces had ranged from "a beat-up old car, which she took when she left, and debts, which she didn't take" to "the family home, several rental properties, jewelry, and a few stocks and bonds." One person claimed his former wife left the marriage with $250,000 worth of jewelry received from him as gifts. Most men, however, reported having had only few assets, which were of limited value. Some had only debts to divvy up.

The property item having the greatest value was the family home; nearly two thirds of the men and their spouses were home owners (see also Weitzman 1985; Fineman 1991; Seltzer and Garfinkel 1990; Garrison 1990). Only six of the men, two with their children, remained in their homes when they separated. The others moved out, and their spouses and children remained in the family residence. Eventually, 15 of the properties were sold as part of the divorce settlement; the equity remaining after legal and other debts were paid was divided according to their legal agreement.[28] This pattern was roughly comparable to that in the state at large in the past decade; according to legal scholar Garrison (1990): "Wives with custody of minor children obtained the home 60 percent of the time in 1984" (p. 245, footnote 98).

Leaving the family residence at the time of separation was an unhappy experience and a continuing, contentious issue, particularly for the men who felt deeply wronged by the ending of the marriage. By moving out and making other living arrangements, they "had allowed" the estranged wife to establish a precedent for retaining both custody and the family home. "I got blindsided, pure and simple, blindsided," said one of the men who had voluntarily left the home only to later discover that having done so undermined his bargaining position.

"Losing the home" was emblematic of numerous losses, including self-esteem (see also Riessman 1990). This father of five refused to move out of the house when his wife insisted on a divorce. She finally took the children and moved into a smaller rental property that they owned, later selling it and going into an apartment. He raised a variety of issues, both practical and symbolic, regarding the family residence and divorce.

There's such injustice in moving out. Here's a person, doing what you can, going to work, you're willing to do all the counseling needed to save your marriage and at least have a place for your children. You shouldn't be forced out of your home, there's no justice in that. You shouldn't be forced from your home. Another thing I think is that a lot of men put a lot of work and effort into their homes. Women do too, but men put a lot of physical effort into their homes and then they lose them. If you take that from a man, what do you leave him with? The other part about saving a man's home, another part of this thing too, is that when a man loses his home, he's forced off into some other place. He no longer has as good a place for his children, he now has an apartment so his activity as a father is limited.

This next person voluntarily left the residence out of concern for his children when he feared the continuing arguments with his wife would lead to physical violence. Later he turned the home over to her on the condition that she remain in it with their children. Coupled with his logic and actions, with which he was satisfied overall, was a lingering ambivalence. That his former wife's boyfriend had begun to stay overnight in the house heightened his mixed feelings.

My neighbor, one day, came up to me, he's an old Italian guy. This is funny. One day he comes up to me, he saw me build the house. In broken English, he says to me, "Boy, you did all this work, building this house, this beautiful house. And now she's got somebody else living there, enjoying it." He says, "What are you going to do about it?" All I could say is, "Such is life." But when I got in the car I was really upset. It's my house, you know? My house too.

ECONOMIC EFFECTS

Divorce visited irreparable economic damage on their lives, in various ways, according to many of the participants. Separating the family into two households and equipping a second residence, losing the wife's "supplementary" earnings, meeting legal expenses, paying child support, and, for several, suffering monetary losses during the divorcing process as a result of emotional distress exacted significant tolls. Although a few men took a dispassionate stance, attributing the economic effects to the inevitable ramifications of divorce itself, most incorporated assertions of sexist legal bias into their assessments. "The legal system killed the goose that laid the golden egg," observed one man whose business earnings declined so dramatically after divorcing that he eventually declared bankruptcy.

Despite the adverse effects, most believed they would recover from divorce. For instance:

> What I ended up doing is that I bought her out of her half; I paid for the same house twice. She didn't pay for it to begin with. But that's the way things are. At first I thought about fighting it. After all she did with all the money she wasted, everything she did, I didn't think she should get half. As it is I probably ended up giving her more than half of the value. But now looking back I say, "Hey, look, I'm making more than she is, a lot more. Let her have the money."

Widespread among the men generally was the belief that financial hardship is common among divorced fathers, but is glossed over in the media and by the courts. In turn, economic conditions of divorced mothers were believed to be grossly exaggerated.

Although there was no way to assess the validity of these participants' overall claims of disadvantage, several incidents raised the possibility that some men relied on narrow measures. And some assessments of hardship may have been subject to outright hyperbole. For example, a person who was one of the top income earners in the group complained extensively about the miscarriage of justice in the economic outcome of his divorce. He argued that he had lost several hundred thousand dollars initially, and even more later, given the interruptions related to the divorce, in his career activity. It would take him several "excellent years" to get back on his feet; in the meantime he would have to "scrape together a living while she [the former wife] lives with riches." Despite being "financially strapped," he and a girlfriend, who had been his guest, had just returned from a 2-week trip to the Caribbean and were leaving the following week for a ski trip in Colorado. "I can't really afford them [the trips], but I really needed them after the year I've had." Another suggestion of exaggeration occurred during one of the two interviews involving several participants rather than just one. In this case, the two men were acquaintances. One, listing his numerous grievances, complained that his former wife had "taken everything, even the one good vehicle." The other informant interrupted him: "Come on, you know that both those cars were junks. You were keeping them together with gum and clothes hangers." "But I drive cars like that. There's holes in the floor, I *have* to wire it together. I *did* give her the better of the two cars. I kept the worst of the two. Yet *she* complained." And six of the participants claiming the economic effects were disastrous and lasting had recently purchased relatively expensive new vehicles. Such discrepancies, although few given the number of participants, were not evident in the accounts offered by divorced mothers in an earlier study (Arendell 1986).

Other men in the study, however, like women in the prior research, showed evidence of the economic hardships they described. Three fathers, for example, each of whom had custody of his children, were driving older vehicles that were visibly rusted. One of these men was limping: "I need knee surgery but just can't afford it." His health insurance plan required him to pay 20% of the needed treatment and "with two teenagers, I just don't have it."

> We have an apartment in probably one of the town's half a dozen slums. It's really crummy. It's very tough bringing up kids in this area—my poor children: All of their friends, given the area, are just so wealthy, it's absolutely mind-boggling. That's been difficult because I have very often written checks and allowed certain things to be purchased, etcetera, that there's no way with any sense or financial honesty to myself, I would have done, no way. I mean, I should have paid the rent instead this month! Silly, but it's true, unfortunately.

And, for example, an unemployed noncustodial father was staying with an acquaintance, after having been evicted from his apartment for nonpayment of rent. "I'm a friend away from a park bench," he said. He was also 18 months in arrears in child support payments.

Thus the respondents' economic situations varied. In general, however, with the exception of several of the custodial fathers and the three men who were deliberately unemployed in order to circumvent child support payments, the men's financial circumstances were higher and more stable than divorced women's generally or those of their former wives, as they described them; the exceptions were the former spouses who had remarried. These variations along gender lines are the common situation in contemporary divorce (Burkhauser and Duncan 1989; Hoffman and Duncan 1988; Garfinkel and McLanahan 1990).

In lamenting the economic misfortunes of divorce, the majority of participants targeted complaints at their former wives. But as with their arguments about the bias in maternal custody, most men's complaints about finances, property, and child support involved few, if any, expressions of concern about children's welfare or well-being. The exceptions were several custodial and co-custodial fathers who were struggling to adequately support their offspring as well as themselves.

In sum, an overwhelmingly consistent theme in the men's narrative accounts was their conviction that men are or stand to be victimized in and after divorce. Their focus was narrow: their own circumstances and well-being. Most men's vision, then, was nearsighted. The position that divorce law inherently discriminates against men *as a class* is contrary to the findings of various studies that conclude that men are regularly favored in divorce (e.g., Weitzman 1985; Polikoff 1983; Seltzer and Garfinkel 1990; Kitson and Morgan 1990; Morgan 1991).[29] Although vehemently asserted, the participants' claims of general legal bias operating against men as a class in divorce are simply not supported by other research and analysis. According to some analyses, even the shift to maternal custody in the early part of the 20th century, which preceded the transition to the best-interests standard, was part and parcel of the shift from public to private patriarchy, made in men's interests (e.g., Brown 1981; Polatnick 1973). Indeed, the encompassing generalization that all men are inevitably subject to inequities in divorce can be viewed as somewhat ironic, as suggested by Franklin (1988): "Basically, in America, men make the laws, men break the laws, and men sidestep the laws—it is all a part of men's culture" (pp. 49-50). Yet, that men as a group have a superordinate social and legal status—belonging to the "white male club," as one participant said sarcastically—does not mean the benefits of that membership are universally available, on the one hand, or recognized, on the other, by those who are privileged relative to others.

Irrespective of the broader context or legitimacy of their complaints, however, individual men's perceptions of having been wronged in divorce had profound consequences (see also Girdner 1988; Milne 1988). Feelings and strategies of action were linked to rights-talk and perceptions of victimization. Although the use of rights to frame divorce experiences may have been "reasonable and logical" from most respondents' perspectives, and functional in various ways, whether it was successful overall was another matter. The paradigm of victimization and the overlapping preoccupation with divorce injustice and the former spouse interfered especially with postdivorce parenting and father-child relationships.

Notes

1. For a theoretical discussion of the relationship between the state and the family, see Cheal (1991), especially Chapter 4. For discussions of the ideology of the privacy of the family, see Morgan (1985), Thorne (1982), Zaretsky (1976), Gordon (1990a), and Abramovitz (1988).

2. For overviews of the pace of legislative reform in family law, see, for example, Freed and Walker (1989), Jacob (1988), Wadlington (1990), Fineman (1991), Marcus (1988/89), and Sugarman and Kay (1990).

3. Using Wisconsin court record data, found to be similar to estimates in Current Population Surveys of national data, Seltzer and Garfinkel (1990) determined that legal representation in divorce results in higher child support awards: "When both parents have attorneys, support awards are higher. . . . In contrast, when neither parent or just the father has an attorney, men's bargaining power is enhanced and women receive less support. When mothers have attorneys but fathers do not, less support is awarded than when both parents have attorneys, but the effect is not quite statistically significant" (p. 103).

4. Legislative efforts of recent years, including in 1991, to bring New York state's grounds for marital termination in line with the other states, thus affording a unilateral no-fault option, were all defeated. Presently, the fault grounds for divorce in New York include cruel and inhuman treatment, abandonment for 1 or more years, imprisonment for 3 or more years, and adultery (*Family Law of the State of New York* 1990). In 1966, New York implemented a no-fault option (Marcus 1988/89; Garrison 1990), requiring consensus and a formal separation of 12 months (*Family Law of the State of New York* 1990).

5. The state of New York is atypical also in that it has a dual court system: Matters pertaining to child custody and support are usually handled within the family court system, under the auspices of the state supreme court system, whereas divorce and property division are adjudicated within the state supreme court system directly (*Family Law of the State of New York* 1990).

6. "Divorce is a conflict medium. Whether or not it produces virulent conflict is determined by the nature of the dispute and the resolution procedures available. Dispute-resolution processes range from avoidance to attendance, from cooperative to competitive, from singularly imposed to mutually accommodated. Dispute resolution may occur through personal and direct negotiations, third-party negotiations, arbitration, adjudication, and mediation, to name a few possibilities. Each process has unique applications befitting particular situations. No one process is universal in its ability to resolve all disputes or meet the needs of all disputants" (Milne 1988, p. 43). See also Arditti (1991).

7. According to the *Encyclopedia Judicia* (1971), a *get* involves a system of divorce in which "there is no divorce other than by way of the husband delivering to his wife—and not vice versa—a bill of divorcement, in halakhic language called a *get pitturin* or simply a *get* (a word having the meaning of *shetar* or bill). . . . In Jewish law, divorce is an act of the parties to the marriage, whereby it is to be fundamentally distinguished from divorce in many other systems of law, in which the essential divorce derives from a decree of the court. In Jewish law the function of the court—i.e., in the absence of agreement between the parties—is to decide the question whether and on what terms one party may be obliged to give, or the other, to receive, a *get*. Even after the court has thus decided, the parties nevertheless remain married until such time as the husband actually delivers the *get* to his wife. At the same time, it is the function of the court to ensure that all the formalities required for divorce are carried out according to law" (p. 125). "Upon divorce, the parties are generally free to remarry as they please save as prohibited by law. The wife becomes entitled to the return of her own property from the husband, in accordance with the rules of law pertaining to the husband's liability therefor. She is similarly entitled to payment of her *ketubbah* and dowry, save where she forfeits her *ketubbah* e.g., because of adultery. Divorce terminates the husband's legal obligation to maintain his wife, since this duty is imposed only during the subsistence of the marriage. For charitable reasons, however, it is considered a *mitzvah* to sustain one's divorced wife more extensively than the poor at large" (*Encyclopedia Judicia* 1971, p. 134).

8. "The dimensions of power in divorce mediation relate partly to gender differences in areas of expertise, perceptions, skills, experience, and resources and partly to the bargaining endowments created by law, and the emotional dynamics of divorce. . . . Little is known at this point of the mediator's strategies and effectiveness in balancing power between divorcing couples" (Girdner 1988, p. 56). For discussions of the need for mediators to be sensitive to power issues, see also Ferreiro (1990), Pearson and Thoennes (1988), and Emery and Wyer (1987a).

9. In her analysis, Fineman (1991) indicts the social sciences for contributing to the unwarranted push for joint custody: "The helping professions' views on mediation, for example, have empowered fathers and fathers'-rights groups. The rhetoric has offered fathers groups a legitimate way to argue for their political goal of removing custody cases from the courts, which they view as favoring women. Fathers'-rights groups see mediators as more malleable than judges and attorneys, who are concerned with laws and rights. They also see mediators as less powerful and exacting and less likely to focus on embarrassing child-support issues when custody and visitation problems exist" (pp. 161-62).

10. For a systematic and thoughtful analysis of the literature and research findings on the limitations of the judicial system in making custodial determinations, see Chambers (1984).

11. For scholarly arguments that maternal custody predominates because mothers overwhelmingly are the primary caretaker and childrearer, see, for example, Fineman (1991), Mnookin et al. (1990), Kay (1990), Furstenberg and Cherlin (1991), Lamb (1987), and Goldstein et al. (1979). For a discussion of a noncustodial parent's legal rights to visitation, see Novinson (1983).

12. As noted in Chapter 1, child custody arrangements varied among the men. Five fathers had primary physical custody. Nine had co- or shared physical custody with their former wives; of these, four had legally assigned joint custody arrangements, and the other five had informally negotiated (de facto) shared parenting although the court order was one of sole custody.

13. "Proponents of joint custody argue that present custody laws favor women and are unfair to fathers . . . , and that presumption of joint custody offers a gender neutral standard which is fair to both parents. Some feminist lawyers, however, are concerned that if gender neutrality becomes the principle for custody decisions, fathers may be given the edge in obtaining custody because of their superior economic status. . . . Feminists are also concerned about domestic violence and the feminization of poverty. They argue that joint custody gives violent spouses continuing control over their wives and children, and that fathers may use joint custody as a bargaining chip to negotiate for less child support" (Ferreiro 1990, p. 423).

14. The Stanford Custody Project is based in California, a state in which both legal and physical custody are specified in divorce agreements (Kay 1990; Mnookin et al. 1990) and where joint custody of both types is far more common than in New York.

15. Also part of the Stanford Custody Project, Maccoby, Depner, and Mnookin (1990) concluded: "Our findings reflect interesting compromises between opposing viewpoints in the joint custody debate. Parents appear to be embracing the norm that fathers should remain involved with their children after divorce. Still, they are not rejecting the idea that children, especially very young ones, should have their major residence with their mothers. The level of father physical custody is not increasing; but joint physical custody is. Most parents [in this California study] elect an arrangement that assigns physical custody to the mother and legal custody to both parents" (pp. 110-12).

16. "Our analysis [in the Stanford Custody Project] suggests that the odds of whether there will be conflict were very much affected by what the father requested in the petition or response, but not by the mother's request. If the father requested mother physical custody, whether combined with mother legal custody or joint legal custody, only 10 or 12 percent of the cases fell into the 'intense'-conflict category. On the other hand, for fathers requesting joint physical custody, 30 percent of the cases involved 'intense' conflict, and for fathers requesting father physical custody, 41 percent fell into the highest category. As it turns out, about 71 percent of the 'intense'-conflict families (Level IV) involved fathers who initially requested joint physical custody or sole father custody, although only 37 percent of all families in all four conflict levels had fathers making such requests" (Mnookin et al. 1990, p. 68).

17. Contrary to most men's assumptions, maternal custody was not always the normative national practice. "The law's treatment of children [in divorce] has gone through four phases in the United States. Until the middle of the nineteenth century, children were considered the father's

asset and responsibility. From approximately the 1850s to the 1940s, as fathers increasingly worked outside the home, children were presumed to belong in their mother's custody because maternal care was considered to be best for the child. Over the course of the twentieth century, judges' decisions subtly shifted the emphasis from maternal preference to the 'best interests of the child,' which, however, generally continued in practice to mean maternal custody" (Jacob 1988, p. 127). Although by the mid-1970s, states began to emphasize gender neutrality in its stated laws (Jacob 1988; Weitzman 1985; Fineman 1991) and some "began to look with favor upon joint custody by both parents" (Jacob 1988, p. 127), a move away from shared custody as the mandated preference is under way in some states (e.g., Kay 1990). For additional historical overviews of legal custody preferences, see Maccoby et al. (1990), Mnookin (1975), Chambers (1984), and Polikoff (1983).

18. Although joint custody is permissible in New York state, the prevailing decision, *Braiman v. Braiman,* has been interpreted as allowing joint custody only when parents are in agreement. For a discussion of the *Braiman* case, see Chambers (1984). Sole custody remains the norm in New York, which has no statutory custody guidelines, where children's wishes may be explored but not used as determinative, and which has no explicit joint custody laws (Freed and Walker 1989).

19. Cahn (1991) noted: "Surprisingly, the exclusion of parental violence as a factor in custody decisions is relatively new. Prior to approximately 1970 both fault-based divorce and custody decisions focused on the morality of parental conduct" (p. 1043). Cahn (1991) continued, "stating that 'the assertion that family affairs should be private has been made by men to prevent women and children from using state power to improve the conditions of their lives' " (p. 1047, quoting Olsen, 1983).

20. For instance, Faller (1991), investigating 136 cases of alleged sexual abuse, concluded that although "19 of the cases were categorized as false and 12 as inconclusive (therefore possibly false), [only] three cases in the sample appear to be calculated untruths, evidently motivated by the desire to exclude the accused parent from the life of the child and of the accusing parent" (pp. 88-89). Among the 136 cases, 94 of the allegations were against fathers, 8 against mothers, 18 against stepparents, 7 against other relatives, 3 boyfriends or girlfriends, and 6 unrelated persons. Of the alleged victims, "49 (36%) were male and 87 (64%) female. The mean age of the victims at assessment was 6.2 years for the boys and 5.4 for the girls" (Faller 1991, p. 87).

21. "Reviewing the evidence from five surveys between 1940 and the present, Hermann (1981) found that one fifth to one third of all the respondents reported that they had some kind of childhood sexual encounter with an adult male; between four percent and twelve percent reported a sexual experience with a relative, and one female in one hundred reported having had a sexual experience with her father or step-father" (Sheffield 1987, p. 184). See also Russell (1986) for a study of incestuous abuse against girls: "One of the most shocking findings of our probability sample is that 16 percent of the 930 women had been sexually abused by a relative before the age of eighteen, and 4.5 percent had been sexually abused by their fathers before this age. If we extrapolate from this 16-percent figure to the population at large, it means that 160,000 women per million in this country may have been victimized by their fathers" (p. 10).

22. In her study of Boston "child-saving agencies," Gordon (1990a) found evidence that fabricating allegations of abuse or neglect by one or the other parent against the other in divorce situations is not a recent phenomenon: "Rejected men, then as now, often fought for the custody of children they did not really want as a means of hurting their wives. One way of doing this was to bring complaints against their wives of cruel treatment of children, or the men charged wives with child neglect when their main desire was to force the women to live with them again. Embittered, deserted wives might arrange to have their husbands caught with other women" (p. 198, footnote 17).

23. Douthitt (1990) analyzed the Wisconsin child support percentage-of-income standards and family expenditures for and costs of rearing children. (Wisconsin was the first state to experiment with percentage-of-income child support guidelines.) She concluded that "the Wisconsin's flat PYS is not punitive to either upper-middle-income or lower-middle-income absent parents in the sense that neither group is being asked to pay more in child support than would have been allocated to the child had the family remained intact" (p. 24). Neither income group was paying a full cost of rearing children. The Wisconsin standard guidelines are similar to those instituted in New York in the Child Support Standards Act of 1989. In New York, however, the formula used to establish child support level uses "combined parental income" so that the noncustodial parent pays a pro rata share to the custodial parent (*Family Law of the State of New York* 1990).

24. Forty out of 60 divorced mothers interviewed in an earlier study were receiving some financial assistance from their parents, and parents' contributions exceeded those received through child support (Arendell 1986).

25. For discussions of the federal reform actions, see Garfinkel and McLanahan (1990), Martin (1990), and Garfinkel (1992). "The 1988 legislation makes the guidelines the presumptive basis for child support awards. Judges may depart from the state guidelines only if they provide a written justification which can be reviewed by a higher court. Further, the Family Support Act requires that, by 1993, states review and update child support awards of Title IV-D cases (those handled by the Office of Child Support Enforcement) at least every three years and directs the DHHS Secretary to study the impact of requiring periodic review of all child support cases. With respect to routine income withholding, the 1988 legislation requires withholding from wages of the child support obligation from the outset for all IV-D cases as of 1990, and for all child support cases as of 1994" (Garfinkel and McLanahan 1990, pp. 209-10). Thus both the child support level established and collection of child support were removed from individuals' discretion. Private agreements are allowed, however. According to the New York Child Support Standards Act (CSSA), in conformity with federal legislation, parents are allowed to enter a private written agreement provided that (a) it contains a written statement that both parents are aware of the provisions of CSSA; (b) a parent not represented by an attorney is given a copy of the CSSA chart indicating what the court would order according to the guidelines; and (c) the child support is at least $25 per month (*Family Law of the State of New York* 1990). See Leehy (1991) for an analysis of the New York state reforms.

26. See New York Family Court Act, Section 413, and New York Domestic Relations Law, Section 240, for a delineation of factors to be considered in establishing child support awards. Although some judges may be adhering strictly to the formula provided by the support guidelines, "combined parental income" is to be considered. Numerous other factors may also be considered (*Family Law of the State of New York* 1990; see also Bruch 1983).

27. New York has repeatedly defeated proposed legislation modeled on the Wisconsin equal division of property rule (Fineman 1991; Garrison 1990).

28. In her analyses of New York data, Garrison (1990) concluded that the implementation of the equitable distribution law had only modest effects on the distribution of the marital home. "Among renters, wives were slightly more likely to keep the family home in 1984 than they were earlier (52 percent in 1978, 57 percent in 1984), but the change was not statistically significant. Among home owners, husbands were slightly more likely to retain occupancy of the marital home under the new regime as compared to the old one, but once again the difference was statistically insignificant. In 1978, they obtained outright ownership in 28 percent of the cases. In 1984, they obtained outright ownership in 28 percent of the cases. Wives, by contrast, received outright ownership in 34 percent of the 1978 cases and 35 percent of the 1984 cases" (p. 88). Although wives lost occupancy, they gained money in that husband ownership was offset more by case settlements in 1984 than 1978 (Garrison 1990, p. 88).

29. See, for analyses of the differential economic effects of divorce on men and women, Garrison (1990), Rhode and Minow (1990), Fineman (1991), Marcus (1988/ 89), Holden and Smock (1991), U.S. Bureau of the Census (1990, 1991, 1992), Burkhauser and Duncan (1989), Duncan and Hoffman (1985), Weitzman (1985), Seltzer and Garfinkel (1990), Kitson and Morgan (1990), and Morgan (1991). See Arendell (1986), Weitzman (1985), Kurz (1995), and Kurdeck (1986) for divorced women's arguments that men are favored in divorce.

PART III

The Majority Story:
Conventional Responses

5

FORMER SPOUSAL RELATIONS
"War Without End"

A majority of the participants, 66 of the 75, relied in the highly ambiguous situation of divorce on the familiar definitions, role expectations, and behaviors associated with American manhood and men in families (e.g., Franklin 1988). They looked to customary views and practices for answers, direction, and self-definition in their efforts to handle interpersonal relations and situations, identity, and emotions. Engaged in the processes of traditionalization (see LaRossa and LaRossa 1989), these men emphasized resistance to divorce-related injustices and, often, resorted to a highly confrontational style. The injustices inflicted on them, according to the men, included having rights repudiated, and being "emasculated," displaced from family and discredited and disregarded as a father and exploited as an income earner. Held in common and defining and reinforcing the perception of victimization was a rhetoric of rights. The focus on an oppositional stance often was so narrow that other issues were disregarded, including children's well-being and the character of parental involvement. The postdivorce situation was understood in terms of the former wife, and actions often were intended for her. Indeed, men engaged in traditionalization viewed the former spouse as the primary player in the divorce scenario, irrespective of the level or character of actual contact with her. Constituting the single greatest threat to rights after divorce, the former wife could not just be ignored or walked away from "like John Wayne riding off into the sunset, no strings attached"; she remained the woman who had been his wife and was the mother of his children. In exerting their authority, they were committed to demonstrating their competency and confidence; they expected themselves to appear to be unaffected by the family disruptions and their own dissatisfactions. Strategies of action, then, centered on resisting the former wife and divorce-related injustices; they also emphasized impression management.

Resistance and Opposition

Not surprisingly, given their dedication to resisting and opposing the injustices inflicted on them by divorce, conflict was a dominant motif in these divorced men's lives. Although it did not govern all former spousal relations, conflict was for most participants an ever present possibility, a defining phenomenon in its potential. Their points of view and perceived interests often differed from and clashed with the former wife's, particularly with regard to their children and parenting. The need to establish and maintain workable living and parenting arrangements—"the most difficult and complex task of the divorce process" (Ahrons and Wallisch 1987a, p. 228; Bohannon 1970)—highlighted the perception that tensions between them as former spouses were inescapable. Most of these 66 men characterized their relations with their former wives in ways similar to two highly conflictual types identified by Kressel et al. in 1980 and discussed by Milne and Folberg (1988): *enmeshed* and *direct-conflict.* Enmeshed couples exhibit extremely high levels of overt conflict and ambivalence about the divorce, engage in prolonged conflict over minutiae, and appear to expand conflict for its own sake. "They appear to be what Hugh McIsaac (1981) has described as 'hostility junkies' " (Milne and Folberg 1988, p. 17). Direct-conflict couples engage in overt conflict and communicate directly with each other, including about the decision to divorce.[1]

Overall, the men committed to the most traditional beliefs about gender differences and thus to the most conventional views on men's and women's appropriate family roles were engaged in, or had been until they ended all association, the more extensive, continuing, and drastic forms of overt conflict with the former wife. For them, strife was far more pronounced than was cooperation. For instance, this father, who saw his children regularly, had been divorced more than 6 years. He explained his "vigilant opposition" to and nearly continuous confrontations with his former wife: "Believe me, if I let a violation go now, she'll cheat more in the future is my philosophy. I stop it now. If you give this lady an inch, then she has freedom for three inches next time. She has to be stopped here, or she'll go there. I lived with her for 8 years, I know. We are engaged in a war. . . . I am not in there to cheat, I'm in there to resolve the cheating. That's who I am. I have to be true to that." And this person said, "I refuse to be defeated. I force myself to be as aggressive as possible. Assertive isn't enough, it makes me look too mild. I'm not taking it lying down." Strife with the former spouse occurred informally and formally, outside of and within the legal system, respectively.

Marital conflict was exacerbated initially by separation (Chase-Lansdale and Hetherington 1990). Because many of the marriages had been conflictual, dissension subsequent to divorce was merely an extension of established routines (see Ambert 1988). For some, conflict waned with time; the tendency was to "give up the fight" and replace confrontation with disengagement and avoidance. Several men "even" moved toward cooperating, although only on occasion, and cooperation was typically accompanied with persistent feelings of deep resentment. An increase in strife subsequent to the early post- separation period was the circumstance for only a few participants. But some men remained, as they reported it, together with their former wives, consistently antagonistic and confrontational over the course of the postdivorce period. A few men ceased "acting out" their opposition when they achieved their goals or when the former wife became "cooperative." Reactivating confrontational approaches, however, remained a viable threat, as this person indicated:

> She got what she wanted. And I think that she thinks that if she causes problems now, that she's afraid that I might take her to court and she might lose custody. I told her, "Look, you give me any more problems with visitation and you'll be back in court immediately. I don't have time for this. I don't want to do it anymore." I fought with her enough and there's no reason for it. Now she's okay, so I hope there won't be any problem. I think now she'll behave. I've learned that if I won't be her wimp, then I won't be her wimp and she understands. I hope.

Continuing conflict between former spouses is not atypical; nor are lingering feelings of resentment and anger. For example, Wallerstein and Blakeslee (1989) found that over half of the participants in their study, divorced 10 years, were still quite angry at their former spouses. Mnookin et al. (1990) found high levels of ongoing conflict: "For 30 percent of our sample there was significant conflict, and for 15 to 20 percent the conflict appeared to be serious" (p. 74). And in their study of former spousal relations at 1 and 3 years postdivorce, Ahrons and Wallisch (1987b) concluded: "We have found that at least half of the sample do have relationships similar to ones depicted in the prevailing stereotypes. . . . In general, what interaction they do have is negative and their feelings toward each other are usually hostile. Some may be indifferent, but many still harbor the anger arising from the marriage and divorce" (pp. 292-93; see also Ambert 1988). Kelly and associates (1988) had similar findings as well.

SUBJECTIVE ASSESSMENTS

Perceptions and assessments of conflict, its intensity and significance, were highly varied and subjective. On one hand, some participants understood their situations to be highly contentious even though their interactions with the former wife were basically cordial and cooperative. These particular men's relations would be classified as low conflict, according to the more objective measures of conflict used in other studies. For example, their differences had not been adjudicated (e.g., Mnookin et al. 1990). On the other hand, some characterized their associations with the former spouse as being low in conflict even though they had been physically violent with each other and involved in numerous court hearings.

Assessments of conflict involved various interrelated factors, including past interpersonal, family, and marital histories; expectations; and gender beliefs. For instance, yelling was viewed by some men as a standard and appropriate interactional style. Noting his frustration about the fact that his former wife "was still terrified" when he was angry, one person observed: "My dad yelled at my mom all his life. It didn't mean anything. Once in a while she would get fed up and let him have it. But my wife [sic] just won't let go of it, she makes a big deal out of it. Just won't let go of it." A former wife's response was especially pertinent: Conflict required reciprocal action such as arguing and threatening to retaliate, if not actually doing so. The significance of the former wife's behavior in the assessment of conflict contributed to the perception that she held center stage in the postdivorce family drama. It also reinforced the argument that continuing conflict was largely her doing.

When responsibility for ongoing conflict was assumed by particular men, it was usually in regard to certain episodes and not the overall postdivorce interactional climate. Such specific conflict was explained as "necessary": A wife's efforts to exercise power and interfere with his rights had to be resisted and certain points "hit home." A not uncommon practice, this man blamed both his former wife in particular for their specific "divorce hostilities" and women in general: "She's [former wife] a real fighter, Irish. Her lawyers kept telling her they could be like sharks in the water and go after me. So we were locked in battles. But she shouldn't have been fighting me. . . . She just didn't know when to stop fighting.

Men know when to call it off. Women will fight to the death. Like piranhas, that's what they are—piranhas."

Postdivorce confrontations were an acknowledged game for several men who relished the power struggle and their ability to intimidate the former wife. "It's a war, a divorce war, and it's been stimulating, kept me going," said one respondent who had numerous court adjudications and police contacts to his record. Rare in his explicit acknowledgment of the satisfaction gained in the continued fighting and haggling with his former wife, he was not unusual in his admission that these behaviors were costly. Continued engagement in the divorce war carried risks; he attributed the dissolution of a subsequent, brief marriage to the continued "warfare" with the mother of his children. Two other men offered similar stories.

HARASSMENT

The most common forms of resistance directed toward the former wife were acts of intentional needling and annoying. Harassment was interactional and reciprocal, but their own actions were "necessary" responses, whereas former wives' comparable behaviors were "unprovoked" instigations. Intentional provocations ranged from acts that were petty and meaningful only because the two knew each other intimately to ones classified legally as criminal. The character of harassment was related, in part, to the specifics of their circumstances. For example, men with greater financial resources relied on attorneys to handle disagreements or establish certain points. This father disapproved of the casual relationship between his young son and his former wife's boyfriend, in which both walked around the child's (and mother's) home nude. "Since speaking to her did no good, I figured I had two options. One was illegal, in which case if I ever got caught my son wouldn't have me anyway. To be honest with you, when I logically thought it out, that [violence, described later as breaking the person's legs] was my only alternative. But the risks were too great. So now I've laid out a few thousand more dollars and hired a private investigator to check him [the boyfriend] out. And I have my attorney send her letters, *lots* of letters." Most men, though, had limited discretionary income and so had to rely on their own efforts and imaginations in their strategies of opposition.

Common actions intended to irritate the former spouse included, for example, returning the children home later than the previously agreed on time, delaying payment of the child support so that she had to request it, providing a check knowing it would bounce, challenging or denigrating her parenting commitment and ability, and deliberately denouncing her in some way in front of their children with the expectation that the message would be conveyed. Other actions were more idiosyncratic. For example, several men noted that they liked to appear with a much younger woman at a school or other function at which the former wife was present, believing "it upsets her." One insisted that "this drives her [the former wife] nuts, insane." A father of three described his "favorite" tactic: "I put the [child support] check in the kids' dirty clothes bag and send it home with them after they visit. I used to put it in the clean clothes but now I put it in the dirty clothes bag." She could not complain, he explained, because, if she did, he would simply stop paying altogether. Continuing, he noted that he was limited in his acts of resistance by his scruples: "One woman told me her husband sent back the kids' clothes with a woman's sock, then, the next time, a woman's bra. I won't go that far, it's too low."

What was provocative was a subjective call because actions involved multifaceted and entangled intentions. This respondent, with a marital and divorce history dominated by conflict and confrontation, was charged with a criminal offense:

> Oh, I got arrested for something. Oh yeah, it was a felony for breaking and entering into her house. That's what it was. She had a one-story house and I used to be able to go around and hit the windows and the kids would come to the windows and I'd talk to them. It would really piss her off. One day, it was 12 o'clock at night and I had this terrible desire to kiss my kids good-night. What I did was I went to her house and I went around to the back and opened up the window, went into the children's bedroom and kissed them good-night and went back out the window and went on home. That's what I did, that's all. It was some months later that I was accused of illegally entering her house and stealing her answering machine. Before that, I used to go see them every night and then I was charged with harassment. Harassment? For wanting to see my kids? Why? Why? Am I the father, or am I not?

Coupled with this person's frequent expressions of righteous indignation over the constraints on his parental access, however, were ones of pride at how he had successfully "irritated and kept tabs" on his former wife over the years since divorcing. Exercising his "rights of access" to his children was an acknowledged bridge to his former wife.

Harassment by Former Wives

Former spouses invited resistance and opposition, insisted numerous respondents. According to well over half of the men, former wives harassed —"misused their power"—in sundry ways. The most prevalent and infuriating provocation, after the legal divorce experience itself, was interference with their fathering. A large majority of participants, including several co-custodial fathers, insisted that their parental relations had been obstructed and undermined by the former spouse. Especially problematic was custodial mothers' hindrance of fathers' access to their children. "Month after month, denial. Will I see my children? Two out of three times, she [the former wife] would deny me. I never knew, never know." Some men encountered persistent barriers: Visits were denied, telephone conversations interrupted or prevented, messages not conveyed, and mail intercepted and not given to the child to whom it was sent. The "cat and mouse game," as several fathers described it—going to pick up their children for a scheduled visit and finding no one home—was experienced by nearly half of the noncustodial fathers. For some, it was a recurring event, as this father of three recounted: "Every time I went to pick them up, they'd be gone. I'd drive all the way [40 miles] over there, as we'd agreed and after I'd called her the night before to remind her; they'd all be gone, every one of them. Even the neighbors were in cahoots with her. They'd insist they hadn't seen any of them the whole day." And another complained: "You drive over to her house to see the kids, you've got it arranged and you go up to the door and either they're not there, or she opens the door, she's on the rag or something, and slams the door in your face and tells you to go to hell. Then the kids don't want to get into it."

Other frequently cited abuses committed by former wives against them included: denigrating them to their children, instigating interpersonal conflict, being uncooperative in legal matters, demanding additional money, and squandering the child support. Complaints also included continued arguing about agreements made, such as when children were to be picked up or dropped off; threatening to involve attorneys or initiating a court hearing; and sending the children off for their time with them with "dirty," "ragged," or insufficient clothing. This father shared parenting time equally with his former wife: "She would send a suitcase so the outward appearance looked good, but it was empty. So the neighbors and all thought she was sending clothes until, one day, I opened the suitcase out in front of the house in the street and threw the suitcase at the house and put the kids in the car and drove off. At that point the suitcase never came out again."

Interference with holidays was an especial affront. For nearly two-thirds of the fathers, the Christmas holidays were a particularly sensitive issue. And Father's Day was deemed crucial by over one-third. "I've never gotten to see my kids for Father's Day though I'm sure that they see their mother on Mother's Day. Can you imagine what it's like not to see my kids on Father's Day? I might as well be dead as far as they're concerned. I saw them the last Christmas but not the other [three] ones. There wasn't much I could do. I was supposed to pick them up for the holidays and I'd drive up there and there'd be nobody there." Holidays took on enhanced symbolic meaning after divorce. Being with their children on special days validated their parental status, importance, and rights. Therefore, many men alleged, the impeding of access to their children on such days was a powerful weapon, misused by custodial mothers who had it made available to them by the legal system.

VIOLENCE

One indication of the volatility and scope of interpersonal conflict between the former spouses, as reported by the participants, was the extent of threatened or actual use of physical force. Forty percent of the men described incidents in which they had threatened explicitly or resorted to acts of violence against the former wife since the end of their marriages. Another 10% implied that when involved in a dispute with the former spouse, they, on occasion, had intimated that they could become violent if "pushed too far." Such messages were conveyed, as one respondent explained, by "you know, using a threatening, stern tone" or, as another said, "sort of sticking out my chest, puffing up, and getting louder, yelling." Specifically, 16 men described incidents since divorcing in which they were physically violent and another 24 talked about having made overt threats to resort to violence "if pushed." Eight others reported having deliberately encouraged the former wife to be cautious, uncertain about what they might do if she continued to "press an argument."

Most men reporting violent episodes insisted they had decreased over time. But eight men indicated such events had not significantly lessened, and several others observed that as verbal conflicts had accelerated over time, so too had the use of physical force. Others who no longer resorted to violence or threats indicated that a recurrence could occur: "It just depends on how far she tries to push [me]."

Confrontations involving violence and threats happened most commonly when children were being transferred between parents—the "handoff," as several men said. Thus children were usually witnesses to their parents' fighting. Nearly all of the episodes of *separation assault* (Mahoney 1991) remained outside of the formal divorce record. And although instances involving threats or force were cited by respondents as examples of conflict, they often were not described as violence (see also Adams 1988; Velicer, Huckel, & Hansen 1989). One father of two, for example, described an episode that led to his disengagement from his children: "I remember grabbing her around the neck with one hand and picking her up with just that one hand. Her head hit the ceiling and I held her up there. I was in shock, I was so surprised that I could pick her up like that with just one hand. I was really surprised. She was choking and gagging, crying. When I put her down on the floor, I said, 'Don't ever let me get this mad again, don't ever make me this mad.' She was full of apologies. Both of my kids were hysterical. So after that, I just quit going over there. I quit trying." When asked if there had been other incidents of family violence, he replied: "Violence? Oh, there wasn't any family violence. I didn't hit her or anything. I often had to threaten her to get her to shut up and listen to me but I never hit her. Actually, the only hitting that happened was one time when she threw a pan at me and it hit me in the shoulder. She was the violent one."[2] Nearly half of the men describing incidents involving the use of physical force claimed that there had been no interpersonal violence before marital separation. "Divorce drove me to it, the divorce she wanted."

An argument made by numerous participants was that women are responsible for interpersonal violence. This view was consistent with the men's commitment to a belief in gender differences and to the marital division of labor assigning women the role of family emotion management worker (see Hochschild 1983, 1989). A common refrain issued by the men describing episodes in which they were violent was that "she drove me to it," and blaming the victim (see Gordon 1988, 1990a)—the targeted former wife—for the use of physical force against her was common. "She set me up, that's what, plain and simple, set me up. She wanted to deny me my kids." Another reported, "She pushes my buttons and I go ballistic. If she wouldn't push my buttons, I wouldn't lose it." Accordingly, violence was a justifiable response, largely beyond their personal control. "I understand how homicide and attempted homicide occurs when your home, your money, your children are taken from you. I can understand that kind of rage. It's what divorce does to men." Differences between the sexes were also used to explain men's use of force.

You know, men have been bred to express their aggression in violence. I think we need war because our society conditions men for protecting, and it gets us psyched up for it and we no longer have an outlet for it. I'm not pro-war, but we are doing our men a disservice. They raise us to be aggressive: one, to go out and fight wars, to be cannon fodder; two, to be competitive out there in the business world and all this kind of stuff. What's a man to do with all this aggressiveness that he's been taught by his father and mother that he's got to have to be successful? Then this poor weakling woman comes along and pushes all his buttons and drives this guy over the edge, and he does hit her. Is that *valid* domestic violence? Isn't that valid? Isn't it?

Over two-thirds of those reporting such incidents claimed that the former spouse had incited their use of physical force in order to justify visitation interference.

The blaming of women for violence against them was not limited to the men who reported their own use of physical force or issuing of threats. A majority of the others engaged in traditionalization insisted that women provoke and initiate violence; they had resisted the former wife's provocations only because of their "great personal restraint," as several described it. Several others noted that becoming violent was "too risky," in that it might keep them from having access to their children in the future. Two men said they controlled themselves out of concern about the possible harmful effects on their children if they were to witness their parents' fighting physically. And one person said, "No matter what she's pulled, I've successfully maintained my cool. My self-respect is at stake here. But she pushes; boy, does she push."

A few men acknowledged that the use or threat of violence against the former wife was effective. Intimidating her served to reassert control in the immediate situation, a function consistent with the position that because their rights had been violated and their power illegitimately diminished by divorce, forceful responses were necessary. The use or threatened use of force was consistent with the norms of masculinity and masculine identity (see Kaufman 1987; Franklin 1988; Connell 1992): Acts of violence served to release pent-up frustrations and anger and to circumvent and avoid seeking other problem-solving strategies. As gender studies theorist Brod (1987b) wrote, males are socialized *"toward* violence. . . . Attitudes are conveyed to young males ranging from tolerance to approval of violence as an appropriate vehicle for conflict resolution, perhaps even the most manly means of conflict negation. From this perspective, violent men are not deviants or *non*conformists; they are *over*conformists, men who have responded all too fully to a particular aspect of male socialization" (p. 51, italics in original; see also Connell 1992). Legal scholar Mahoney (1991) concluded that separation assault is about power and control: "The fact that marital separation increases the instigation to violence shows that these attacks are aimed at preventing or punishing the woman's autonomy. They are major—often deadly—power moves" (p. 65; see also Alder 1992; Kurz 1995). Indeed, "in one study of interspousal homicide, more than half of the men who killed their spouses did so when the partners were separated, less than ten percent of women who killed were separated at the time" (Mahoney 1991, pp. 64-65).

Ten participants insisted that women's violence against men is more injurious than men's against women. It was only on this issue that men belonging to fathers' rights groups differed from the others: Nine of the ten arguing that men are disproportionately victimized by domestic violence were associated with men's groups. Clatterbaugh (1990), a men's studies scholar, after summarizing the arguments made by men's rights organizations with respect to family violence, refuted them: "The use by men's rights advocates of the new domestic-violence studies suggesting women's violence against men is misleading and only compounds the problem of violence against women" (see also Brod 1987b; Mahoney 1991; Cahn 1991).[3] And, contrary to some of the men's assertions, both social science research findings and FBI data show that men are disproportionately the perpetrators in domestic violence and inflict greater bodily harm (e.g., Harlow 1991; Gelles and Straus 1990; Dobash and Dobash 1992; Sigler 1989; Finkelhor, Gelles, Hotaling, and Straus 1983).

Some respondents, again especially those belonging to fathers' rights organizations, also argued that spousal or former spousal violence should be wholly excluded from custody considerations. Family violence was not a required consideration in divorce and child custody proceedings in New York, as was the case also in 30 other states (see Milne, Salem, and Koeffler 1993, p. 37) nor were the participants asked directly about this issue. Thus these men were voicing concerns piqued by media coverage of various groups' calls to require consideration of domestic violence in custody and visitation determinations, not by actual policy mandates.

Stalking

Nearly one-quarter of the participants had surreptitiously followed the former wife or positioned themselves near her residence during the early months after separation and divorce. "Spying," as some termed their actions, was done especially in the early postseparation period to "gain information." But five men had continued their spying long after their divorces were final. One had been physically violent with his former wife during that time. Stalking was done usually in response to a remark made by a younger child about "mommy's boyfriend" or a sudden evasiveness by an older child about his or her mother's activities.[4]

Fantasies

According to nearly one-quarter of the participants, fantasies of violence were substitutes for or a "safe alternative" to physical force, as one person, who described his history of marital and divorce violence with vivid detail, noted. Such mental imagery allowed expression of anger and hostility without directly jeopardizing access to their children, as might have occurred had the acts of violence actually been carried out. The range of "acceptable" fantasies was broader than allowable action. For example, a person who saw his children regularly reenacted in his mind a remembered movie scene: "I fantasize about killing her that way: hanging her up by her wrists and skinning her alive. I hated her so much and that had to be a very painful way to die. But that's fantasy; I don't do these things, as much as I hate her." His assertions about the possibility of his carrying out such actions were contradictory:

> Given the right circumstances, she could be gone, but the probability for that is very low because, getting back to basics, I, *I,* am not going to go out and murder anybody. Don't get me wrong. I'm not a romantic idealist: I could kill. But I haven't threatened her [seriously] or anything. Obviously she never interfered [with visitation] too much since she's still alive. When you come right down to it, it would have to be an unusual circumstance. I tell myself that if we got something really bizarre like a nuclear war, she's gone. . . . And there's the concept that if I kill her, I'll end up in jail and then my kids will have neither one of their parents. That's why she's alive today.

Where fantasy left off and action occurred, or could occur, was unclear in several men's accounts. And various men said they controlled their "homicidal rage" at the former wife for the sole reason that their children would become orphans if they did not.

CHILD ABDUCTION

An ultimate act of protest and resistance to the postdivorce situation and the "disregarding of fathers" was "child snatching," the taking of children without the custodial parent's knowledge or permission (Finkelhor, Hotaling, and Sedlak 1990).[5] Nine fathers volunteered that they had taken their children in such a fashion subsequent to divorce.[6] Additionally, some men's children had been taken clandestinely by one or the other parent in the immediate postseparation period, before the finalizing of custody. Five men whose former wives had initiated divorce proceedings and been granted custody claimed that their offspring had been kidnapped from them through divorce.

Child snatching after divorce was an act of last resort, these men insisted, "done out of desperation." Had their rights been protected, such actions would not have been necessary.[7] But as with other facets of their situations, men's abduction of their children was more complicated than the alleged resistance. Protest was entangled with and inseparable from revenge. That is, questions of access to and authority over children were intertwined with antagonisms toward the former wife. For instance: "I believe that I took the children in order to try to shake her up and get her to see: 'Now you go and see what it's like not having the kids. This is a scare, see? So that you'll be able to think more rationally and come around to my point of view. I really do want to share the children with you but I am protesting against the system.' " This next noncustodial father had his child "snatched away from his mother" by having him picked up while playing at his neighborhood school in a western state and put on a train to New York. Court hearings and delays extended over an 18-month period, during which the boy remained with his father.

> My "child snatching" was a huge success. It was a big score. But the judge upheld my ex-wife's custody by ruling that my son was "too young" to be with me. Besides, I didn't really want custody. My son was a kid and needed his mother, I knew that. And I wanted my freedom. But it was all-out divorce war. It was just like an A-bomb: I wanted my son for a while and got back at her, all in one fell swoop. I legally stole him, just simply resorted to child snatching. I'd never really wanted custody. I just needed to flex my rights. After all, I *still* was his father; I wanted to have some say in his life. I needed for her to know that I still had some control around here.

Seven of the nine men who snatched their children voluntarily returned them to their mothers after "keeping" them from between 10 days and 3 months. The other two fathers returned their offspring only after being ordered to do so by a judge. One described his motives and the first of three abductions:

> I took the kids down to North Carolina. I only wished that I'd had the guts to be more radical. . . . I knew what the problems are in trying to start a new identity. I know all about that stuff about having to get birth certificates and Social Security numbers and everything, and I even started the process of doing that. So I'd go to the library and I'd look up kids who came from New York who died in 1940 and then the idea would be to send away, and at that time they hadn't clamped down yet, and send away and demand from the Department of Health the birth certificate because you lost yours.

Because of his "skillful handling" of the situation, his children were not harmed by the 7-week abduction, he argued. "The kids couldn't have been better; I never told them we were staying. I told them we were going on a big trip. My daughter had her sixth birthday on the trip. We went down to Disney World. That was great, it was enchanting." He returned the children after learning from his sister that a warrant for his arrest had been issued. Despite his attorney's warnings, he was not jailed. "So I got to town by September such and such, turned the kids over. The judge wasn't a bad guy at all. I was very forward. I said, 'I didn't do anything wrong at all. All I did was go on vacation and I deny I absconded, I deny everything.' I would have made a good lawyer. I had given the kids back to her. So what was the big deal?"

About a year after returning the children, he abducted his son as he was leaving school one afternoon. He did not take his daughter, fearing that she would call her mother or the police to report their whereabouts. This absence lasted about 5 weeks, until his money was gone and he was unable to obtain a job. Almost a year later, when he was feeling especially depressed after the death of a long-time friend, he took his son once again. The repercussions were more serious this time:

> I never saw him for a long time after that, 18 months or something. I used to wait by the corner. Since I didn't work regular hours, I looked like a bum, I guess. I'd wait by the bus stop. She [former wife] changed his route. She was so cruel. Maybe I shouldn't characterize her that negatively, she was that fearful maybe, but she should have known I didn't have resources to take him away and keep him. The court had revoked my rights so she had the power to deny me that way.

Irrespective of its objective, the taking of children without the custodial parent's permission or knowledge had largely adverse consequences on the fathers. Rather than expanding their parental access, abduction typically led to a strict curtailment of visitation.

Nationally, the taking of children in violation of a custody and visitation agreement is done most commonly by nonresidential fathers. But child abduction is not restricted to men: About one in four parent abductors is a mother (Finkelhor et al. 1990). Among this group of men, five former wives had relocated their children outside of New York. Two men, who knew where their children had been taken, obtained legal custody after contending with states' jurisdictional questions. After living with their fathers for some months, the children of both men insisted that they be allowed to return to live with their mothers. In another case, a father of two was granted temporary custody while an investigation was undertaken to assess police reports of physical abuse by the mother's boyfriend and to determine legal jurisdiction. Aided by several male relatives, the mother abducted the children from a public park where they were playing and took them once again from the state. Although the children were quickly remanded by the authorities into the temporary care of their grandparents, months of legal wrangling ensued before the children were returned to their father.[8] Two other men, whose children had been taken by their mothers in violation of joint legal custody agreements requiring the other parent's written consent for taking children across state lines, had not located their children.

In addition to the nine fathers who took their children for periods lasting more than a week, three others "temporarily abducted" theirs instead of returning them home after a scheduled visit. They did so, they explained, after concluding that the former wife was too upset to care properly for them. One explained: "I came back to drop her off at the appointed time and found a hysterical woman who believed I was going to run off to another state and get lost with her and so on [after taking the baby out of state to visit his parents, whom he depicted as "quite elderly"]. Seeing her in that condition, hysterical, I decided I wasn't going to leave her. So I took my daughter back to my parents' home." After his former wife and her parents located and "kidnapped" the 14-month-old child, "it cost me some $4,000 to hire a private detective to find out where she was after that. And it took many court hearings for me to even reclaim my visitation rights."

WITHDRAWAL AND AVOIDANCE

Not all men engaged in traditionalization were committed to "winning the war" by direct action and interaction. The relatively more moderate men, however, were also not neutral in their stances toward the former wife. Some, indeed, were intent on avoiding her "at all costs." For example, in their dedication to eluding their former spouses, four men refused to adhere to the visitation schedule and so saw less of their children than they otherwise would have. One explained:

Look, she's tried to kill me. She ruined my life [by getting the divorce]. She broke me financially. She took my kids away from me, stole my kids from me, and I was a good father. I do everything I can to avoid her. Simple as that. . . . By refusing to follow the schedule, she can't exploit me again and again [by making other plans, free of the children]. If they want to see me, they call and arrange it. I never meet them at her, their, house—it *was our* house. I refuse to go there. No way. Never. Maybe I'd see them more if I followed the court schedule. But this way I totally avoid seeing her. And if I run into her on the street, I turn and go the opposite direction.

And this person declared: "She presented herself as 'Susie Q Homemaker' to the judge. He bought it all, every bit of it. You'd have thought she was the mother guiding light for the ages the way she acted in family court. If I could have spanked her right there and then and set her straight, you can bet I would have. Now I just stay away, avoid her. Why bother? She's made me a prisoner in my own life. The trick is to avoid the jailer, that's what I've learned." In his concerted efforts to avoid his former spouse, this person saw his children only several times a year. Another respondent explained his commitment to "seeing her as little as humanly possible without moving away"; he saw his child once or twice monthly. "Seeing her, not even having to talk to her but just seeing her, gives me a blinding headache. She knows it too. Last week she had my daughter invite me to a graduation party she's [the former wife's] having for her. She's graduating from eighth grade. She knows I won't go. So why does she set me up, set my daughter up, like this? She's just trying to antagonize me. That's what she does." In withdrawing, some fathers became totally absent, whereas others became as disengaged as possible while retaining some contact with their children. One said, "I cut my losses, just cut my losses." Those without ongoing association with their children, with only several exceptions, were the more traditionalist in their positions about family and women's and men's roles. But, in turn, several with the more conventional and rigid views and positions remained involved with their children, although in highly defined, circumscribed ways. This father saw his children, usually several times a month, on the first and third Saturdays, unless he had the option to work overtime.

> See, what I did was make her so uncomfortable that she quit going to our church. She avoids *me* so I don't have to make so much effort to avoid her anymore. I'd stare at her, you know, sort of glower. Or I'd refuse to speak to her even if others were standing around. Like she'd start to talk and I'd just turn around and walked away. It felt great. Everyone saw it. She had to be embarrassed. It serves her right. Who is she to be so self-righteous? Besides, it was *my* church. She joined only because of me, because I decided we should.

Most of those who had withdrawn, "dropped back" as one described it, from interacting with the former wife had been overtly confrontational in the early period after divorce. The decline in contact and reduction in hostility came about as a result of "fatigue" or being diverted through a serious involvement with someone else, and usually was gradual. Several withdrew from active opposition because of legal action against them.

SUPPORT NONCOMPLIANCE

Refusing to pay child support was a line of resistance available to all of the participants who had formal child support orders and whose wages had not been garnished. (Once the mandates of the Family Support Act of 1988 are implemented fully in New York, under the auspices of the Child Support Standards Act, child support will be deducted automatically from payroll checks so not paying will cease to be an option.) This strategy was independent of the character of the interpersonal interactions between the former spouses. That is, even several men who were seeing their children and who were not intent on engaging in conflict with the former wife at every opportunity withheld child support.

Most respondents complied with their child support agreements. Yet nearly all shared the view that choosing not to pay was one of the few areas of discretionary authority left to them (see Arditti 1991; Seltzer 1991a). To comply with support orders "was to be reduced to a money machine for my ex," as one person said. Paying support irregularly or not at all was used also to sanction the former wife. "I pay but I don't pay all that I'm supposed to pay. Actually, I don't defend it morally. I intended, I even told her, I wanted to pay the money. But I just didn't get around to it. I have a lot of other bills. And, really, you know, she asked for this."

Those men most tied to the conventional ideologies and roles of the good provider and family authority figure had the highest rates of support noncompliance. The provider role was entwined with the intact family and thus was severed on divorce, as far as these men were concerned.

> I was ready to go to jail and not pay my ex-wife anything, not because I didn't have the money but because it was just so unfair. That is all they seemed to want from me as a father, the legal system: "Provide for the kids but there are no benefits for you. You're just a cash register. And that's your main value as a father." I would not pay— that injustice. She says, "I'm taking these things from you, taking them from you, and now pay me." I say, "But that's not fair." They take your children away and then charge you for it. Part of it, too, is the hurt, the emasculation, the pride; all of that is involved.

Not paying support was an exertion of power, a symbolic and compensatory act for the loss of authority inherent in being ordered to pay support at levels determined (or approved) by the court. This participant, with unusually high financial resources at his command, "bought out" his wife in order to avoid having to make child support payments.

The arrangement is such that I was willing to do anything that I could for the child as long as it involved never writing a check with her name on it. Accordingly, I pay a larger percentage of certain expenses but I pay them directly. She walked away with lots, *lots*. But I pay *zero* support. I refuse to ever again; that's the one thing that keeps me psychologically sane about her, is that knowing I will never write a check to her in her name, for anything, ever. And I won't. I feel that because I let her walk away with so much that I don't have to.

Several participants justified their support noncompliance as being a response to a former wife's remarriage. This father of four teenagers explained:

Why should I pay to support children with whom I do not live? In paying support, I am simply reinforcing my ex-wife for having left the marriage. Why should I have to add to my losses by paying out my hard-earned money? Not only would I be paying money to her that she could then spend on herself, and not the kids, but she has a husband who can support all of them. He lives with them; he can support them. We are no longer a family. Why should I pay?

A former wife's remarriage confirmed the perception that their own family was broken, ended. But the logic of the relationship of remarriage to support noncompliance had a dual character. Several men stopped paying support when they remarried: Remarriage increased financial encumbrances, and "there's only so much to go around."[9] "The only difficulties we've had in this marriage have involved her [the former wife] and her constant demands for 'more,' 'more,' 'more.' I quit paying. We need the money here; why should I risk this marriage to please her? She [former wife] would just love to see this marriage come apart," explained a father who saw his two teenagers several times a month.

Failing to comply with support orders was not without adverse consequences. It was legally indefensible, irrespective of visitation interference or other offenses, and left the violator vulnerable to court action (*Family Law of the State of New York* 1990). Further, and more subtly, it reinforced a lingering suspicion that access to their children in the postdivorce situation was being bought: "Pay, I see my kids. Don't pay, I don't." The link between support and parental access was tacitly allowed if not officially condoned by the courts, argued various participants. That is, involvement with their children—"being allowed to be a father"—was contingent on their support compliance, a point also made by some divorced mothers in other studies (e.g., Arendell 1986; Kurz 1995).

Several of these men were so committed to not paying support as ordered that they insured the futility of court action by remaining unemployed or seriously underemployed. This father of four, who saw his children twice monthly, resided with his parents out of economic necessity. His only income source was a small, monthly stipend from the state's General Assistance program. "I have no economic incentive to get on my feet. Let me get you angry. In order for me to feel comfortable about taking a job [in middle management], I have to immediately or in a very short time be getting $60,000 a year.[10] That is not my grandiose ego or anything else. . . . If you offer me a $40,000 job, I'll say big deal, it's nothing because of taxes and the back support. If I can get a $60,000 job, then it might be worth it." Continuing, he noted that an alternative was for him to be granted custody of the children: "I'd have only my regular taxes and the 10% garnishment, so I could go take a job for the less than $60,000. Even without any contribution from her [the former wife], I could probably make it." The belief that child support was costing him, or would if he were paying it, more than it would cost him to raise his children was a view shared by other participants, as well, and pointed again to the tendency to miscalculate the costs of childrearing.

The men who deliberately kept themselves in economically disadvantaged positions argued that their actions did not adversely affect their children. Indeed, rather than being harmed, their children were benefited, these men insisted, because, among other things, they remained in the state "within ready reach." The alternative was to simply disappear by moving to another state where there was less likelihood that their wages would be garnished.[11] After talking at length about his chosen unemployment, this father concluded:

> So you see, my poverty is a way of nurturing my child. What I did was, where her mother and husband, current husband, are rather affluent, very affluent, I went the other direction . . . to not emphasize the material aspects because I could not compete with that. One of the things we have to teach children is how to deal with our feelings and to know that you basically treat people right, the Ten Commandments, all of this, that whether you're rich or poor, these values hold true. So, since her mother provided the forum for doing it on the material side, I decided to do it on the nonmaterial side where we were poor.

Unable to pay child support, he was also financially strapped during his time with his daughter. "I don't have money to take her to the movies so her and I together go out and pick up cans. She doesn't feel funny about it either. We find that it enriches our lives because of the interaction that we have in doing it: 'There's one, go get it.' Then we use the money to go to the movies with or to buy a coloring book or something."

In addition to three men relying on unemployment and another two on underemployment to circumvent child support orders, another 10 intimated that they participated in the underground economy. As long as they did not report it, supplementary cash income went undetected and so was not included in official child support calculations. Changing jobs was another strategy used to reduce child support obligations. But more men reported being falsely accused of trying to circumvent child support orders through unemployment, hiding earnings, or changing employment than acknowledged deliberately doing so. One, whose earnings dropped more than one third, about $20,000, when he changed jobs soon after separation from his wife, said, "It's just that I needed to make these changes [divorce and a job change] about the same time. I wasn't trying to cheat her [former wife] out of money by changing jobs. I was stagnating in that job. My whole life was stagnating. I was determined to change it all."

When legal and judicial intercession was sought with regard to child support orders, it was typically initiated by the former wife in response to a pattern of father noncompliance. Six men, however, had sought judicial relief from support orders or payment levels, mostly unsuccessfully. But one father, in a unique situation, requested and was granted a cessation of the child support order as a response to his children's illegal removal by their mother from the state.

Former wives, reported more than a few respondents, falsely leveled charges of inadequate child support payment, trying to justify their visitation interference. Explaining the experiences leading to his eventual withdrawal from his children, this father, for example, said, "She kept insisting that I was hiding money, that I had lied to the judge by filing a false income statement. She knew I was unemployed and that I was only behind in making support payments because I didn't have a cent. Yet she announced that 'if you don't pay, you don't get the kids.' The fact that I had lost my job was totally meaningless to her. Actually, she believed I quit that job on purpose so that I wouldn't have to pay support. That's what she kept telling her attorney and my kids. It's a lie."

CUSTODY CHALLENGES

Another action taken primarily, although not solely, to harass and oppose the former wife was the challenging of child custody. More than three-quarters of the fathers without primary custody had threatened a custody fight subsequent to the divorce, and nearly one-third had issued a formal threat through an attorney. Dissension could be repeatedly played out by challenging, or merely threatening to challenge, maternal custody. (Two fathers had sought and obtained custody during the divorcing process; these men, like the other three who became sole custodial parents without a custody contest at the time of divorce, were raising their children as single fathers.)

Predominantly at issue in custody challenges was the relationship with the former spouse. Claims of parental access or children's well-being were often a ruse: Threatening to fight for a change in custody kept the former wife "in line." This father, for example, although he believed he was the "better parent," was most intent on "bringing down" his former wife. Discussing his repeated custody challenges, he accounted for his lack of success by charging sexist bias. He believed that sex differences are both "natural" and used unfairly against men by the judiciary.

> After that particularly nasty fight over visitation, I took her to court again. I got the usual crap from the judge that "it's just awful that you fight this way" and that "you should be ashamed." Judges always look at me when they say that; their eyes are on me. I think what they mean is that "you are the only one here who has rationality, you should be stopping this. Also, you're male so you're inherently wrong, that's why I'm looking at you." And he refused to change the custody even though he agreed with me that I was correct and she was wrong. He told her not to do it again. Judges would never let men get by with these violations, but women get by with murder in these cases. She wins. I lose.

But several men used custody challenges both to manipulate the former spouse and in the hope, "however thin," that they might actually win. Men's attempts to alter the custody arrangements were almost always denied by the courts. Only three had successfully obtained a formal change in child custody. All three eventually returned the children to their mothers; two then joined the ranks of absent fathers because they were, as one put it, "weary of warring with the ex." "High noon," he said, "has come and gone."

Interference with their parental access led some men to initiate court hearings, a not uncommon action because visitation issues are second only to support complaints in involving divorced parents in litigation (Fox 1985), and repeated court hearings are typical. Ahrons (1983), for instance, found that 1 year after the divorce 44% of non-custodial and 7% of joint custody fathers had either returned or were planning to return to court.[12] Despite judicial rulings in some participants' cases, visitation interference often persisted, or resumed after only a short lull. An ultimate threat by a judge was that continued interference could lead to a change in custody. But it was mostly an idle threat, as this person explained: "But now the court claims, 'Well, you know, we can't figure out what is going on.' The court's reluctant to take any action. Her lawyer tells the judge, 'If you change custody and anything happens to this kid, it's on your head.' But look what he's going through this way. And what about me?"

Half of the custodial fathers reported having interfered on occasion with the former wife's visitation access but "always only for cause." One had been "wrongfully" challenged in court by his former wife for his "supposed infractions." As with conflict generally, the bases for and definitions of interference were subjective, dependent on one's particular perspective and position in the postdivorce scenario.

That children frequently were used as pawns in their divorced parents' struggles was clear in these men's reports. For example, this father's son was 4½ years old: "One day I didn't know what was the matter with him. He cried when I picked him up. For 2 days he wouldn't talk. When I finally sat him down and said, 'What's the matter?' he cried and said, 'My mommy says you're going to take me away.' She was living her own fears through him and destroying him. I asked her, 'Why do you tell him these things, why are you frightening him?' Now she must tell him not to tell me anything. Now he won't tell me anything." Such use of their children in the former spousal conflicts was not unique to these men or their former wives. For instance, researcher Maccoby and associates (1990, p. 152) noted that one of three primary ways divorced parents can handle conflict is to embroil their children in "loyalty conflicts and cross-pressures, and continuing to fight." (The other approaches are to cut off all direct contact with each other or to separate their parental functions from other issues [Maccoby et al. 1990; see also Ahrons and Wallisch 1987a, 1987b; Ambert 1988].)

Putting a young child in the position of having to choose between the parents was another strategy of interference. This father of two young children recounted an episode when his older child was "put in the middle," between the parents, by the mother. Initially expressing concern about his child's well-being in such a circumstance, his focus shifted as he continued talking.

> So she was looking back and forth between us, confused. She didn't know what she should do. It wasn't fair to her. There have been other times when there's been a show of power and force where she's actually kind of proven to my daughter, my son is too young, that 'if you don't do what mommy tells you, there'll be some problems because daddy can't protect you.' I kind of

got gypped out of my time there. The thing is that daddy is learning very rapidly that he does have rights and he can take and protect them if he just stands on his own two feet.

Identity Management

Traditionalization was about exercising control over their situations, former wives, and offspring. It was also, however, about identity and emotion management (Goffman 1959; Hochschild 1983; Perinbanayagam 1985), the reaffirming of self as efficacious, dominant, and autonomous— as masculine. The men confronted a dilemma. They understood the post-divorce circumstance to be one in which they were oppressed, stigmatized, and marginalized. Divorce involved an undeniable loss of authority and status, particularly for noncustodial fathers (Riessman 1990; Seltzer 1991b). Personal identity was brought into question and emotional duress common (e.g., Gore and Colten 1991; Riessman and Gerstel 1985; Riessman 1990; Wallerstein and Kelly 1980). Yet they expected themselves to be a powerful player, if not the dominant one, in the family, consistent with their former roles, or at least their idealizations, as husbands and fathers. Self-expectations remained high despite the various challenges posed by marital dissolution. Particularly because relationships and interactions with others were involved, living up to these expectations was a continuous, challenging task.

Self-esteem was often deeply shaken by the ending of the marriage. The frequently used phrase, "my failed marriage," implied a relationship between the expected "successful marriage" and a competent self. This father, for example, explained his "ferocity" in continuing to fight for custody: "If I lose custody, I'll lose my identity, my self-respect, my future. I'd already failed at my marriage; she'd insisted on ending it, ending it all. I wasn't about to let them [the legal system and his former wife] do this to me. What kind of man lets them do all of this to him?"

Convincing others of their competency and resiliency was one objective: "The individual does not go about merely going about his business. Rather, he individually goes about trying to sustain a viable image of himself in the eyes of others" (Goffman 1971, p. 185; see also Perinbanayagam 1990).[13] And convincing themselves was integral to convincing others (Goffman 1959; Stone 1962). In seeking to demonstrate and reconfirm their identities, these participants turned to the "taken as given" or core facets of their identities (Foote 1981, p. 338), their *gendered* selves (e.g., Chodorow 1978; Epstein 1991; Arendell 1992b). To be conveyed to others, irrespective of the particular activity or other person involved, was a confident, competent, and controlled man who was coping successfully: "People needed to know I was okay, still in charge, you know?" That they were shaken by divorce was to be kept closeted. The presented self was to be "rational" and active, not preoccupied with or immobilized by emotions and uncertainty, or intimidated by confrontation and challenge. Difficult or painful experiences were disclosed only selectively, if at all. Yet divorce and, for most, the subsequent family developments were emotionally intense experiences (Jacobs 1982, 1983). This person, for instance, did not know where his daughters had been taken by their mother. He isolated his personal pain from his public life, defining that segregation as "appropriate male behavior."

> Take my work environment: I feel that to talk a lot about my situation, how I feel, would be damaging to my work relationships. I know it has damaged my working relationships even without my talking about it. For me to talk about it more, to let on how deep the feelings of grief are, or the frustrations, would not have helped any, as far as I know. I don't have any problem talking about it. But when you talk about it in other contexts, it can have a—this may be me, I don't know, those relationships—you know women tend to talk more about things. You know I don't talk about any illness or infirmities I have to any great extent in my work relationships either, but I perceive it that women would be more likely to do that. Or they would be more likely to be self-effacing or whatever. Men just don't do that.

Feelings contrary to confidence, such as pain, vulnerability, insecurity, or confusion, were redefined or reconstructed, for the most part, by being positioned within the context of experienced injustices. By emphasizing the securing or protecting of *rights,* specifically, they were able to blunt the power of their feelings and assert that they "remained in control" or, less commonly, were "working on regaining control." Thus feelings could be manipulated in ways that allowed acceptable action: "To be tough and to hold it together," as one respondent noted, was possible through taking real action, not through "sitting around and suffering." Such a stance— distancing oneself from one's feelings by engaging in action—was entirely consistent with the dictates of masculine identity: "For one of the most powerful archetypes of manhood is the idea that the real man is the one who acts, rather than the one who contemplates" (Schwenger 1989, p. 110). As Riessman (1990) concluded in her study of divorce, "Men's various manifestations of distress [in divorce] have one thing in common: the distancing of self from feelings of sadness" (p. 153). This occurs, she also observed, through moving "into the realm of action" (1990, p. 159).

IDENTITY AND THE FORMER WIFE

Identity issues and transitions raised by divorce were integrally tied up with the former spouse. But more was involved. Identity had been reinforced, negotiated, and exercised during marriage in relation to the wife. She had been the "primary other," the principal source of support, for a significant period of time: "Because of social inhibitions that keep males from expressing their emotions, especially to other men, wives are often the only source of emotional relief for men" (Basow 1992, p. 194). The relationship between the former spouses was often intensely emotional. A relationship initially formed on the basis of shared intentions and hopes was ended. Left were feelings of disappointment, bitterness, and uncertainty and the sense that interpersonal struggles were inevitable. The affective interdependency with, or dependency on, the former wife was further complicated by the gender dynamics through which men attribute to women the power to validate (or undermine) masculinity (Pleck 1992a, p. 21). Divorce severed the systems of emotional support and validation (see also Riessman 1990).

The situation between the former spouses was paradoxical: They were no longer married, yet they were entangled in various and complicated ways as parents (see also Ambert 1988; Ahrons and Wallisch 1987b). Many men claimed that despite continued interpersonal tension, conflict, and strong feelings about various, and often unresolved, matters, the need for communication between them as parents was greater than during the marriage. Men who had been in marriages in which the wife had done most of the child care and/or whose children were too young to be relied on to make their own visiting arrangements or adequately convey messages between the parents found the need to interact with the former spouse especially pressing. Similarly, and based on data obtained in the Stanford Custody Project, Maccoby and associates (1990) concluded that children's ages affect postdivorce interparental contact: "Parents were more likely to be disengaged if their children were older than if they had at least one child under the age of six" (p. 152). As one father in this study, whose direct parental involvement with his preschool-aged children had increased substantially subsequent to divorce, observed: "We have to talk more now about the kids than we ever did when we lived together. I often think we might just as well have stayed married. We still don't get along, but at least then we'd be in the same house when we have to talk. And actually, as I think about it, if we lived together, we'd have less need to talk to each other about the kids."

The emotional quagmire resulting from a terminated marriage but continued parenthood was especially deep for those adhering to the view that the former wife constituted the opposition—"the enemy"—in a divorce war. Trust was necessary, given their circumstances, and at the same time, it was impossible, given their conflicts of interests. They were not atypical divorced persons in this regard: 70% of former spouses indicated in another study that they would not relate to one another if they were not parents together (Ahrons and Wallisch 1987b).

Dependency on the former wife for both identity issues and the facilitation of the father-child relationship usually lessened over time, particularly for those men who had remarried or were involved in a sustained, intimate relationship with someone else. For most participants, however, the significance of the former wife persisted. Their shared parental status kept alive to varying degrees the memories of a prior emotional relationship and set of expectations and disappointments, all of which muddied the postdivorce experience. Being parents together precluded a total emotional and logistical divorce: "When the kids finally leave, when there's nothing to fight over—the kids, the support, schedules—then you're as close as you'll ever get to resolving your divorce."[14]

A primary tool in the processes of managing emotions was the fostering of anger. By defining a situation as a threat to or an assault on one's rights, feelings could be interpreted as anger and other possibilities obscured: "In managing feeling, we contribute to the creation of it" (Hochschild 1983, p. 18). The former wife was the most common target or source of the anger.

> I was so depressed at first, it almost killed me. I couldn't even drag myself out of bed. But then I got to realizing that she had shafted me, *shafted* me. We made a deal, a vow, that's what marriage is. And she didn't honor it. She thought she could just up and break it off. Break a contract, a contractual arrangement. I became very angry; it was true I would yell at her from time to time. I can't imagine anybody being more angry than I was. I think I had good reason to be angry.

Anger was acceptable, even expected. Because the postdivorce situation offered up innumerable provocations, anger became a blanket emotion. At the same time, performances of righteous indignation and outrage, regardless of the incendiary event or source, could be used as a cover for one's own provocative actions, such as the "pulling" of the former wife into court for transferring their children 3 hours late: "She caused me to act this way. I don't do it because I like it. I don't. But she leaves me no choice."

Eliciting and expressing anger did not preclude other emotion management strategies, although anger was entwined with most others. In addition to those who avoided their former wives and children, others regularly issued threats to become absent. Over one-third of the sample reported excessive alcohol use. A smaller proportion reported using drugs, particularly cocaine. Social isolation was some men's response but more common was increased social activity, especially the seeking out of a number of women for casual relationships. These responses were not unique. Reviewing the divorce literature, Chase-Lansdale and Hetherington (1990) concluded that although men are less likely than women to seek out emotional support, "they tend to develop a very active social life soon after divorce and to engage in a 'frenzy of heterosexual and self-improvement activities' " (Hetherington and Hagan 1986, p. 115; see also Riessman 1990). Most respondents had increased their work involvement substantially, at least for a period of time. Some initiated interpersonal conflicts with friends and other family members; most of these disputes involved the former wife in some way. Suicide was contemplated, at least briefly, by nearly one-quarter of the participants. This next person eventually sought professional counseling in order to improve his relationships with his children. He described a gamut of divorce responses, both emotional and behavioral, similar to those characterized by others. His actions had impeded his fathering for many months immediately following divorce.

Now, I didn't smoke, snort, or drink and hadn't for 10 years, got into this divorce thing, and that's one of the things as to how I cope. I went through such a severe depression, I crashed. I get, got, drunk a lot. That's a kind of sincere statement. Just so totally disoriented. All of a sudden what was right wasn't right, you know? Our church was right but I didn't find it all that supportive. My former wife, my best friend, hated my guts. My kids were caught in the middle but there were just so many things going on at the same time [that] I was trying to deal with a personal relationship with my former best friend and the relationship with my kids, who were sort of caught in the middle at the same time. And I have ties over here from my job, compelling me for my time. All of a sudden I'm spread thin. I'm out of the house, and I am disoriented. I am confused. I am forgetful. I am anxious. I do have anxiety. I am an insomniac. I can't get to sleep. When I do get to sleep, it's interrupted. So I see my doctor. He gives me medication. It take 2 hours for the medication to work and I get up in the morning and it doesn't wear off until 4 or 5 o'clock in the afternoon when the workday is all done. So it's much easier to rationalize and instead do a little Canadian Mist (liquor) and it takes effect in about 20 minutes. And, you know, you wake up the following morning and there's really no problem but you have a cup of coffee to crank you up and get you going, and it's only incidental that you have the cigarette. That's how I coped. But did I tell anybody, besides the doctor, what shape I was in? Oh no, not me. Couldn't do it. I didn't even tell my doctor the whole nine yards, not even my doctor.

By seeing a counselor and "just getting my shit back together," he was, he reported, "now fully recovered." Like others engaged in what they viewed as behaviors appropriate to them as men, he expressed supreme confidence that an assured and competent self was seen by others. Thus the management of feelings was now successful, and damage done to his identity by divorce and the emotional assaults by his former wife rectified. His continued anger, he argued, was "reasonable, pure and simply reasonable."

Other research has found similar impression management by divorced men as that described by these participants. For instance, in their study of families before and after divorce, Block, Block, and Gjerde (1988) assessed the relationship between self-descriptions and ones offered by the spouse: "After divorce, fathers providing their own characterizations, ascribed largely positive qualities to themselves that in interesting ways are convergent with the largely negative descriptions of them offered six years earlier by their then wives. These fathers viewed themselves as independent, even rebellious and unhelpful, self-controlled, not easily disturbed, and curious. Overall, the fathers' self-picture can be seen as the obverse of a personality described earlier by wives as assured but unrelating and unsupportive" (p. 211). For the participants engaging in conventional actions, then, the former wife was the principal but not sole audience for their impression management; she was the motivating force underlying their efforts to direct their emotional lives and responses in specific ways. At the core of their efforts at identity maintenance and repair was defiance and protest.

Notes

1. Of the other two types of former spousal relations identified by Kressel et al. in 1980, disengaged couples demonstrate a low level of ambivalence about the divorce, appear to be ready to terminate the marital relationship, and display a lack of interest in each other, whereas autistic couples display "a relative absence of overt conflict accompanied by minimal communication and mutual avoidance during the decision- making stages of the divorce" (Milne and Folberg 1988, pp. 16-17).

2. After this interview, I exercised great caution to avoid labeling described actions.

3. Clatterbaugh (1990) summarized (and then rejected) the positions taken by men's rights organizations with regard to domestic violence: "Men's rights groups are aware of the fact that domestic violence against women is a serious problem; they often note the number of shelters and special domestic violence teams that seek to protect women. But they also cite the highly controversial studies by researchers M. Straus, R. Gelles, R. L. McNeely, and Gloria Robinson-Simpson that indicate a change in the patterns of domestic violence from 1975 to 1985 (Farrell 1987, p. 228; Men's Rights Incorporated 1985). These studies have concluded that whereas men were more often violent against wives in 1975, severe violence against women has decreased and violence against men has increased such that men and women are currently equally violent toward

one another in domestic situations. This is true of both the degree of violence and the frequency (McNeely and Robinson-Simpson 1987). The Coalition of Free Men included this report in its January-February issue of *Transitions* in 1988. In a similar vein, Roy Schenk has argued that violence is reciprocal between men and women, but because 'the physical . . . violence that men do to women [is] usually more visible' and because 'women are more vocal,' 'the violence men do to women . . . receives more attention' (Schenk 1982, p. 87). In short, society is more tolerant of and responsive to violence against women than violence against men" (pp. 75-76).

4. In 1990 California became the first state to enact an antistalking law, with other states later following suit. Enforcement, however, has been generally lax. Furio (1993, p. 91) observed that battered-women groups have been saying for years that police officers, district attorneys, and judges need to take the problem seriously.

5. "The term 'Family Abduction' typically refers to a situation where a parent absconds with a child in the course of a divorce/custody dispute" (Finkelhor et al. 1990, p. 43). The problem is sometimes referred to as child snatching; definitions vary by state. In a study done for the U.S. Department of Justice of 1988 data from various studies collectively referred to as NISMART, researchers Finkelhor et al. (1990) characterized family abduction as two types. One is *broad scope,* which "conforms to a more legal conception and includes many short-term violations of custody arrangements or decrees" (p. ix). "There were an estimated 354,100 *Broad Scope Family Abductions* in 1988," defined as "situations where a family member 1) took a child in violation of a custody agreement or decree, 2) in violation of a custody agreement or decree failed to return a child at the end of a legal or agreed-upon visit, with the child being away at least overnight. . . . Most of the . . . abductions were perpetrated by men, noncustodial fathers and father figures" (Finkelhor et al. 1990, p. xi). The second, *policy focal,* is "closer to popular conceptions of 'child snatching' and is limited to cases of concealment, transportation out of State, and intent to keep the child or alter custodial privileges" (Finkelhor et al. 1990, p. 45); some 163,200 children were taken within this category. Additionally, there were an estimated 3,200 to 4,000 *legal definition nonfamily abductions* known to law enforcement in 1988 (p. xii). Family abduction, the researchers concluded, is a fast growing phenomenon and is probably the fastest rising form of missing children: "The Family Abduction problem has proved to be substantially larger in this study than most people had anticipated. The 354,100 Broad Scope cases make this more than three times larger than the largest of the widely quoted professional 'guesstimates' " (Finkelhor et al. 1990, p. 61).

6. The dominant characteristics of family abductions, according to Finkelhor et al. (1990), are as follows: (a) children involved are primarily between ages 2 and 11; the rates of abduction are lower for infants and older teens; (b) children most commonly are from families affected by divorce and separation; (c) the rates are higher in the South and lower in the Midwest; (d) three out of four perpetrators are men; (e) 81% of the cases are parental abductions; (f) over half of the abductions occur more than 2 years after the marital relationship has ended; (g) half of the abduction episodes involve failures to return children to the other parent or caretaker; (h) most takings are from the children's homes; (i) takings are more common at the end of vacations, with the two primary months of takings being January and August; (j) 46% of the takings last 2 days to 1 week; only 1% of those missing were not yet returned at the time of the study; (k) one in 10 children is taken out of the state; (l) caretakers know the whereabouts of more than half of the children taken, whereas in 17% of the cases, the children's whereabouts are entirely unknown; and (m) police were contacted in 44% of the incidents. According to the primary caretakers, 40% of the children taken experienced some mental harm (p. 63).

7. Fox (1985) noted that "the two major patterns that have emerged in response to problems with visitation [in divorce] are quintessentially American: On the one hand, childsnatching—an individualistic, taking-the-law-into-one's-own-hands response—and on the other, fathers' rights advocacy groups—a formal organizational, voluntary association response. Interestingly, both 'movements'

appear to be pushing state legislatures in the same direction, that is, to clarify the nature of visitation and to strengthen the enforcement of visitation orders" (p. 405).

8. A year after interviewing this respondent, I received a letter from him in which he informed me that the courts had finally awarded him sole custody of his children and that their mother was denied access of any sort to them. He had remarried and the entire family was leaving the state for another part of the country "to build a new life together, where the children will be safe." He reported that his children were happy to be living with him and their new stepmother, and that they had all been involved in family counseling.

9. For discussions of the effects of remarriage on former spousal relations, see Ahrons and Wallisch (1987b), Furstenberg (1987), Furstenberg and Spanier (1984), Giles-Sims (1987), Gusinger, Cowan, and Schuldberg (1989); Hetherington et al. (1987), and Visher and Visher (1989).

10. An annual earned income of $60,000, at the time of the interview in early 1991, was more than double the median household income in upstate New York where this respondent resided.

11. The recent passage (November 1992) of the so-called deadbeat dad legislation —SB1002—is intended to end the practice of "skipping out of the state" in order to avoid child support payments (U.S. Congress 1992).

12. Ilfeld, Ilfeld, and Alexander (1982), assessing court records, found that in Los Angeles County, 32% of sole custody parents and 16% of joint custody parents had returned to court to litigate a dispute. And earlier, but widely cited, figures from Foster and Freed (1973) indicate that one third or more of all parents appear in court at some time subsequent to their divorce in a dispute concerning their children. See also Weitzman (1985), Mnookin et al. (1990), and Weisel (1989).

13. "A person dresses himself in the 'appearance' of the identity, value, mood, and attitude that he wants his audience to take to be indeed his identity" (Perinbanagayam 1985, p. 64; see also Burke 1962).

14. Similar statements were made by divorced mothers in an earlier study (Arendell 1986).

6

TRADITIONALIST FATHERS
Disengagement and Absence

Fathering behaviors and notions were consistent with these men's overall strategies of action. The congruity is not surprising: Men enter fathering with attitudes, values, and standards that inevitably affect parenting practices. Fathering is not separate from masculine gender identity (Franklin 1988; May and Strikwerda 1992b), as these respondents' narratives demonstrated repeatedly.

Men engaged in traditionalist responses to divorce had less to say about parenting and their children than about most other facets of divorce. This was the case for both traditionalist and neo-traditionalist fathers. Whereas these men approached various topics and relationships with confidence and generally unqualified certainty, buttressing their points of view with numerous illustrations and arguments, their stances toward their children and parenting were often tentative, vague, and either upheld with contradictory or inconsistent evidence or unsupported with examples. That is, although most readily expounded with detailed specifics about their associations with the former wife and her unique characteristics and failings, the particulars of the postdivorce situation, and the machinations of di-

AUTHOR'S NOTE: An earlier version of sections of this chapter dealing specifically with father absence appeared in Arendell, Terry, *Gender & Society, 17*(1):30-34, copyright © 1992 by Sociologists for Women in Society. Reprinted by permission of Sage Publications, Inc.

vorce law and the legal system, many men were relatively inarticulate about their children. And much of what they did have to say about their offspring and their parental relationships was negative and conveyed detachment and disenchantment. Over two-thirds of the nonresidential fathers characterized their parental relations as being at least somewhat strained or superficial, untrusting, and unfulfilling (see also Seltzer and Brandreth 1994). Most estranged from parenting and their children were the traditionalist fathers, many of whom were absent from their children or only occasionally visited them.

Parental Separation

By their own reports, 9 of the 75 participants were absent fathers: They had neither seen nor had contact with any of their children during at least the past 12 months. Nearly two-thirds of the children from whom these men were absent were daughters, a pattern consistent with other research findings that show that nonresidential fathers maintain greater involvement with sons than with daughters (Marsiglio 1991).[1] A majority of the respondents' disaffiliated children were older than 10 years. Four additional fathers were absent from one but not all of their children; only one of their disaffected children was a son. Another father had occasional contact with one but not the other son or two daughters. Numerous other participants were disengaged or distanced fathers; they had some contact, although usually minimal, with their children and were emotionally distanced from them. Their children, as a group, were somewhat younger than the absent fathers'.

The proportion of divorced fathers among this sample of 75 who were absent, about 15%, was significantly lower than the national figure.[2] Estimates of paternal absence, based on representative survey data, range from approximately 30% in the latest surveys (Seltzer 1991b) to nearly 50% of all divorced fathers in somewhat earlier studies (Furstenberg et al. 1987; Furstenberg and Nord 1985). Furstenberg and Cherlin (1991) commented on the apparent decline in father absence: "The most recent of these studies indicates a slight rise in the proportion of fathers who have regular contact with their children (Seltzer and Bianchi 1988; Seltzer 1991). Perhaps children of divorces are seeing more of their dads. But the pattern of modest initial contact and a sharp drop-off over time is strikingly similar across studies" (p. 36).

Length of time divorced was associated with absence and disengagement: The longer divorced, the greater the proportion of father withdrawal

(see also Furstenberg et al. 1987).[3] Paternal involvement generally declined over time, as is the case nationally, and all but one of the participants
already absent from their children had been divorced more than 3 years.
Summarizing the earlier analyses of the NSC data with regard to "fading
fathers," Furstenberg and Cherlin (1991) stated: "Almost half of the
children of recently separated couples saw their fathers at least once a
week, and one-third had not seen them at all in the past year. Among the
children of marriages disrupted for ten or more years—that is, since early
childhood—only one in ten had weekly contact with their fathers and
almost two-thirds had no contact in the past year. . . . Over time, the vast
majority of children will have little or no contact with their fathers"
(pp. 35-36). And Hetherington and associates (1985) found that fewer than
one-quarter of noncustodial fathers were seeing their children once a
month or more after 6 years after divorce.

Paternal disengagement was not irreversible, and change in parental
involvement among the respondents was not strictly linear, moving only
from higher to lower. Rather, some men's shifts entailed swings between
relatively more and less involvement. Several fathers had reconnected with
their children after a period of no direct association. For instance, one
person, after abducting his children several times and having his access
strictly limited by the court, withdrew totally for nearly 2 years and then
resumed contact: "I just called them up one day out of the blue—I'd been
missing them—and said, 'Hi, how about dinner tomorrow?' " Another
father, preparing to leave within weeks for employment abroad, was not
concerned about his upcoming and probably protracted absence from his
child. He explained: "I was in the Army for her first 3 years anyway and
didn't see or talk to her then. If I want to, I could write her, I guess." And
three fathers who saw their children occasionally had assumed custody
earlier, informally, for a span of months.[4] But as is the case nationally (see
Aquilino 1993; Furstenberg et al. 1987), once in place, paternal disengagement was not usually reversed.

The character of paternal disengagement and absence was multidimensional, and its functions interrelated and overlapping. Withdrawal was both
an actual practice and a perceived option and was an emotion management
strategy. Other men's parental absence served as a standard of comparison.

ABSENCE AND DISENGAGEMENT
AS PRACTICE AND OPTION

Despite the rhetorical explanation that men are driven out of their children's lives, parental separation was a course of action, an option among

others. Absence was an acceptable route for divorced fathers generally, "under certain circumstances," according to a large majority. Over one-quarter of all of the respondents indicated that their own total withdrawal was not inconceivable. Moreover, paternal absence was not met with wholesale condemnation from others. Sometimes it was even encouraged, as this father of three recounted.

> Do you know what my first lawyer told me, off the record? He said, "Get an equity loan from the house, saying you're going to buy a condominium. Go buy anything you want. Lay it all out, make it look good on paper. Whatever, give them a couple of hundred, you're going to lose that anyway. Get the check, go to the bank, cash it immediately, and hit the next plane to California and write the bank and say, 'lots of luck, pal.' She'll end up losing the house because she won't be able to make the payments." And I said, "Yeah, and I'll never see my kids." He said, "Yeah you'll lose your kids but you'll get on your feet financially. You'll have a life."

Absence was not always the result of a deliberate decision but evolved as time between contacts was allowed to increase. Thus the boundaries between disengagement and total absence and between withdrawal as a practice and an option were not always discrete and identifiable. Indeed, half of the fathers fully absent from their children's lives pulled away gradually, allowing longer periods of time to elapse between contacts until absence became the condition. "I never planned for this [prolonged absence] to happen, it just sort of did." In addition to those who were fully withdrawn already, eight others perceived their relations with their former wives and children to be so tenuous and emotionally costly, and were having such infrequent contact with them, that becoming an absent parent in the very near term was possible, even probable.

Only two of the absent fathers had sharply restricted visitation access, both being limited to supervised visitation. None of the occasionally visiting fathers had legally curtailed access. With one exception, each of the sporadic visitors and nearly all of the absent fathers insisted they wanted more contact with their children. That they were basically powerless to be more involved given the situation was a common lament. Had their former spouses been agreeable, insisted the men, they would be sharing more fully the rearing of and caring for their children. They, and thousands—"tens of thousands," one asserted—of men like them were "locked out" in divorce by the actions and attitudes of the former wife (see Doyle 1985; Bauer and Bauer 1985). In point of fact, parental disengagement and absence were choices, not inevitable conditions imposed on them.

Parental separation was used to handle threatening or unsatisfactory situations. Consistent with their traditionalist priorities, parental withdrawal was grounded principally in the relationship and continued antagonisms with the former wife (see also Koch and Lowery 1984; Fox 1985; Kruk 1991). This father of two, for example, who had his son "snatched" from a school playground in another state, explained his later "parental retreat" in terms of his former wife's behavior. "I finally decided that I was putting too much energy into this divorce war with my ex-wife. We'd played this game [each initiating court hearings] for over 4 years. So I pulled out; she didn't even know when to say 'uncle.' That's what kept it going, after all. She didn't know when to quit. Someday, if my son wants to get to know me, he can find me. My daughter, she could care less. She's been totally brainwashed by her [the former wife]." More important, ultimately, than parental involvement for these disengaged and absent fathers was resistance against divorce injustices and, therefore, the former spouse: "taking an irrefutably clear stand and remaining a man, not a weakling" as one described it. As another indicated, "First things first. Being a father requires being a man."

Through withdrawal further hostile interactions with the former wife could be precluded. These men, with only several exceptions, had post-separation histories fraught with interpersonal conflict, including to varying extents, violence and repeated involvement of police and use of the judicial system. Avoiding conflict was especially important for some because their anger was so deep and the exchanges between them so volatile that the risk of inflicting serious bodily harm on the former wife was increasingly great. That parental conflict is more significant in the postdivorce father-child relationship than custody and visitation arrangements per se is a consistent research finding. For example, based on their analyses of the NISMART data, researchers Donnelly and Finkelhor (1992) concluded: "Level of parental disagreement appears to be of more concern for the parent-child relationship than custody type per se" (p. 844). And based on data from questionnaires with 84 fathers having infrequent or no contact with their children, Dudley (1991, p. 281) too found that former spousal conflict was the primary explanation for fathers' parental disengagement: Of the 84 participants, 33 "fathers identified their former spouse as their obstacle, and 22 identified personal problems or circumstances" as their primary obstacle to more active parenting" (Furstenberg 1987, p. 57).

Antagonisms with others were avoided or reduced by father separation. These conflicts, or potential ones, also usually involved the former wife, however. For example, second marriages were affected by repeated fighting with former spouses. Four men partially attributed their erratic or decreased involvement with their children to pressures from a present wife. She, the men reported, wanted them to focus their attention on her rather than the children of a past marriage and, even if only indirectly, the former wife. Several fathers noted that tensions between stepchildren, with whom they lived in the remarriage situation, and their own offspring made visits unpleasant. Said one of these fathers, "To keep the peace on the home front, I just don't see them [the two children from the first marriage] very much. It's just not worth the hassles."

Other reasons given for disengagement involved logistical issues, such as work conflicts, time, money, and geographical distance. A lack of space in which to entertain or lodge visiting children and conflicts with their schedules were also cited. Claimed too was the expense specifically of visits (Seltzer and Brandreth 1994). This father, for example, had quit his management position after divorcing and was trying to establish himself as an entertainer. His earnings were sporadic and he had ceased paying child support soon after divorcing. He explained: "When he comes here it costs me a fortune. He eats everything in the place and then some. He always wants to eat out since there aren't many fast food places there [rural New York]. And he wants to see a movie and always wants to throw money into the video arcade. It adds up. I can't afford it. And last time he was here, I was completely exhausted by the time he left. He thinks visiting me means party time, play time." According to this next person, who talked with his children only rarely, his former wife had moved out of state 3 years after divorcing, "in order to screw me," taking the children with her. "They [both children] visited once during a Christmas vacation. But it cost thousands of dollars— airfare and phone calls. Visits cost more than child support, which was part of my reason for not paying support. It's like buying a car in New York and having to go to Montana to drive it. What good is having [legally specified] visitation if your kids are across the country?" Despite the strength of these arguments, however, logistical and financial issues did not sufficiently explain father disengagement. Others confronted similar, and sometimes greater, difficulties but found ways to handle them without disconnecting from their children.

Father absence was also about control: Unable to force their expectations or preferences, these men "took charge" by refusing altogether to cooperate or compromise with their children's custodial parent. For instance, several men withdrew totally from their children's lives after spending numerous months "unsuccessfully" embroiled in dissension with the former spouse over arrangements for their children. One of these fathers characterized his absence as "a response to the condition of 'forced impotence,' a response to the total denial of my rights." Another person, who became an absent father after unsuccessful attempts to obtain shared custody, offered a similar explanation: "I will not be a visiting uncle. I refuse to let some woman [former wife], judge, attorney, or social worker reduce me to that status. I'm a parent and parents do not *visit* their children. If I see my child only every other weekend, I become nothing more than a visiting uncle. I am a father in name only at this point. Until and unless I can be a father in every sense, I simply refuse to have any part of this." And one more, who saw his children every few months for a part of a day, said,

> Visitation puts you in the position that you're a visitor to your child. The connotation of a visitor is, well, you know how when you go to visit somebody's home, you can't tell somebody in their home what to do? You go visit another country; hey, you have to respect their culture. I'm a visitor in my child's life so I have no control, I have nothing to say. I'm just there. One day you're a father, the next day you are a degenerate. Or you're a bum, you're a something, but what you're not is normal. You're not part of the family, part of the society anymore. You really don't have a proper place, a place wherein you have input into what goes on in your life and your child's life. If anybody says, "Hey man, you're overreacting," [let me ask], "How much control does any noncustodial parent have in their child's life? How much input, how much input?"

These fathers, as did nearly half of the neo-traditionalists also, complained that visitation put them in the position of baby-sitters. As such, they were exploited by former wives who used the visitation time to pursue their own activities or interests without having to pay someone to supervise their children. "It's a racket. She dumps them off on me and goes off with her boyfriend of the week." Moreover, numerous men insisted, it was their child support monies that financed the former wife's leisure activities. Seven fathers asserted that they should be paid for visiting their children because it constituted a baby-sitting service, and several suggested such charges should be deductible from child support payments. If these changes occurred, they noted, then they would become more involved parents. They would also, not incidentally, acquire greater control over the former wife's actions.

This next father was atypical in that, although he was a traditionalist, refusing to contribute any child support and "frequently fantasizing" about how he would murder his former wife, for example, he "continued to exercise" his visitation rights, seeing his three children for overnight visits on alternate weekends. Describing his relations with the adolescents as "weird," he explained that "without exception, I demand that they adhere to the visitation schedule. I'm their father. See, I've never believed in this idiotic concept that sole custody and visitation might be abridged because of activities of the children. There's absolutely no reason they can't do their activities out of my home. We didn't live basically close but there was never any resistance, ever, on my part to take my kids up to where they needed to be." For him, adhering "rigidly" to the visitation schedule while rejecting the mandate to contribute economic support was one way to exercise control over his children in the divorce situation.

Offered by highly involved as well as disengaged fathers, the explanation that fathers are pushed out of their children's lives by a conspiracy between an unjust judicial system and the former wife, which makes conflict inevitable, was also about control. In keeping with their overall arguments, the explanation was about lack or loss of control. A father involved with his children to the full extent detailed in the visitation agreement explained paternal absence:

> There's all kind of forces at work telling fathers to abandon their kids, telling me to abandon my kids, because it's such a lousy deal. . . . Most of us [divorced fathers] do walk away from our children. Half our kids don't see us at all. As a group, there's still no recognition of our status of slavery, we're just a group of economic slaves. At least the world recognizes that apartheid is evil. The world does not recognize that the loss of fathers is evil, or at least they haven't implemented this in our law, in our daily practice. It is legitimate for a father not to want to pay child support. It is legitimate for a father not to want to be involved with his children because to want to be involved with his children, a father has to be a masochist. Our government and our courts have no right whatsoever to make that kind of circumstance.

Being an authority figure to their children was a common goal among the traditionalist fathers, an emphasis consistent with the conventional cultural expectations of fathers (e.g., Rotundo 1985; LaRossa 1988). The postdivorce challenge, as a father of three described it, was one "of trying to maintain a hand in their discipline, despite the noncustodial situation." This next person's contacts with his children were sporadic.

> I want my kids to see me as the father, to treat me as the father. In that respect, it's been hard. Just getting together and doing things like a father and son. It's a funny instance in which I still command a respect. My son was late showing up, he was driving. I didn't see him pull in the driveway and I opened the door to do something and the dog runs out. I go running out, yelling, and I hear my son saying, "I'm sorry dad, honest, I'm sorry." See it was "dad yelling at me" type-thing. I was going, "It's all right, it's all right [that] the dog is out." See, I still command that type of respect: "Oh, dad is pissed off at me." See I was still the father figure.

But children often resisted rather than acquiesced. Parental authority —their "prerogative as fathers"—was undermined by their family displacement and limited involvement, the "unnaturalness" of visits, and their children's mothers' negativity.

Children's resistance sometimes evoked anger. This father, for instance, discussed the quandary he faced as a noncustodial parent. "I found that I really couldn't control my kids except by getting angry. They just argued and fought when they were around. Every visit was incredibly tense. We were like coiled rattlesnakes just waiting to strike. I'd end up losing my temper, which just made it worse because they treated me like I had no right to punish them anymore, you know, to discipline them."

Children's Coerced Complicity

Children, especially older ones, were complicit in father disengagement and absence, according to various men. Their collusion was due to uncritical loyalty to their mothers, devotion that was often a result, these fathers argued, of "maternal brainwashing" or, as one said, of "being hoodwinked." One person, whose children refused all contact with him because of their support for their mother in her claims of extreme physical abuse during marriage and after separation, which he denied, insisted: "My children were brainwashed and my wife and children conspired against me. They were felonious charges, felonious." Children's assertions of different viewpoints were seen as evidence of disloyalty, and their intentions confounded with what the men assumed were the former wife's. That children were less mature and at different developmental stages than their parents went unseen. These fathers also failed to see how their children were relatively powerless in the struggles between the parents.

That they bore any responsibility for their children's rejection was denied mostly out of hand. This father, for example, explained his disassociation with one of his four children: "I don't see my older son [who's 11 now] at all. I haven't seen him in 2 years. What happened was it was Labor Day weekend. [When we said good-bye,] we were hugging and he said he loved me and all that stuff." Due to miscommunication about an appointment with the attorneys, he missed the meeting the following week. He continued: "I later went to pick up the kids and he, the oldest one, kept saying, 'You weren't there for mommy, you weren't there for mommy.' I asked her why they even knew about the lawyers. 'They know everything, everything,' she said. And she hadn't even been there herself. She found out from her attorney that I wasn't inside [the courthouse]. These kids are still babies. They don't need to know these things. My son hates me, he hates me. What have I done to deserve this?" This father later reported that his son and former wife alleged that he had physically assaulted the boy on the sidewalk outside of the family home. Further, they had "conspired" with a neighbor who supported their claim: "She [the former wife] stops at nothing."

This next person also discounted any responsibility for his adolescent daughter's actions and attributed *her* withdrawal to her collaboration with her mother, which occurred after he had failed to return her home as planned a second time after a visit. He speculated about a possible future interaction in which he would further solidify the separation between him and his daughter.

> You can imagine all kinds of scenarios. A kid doesn't want to get caught in the middle, but nothing like that is going on. I'm not cursing out the mother every 2 days; the mother doesn't curse me out. We've pretty much quit doing that stuff. I don't know what the hell is the problem. The only real difference is this: If I and the mother had never got divorced, the girl might have problems, especially this stage of puberty, and her mother and all. There's all kinds of problems. However, I would have had some ability to cope with it, some appropriate response would be called for. As it is now, I'm not really her father. I'm a guy who pretends to be her father and it's up to her to allow me to fulfill this pretension or not. I think it's a very unnatural and bad situation. It's kind of like a cold way to put it. But I'm getting very resentful towards her. When the day comes, you know—there's the old story, you know, it's usually put this way—when the day comes and she wants to go to college and she comes to me and says, "Dad, I need a few thousand dollars," I feel like saying, "Well, who am I? What, your father? Not I."

At another point, he wondered what he would do if he ran into her on the street: "Slap her silly is what I'd probably do, slap her silly. That's how angry she's made me."

Three fathers ceased all contact with their children after being formally investigated for charges of sexual abuse. In each case, according to the men, the charges were dropped due to a lack of evidence. The children, two teenagers and the other a preteen, stood by their stories. These men feared that they could be recharged and convicted, albeit "wrongfully," of child sexual molestation, as this person said,

> I cannot come near my children for fear that I'll be brought back into court, because this situation could arise at any time. It's just nailed me shut. I can correspond. I can do anything I want. I just don't. There's been no court order. This did go through the courts but they had no, the judge told them, in

essence, that, "You don't have a case." This was just 2 years ago. My feeling is: "Fool me once, shame on you. Fool me twice, shame on me." I have no choice. I can be landed in jail, all it takes is one more accusation. And I've seen how the system works and I can guarantee you that I will be in jail. I cannot be protected by the law.

According to him, his former wife played to both sides of the situation.

Even my ex-wife says, "Why don't you take the children and have a lot of people around you?" I say, "How many more? I had six people there and it did not protect me, why should it protect me now?" So with the idea that I could land up in jail, "I must protect myself because you have, in essence, brought up these children in this way where I cannot trust them." It was their mother. It was her words, her thoughts. She was behind this. My daughters couldn't have come up with this on their own.

These three men's explanations for their parental disengagement were, however, more complicated than their fears about false charges of sexual abuse. These allegations were entangled with other issues pertaining to the former wife, the "failed" marriage, and stereotypes about women. For instance: "The other parent, usually the mother, has got to build a case so they make you out to be a criminal. It's like sticking your hand in a fire. Every time you go to visit your kids with these sadistic women, it just isn't worth the emotional pain to get involved with them. It's like the Elizabeth Morgan case, do you know it?[5] Look at what she's done. She's poisoned those children against their father. Fathers have nothing, nothing. Mothers have their children."

Other men whose parental involvement was sporadic also considered their children to be complicit in making them feel unwelcome as fathers. Especially younger children, according to the fathers, were reluctant to leave their homes or their mothers or to adhere to a visitation schedule. Some young children resisted visits because they disliked interruptions in their television viewing, and others preferred staying home during weekends to play with neighborhood friends, reported fathers. Older children more typically had competing demands on their time or were reluctant to make advanced plans, fearing that they might be shutting themselves out of other, "more exciting" possibilities.

Many fathers bridled over what they perceived to be children's passivity about frequency of visits: Their parental involvement would increase if the children were more assertive and insistent with their mothers about their rights to be with their fathers. "My kids don't want to be bothered getting themselves out here to visit me. It's true, it requires a 2-hour bus ride and several changes. But why should I have to drive there, pick them up, and then drive them back again? I'm their father. If they want to see me, they know where I am. I'll tell you, if their mother had been supportive of my remaining an active father, the kids would be making the effort it takes today. She isn't."

Gradual but steady disengagement by some fathers was a response to feeling that they were unappreciated or even rejected by their children and particularly by older children who were more likely to enter into the ongoing parental conflicts. Some children openly "took sides," seeking to explain or defend their mothers' actions. Other children expressed their anger or resentment about the economic conditions experienced, implying that their fathers were responsible, sometimes for capricious or vengeful reasons, for their mothers', and therefore their own, reduced standard of living. This person was close with his youngest child but estranged from the older ones.

> It's always been the situation where it was private school where the tuition is due and somehow I would come up with the money, whether it was from working extra hours overtime or getting a windfall, getting a stock sale or an interest refund or something. There was always a little extra shot of money that provided at least part, if not all, of the extra payment for something. And those things are becoming fewer and fewer, the money's just not there. However, the expectation that because it was always there it will continue to be there continues. So when it stopped being there, the word was, "Well, you obviously don't care about me and you don't care about supporting me." So I, my feeling at this point is that I'm trying not to do the hostility thing but I'm, you know, I'm irritated about it. I'm very strapped at this point and getting further into debt. Besides, I urged them to transfer to state colleges where the tuition wouldn't be so high. But, "Oh no." And their mother agreed with them.

His situation, though, was more complicated than his "children's selfish interests" in that he voluntarily changed employment after separating. The new position paid less. His children, apparently, interpreted his willingness to forgo income as a lack of concern for them.

Children's demeanors were also taken to be messages of disapproval. Several fathers who saw their young children on occasion complained that they were stiff and formal. For instance, "She just never relaxes and acts like a kid. She's perfectly behaved, don't get me wrong. But she's 'too good,' do you know what I mean? It's not normal for a kid to act like this. She doesn't trust me."

DISENGAGEMENT AS EMOTION MANAGEMENT

Managing or handling emotions (Hochschild 1983) was another function of paternal withdrawal after divorce. Such emotion management was implicit if not explicit in nearly all of the disengaged fathers' accounts, and most others' as well. Strong feelings were anathema to their expectations to be in control of both their responses to divorce and overall situations (see also Riessman 1990). The persistence or occasional reappearance of feelings such as sorrow, anger, fury, and confusion—having to do especially with their ended marriages, disrupted family life, and rocky relationships with their children—threatened to subvert their constructed personas of competency and mastery.

Distance from experiences likely to elicit painful memories was established and maintained through avoidance. Especially significant in numerous men's diminished contacts with their children were the unresolved, sometimes intense, feelings of loss about the ended marriage and the former partner. For instance, the emotional turmoil prompted by his former wife's remarriage pulled this person totally away from his children: "Her marriage was the final nail in the coffin." Another saw his children "rarely," and not at all in the past year and a half, because he had "only finally begun to heal" from the loss of his wife and the end of their marriage: "Seeing my children simply reopens old wounds. It's better to avoid the reminders of the past."

Visits did not occur in an emotionally neutral or affirmative context. Powerful reminders of the failed marriage and broken family, visits, at least in part, were aversive and further complicated by feelings of resentment at being relegated to a "visiting" parent (see also Loewen 1986, 1988). "Weariness" and "fatigue" with the stress, uncertainty, and frustrations of the postdivorce situation and interpersonal interactions undermined whatever commitment existed to remain connected with their children: "It all just got to be too much. They wore me out. Wore me down." Furthermore, because contacts between these traditionalist fathers and their children often consisted primarily of brief telephone calls or cards sent to acknowledge a holiday or birthday, face-to-face encounters, infrequent as they were, lacked a sense of familiarity and ease. Without a base of developed and maintained intimacy from which to draw, trying to reestablish a personal connection was awkward, at best.

> There were times when I would try to be a parent; it was difficult because there were so many pressures being placed on myself. It was difficult to, sometimes, to act rational. You know, like picking up the children, "Well,

kids, nice to see you after 3 months. Where were you?" Sarcastic-like. Once I was with the children, sometimes, I would rant and rave on and realize it was a weakness of mine to go on, like, "Your mother is driving me nuts, kids." I realized it was a mistake so fortunately didn't do it too often. But I found myself doing it sometimes. Well, I guess for a while it was a lot of times. It was hard to know what else to say. And I was just so, sometimes, just so frustrated.

Several, for whom visits were consistently stressful, had begun deliberately to avoid their offspring, screening telephone calls through answering machines and canceling or neglecting to arrange visits. "I just stick the check in the mail now [rather than deliver it in person] so as to avoid all contact with them all. It's easier. If only I didn't have to send the check!"

A few fathers attributed their decreased parental involvement, bordering on full disengagement, to a gamut of painful feelings having to do specifically with their children. One father, unusual in the degree to which he distinguished his child from his former wife and his feelings of sadness from anger, found that relating to his son "as a visitor" prompted unbearable feelings of sorrow and loss. He described his experience and explained his absence of nearly 9 months.

Every time I pulled up to the driveway to let him off, it was like part of me was dying all over again. I could barely keep myself together long enough to give him a hug good-bye. I knew it wasn't good for him to leave seeing me so visibly upset each time. He would open the door, step out of the car, and I would feel as if I would never see him again. He would walk up the sidewalk and a sense of grief would utterly overcome me. It would take me several days to pull myself together enough to even function at work. I'd have to keep his bedroom door closed; I couldn't bear to see his empty room. I had to break it off totally just to survive. The visits themselves were terrible because I had this constant unease, knowing what was coming.

This respondent described the turmoil created for him by the inadequacy of visits with his children.

Three times out of three I would be an emotional wreck. It was awful, awful. By the time your coat is off, you're not interacting, you're worrying about when they'll go back. You're tearing your heart and guts out saying, "You're [I'm] only going to see them for a few hours." It's like, "I can touch you." It's awful, it's awful. A slightly earthy comparison is that you're crazy in love with someone and you're allowed to see them fully clothed for 3 hours and not touch them. It's nonrequited [*sic*] love, especially the 3- or 4-hour visit. It's bad. You're disoriented and it's hard to interact with your children that way.

This next father had assumed primary custody for a period when his former wife became ill. After their children returned to live with her—a move made at their insistence—he eventually withdrew altogether.

> I don't know, there comes a point when any man or any woman says, "I don't want to fight anymore." That's where I was. I don't want to fight anymore: "I want to get rid of it. It's burning me up, it's destroying me." I had high blood pressure. I think all those things are related to stress. I said, "I have to get out of this, I can't continue this." So I let go. And what happens is you let go emotionally and you lose your kids. "Okay," I said to myself [and to the former wife], "Okay, you want everything, you wanted the kids, you wanted the house. Okay, take it, but that's it. Then we're finished. There's no more of me, for them, for you." I said, "That's how I feel. It's over, all gone."

And this father justified his total parental withdrawal as a response to his children's rejection of him. "They didn't care about me anyway, it was clear enough to me. They never even called on Father's Day. The last year [I was in touch with them], they even missed my birthday." Yet the situation involved more than his offsprings' rejection. This father was one of nearly one-third of the men who was uncertain about the dates of his children's births. Like many other participants, he had depended on his former wife for handling holidays and special events. Since separating, he had missed their children's birthdays and ignored the recent Christmas holidays. He expected more of his children with respect to acknowledging their relationship and his existence than of himself.

Various behaviors were construed by fathers to mean that the parent-child relationship was being denied, even if subtly, by their children. Children most often conveyed their rejection and resentments through unspoken messages, especially sullen attitudes. A conundrum of noncommunication prevailed. "My kids tell me almost nothing. What I do hear, I have to drag it out of them." This next father, who had not talked for several months with his children, who were 12 and 14, was concerned about discussing unplanned teenaged pregnancy and AIDS with them.

> I've been afraid to approach the subject of sex education with my kids. I don't feel that we have that kind of relationship even though I'd really like to talk to them about this. We're just not that close on stuff like that. And part of it

> is my own shortcomings in terms of how to deal with it. I suppose if I really pushed it and developed a technique to approach it, I could take the old attitude that parents *should* talk about this, and do it in a way that they'd listen, that they'd *have* to listen. I realize that this is a problem in intact families too, not just divorced fathers. I realize that mothers also have problems talking about sex and some of these other problems. But we don't even talk about the basic stuff, like, how they are doing in school or who their friends are or how they are. Nothing. It's a total shutout.

Because he believed that "children should respect their parents, not the other way around," he was unwilling to initiate broad changes in their communication system.

Failures, then, of both communication and imagination added to the postdivorce interpersonal and emotional quagmire involved in paternal disengagement. Two fathers, for example, wanted to reestablish contact with their children, but did not know how to do so and were fearful that if they put forth some effort, they would be openly repudiated. One, absent from his children for over 3 years, asked, "How do I explain to them my absence from them? How do I explain that even though I gave up, I still am their father? I have a difficult time rationalizing that myself."

Adding further injury to feeling rejected by their offspring was the assumed intimacy between children and their mothers. This perception was fueled by children's typical reluctance to discuss their mothers. In discussing his children's reticence with him, for example, this father shifted his focus to his former wife, a common phenomenon.

> They talk about her very little. The younger one has opened up a little bit, like "mommy said this," and "mommy said that." Not so much the bad things, you know, but some of the good things. I guess the only comments are when I bring something up. Like I received a letter from her a couple of weeks ago saying, "The children are changing schools and don't plan to do anything about it," or basically saying that. She just wants me out of the picture. I asked my kids about it, and neither had anything to say. They just sat there, hanging their heads. The younger one finally said, "It's okay, dad. Don't worry about it."

Several of these fathers observed that the level of disclosure between them and their children was not significantly different from their relationship before divorce. But because it was ensconced in a restricted period of time and more direct, occurring without the mother's involvement, the relationship seemed even more limited.

Success at managing their feelings about their "lost" or "denied parenthood" or "fears of losing their children" added to the sense of parental alienation. Most "worked at" distancing themselves emotionally from their children: "I do what has to be done to survive," is how one father explained his efforts. Specifically, for him, that meant having no contact with his two young daughters. The process of creating emotional distance was facilitated by the tendency to mix children with their mothers, and sometimes with their siblings, objectifying them and so losing sight of their distinctiveness.[6] For instance, efforts made by children to express their feelings were attributed to the former wife's "biasing of them." Thus the possibility that their offspring had unique perspectives or responses to family developments and relations was ignored or denied.

A paradox existed with respect to emotion management. Paternal separation was explicable and defensible as a technique for deflecting or minimizing painful feelings. It was also "regrettable": the source of "loneliness," "sadness," and even "grief," as these men variously said. Disengagement, or absence, was not an easy emotional route, but was necessary or advisable, "given the circumstances," insisted numerous men. Other researchers have observed the fundamental inconsistency between fathers' expressions of feelings of loss and regret about their nonparental involvement after divorce and their failure to maintain contact. For example, Spanier and Thompson (1984) concluded from their research that "among men, *none* of the child-related variables was a factor in well-being after separation. . . . Even longing for the children—a common form of loneliness among fathers—was unrelated to well-being" (p. 222, italics in original). Mothers' well-being, in contrast, was found to be dependent on their relationships with their children; moreover, noncustodial mothers maintained significantly more sustained and active relations with their children over time after divorce than did noncustodial fathers (see also Furstenberg and Nord 1985; Aquilino 1993; Fox 1985). Fox's (1985) assertion that this inconsistency "can be resolved by considering the *intensity of conflict* in the postseparation or postdivorce family" (p. 404, italics in original) pertains to these traditionalist fathers.

ABSENCE AS A STANDARD OF COMPARISON

Another aspect of postdivorce father absence was its use as a standard of comparison: Nearly 80% of both traditionalist and neo-traditionalist fathers having some parental involvement compared themselves to absent fathers. Most knew few, if any, divorced men who were extensively engaged with their children, but nearly all knew fathers who were disengaged. Any involvement with their own children was evidence, then, of good effort compared to men who were absent fathers. Parental association of any kind evoked a stance of self-congratulation. For instance, "I occasionally have to acknowledge that maybe I could have handled most of this better—better for my children—by not insisting on having the last word always with my ex. But at least I haven't checked out like lots of guys in my situation have. I've hung in there and struggled. But most guys just leave, hang it up and leave."

A few fathers, all of whom had regular association with their children, took issue with the phenomenon of paternal absence, describing absent fathers as "derelict dads," "deadbeat dads," and "bums." An active member of a single-parents' organization, through which he had numerous contacts with other divorced parents, this person explained, at some length, his critical position on divorced men's noninvolvement with their children.

> As a general rule, if there's an abandonment of the children, it's the father. I've seen that. I know it's not 100%, not always the male parent who abandons the child, but as a general rule if someone is going to, then it's the father. And the argument is that they "get run out." But I don't think that's true. I think that if you have a court-ordered agreement, the ability to enforce the agreement is there for both parties. Yes, you will find that the relationship with the ex-wife will prevent additional visitations, or create them, depending upon the relationship, so it has an effect, but it's not the only factor. If a father has visitation rights and wants to see his child, there is no way legally for the mother to prevent that, other than to run away [with the children]. If the mother has sole custody, then she has the right to move out of state and that effectively cuts it off.

Continuing, he discussed the power held by a custodial parent, concluding that, nevertheless, father absence is not ultimately the "fault" of mothers:

> I've seen and heard women say that, "If he doesn't pay, I'm not going to let him see the kids." I've also seen most of them break down and figure that it's more important for kids to see their father. What they will do is not give something extra. It's his birthday. He doesn't have visitation this week and wants to see them. "Too bad!" I've seen that. It's Christmas. "They're mine by agreement this week or this year, too bad!" She's having a special party for one of the kids and he wants to come. "Too bad," [she says]. So yeah, it has an effect. But most of the women I've seen who have sole or full custody, whatever you call it, need a break too. And from their own emotional standpoint and well-being, they want the kids to go to their fathers'. The ones whose ex-husbands don't come around to see the kids are very jealous of those whose ex-husbands are around and take them on a regular basis. No

question about it. And any man who says he doesn't see his kids because his ex-wife won't let him [then] he's not trying too hard. That's my perception. That's my perception, real unusual to be denied visitation. And you don't have to be rich to get a hot shot attorney like I did. You can go to family court, and it's just as lenient with a court-appointed attorney or without an attorney to get a court-enforced order. But they have to bother to do it. So I don't buy that, at all, that "it's the fault of the ex-wife." It affects, but doesn't prevent [father involvement].

The respondents denouncing absent fathers most vehemently, including the father quoted above, however, were the few men who had successfully dictated the terms of their divorce settlement and child custody arrangements. Able to assert themselves because of their relatively extensive economic resources, they disparaged other fathers who, they argued, simply needed to exert more effort and assertiveness to shape the postdivorce situation: "As my attorney told me, all most men need in divorce is to show they've got balls." But the majority did not have the means to impose their desired divorce outcomes unilaterally, and for the most part, they sympathized, and often identified, with the experiences and choices of absent fathers.

INVOLUNTARY ABSENCE

One person stood in stark contrast to the fathers who, despite their claims that they were forced into parental separation as a last resort, were disengaged basically by choice. Without his consent or the court's knowledge, his two children had been removed from the state to unknown whereabouts by their mother. Sorrow and resignation prevailed in his accounts. "If you lose a child through an accident or some way, there's social supports and society lets you express your feelings. There's ritual and patterns. When you lose your child this way, the way I have, there's no way to give recognition to it. For the hostages in Iran, people wore yellow ribbons, remember? You can think of—it's one of those passages in life for which you suffer silently. I keep thinking there should be some kind of ritual to mourn the loss." Although frustrated by legal and judicial events, especially the slow pace at which rulings had been made, he was not preoccupied with the failings of the system or anger toward his former wife. There had been little communication or overt animosity with her or their offspring subsequent to divorce; the former wife had left the marriage in order to marry someone else. The probable explanation for the disappearance, according to the respondent, was his former wife's apparent intention "to fully close the door" on the past, which required prohibiting contacts between the children and their father. The children were seemingly cooperating in maintaining the secrecy of their whereabouts: Both were elementary school aged and, so, presumably, could have contacted their father by letter or telephone independent of their mother's knowledge.

Attempting to locate his children, this man had pursued court as well as other assistance, including the hiring of private investigators. He sought also to compensate for the lack of direct contact with their children, although such efforts were "small change, very small change" compared to routine, direct involvement. He regularly wrote letters to his children.

> I write them every week. The address I have is their maternal grandparents. I write them every week through them, but I don't know if they get them. They [the grandparents] would be reluctant to answer if I directly asked them. I plan to keep writing weekly letters. I keep copies. It allows me to keep good perspective. This way I have a log, a sort of diary, of what's happened in my life. So that would give them a chance to see. It's sort of like an open diary.

Talking about the pain of involuntary parental absence and, at the same time, his willingness to be interviewed, this father noted, "I wanted to communicate it because I think that what happened shouldn't have happened. It's sick, a sickness in our society. Children should not be turned against their parents. It's too late to help me, but I just hope something can be done about it."

Assessments of Children

The traditionalist fathers were nearly unanimous in their belief that their children were experiencing serious behavioral and psychological problems. Absent or disengaged fathers were most vehement in their negative appraisals. This father assigned his absence to the allegations against him of sexual abuse.

> One daughter is drinking, the other daughter is smoking. We're talking, here, the drinking one is 16 going on 17. The one who is smoking is 12. I don't consider that good. The one child, the youngest, is totally overweight. She has lost love of herself. She has, she cannot hold a social relationship with anybody, anyone on her own plane. My other daughter is quite similar in that aspect. She is not socially evolved, totally, I mean. At 16 years old she prefers to be with 11- or 12-year-olds where she's not socially on demand. And this is totally because of the fact that I have not been able to participate in their

parenting. I mean, their mother wants them to be that way. . . . They are becoming antisocial and there's nothing I can do.

Because these men had little or no direct contact with their children, their assessments were based largely on dated information and speculation. Only a couple of the absent fathers had heard about their children from reliable sources in recent months. One was periodically informed about his children by his own parents, the children's grandparents, and the other by a former neighbor who continued to live next door to the children and their mother in what had been the marital home.

Negative assessments of their children invariably involved some appraisal of the former wife also. For instance, this person, who remained in contact with his son only, described his daughter's general character and simultaneously denigrated his former wife.

> My daughter's cold. To be so self-standing, to be like the stoic philosopher and you're there and the rest of the world can go by, nothing affects you. She, at her age, only 13, talks that way. She says, "I don't need anybody." Now that's a really pitiful thing to say. I don't know what goes on with her. Her mother, typically, has never got around to asking her why she's doing or not doing what she's not doing. Well, I never did credit her with too much brains in this area when it comes to things that would require, I don't know, forcefulness and intelligence to try to solve a problem. She'll [the former wife will] always be found going the other way, like "I don't know." But I worry about her [the daughter]. Evidently she's icy cold about the whole thing. She doesn't give a shit about what her father thinks.

The fathers who were out of contact with one or more but not all of their offspring were in peculiar positions: Kept informed about the "absent" child through association with their other children, the child presumably was similarly kept informed about his or her father. Coupled with the anger about the child's rejection was concern that the other children would also come to refuse further connection, influenced by their mother with her "behind-the-scenes omnipotence," and by the recalcitrant sibling.

That their children were "screwed up," language used by nearly two-thirds of the traditionalist fathers, was proof, they insisted, that the decrease in paternal authority following divorce had harmed their children. The lack of a "strong father figure [in their lives]" was a major factor in children's problems. Moreover, children's behavioral and emotional problems vindicated their own, usually earlier, efforts to retain "some control." Denied the role of authority figure and assigned instead by divorce to being "an open checkbook and a visitor," they could do little, these fathers argued, to offset the consequences of the lack of their guidance. This next father, for example, blamed his former wife for his children's difficulties, including those experienced prior to divorce. She had "poisoned" them with lies about him and interfered with his efforts to provide discipline. "My second oldest daughter is trying to kill me. She hates me. I saw her in court [over child support noncompliance] 2 months ago. She came with her mother. She's still hostile and yelling things at me. And she's turned my son against me too. Their mother has done a real job on them." After describing her "delinquent" behavior, which he related to a "drug syndrome" but which, he said, did not actually involve drugs, he went on to characterize his son. "My son is into drugs now. He wasn't until I left. It's his way of coping with his mother and sister. Nobody's dealing it with it. My wife [sic] will just keep acting like it's not going on. But I talked to the neighbor who described some of the kids my son is hanging out with. It's not good, not good. Has to be drugs."

Numerous fathers said that boys take divorce harder than girls. For instance: "My son's coming around now. He was doing some excessive pot and alcohol, that sort of thing. He was doing very poorly in school too, dropped out. He hasn't been able to keep jobs. He got hurt by all of this. I had an angel and a devil. But even my daughter's been hurt by this. But boys take divorce harder. And their mother just couldn't cope with them; she was too busy 'looking for herself.' " Contrary to these men's assertions, the research evidence with respect to the differential effects of divorce on boys and girls is mixed (Chambers 1984; Chase-Lansdale and Hetherington 1990; Emery 1988; Kline, Tschann, Johnston, and Wallerstein 1989; Furstenberg and Cherlin 1991). A concern related to that about the lack of a strong father figure was that their sons might be or become homosexual. "I was getting very upset too because the woman [former wife] is so controlling and [that] is supposed to be so very bad for boys. I guess that's a whole story, but at least he [the oldest] seems to be changing and seems to be okay. I just heard on the radio today that domineering, controlling mothers lead boys to homosexuality. I said, 'Like what? Is that what we have here?' " Voiced by each of the traditionalist fathers, the view that homosexuality was a behavioral and developmental danger in the divorce situation was held also by many neo-traditionalist fathers. In total, more than two thirds of the nonresidential fathers with sons raised the concern of homosexuality, framing it as a "problem" resulting from "excessive" mother presence together with father absence from the home: *Their* not being present as full-time fathers to moderate the mother's effect jeopardized a son's sexual (heterosexual) identity. An orthodontist, this father had an arrangement that amounted to de facto shared custody.

My son is a very loving child. He is slightly, well, I told you I was worried about his sexual identity. He may have homosexual tendencies, you know? I was worried. He is a very gentle soul, very loving. And his mother is very domineering, *very* domineering, overprotective. He definitely doesn't appear to be homosexual but certainly isn't very macho. I don't know, but I don't think he's going to be that way. He's studious, he's a good kid. He's terrible at athletics, but I wasn't very good myself. And I don't have any problems that way. But then I didn't have his mother.

No father in the study raised such concerns about a daughter's sexual identity, not even fathers with primary childrearing responsibilities for daughters. Moreover, there is no evidence that father absence or parents' marital dissolution "causes" homosexuality (e.g., Pleck 1992b).

These men's overall contentions that children are adversely affected by their parents' divorce and fathers' limited or nonparental involvement has some research support (e.g., Wallerstein and Kelly 1980; Wallerstein and Blakeslee 1989; Hetherington et al. 1978, 1982, 1985). But other scholarly analyses of empirical data challenge the conclusion that paternal involvement is significantly related to children's well-being and adjustment after divorce. For instance, researchers Furstenberg and Cherlin (1991) summarized the findings from the National Survey of Children (NSC): "The amount of contact that children had with their fathers seemed to make little difference for their well-being. Teen-agers who saw their fathers regularly were just as likely as were those with infrequent contact to have problems in school or engage in delinquent acts and precocious sexual behavior. Further, the children's behavioral adjustment was also unrelated to the level of intimacy and identification with the nonresidential father. No differences were observed even among the children who had both regular contact and close relations with their father outside the home. Moreover, when the children in the NSC were reinterviewed in 1987 at ages 18 to 23, those who had retained stable, close ties to their fathers were neither more or less successful than those who had low or inconsistent levels of contact and intimacy with their fathers" (p. 72; see also Furstenberg et al. 1987; Emery 1988; Aquilino 1993).

These participants' assessments of their children's adjustments to divorce and the effects of paternal noninvolvement may well have been distorted. Children and the residential parent often do not establish family stability for a year or more subsequent to marital separation (Hetherington et al. 1979, 1982; Wallerstein and Kelly 1980; Chase-Lansdale and Hetherington 1990), by which time most of these fathers had tenuous relations with their children. Also, for the most part, their families had been highly conflictual prior to divorce. Marital turmoil itself negatively affects children (Block, Block, and Gjerde 1986; Block et al. 1988); according to various researchers, children's postdivorce adjustment is most related to the level of interparental conflict (e.g., Johnston, Kline, and Tschann 1989; Furstenberg and Cherlin 1991; Emery 1988; Ferreiro 1990). Scholars Chase-Lansdale and Hetherington (1990) summarized the research findings: "Most children, and especially boys, enter the divorcing period at a distinct disadvantage, having already experienced marital conflict for a number of years. The divorce itself in the immediate aftermath may exacerbate ongoing behavioral difficulties. . . . For example, the escalation of parental conflict after most divorces likely contributes to significant deterioration in children's psychological functioning over the course of the first year or so postdivorce" (p. 121).

Discussed as having or being at risk for developing serious problems, children were also talked about as *being* problems. Their financial support was a burden and their presence, even existence, an inescapable reminder of the former wife and failed marriage. "Not until they've reached 18 will I be free" was a common refrain. One father went so far as to say, "All in all, I'd be better off had they never been born." Another said, "If they'd all [former wife and their children] just died, you know, maybe a car wreck, I'd be a free man."

In conclusion, unable or unwilling to disaggregate the former spousal relationship and roles with the parental ones, or their former wives from their children, the traditionalist fathers were emotionally disconnected from their children. Finding their contacts enormously dissatisfying and frustrating and feeling displaced from their rightful positions, most withdrew to varying degrees from parenting. Paternal absence was viewed as being a logical and reasonable response to the divorce circumstance.

Notes

1. "Using data from the NSC, we find [in intact marriages with children] considerable evidence that fathers are actually more involved in rearing sons than in rearing daughters. Judging from the reports of both mothers and children, sons are closer to fathers than are daughters; according to the children, fathers participate in more activities with sons than with daughters; and children and mothers report that fathers are more involved in rule setting and discipline for boys than for girls" (Morgan, Lye, and Condran 1988, p. 123).

2. One of the unanswerable questions of this study is how do the vast majority (even in just New York state, the site of the research) of absent fathers who were silent —who did not participate in this study—differ from the absent father participants?

3. A decline in paternal involvement over time is related to a decrease in association between divorced parents: "Overall, former spouses still shared a moderate amount of co-parenting at 1 year after divorce. At that time, about 21% of the former spouses 'always' or 'usually' shared in seven or more of the ten areas asked about, and another 21% 'rarely' or 'never' shared in seven of

the ten areas. The remaining 59% 'sometimes' shared in these areas. There was a significant decrease in the amount of co-parental sharing by 3 years postdivorce, at which time only 9% still had a high degree of sharing. There was also a significant decrease over that period in the amount of time they spent together with each other and their children. At both 1 and 3 years, satisfaction with the amount of sharing was positively related to the actual amount of sharing. However, while the amount of sharing decreased over time, the respondents' satisfaction with this amount did not significantly change. Satisfaction with the co-parenting relationship overall did decline over the 3-year period for the fathers, although not for the mothers. The amount of conflict and of support in the co-parenting relationship did not change between 1 and 3 years postdivorce. There were no significant differences between former husbands and wives in the amount of co-parental sharing, conflict, support, or satisfaction reported at either time period" (Ahrons and Wallisch 1987a, p. 235).

4. More research attention needs to be given to ascertaining the informally negotiated movement of children between parental residences after divorce. In the Stanford Custody Project, involving over 1,000 families, it was found that approximately 3 years and 6 months after divorce, "there was a certain amount of shifting in and out of each of the residential arrangements, but 79% of the families having one of the three major residential arrangements at Time 1 (mother, father, or dual) retained the same arrangement at Time 2" (Maccoby et al. 1990, p. 144).

5. The case involving Elizabeth Morgan, a mother who because of her noncompliance with a court order to turn her daughter over to her former husband for visitation went to jail for nearly 2 years, was being covered in the newspapers and television news during the time of the earlier interviews. Her refusal to allow visitation was based on her belief that her daughter, and a child from her former husband's first marriage as well, were sexually abused by him. Elizabeth Morgan eventually joined her daughter in New Zealand, where she was granted sole custody. The case was mentioned by about one third of the fathers in the study; with only two exceptions it was cited as evidence of how fathers are mistreated and abused by the legal system and women intent on denying fathers their children and rights. See "As Far Away" (1990) and "The Morgan Case" (1990).

6. The flip side of the men's tendency to merge their children with their former wives was their tendency to merge their former wives with their children, especially in the processes of devaluing them as wives and mothers. Arliss (1991) suggested that such merging is an interactive process that is interrelated with the gender hierarchy: "Perhaps, as most subordinate populations, women have cultivated strategies that are nonthreatening to their 'superiors,' but also effective in obtaining desired outcomes. . . . So, the husband-wife relationship may resemble the parent-child relationship more closely than most married women would like to acknowledge" (p. 210). See also Goffman (1975) and Morgan's (1985, pp. 244-45) discussion of analytical approaches to patriarchy—"the role/rule of the father."

7

NEO-TRADITIONALIST FATHERS
Shifting Priorities

Principal concerns of the neo-traditionalist fathers were creating and maintaining meaningful relationships with their children as well as resisting the indignities of divorce and the actions of the former wife. Apprehensive about losing all parental involvement, they managed the former spousal relationship more successfully than did the traditionalist fathers. The noncustodial fathers especially were engaged in a balancing act. They "needed" to withstand the injustices of divorce without totally alienating or infuriating the former wife because, as a father of three said, "She holds the reins as to whether I get to parent my kids or not; hell, whether I get to see my kids or not."

Levels of Parental Involvement

Most neo-traditionalist fathers were nonresidential fathers, but three were co-custodial and two were custodial parents. Three saw their children only occasionally. The others had regular contacts, ranging from once or twice a month to several times a week. Over half of the 23 regularly visiting fathers met with their children for a weekly evening visit in addition to the allotted alternate weekends, and more than one-third had frequent telephone contacts beyond those used to make or confirm visiting plans. Men

166

who saw their children infrequently had little other contact with them. Data from a national survey also show a relationship between types of contacts: "Among those who did not visit at all during the past year, only 10% had any contact by telephone or mail, and most (77%) of those who visited regularly (i.e., at least 1-3 times per month) also maintained regular contact by telephone or mail. . . . Fathers and children who maintain close touch through visiting communicate regularly in other ways as well" (Seltzer 1991b, p. 85).

With the exception of telephoning, most men's access to their children was circumscribed, defined by and limited to that stipulated in the custody and visitation accord. Flexible or liberal access, whether assigned legally or developed informally between the parents, was rare in this New York sample; custody and visitation arrangements vary by states, affected by both family law statutes and customary practice (Riley 1991; Jacob 1988). Only five of the visiting fathers had relatively unfettered access to their children. Yet nearly half of the others, although complaining about the limits of their parental access, had less contact with their children than formally specified. Further, most communicated little with their former wives regarding their children or parenting. Their arrangements constituted *parallel parenting* in which parents "maintain separate and segregated relations with each of their children and have a tacit agreement not to interfere in each other's lives" (Furstenberg and Cherlin 1991, pp. 39-40).[1] "Only a small proportion of divorced spouses develop a cooperative, even friendly, relationship with each other, indicating that the pattern of cooperative parenting, so widely portrayed in the popular media, is, in fact, rather rare. Indeed, former spouses appear to be reluctant partners in the childrearing process," and children often provide the link between the parents in terms of communication (Furstenberg and Nord 1985, pp. 899-900).

Six of the visiting fathers had unusual levels of parental involvement. Mostly limited to set visitation schedules, each handled a particular parental responsibility, in addition to contributing economic support, and five of the six engaged in joint decision making with their former wives. One father managed his child's singing career and earnings. Two handled their children's religious upbringing and activities, and two directed their offsprings' education. Another managed his daughter's education and religious training:

She [the former wife] said she would send her to public school. My daughter's private school is, I think, three times the level of the public schools around. It's an excellent school. She said she'd send her to a public school and I said I wouldn't sign any agreement unless she agreed to send her to yeshiva. So we agreed that as long as I pay for it, she must stay there, which is fine. It's my investment. It's my future. I have control over her education which I think is one of the most important things, even though I don't have custody.

Three of the fathers having some particular sphere of parental responsibility concluded that they were "more aware" fathers as a result of divorce. One, who "was allowed" responsibility for his children's education, acknowledged that he previously subordinated his children and parenting to his career.

Maybe I'm a more attuned father than I might have been because when you're living together, it's like sometimes you get more carried away with your work and you're so involved with all your daily routines, that even though you set aside some time for them [the children], it's not as much time really. Actually, when I think about it, I spend more time now probably than I used to because there it was an hour a day, although I did spend weekends with them then too. But I do give my undivided attention now. I do think it probably is better.

The changes brought about by divorce were sometimes dramatic, as they are for substantial numbers of fathers who divorce. Wallerstein and Corbin (1986), for example, observed that "by eighteen months postseparation, one half of the father-child relationships were significantly different from their dominant cast during the marriage" (p. 109). These researchers also reported that "there was an extraordinary lack of significant linkages between the predivorce father-child relationship and the frequency or regularity of visiting patterns and child support." Responsible for his son's religious upbringing, this next father had sought joint physical custody. Having his earlier petitions denied, he was again pursuing a custody modification, arguing that the lack of shared custody pushed him into an unfair and untenable position as a parent. During marriage and family, he had been "a modern father" involved in the daily care of his child. Unlike many other participants, he was able to detail these care activities. Through divorce, he went from sharing daily parenting work to seeing his son weekly for church services and on alternate weekends for a more extended visit.

This [standard visitation] isn't enough. I'm saying in order for a father to remain a father, he needs day-to-day responsibilities. A child needs substantial access to a father. A father needs substantial access to his child. All I wanted was for my son to have daily access to both of his parents—substantial access to both of his parents, even if it was 30 or 40% rather than 50%. But the routine agreement of every other weekend amounts to 15% and, with 15%, I'm just a playmate and a visitor. So I think this has hurt my child. It's hurt me. I have no authority; I'm just a visitor and a playmate now. Without day-to-day responsibility, my child perceives me to be a secondary parent. He perceives his custodial parent as being his principal parent, his—I don't like the word boss—but his authority. Noncustodial parents do not have the authority that custodial parents do. But having a visiting father is better than having no father at all.

His argument that time together plays a significant role in a noncustodial fathers relationship with his children is supported by some professionals working with divorced families. Psychiatrist Williams (1988), for example, argued: "There are those who would believe that one can maintain a good sense of parental identity by 'quality' visitation contacts—even if those contacts are infrequent—compared with quantity of custody contacts. That is just not so. Each of our identities—be it our professional, or marital or our parental identity—is fulfilled by both the quality and quantity of our experiences" (pp. 2-3). Like the professional who is only able to practice occasionally, he continued: "So too, when fathers and mothers are wonderfully interactive, responsible, and loving with their children two to three times a month, when they have been used to being with their children most every day, they no longer truly feel like a parent" (Williams 1988, pp. 2-3).

None of the neo-traditionalist fathers with atypically high levels of parental involvement—the six highly involved visiting, three co-custodial, and two custodial fathers—believed a genuine parenting collaboration with their respective former spouses was possible. Seven of the eleven had continuing antagonisms with them. One person, for example, whose associations with his former wife "had simmered down some over the years," nonetheless saw himself as being locked in an "unending, necessary, and open divorce war." In his quest to increase his and decrease her parental involvement, he had initiated several dozen judicial hearings. Although his confrontational style was comparable to, and even exceeded, that of some fathers who gradually disengaged from their children, parental withdrawal was out of the question for him. He remained both a combative former spouse and an engaged parent, believing that not having been granted sole custody from the initial point of separation was "a grave legal and moral injustice."

I kept fighting. They'd [attorneys would] say, "We'll bargain, like horsetrading." I said, "My children are not horses." Eventually [after 4 years of legal negotiations, court hearings, and psychiatric evaluations], her lawyer said, "We'll give you three weekends a month and all of the summer." So anyway, three weekends a month, I choose the three. So I was treated as noncustodial in various custody battles but the order was finally joint legal custody with what amounts to 36% physical custody. I chose three weekends a month so when there's 3-day weekends, I always choose that. Thanksgiving and Christmas every other year. On the off years, I get the first days of the vacation. She goes wild about this. She's out of control. In the summer, she's able to pick only 2 weeks out of the 17. I have them almost 60 days then, depending on the weekends.

The reluctant custodial father, although extensively involved with his child as his primary parent, also resembled the traditionalist fathers in his attitudes.[2] He had expected, after forcibly removing his wife from the family home, that she "would get her act together and behave like a mother" and assume responsibility for their child. He blamed the collapse of the marriage and her "inadequacy as a mother" on her immaturity and history of drug dependency, which he had shared earlier. After divorcing, he relied on his sister for assistance in caring for and rearing his child for several years. A "falling-out" with her over her strong disapproval of his active social life and parenting style brought him to his "current coping strategy": "Now I let the therapist do the nurturing thing [during a 1-hour, once a week meeting]. That's what I'm paying her for. If she can't come up with anything better, I'll find another therapist." He continued, describing his feelings of resentment about, together with occasional moments of pleasure with, primary parenting:

To be a father means a lot of responsibility. And it means that you are the *one*. That there is someone who counts on you for everything. And it really stinks because you just don't get a chance to live your life and do what you want to do when you want to do it. But then there are those rare occasions— like last Sunday was the All-Star game. They announced his name and he was out there and you get all teary-eyed and you feel good about life. And that happens a bit. He's really made me proud of him in a lot of ways, and I love him dearly, and I wouldn't—if I had to redo the whole thing other than not get married and not have him—I wouldn't want to have it this way. I'd put him in boarding school next year if I could find one I can afford. And I could use the break. I have to deal with him 24 hours a day and it's really a pain in the neck. Just kidding! Well, maybe not.

This father was affected also by his attitudes and expectations that women are to mother and men are to be left free "to live their lives." Missing in his account, as in most neo-traditionalist and traditionalist fathers, a majority of whom typically spent less time with and did little caregiving of their children subsequent to divorce, was evidence of "a [parental] commitment that is central to his self-conception" (May and Strikwerda 1992a, p. 81).

ROLE AMBIGUITY

Who they were as fathers was disrupted by the dissolution of their marriages, and yet what being a divorced father meant in practice was largely unclear. Most, particularly the nonresidential fathers, felt displaced and disregarded. The disruption in parental identity was believed to be singular, not shared by the former wife whose role and status as a mother were relatively untouched by divorce. This difference was attributed not only to the unique relations between mothers and children but also to the cultural and legal support granted to motherhood. Thus these fathers' uncertainties were juxtaposed over and against the relative clarity available, it seemed, to former wives: Women were mothers irrespective of their marital status. The cultural idealization of motherhood (Glenn 1987; Backett 1982, 1987), which most of the men accepted and often explicitly expounded, even the custodial fathers, was not coupled with a comparable conception of fatherhood.[3] This father, for instance, complained about the different cultural values placed on fathers and mothers:

> I don't know, maybe the child means too much to me but I mean a lot to him too, and I honestly believe that the father is important in a child's life, especially a young boy. Some people don't really understand the bond that can be between a father and a son. A lot of people seem to think that fathers are entirely remote from their kids, that they don't care as much about their kids as mothers do, that somehow we asked for it [divorce]. "We don't really want our kids as much as we say we do and, even if we did, we wouldn't know how to take care of them." Well, that's not true. Being a father is a mission for me, in the spiritual sense. Whatever sense, it's the most rewarding, fulfilling mission that I could possibly go on. I'd rather be a father to my son than be Donald Trump, Ted Turner, or George Bush, or whoever. It makes it all worthwhile. I don't know how you describe it, and I don't mean to sound like a martyr or anything, but I'd walk over hot coals for the opportunity to have these times together with my son. It's amazing. As soon as I pick him up I feel this whole smile coming across my whole face. My life is just so much more complete. I feel like I'm me again, I'm natural again. I just feel natural when I'm being a dad, and unnatural when I'm not being a dad.

The problems of fatherhood became particularly pronounced in divorce. Backett (1987, p. 79), analyzing men's parenting involvement in English middle-class families, concluded that most fathers deal with general domestic and family matters and negotiate acceptable parental behavior in relation to the mother, but do little in the way of developing direct relationships with their children, in contrast to mothers. This presents a unique handicap in divorce, as clearly evidenced by these men's experiences. Not only were their parental relationships shaky and tenuous but they had to look for reassurance that their children, especially, and other people as well recognized them as fathers. For instance: "With parenting I think I've kept the image of parent, of the father, even though the ex-wife was trying to make one brother-in-law into a father, in all actuality. I think I survived through this whole thing because the kids are still like, 'that's my dad' type-deal."

The insult of being displaced by divorce from parenting was heightened further for the neo-traditionalist fathers because they had been, as several claimed, "contemporary" or "modern" fathers. Compared to their own fathers and others of earlier generations or, for that matter, most men they knew in their own age cohorts, their childrearing and child care involvement was high during marriage. Other men were their reference points, not their wives or the division of labor between them before divorce. This father, for example, desired a more active role in his child's rearing, comparable to what he had before divorce.

> Most divorced fathers do not get support and understanding from their own relatives. Most of us have been raised by our mothers. You know, my father was a self-employed businessman; he worked long hours. He was a loving father, but day-to-day responsibility for whatever was involved—laundry, cooking, housekeeping, whatever —was my mother's. My father worked outside the house and brought home the money. He was there. We saw him every day. My brothers are traditional fathers and I would say that their wives are traditional women. Of the five brothers, I'm the one with the most education and the least success in marriage. My seven nieces and nephews were not born in the presence of their fathers, okay? . . . So none of them [adult family members] understand why I'm so miserable with this arrangement.

Nearly all, especially those with children about age 10 and under, pointed to their presence at the child's birth as evidence of their greater involvement and commitment (see May and Strikwerda 1992a; Ruddick 1993; Laqueur 1993).[4]

Whatever the character and level during marriage, many of these men's family activities were not easily carried over into the post- divorce situation. Nor was the status associated with these activities easily transported or converted. Although continuing financial obligations were clear and definitive, even if sometimes unmet, other parental responsibilities or opportunities were not (see Seltzer 1991a; Tepp 1983). In this ambiguous context, resisting exclusion required vigilance, effort, and loud protestations. But individual efforts alone did not alter institutional arrangements or cultural assumptions. Nor did such efforts compensate for limited cooperation from the former wife. For instance, this next person's former spouse held him to the court-approved access schedule and reported violations to the courts. "I've had judges lecture me, saying, 'How dare you call that house? You're only supposed to call that house on Tuesdays and Saturdays and you called on Wednesday.' I mean, who gives a shit when you call on the phone to talk to your own kids? This is somehow bad, because they wrote it on a piece of paper and somebody made a decision? You tell me: Why? Why?"

Like the traditionalist fathers, these men saw their parental roles as involving primarily the particular disciplinary controls "only men" or "only fathers" can offer. Similarly emphasized was the importance of being male role models to their children, particularly to sons. Conveying skills was stressed also. For instance, "She [the former wife] complains about my teaching them to shoot and hunt; she says it's dangerous and unnecessary. 'Too macho,' she says. But what's really bugging her is that she can't stand it that I have something to offer them that she can't. They're boys. I understand that. She doesn't. They need this sort of input from me. She can't give it to them." These fathers also wanted their roles to be broader than the conventional ones assigned to fathers. At the same time, most were uncertain about what expanded roles might entail. Distinguishing between women's and men's natures and relations with children, they insisted, in varying ways, that "women do the mothering thing, the nurturing thing" as one characterized the "natural" division of labor. One father, for example, insisted: "I still can't hold a baby. Just keep them away from me. Give them [children] to me when they're about 3, or better yet 4, then they can be talked to." Having a co-custodial parenting arrangement, achieved by threatening to fight for sole custody, he was "furious" that his 4-year-old son had been given a doll: "He's not allowed to bring it here, no way. How's he supposed to grow up to be a man [when] playing with dolls?" These men were constrained in their parenting, then, both by their circumstances and adherence to the conventional gender belief system (May and Strikwerda 1992a).

Contributing also to role ambiguity and not lessened by the passage of time, except for the few men having sole custody, was concern that the former wife would remarry or, if she had already, worries about the influence of the stepfather on their children. The possibility that they would be further displaced from their children's lives by another man was a persistent fear. For instance: "One of the biggest adjustments has been to the pain [of knowing] that they will eventually be living with another man. That's very disturbing to me, that another man will serve as their father and be a father role. That hurts me tremendously and bothers me a lot. I don't want another man to step into their lives as a father. I dread that day." These concerns were not unfounded. Research indicates that non-residential fathers' involvement often decreases when a stepfather lives with their children. Seltzer and Bianchi (1988), for example, concluded: "Our findings suggest that contemporary American society constrains children to two or fewer parents. Even children who live apart from biological parents, and know for certain that their absent parent is still alive, are unlikely to maintain ties with their parent when an alternative step-parent, adoptive parent, or other adult caretaker is available within the child's own household. . . . Noncustodial parents discard ties to their biological children with divorce, and the ties are replaced through remarriage. Children alternate between having one and two parents" (p. 674; see also Furstenberg and Cherlin 1991).

Several participants anguished over the former wife's and her new husband's expectations that their children refer to their stepparent as father. The appropriation of the relational title was symbolic of the broken family and their own ambiguous positions.[5] This person's child was 5 years old:

> The minute they got married, they instructed my son that *he* was "daddy" and that caused a lot of problems. I heard them on the phone. I said, "Don't you tell *my* son to call you daddy." They didn't have any of their own children, now they do. Now they're saying, "Oh well, they're siblings. He hears his brothers saying it." At the time this was first said his brother was a baby and couldn't even talk. It was things like that, you know. They're doing it to goad me, to irritate me, to destroy the relationship between me and my son. It's easy to do when you take another man's child and hold him on the stairway and say, "I'm your daddy, right?" This is the way the guy is, and I'm standing there, and my son would say, "Yeah, right." He was ordered at one point never to call me daddy. The judge told them that they were not to insist that he call him daddy.

Parental Relations and Discontent

Dissatisfaction with their parental situations and relationships was the norm among the neo-traditionalist fathers. Only two were pleased with their overall parenting arrangements, and only four felt close to their children. Irrespective of their prior parental involvement, divorce and the maternal custody arrangement resulted in a loss of daily and routine interaction. A few fathers compared their parental relations to those of strangers, and a majority expressed fears that they and their children would become like strangers. They were neither prepared for the changes in family dynamics prompted by divorce, including the emotional stresses of the immediate postseparation phase, nor familiar with negotiating the parent-child relationship independent of the children's mother. A father of three observed, "My ex used to decode what the kids were saying. Now I'm on my own." In relating to their children after divorce, these men were left trying to "plow new ground with old equipment": "That I only knew how to cook a few kinds of meals wasn't the biggest problem when they came over. It was that I didn't know what to do with them, how to entertain them, how to get them to talk to me." And this father described a typical exchange with his 8-year-old daughter: "I ask her how she is, how she's feeling about things. She says, 'Okay.' So then I try, 'Well, what have you been doing?' She says, 'Nothing.' Then I try, 'Well, how's your mom?' 'Okay.' 'Just okay?' 'Yeah, okay.' Maybe it's normal. I don't worry much because I know she's close with her mother and talks to her about what's bothering her. Kids generally are closer to their mothers that way, it's just natural. But it sure leaves me out, out in the cold." Researchers Furstenberg and Cherlin (1991) commented on this phenomenon: "Many men don't seem to know how to relate to their children except through their wives. Typically, when married, they were present but passive—not much involved in childrearing. When they separate, they carry this pattern of limited involvement with them; and it is reinforced by the modest contact most have with their children" (p. 74).

This next person, like others with older children, found his teenaged son reluctant to discuss personal matters. So he speculated, expanding on limited information.

> My older son [16 years old] is so-so. He's like, "Well, I'll tolerate this." He's dating as far as I know. I guess one of the things that made me feel a little bit better that he's normal [heterosexual] was that a couple of months ago he was working on his car, you know, and I went to open his trunk to get something and I saw a panicked look on his face. I was going, "Huh?" It was Millers [beer]. I just said, "Oh, some Millers! Well, I never. Well, maybe a few times." He reacted to everything by avoidance, not acting out, just sort of going with the flow. He was always pretty much a quiet kid. That's why now that I'm finally getting to see him on a more regular basis and can see some kind of rebellion and get to talk to him a few times on the phone—I don't know what his schedule is. But he's been giving me a call sometimes.

These fathers, like the traditionalist ones, had difficulty separating children from their mothers and parental from former spousal issues. For instance, the father cited above continued: "We're sort of talking about his plans for college. But I had to tell him that 'with your mother getting 40% of my net

pay, it will be quite difficult for me to help out. She has soaked me dry.' "
Unlike the others, however, the neo-traditionalist fathers sometimes recognized that the propensity to mix up children and their mother contributed to
the distance between themselves and their offspring.

OTHERS' CHILDREN

Relations with others' children were also circumscribed and tenuous.
For example, four noncustodial fathers who had maintained some association with their offspring after divorce had separated totally from a step-
child with whom they had lived while married. The emotional ties with
these children were so weak, apparently, that divorce eroded them fully
and seemingly easily.[6]

Children of girlfriends posed problems. Twenty fathers, including both
traditionalist and neo-traditionalist ones, indicated that since divorcing,
relationships with girlfriends had ended primarily because of disagreements over her children and, on occasion, his. Three men attributed the
ending of second marriages to differences over childrearing. Claims also
were made that, although their relations with their own children were less
than satisfactory, they became substitute father figures to the children of
other women. Having only occasional contacts with his children, this
father remarked: "Many of us do end up becoming like fathers to girlfriends of ours who have children, as it is in my case. And in my case, my
girlfriend's case, her husband, who is still her husband, fits all the stereotypes that are the stereotypical description of the deadbeat dad, my girlfriend's husband. He could care less about those kids." Such "serial
fathering" on their part was tenuous (Furstenberg 1988): None of these
men had continuing contacts with the children of former girlfriends even
though, they argued, they had been significant adults in the children's lives
for a period of time. Four men noted that their children were emotionally
upset when they ended a relationship with a particular girlfriend because
bonds had developed between them. In three instances, girlfriends had
children also who had become close with the men's offspring.

SOCIAL LIVES AND CHILDREN

In various ways, children interfered with their social lives, reported a
majority of neo-traditionalist fathers. The reluctant custodial father, for
example, who was a college administrator, worked a second job because
"both my kid and I like expensive clothes, cars, and skis and because I love
to travel and date and it costs money, and I have to cover baby-sitting for

my kid." His biggest hope about being a custodial parent met with disappointment: "I thought my being a single parent would be a kind of calling card, a 'Hey, what are you doing?' 'Oh, you're a single parent, you have custody of your kid?' But I haven't really met many women who thought that was terrific. It has scared a few women away. I don't know. Some people think it's good, some don't. I would have thought it would be a springboard to meeting more women, but so far [4 years], it hasn't." Others said they had thought, mostly erroneously as it turned out, that being a visiting divorced father, rather than an absent one, would be attractive to women.

Like the custodial father cited above, a co-custodial father also relied on baby-sitters for his young child in order to keep up his social life. He justified leaving his child routinely: "If I'd stayed married, he'd have a baby-sitter every Friday and Saturday night. Why should that change? Besides, it's good for him." But most men complained that the burden of child support obligations precluded dating. So too did regular visits with their children. This father, for instance, saw his children frequently.

I'm hindered by my time with the children, which is the wrong way of putting it. But my finances and my divorce settlement prevent me from really getting involved with a woman. You kind of pocket your needs and you go on, and you really don't think about it. You just don't think about it. I talked to a woman in the club last night, and I could relate to everything that she was saying. And she's a female. It's amazing, you know, you have a great rapport with them [women], but at the same time you say, "If I get together with one of them, look at the mess we've got." . . . There are so many drawbacks in the bond between you and a divorced woman with kids. But there has to be something stronger. You have to work so much harder if you want it to grow. This idea of the man with the wine rack and different women every night is a joke. I think for most men, most of them don't do it, can't afford to do it, and emotionally don't do it. Those who do, do so to drown out the horrible sorrow over the loss of their children. I truly believe that. Or, as in my case, there's just not time since my main activity has been parenting. So my social life has been basically nil. A high price, huh? And I'm not getting any younger, as they say.

Parenting

Given the postdivorce situation in which the former routines of family life were disrupted and particularly in light of the constraints imposed by visitation, involvement as a noncustodial father required some deliberation and intent. Yet most of these participants had not developed strategies for parenting and relating to their children. For example, having been divorced nearly 2 years after a separation of over a year, this next person continued to see his child, although his involvement had been declining steadily over the past year. At the time of the interview, he had neither seen nor talked to her for nearly 4 weeks. Because he anticipated that she would ask when they would get together next, he avoided telephoning. Feelings of guilt about her circumstances and frustration about his own interfered with his commitment to maintain frequent contact (see also Wallerstein and Kelly 1980; Fox 1985). Moreover, he was unsure what to do with her when they were together.

> How many times in one day, after all, can I take my daughter to McDonald's or to the park to swing? I just don't know what to do to entertain her. So we end up renting videos and spending hours just sitting in front of the TV screen. I am restless and bored. She is unhappy and bored although she tries, she really does seem to try. She needs to be out playing with her friends, not stuck here with me.

How to maintain a relationship within the visitation context, let alone promote a more satisfactory one, seemed a bewildering task.

VISITATION ROUTINES

Fathers who saw their children regularly were less disadvantaged by visitation awkwardness than the others. Even though few had clearly defined parenting plans, some had established fairly standard and workable routines. This father, for example—the only one of the nine men who brought a child (or children) to the interview who also carried along items with which she could occupy herself—turned to his young daughter during the discussion and asked,[7]

> What do we do on Fridays? I pick you up and then what do we do? I get her three weekends in a row, from Friday night to Sunday night. The fourth week I get to see her one night during the week. [This atypical visitation schedule was a result of an unsettled custody challenge.] It was at the baby-sitter's and now it's at her mother's [that I pick her up]. Usually we spend Fridays, we usually come right home and cook some supper or something. I try to shop the night before so I don't have to drag her to the store. Then we'll watch TV and pop some popcorn. Then Saturdays can be anything. Breakfasts are cereal, Cheerios or something. Then what we do depends on the weather. Especially during the summertime we go to the beach; we're always doing something. We go down to the docks and feed the ducks. We're always doing

something together, at a playground, whatever. So we have quality time together on the weekends. Sometimes we visit friends. Sundays we go to church in the morning and then we do something. Like today, when we're finished here, we're going to some friends who have kids her age; they're going to roller skate. Some Sundays we go see my sister and her family. I have to have her home by 6:00.

This next father was also atypical. He described several of his deliberate strategies for reaffirming his parenting presence in his child's life:

On the phone she tells me about her school and her friends, she tells me about her homework and her report card. I help her with her homework. I've been helping her with that report I was telling you about; we've gone to the library to work on it. She has just great report cards and I get her gifts for her report cards. She loves to do art work too. See those pictures on the wall there? She did those last weekend while we were here [in the office]. Said, "Here, daddy, I made you a present." Aren't they good? She's only 7. . . . I make sure I take pictures. What I do is take pictures of everything we do. Here, let me show you. I make two of each and make her an album of each thing. I think that's important. She'll have a record this way.

The advantages for nonresidential parents of having regular and frequent visits were summarized by Chase-Lansdale and Hetherington (1990): "Those few fathers who do see their children regularly and frequently are more likely to develop close relationships with them, especially if they establish a home where the children can visit and stay overnight. . . . This permits the enjoyable quotidian family activities that stand in marked contrast to the superficial, 'every day is Christmas' or 'tour guide' quality of the short and isolated visits to amusement parks, shopping malls, and restaurants typical of most father-child outings" (pp. 112-13; see also Fox 1985; Hess and Camara 1979).

Pursuing recreational activities in and outside of the home, watching television or rented videos, and sharing meals dominated the time regularly visiting fathers spent together with their children. Indeed, parenting and parental relations were repeatedly described in terms of the activities shared with children: Being a visiting parent was synonymous with sharing in recreational pursuits. One who emphasized the struggle to maintain the authority role of father, this person explicitly equated a "good father-son relationship" to joint participation in activities.

My relationship with each of my three boys is very good. I have found something unique to do with my boys. They enjoy doing the survival games where you run around playing soldiers in the woods; you have guns that shoot paint pellets. It's like the *gotchee* games on campuses. The boys enjoy doing it, especially the two older ones. It's like the one thing I can do with them that's unique to do with their father. It lets me be a parent.

Met through recreational activities were the goals of "keeping busy" or "filling time" and avoiding awkward silences or interactional dead ends: "Just sitting around, looking at each other, is torture, like Chinese water torture." Also, by sharing pursuits intended to be mutually enjoyable, these fathers hoped their children would be pleased, eager to get together, and impressed, convinced that their father was a distinctive, even special, person: a man with particular interests and abilities and not the person the mother may have been portraying him to be. That these fathers emphasized play and entertainment is not unlike fathers' general activities in families before divorce, according to a variety of studies (e.g., Lamb 1987; Douthitt 1989; LaRossa 1989).[8] Regarding fathers in intact marriages, Backett (1987), for instance, noted, "Playing with children and being a source of pleasure were thus highly meaningful ways of demonstrating father involvement. This was an area of activity which the father could carry out spontaneously and voluntarily with the minimum specific knowledge or consultation with the mother being necessary" (p. 86).

Several fathers sought support and guidance in how to be "a successful divorced father" from area chapters of Parents Without Partners, a national single-parents' organization. Parent education classes and recreational activities were the primary attractions. This person, for example, saw his elementary school-aged children every few days and believed his relationship with them was steadily improving, primarily because of his participation in such a parents' group. Describing his visitation routine, he also assessed his parenting involvement.

[Thursday alternate visitation] generally consists of my picking the kids up and us going to eat somewhere at a restaurant, and then we'll go to the library. And then we'll listen to tapes or we'll get books, and I'll read to them or any variety of things. And then, when I've got them for the whole weekend, I'm active in Parents Without Partners. That's where I got the idea of using the library and the importance of sticking to the Thursday evenings. And so there are a lot of children's activities. It's not the proverbial meat-hook-type place, meat market, I guess is what they call it. At least that's not how I look at it. I look at it as fostering and encouraging my own parenting. So we have a variety of activities through there. . . . Three of the guys and I take our kids and go fishing. So I've found it to facilitate my being a parent by providing me with a constantly changing availability of activities. I think that's one of the things that most fathers, not just me, have a problem adjusting to. Being involved in the children's lives every day is suddenly taken away from you as the noncustodial parent and a lot of it is adjusting to that—the not knowing what to do in the time you do have, and yet still realizing that you are a parent, that you do have effect even though it has been curtailed significantly.

Several fathers who saw their children regularly tried to include other adults in their planned activities. They created a kind of limited "fictive kin" with some friends.[9] Having others present eased interactional tensions, added moral support as well as a sense of normalcy to father-child relations, and reinforced and legitimated paternal status. "I prefer to share my children with my friends. I find greater joy in terms of sharing opportunities with my kids, preferably with other people. It's best if it's a sharing experience, you know. It helps draw the kids out, it helps draw the father out." And one father, discussing his daughter, noted: "The child needs to know that the parent is parent not solely because you said so, but because there is a social agreement on the fact that it is indeed that. And that the relationship exists and these other people come into play, how other people relate to you and recognize the relationship."

Subsequent to divorce, nine men had coached sports teams to which a child of theirs belonged. With one exception, the coaching involved boys' teams. Suggesting that they had more discretion in the nature and extent of parental involvement than they usually allowed, six men had overcome their former wife's resistance to their coaching. At the same time, such "successes" were not secure: Three fathers were left with team responsibilities after their children quit, actions each of the men blamed on his former wife. Numerous traditionalist and neo-traditionalist fathers, particularly of sons, lamented their exclusion from coaching their children's sports teams. Being shut out of this role denied them the opportunity "to connect" with their children in a "uniquely meaningful" way (see Messner 1992). That their children were not more active in sports was attributed to the parents' divorce and the former wife's failure to understand the significance of sports for boys' development.

Stressing recreation during their time together had varying degrees of success and was related typically to the frequency of visits, children's ages, and the kinds of activities that could be chosen given the men's respective financial resources. Frequent visits, younger children, and discretionary income contributed to the success of shared affairs. Time of year was also a factor: Over half of the visiting fathers with children who were not yet teenagers found the winter season especially difficult because it curtailed the range of outside ventures. And relying on activities as a way to connect with their children had a downside. It fueled their doubts about the meaning of their parental involvement, making it seem superficial and insincere. Hired baby-sitters could both entertain and supervise children, and besides, baby-sitters cost the custodial mother money.

In their efforts to please and entertain their children, some visiting fathers indulged them with treats and toys, especially younger children, or vacation trips. Each of these men complained of being criticized by the former wife for this kind of spending on their children.

> For a while I was buying them things, you know, little things. Then she said to me that she didn't have money to buy them things. She said I was buying their love and I should stop. So I thought about it and decided maybe I was. So I only buy for their birthdays and things. I agreed. But she buys them things. So I can't buy them things but she can? Now when they tell me to buy them things, I tell them no. "I'm your father, not your uncle-daddy." I had an uncle who bought us things like that.

More common than descriptions of lavish spending, however, were complaints: Financial constraints prevented greater spending on their children. Such limitations were usually attributed to child support obligations; most respondents missed few opportunities to link the burdens of child support payments to other matters.

Geographical Distance

Proximity facilitated regular visitation and shared participation in routine activities (Furstenberg et al. 1987). But determined fathers found ways to handle the additional barrier of geographical distance when it was a factor. This next person had a convoluted situation. As established in the custody agreement, he could visit on alternate weekends, beginning Friday afternoons and ending late Sunday evenings. But to see his son, he had to drive the nearly 300 miles to where his son and former wife lived. To accommodate the commute, he had created a flexible employment situation by quitting his hospital administrative position and working as a substitute nurse anesthetist. He lived with his parents out of economic necessity. He too likened the sharing of recreational activities to paternal involvement and commitment.

> I've got a van so I bring down a lot of toys, remote control cars; we're both into sports so I've got all kinds of sporting equipment. I bring two bicycles down. So I pick him up from school on Friday and we go out and throw a ball around or do whatever. Go downtown then Friday night. Typically, on a

Saturday morning he has a soccer game so I bring him to the soccer, or basketball. Those are the two leagues that he's in. Saturday afternoon we do whatever the weather seems to call for. We find a park and ride our bikes or throw a ball, watch some TV. I bought him a GameBoy and he likes to play that, you know, Nintendo.® Maybe we'll rent a movie and a VCR, or do whatever we can to fill the time, and the time goes awfully fast. We always have a wonderful time. We're pals. We both really love sports. The hotel is usually the same hotel so it's like second home for him. We have a wonderful time. The hard part of it is getting down there and getting back. You can't imagine what a drag it is. It's back and forth and back and forth, 300 miles each way over the same highway. It's been over 200 [alternate] weekends without a miss. I'm drowning in debt.

Geographical distance was handled in various ways. Several fathers whose children lived more than 2 hours away negotiated an altered visitation schedule so their children stayed with them less frequently over regular weekends but for longer periods during vacations and long holiday weekends. Two of these fathers were spending more time in total with their children under the revised arrangement.

This next "highly involved" visiting father, who lived several hours' driving time away from his daughter's residence with her mother, was unusual in his actions, general pleasure with the present situation, and open affection for his child. Initially encountering repeated visitation interference, he had involved attorneys to secure a satisfactory arrangement, defined as "liberal" visitation. He spent more than $20,000 and invested 18 months in obtaining the change. "I get my daughter every other weekend, and I can take her to dinner one night a week. I can call her Monday through Thursday between 8 and 8:30 p.m. Also, I get every other holiday, and I get between 2 and 3 weeks in the summer. That's what I had to fight for." Although having occasional "fantasies of raising her alone," he had not sought sole or joint custody because he did not want to either deny their child or her mother their "special" relationship or impede his "freedom to continue climbing the corporate ladder." His definition of his parental responsibility was unique: economic provision and emotional and logistical support for both his former wife and their child. For instance, he encouraged his former wife to work only part-time until their daughter was older and voluntarily compensated her in the meantime for forgone earnings although he successfully had resisted a formal court order to provide any maintenance (spousal support). And he adhered to his former wife's atypical dietary plan, to which he was not personally committed, for their child. His actions, he explained, were guided by the teachings of his religion, Judaism. He was a more involved parent now than before divorcing.

I look at it this way: I see her more than most fathers who live at home. And I control the education. And she's fine. I also take care of medical and dental [coverage] and this way I make sure she has good health care. I have a very close relationship with her. I speak to her every night [by telephone]. I make sure I never miss a weekend [of assigned visitation]. I see studies that show that the average father spends about 8 minutes a day with his child. I say that's absurd. When I have her for the weekend, it's like she's my "little woman," you know. I don't go out that weekend or anything, I just spend it with her. I spend quality time with her. I take her out and take her to where lots of kids who are home [with both parents] never get to go. It's constant activity, we constantly do things together. So under the circumstances—it's like she tells me, "You're my best friend." She says, "Daddy, Annie's father is never home." She says, "I see you a lot more than Annie sees her father." It's funny. I see it here at the office too. Some of these guys almost never even talk to their kids. She's a great kid. My problem is getting her to go home after the weekends.

Although using a metaphor more commonly used to characterize a relation-ship with an adult woman—"she's my little woman"—he described his relationship with his child with detailed examples and specifics.[10] As he continued talking, he again compared himself to other fathers.

I try to visit her school whenever she has a play or something. I'm one of the only fathers, it's an amazing thing. I have to drive more than 2 hours after work and still get back later, and I'm one of the only fathers, sometimes *the only* father, there. She has a play coming up. I haven't missed any plays. I try to go to at least one parent-teachers' meeting each year. My ex-wife and I usually go at separate times. The teachers always tell me the same thing, that if they didn't know the situation [parents being divorced], that they wouldn't know from the child, which is important. It's great, just great.

National survey data support this father's claim that he is unusual as a divorced father in his participation in his child's education. For example, Teachman (1991a) summarized the findings: "Fewer than 1 father out of 27 regularly assists his children with homework or attends school events. Over three-quar-ters of divorced fathers have never participated in the schooling of their children" (p. 360).

"Visitors"

Generally, the nonresidential neo-traditionalist fathers were not in-cluded in routine parental decision making; the exceptions were five of the six highly involved visiting fathers (who had obtained a particular, even if limited, sphere of parental responsibility). Over half were not involved either in the more weighty decision making, such as that regarding children's schooling, religious training, health care, or day care arrangements (see Seltzer 1991b; Furstenberg et al. 1987; Furstenberg and Nord 1985; Ahrons and Wallisch 1987b; Maccoby et al. 1988). Overall, although handling basic care needs when together with their children, these visiting fathers had little responsibility for or involvement in the larger range of activities involved in primary parenting (see Chambers 1984; Marsiglio 1991). Few fathers, irrespective of frequency of contact, assisted their children with homework or projects, handled health or dental care appointments, or scheduled or organized lessons or other activities. And, for example, children's personal items typically were provided by their mothers, and clothes were returned unlaundered after visits. Thus these fathers' involvement with their children constituted, for the most part, visits. Time parameters, role ambiguity, emotional distance, and inexperience were all factors in their limited caregiving, nurturing, and supervising activities. Furstenberg and Cherlin (1991) concluded similarly with respect to the involvement of nonresidential fathers who continue to see their children: "Even in the small number of families where children are seeing their fathers regularly, the dads assume a minimal role in the day-to-day care and supervision of their children" (p. 36).

OUTSIDE INFLUENCES

Many neo-traditionalist fathers railed against not only their former wives for their limited inclusion in their children's lives. They also condemned society more generally. That their parental status and roles were ambiguous was reinforced by the particulars of their immediate situations and also by the underlying assumptions of social institutions and arrangements, and attitudes of the professionals working with their children (see Risman and Schwartz 1989; Risman 1989; Fassinger 1989). This father had divorced when his children were still babies.

> To parent, to nurture, to protect your children requires that you be involved in the community *as a father* and that causes me to remember that in the court one day, this attorney kept asking me, "Well, why, *why* are you doing all of this [seeking a custody change]?" "Well, I'm their father." "No, no really, why are you doing all of this?" "I'm their father." "Why are you here?" "I am their father." [yelling] Finally they got the message. The word father didn't mean anything until I yelled it loud enough that it was heard. But that

attorney and the court were not the only ones who did not hear. The parochial school that my children went to did not hear it either. In fact, they treated me as a troublesome entity in their lives and that if I wanted to know anything or if I wanted to be involved in any of the activities at school, I had to get the permission of their mother to be there. I had no social supports such that I could function as a parent. I couldn't access the school. I couldn't access the church. I couldn't access their friends, health care. I had problems trying to get information. People didn't even know I existed. No, they didn't want me to exist. They denied—deny—my existence, period.

Others also complained bitterly about their exclusion from child-related matters by various persons in positions of authority. School and medical personnel were common objects of complaint. This father became, as he put it, "a pain in the ass" in his efforts to obtain information:

I've gone to the medical center and talked to the pediatrician. I said, "Wait a second, when my children are here I want to know about it, and I want to know what the problem is." As a noncustodial parent, in order for me to find out anything about my children's medical records, I have to make an appointment 2 weeks down the road before they'll tell me anything. But damn it all to hell, they'll bill me right away. I felt like telling them, "Screw you." I've even taken it a step further and I've gone to the school and said, "Listen, I want to participate with my kids. I want to know where they're at." And the teachers have been really quite helpful. Initially, they gave me lip service and weren't helpful but now, since I talked to the teachers back in mid-November, I think I've received one piece of correspondence a month now. . . . But I'm estranged from it all unless I seek the initiative and go out and go after my rights. I lose them by benign neglect. Unless I assert and almost assault— that's what I had to do with the health care provider, I had to literally say, "Listen, I have a right to this information." They really don't want to give it to me. They say, "Well, have your wife call you." "Well, listen, if we got along so damned well, we probably still would have been married." See, all the institutions see us as visitors too, and they don't want to get stuck in the middle so they say, "The custodial parent is *the* parent." . . . What you're dealing with is institutionalized sexism of sorts. Because, if in fact there were in truth joint custody, where both parents were meaningful participants—and that's the crux, *meaningful participants*—then you could literally have a happy divorce where the kids are not embroiled and stuck in the middle. And fathers would be recognized as parents.[11]

"Being shut out" of segments of their children's lives, however, was a continuation of past patterns: While married most of these men were involved only peripherally in the logistical arrangements for their children. The children's mothers typically had mediated between social institutions and personnel and the family, reporting back to their husbands. Thus the cessation of the former spouses' mediation efforts was at the root of most men's objections about exclusion and consequent efforts to obtain information and inclusion through other channels. Moreover, professionals working with their children could find themselves in difficult positions, called on to negotiate between the divorced parents, as various fathers acknowledged. This person's description of a particular incident is suggestive:

> The school psychologist called me in and the first thing she was explaining to me was that my youngest son was having a lot of trouble in school. I said, "Yes, yes, I know." She was explaining to me that I "just must be involved with my children." This was about a year and a half after the divorce. The school psychologist tells me that I should be involved with my children, I should see my children, and I was sitting there going, "Wait, what are you talking about?" And she goes, "Well, according to your ex-wife you don't see your children. You have nothing to do with your children, blah, blah, blah." "Now wait a minute here, wait a minute. When I didn't see them, it was only because she gave me so much grief when I tried." In fact, she had stated to the school psychologist that "there was no sense in bringing him in to talk to him, he'd refuse to come in." Of course, as soon as I was contacted, I went in. "What's the problem here?" She was doing everything she could to paint me the bad guy, the bad person. The school psychologist brought out a lot of these problems and I said, "What do we do?" She said, "Well, the situation is serious enough, I'd like for him to go to counseling with you and your ex-wife." I said, "Fine. If you can get her in here, fine, because I've tried and she's refused." I said, "Fine. Provide me with a date and time, and I will be here." We met at the school several times with the school psychologist; she was nice enough to give several private counseling sessions. We came into the counseling session and after about a half an hour she [the former wife] went out of the room ranting and raving, saying she wasn't going to be involved with this sick person, such as myself, blah, blah. That's how it goes. I said to the school psychologist, "See what I mean? She's just impossible." See? I wasn't the problem.

Assessments of Children

Neo-traditionalist fathers' evaluations of their children's development and well-being were closely tied to their level of parental involvement: the less involvement, the more negative the assessment. Over half of the neo-traditionalist fathers were pleased with and proud of their children and optimistic, at least somewhat, about their futures. Common evaluations were that "they're okay" or "I really think they're fine. They've adjusted." The fathers still embroiled in conflict with the former wife were less positive. Yet variations occurred here too. For example, this next father was highly involved with his children. Unusual in that he had attained a shared custody arrangement after numerous legal struggles, which both he and his former spouse continued to initiate, he was ambivalent about his children's development. His biggest fear was that his son might be homosexual as a result of the divorce. He considered the effects on his children of the parental struggles, posing several rhetorical questions to himself:

> They've got a few friends. They're more with me than with their friends. Their schedule is rigid. They have to please her. They know both parents are extremely aggressive about time with them. Has it been harmful for them? I don't know. They're very good kids. They know what their mother is like. They've seen a lot; I haven't had to tell them. When I ask their opinion, like about those two contested days recently, they try to stay out of it, especially my youngest. So I think they're good kids and relatively unscarred. My daughter has said she's never seen her parents interact in a way that wasn't hostile and angry. She showed me an essay she did for school [in which she wrote] that she'd never seen her parents interact in an amicable way. Could I have done something different? Yes. Should I have done something different? That's a very good question. Again, we're talking about least detrimental alternatives. Should I have stayed on my career track [rather than shifting to part-time work]? That too is a very good question. But you and I both know I would never have gotten my 36% physical custody if I had. I'd have money, but I'd have lost this battle, a real Waterloo.

And this father argued that his former wife had deliberately relocated to create barriers to his relationship with their son, knowing that he hoped the son would want to live with him one day. Claiming that she owed him money from the equity in the marital home and knowingly flirting with further court action, he refused to pay child support. The contacts between them, kept to a minimum by both, were tense and sometimes outright hostile. He described their child:

> He's doing remarkably well. I'm really pleased at how well he's doing. The outward signs, seem to indicate that. When he's with me it's beautiful. There's no friction at all. We have a wonderful time together, it's affectionate, cooperative. He seems to want to please me and I want to please him. We get along very well. He's bright. He's bubbly. He's a personable kid. He seems very well-adjusted and there's been no trouble at all. He's an easy kid to please. He's not a sarcastic or a troublesome kid at all. He's very mellow.

Five of the six who had areas of particular parental responsibility were unequivocally positive in their evaluations of their children's well-being and development: Their children were "fine," "wonderful," and "normal." Having unsuccessfully gone the mediation route in an attempt to gain the cooperation of his former wife, this father was now seeking a legal change from maternal to joint custody. But he was moving slowly to prevent his son from being dragged into the dispute: "I will not put him in the middle." Also, he continued to pay child support regularly and fully despite a salary reduction effected by the state agency for which he worked as a response to the continued economic recession. Reviewing his child's adjustment and development, he also discussed the meaning of fathering to him.

> My son is healthy, normal—as healthy and normal as could be given the circumstances [of a divorce and two-household living situation]. He got A pluses from his teachers in the second grade, in the first grade, and in kindergarten. I have his latest report card, which I can show you. They all describe him as a very nice boy who's a joy to have in the classroom. The positive is that he relates well to the children in the neighborhood here. He looks forward to seeing the next-door neighbors and his other friends. He's starting to share things and he's getting better every year. I enjoy watching him grow, develop, and change. He's a joy to have around. We look forward to seeing each other. We go places and we do things. When we don't swim, we do archery. He got me interested in it. We see movies together. I don't know, I can only compare my life before parenthood. That changes everything in terms of priorities and values. In other words, he is the most precious aspect of my existence. That is the positive that I can say to you about him, that I am very happy about him as a person, very happy with his growth and development.

He continued, expressing some concerns about the possible adverse effects of divorce and the two-household arrangement.

> I feel that, I feel a little bit guilty about his being deprived of day-to-day access to his father, and I feel bad about his not having a nurturing male role model in his life on a day-to-day basis, and I try to compensate and try to make up for it every other weekend and for a few hours on Wednesdays. And I look forward to the precious moments I have with him. If his mother were civilized, she would let me have more time with him. There are a lot of things I could do to be more actively involved in his life that I have apprehensions and anxieties about.

Like only several others among the neo-traditionalist fathers, he seemed a likely candidate for becoming an innovative, nurturing father had he and his former wife been able to work out a workable parenting partnership. Although his former wife's perspective on their situation and thus her explanation for resisting such an arrangement are missing here, what was striking was this father's commitment to keeping their son as unaware as possible of the tensions and differences between the parents. Also noteworthy was his strong commitment to being a wholly engaged, caring, and responsible father despite the bitterness he felt toward his former wife and the tensions that prevailed between them.

In sum, neo-traditionalist fathers more or less successfully straddled the competing desires to effectively stand up against the injustices of divorce and the former wife, and to achieve and retain meaningful associations with their children. Being a divorced father, especially for those with restricted visitation access and involvement, brought few satisfactions, or as many phrased it, "few benefits," and much emotional ambivalence, frustration, and resentment. The predivorce father-child relationship typically proved too tenuous to be carried reasonably intact over the divorce precipice and into the circumstance of altered arrangements and dynamics. There was near unanimous agreement that they deserved more input in their children's lives. Yet these men were largely unclear about what fathering after divorce could entail. Mostly they were unwilling to extend themselves toward greater collaboration with their children's other parent.

Notes

1. Various terms are used in the literature to describe parenting arrangements in divorced situations. For instance, Furstenberg (1988) distinguished between *co-parenting* and *parallel parenting:* "The term 'co-parenting', coined by social scientists to describe the collaborative efforts of parents who live apart, implies a certain level of cooperation in the common task of childrearing. . . . The more common pattern among families in which fathers continue to see their children might be characterized as *parallel parenting.*" Furstenberg (1987, pp. 57-58) noted that parallel parenting may be functional in that it reduces conflict by segregating a parent's respective activities, reduces strain by limiting possibilities for observing the other parent in relation to the child, and reduces competition between parents and stepparents. In contrast to Furstenberg's terminology, Ahrons and Wallisch (1987a) used the term co-parenting to refer to the involvement of both parents with their children after divorce, irrespective of the level of cooperation: If a minor child is involved then the parents have "a 'co-parental relationship' of sorts that could range from minimal interaction to high involvement with each other in areas relating to the children" (p. 235).

2. Trost and Hultaker (1986, p. 97) proposed nine possible interaction patterns between parents' wishes with regard to custody in a cultural context in which normative pressures regarding custody were lessened; parental attitudes fall into one of three alternatives: positive, neutral, and negative. The situation with the "reluctant custodial" father falls into the category in which both parents are negative about having child custody: "The parent who would be a custodian against his or her own wishes will be in a difficult situation, and the same is true for the children; they will be as bad off with their mother as with their father."

3. Divorced mothers in an earlier study, although insisting that they wanted their children's fathers to be involved with parenting and their children, also did not idealize fatherhood or the roles of fathers, other than several who subscribed to the perspective advocating the importance of a male role model for children (Arendell 1986).

4. Responding to Laqueur's description of his participation in childbirth, Ruddick (1993) asserts that the focus on men's role in childbirth is linked to "the shrinking significance of female birthgiving in the story such a good father tells" (p. 181). She continues: "Hence Laqueur effectively leaves fathers with emotions no one doubted they had, without the physical labor such emotions might rightly entail, but (at least in Laqueur's circles) with their minds intact but elsewhere. Most mothers are thus left not only with emotions everyone takes for granted but also with the physical labor that has been rightly thought to be theirs, and without the minds that no one thought they had anyway, unless, like fathers they 'go to [intellectual] work' " (Ruddick 1993, p. 182).

5. For other discussions of biological parents' distress about their children's referring to stepparents with kin terms typically used for mothers and fathers, see Furstenberg and Cherlin (1991) and Furstenberg and Spanier (1984). See Chambers (1990) for a discussion of the societal and legal ambiguity surrounding stepparenting and the stepparent-child relationship; see also generally Pasley and Ihinger-Tallman (1987b).

6. The role of stepparent is often ambiguous even in an intact family (see Hetherington 1987; Ihinger and Tallman 1987b; Ahrons and Wallisch 1987a). Chambers (1990), specifically, explored the lack of legal as well as cultural definitions of stepfamily relationships, including when divorce alters living arrangements.

7. I had not anticipated that fathers would bring their children to the interviews because the respondents chose the time to meet and were told in advance that prior interviews had lasted several and more hours. After the second time when a young child was brought along without materials with which to entertain him- or herself, I put together a packet of items, including coloring books, plain paper, crayons, and felt tip pens to have in case the need arose at future interviews (which it did). Children were particularly interested in the tape recorder, and I let them play with it during the initial minutes of the meeting when we were all becoming acquainted and, then, with their initial agreement, for a longer time after the interview was basically finished.

8. Marsiglio (1991) summarized survey data regarding fathers' involvement: "Consistent with previous research on fathers' involvement in their children's lives, fathers' most frequent interaction with children in both subsamples involved playing with them at home. Indeed, among the fathers in the preschool subsample, almost 76% reported that they played with their children every day (86% of those with children), and less than 1% indicated that they never played with their children. In contrast, a much higher percentage of fathers in the preschool subsample reported that they *never* take their children on outings or read to them, 10.5% and 15.4% respectively. Among the group of fathers in the school-age subsample, 17% indicated that they spent time playing with their children or working on projects with them almost every day. Again, only a small minority of men, 5%, said that they never play with their children" (pp. 979, 984, italics in original).

9. Gerstel (1988) summarized her findings regarding divorced parents' reliance on kin, including gender differences: "Children serve as integrators with kin for both mothers and fathers, but in very different ways. For men, they provide access to kin as emotional providers; for women, as instrumental ones. This gender difference is perhaps best explained by the patterns of custody characteristic of our sample and the nation as a whole. Women, who typically provide the daily care of children, turn to kin for practical help. In contrast, men typically have only weekend care (if that) of children. As other studies show, one of the major problems of such 'visiting' fathers is keeping the children entertained, finding them social and leisure activities to enjoy. . . . Conse-

quently, as our study suggests, these fathers turn to and receive help from kin in ways that ease their 'special burden' " (p. 217).

10. The terminology, "she's my little woman," as well as another father's buttressing his assertion of high parental involvement by noting that he had given his children his business card suggests a limited or impoverished vocabulary for caring and affection related to the norms and conventions of masculinity (see, e.g., Tannen 1990; Sattel 1976; Cancian 1987). Both uses involve an extrapolation from other kinds of social relations to those of parenting. Tronto (1989) proposed a broad explanation applicable to the society at large with regard to caring issues, an explanation that has particular salience for men who typically do less caregiving than women: "Perhaps the impoverishment of our vocabulary for discussing caring is a result of the way caring is privatized, thus beneath our social vision, in this society. The need to rethink appropriate forms for caring also raises the broadest questions about the shape of social and political institutions in our society" (p. 185).

11. Perhaps educational and medical care personnel believe that parents collaborate, or *should,* about childrearing irrespective of divorce. Divorced parents believe they *should:* "While most of these parents think they should have frequent interaction around childrearing, the reality is that three years after divorce most are not doing so" (Ahrons and Wallisch 1987b, p. 281).

PART IV

The Minority Story: Innovative Responses

8

PARENTING PARTNERSHIPS
WITH FORMER WIVES

Nine men behaved in ways not typical of the others in the study. Seeking to maintain active parental involvement and to protect their children from parental dissension, these men engaged in innovative strategies of action. Where they perceived they could, they "departed from traditional formulations of men's lives" (Cohen 1989, p. 228). Two participants said that they played a "different ballgame" than most divorced fathers. Other researchers have also located parents who develop highly cooperative relationships after divorce, although they consistently constitute a minority group within samples. For example, Giles-Sims (1987) concluded: "Almost all of the families in this study reported that the divorce had produced negative emotions. But some former spouses managed over time to put the negative emotions aside, put the interests of the children first, and actively cooperate with each other for the benefit of the children" (p. 148; see also Wallerstein and Blakeslee 1989; Maccoby et al. 1990; Ahrons and Wallisch 1987b).

Behaving in innovative ways entailed both choice and opportunity. "'Choice,'" Cohen (1989) observed in his examination of men's roles as husbands and fathers, "is related to 'role attachment' . . . in that the degree to which men choose to enact a role depends largely upon the degree of role attachment they possess. 'Opportunity,' on the other hand, is dependent largely on the commitments they have made and the consequences of those commitments" (p. 222; see also Ferree 1990).[1] Innovation required three conditions. The first was an awareness of options so that conventional practices and definitions could be rejected. The cooperation of the former wife, their children's mother, was the second necessity. The third requisite was at least somewhat flexible work circumstances. Given these three needs, both the standard familial and gender discourses were eschewed by these men.[2]

Similar actions were pursued by these nine men: engaged, nurturing parenting *and* collaboration with the former spouse. Caring for and rearing their children was a team effort, requiring extensive cooperation between the parents: *Together* they created and maintained *parenting partnerships.* Thus the former wife was seen and treated as a close associate, not an oppositional figure. Mutual concern for their children's well-being enabled them to transcend their differences and residual feelings about both each other and the demise of the marriage. Volunteering the notion of "best case scenario," this father of one explained: "It *is* possible to have a best case scenario: I'm sure the system is not fair. I don't think the system is fair in any kind of law. It can not be perfectly right or wrong, but I think a lot of the tension and a lot of the problems in divorce are caused by the individuals themselves. We decided that we were going to work to have a best case scenario in order to protect our daughter, to keep our daughter the central person in all of this." He explained that some of his views differed from the ones dominant in the fathers' rights group to which he belonged, and so he had offered to participate in this study in order to convey the "positive possibilities" in divorce.

> So I ask: "Is divorce positive?" No, I don't think it is. But it's not necessarily deadly either. What about the kids? They didn't ask for any of this. Children are better off with both parents involved with them. I hope people will realize that it takes two people, no matter what the law says. Whether they're married or divorced, having children without a marriage or whatever, it doesn't make any difference, it's still going to take two people, both parents. "How did it get like this: that one or the other parent is a better parent? When did it stop being both of you and start being single?"

No demographic, educational, class, or marital status variables alone or in combination clearly distinguished this subset of men from the others.[3] Although as a whole this subgroup was well-educated, with most having attained a college degree and three having completed graduate school or professional programs, several had gone no further than high school. Two were employed in the manual trades, two were self-employed in enterprises conventionally categorized as working-class occupations, and the others were employed in the white-collar sector—managerial, educational, and administrative occupations. The majority of these men's children were young at the time of divorce: preschool or early elementary school-age children. Three were preadolescents, but no child was yet a teenager at the time the marriage was terminated. In practice, seven of these nine men shared childrearing to varying extents with their former wives. The other two had primary custody, and their former wives, reported both men, were available to and extensively involved with their children. But custody status was not a determining factor in innovative strategies and collaborative parenting partnerships: Two other co-custodial and three other primary custodial fathers engaged predominantly in neo-traditionalist lines of action. Highly involved fathers, these men, nonetheless, related to their children through the prism of the relationship with and feelings about their former spouses.

The nine innovative men were concerned about protecting their relations with their former spouses and were insistent, therefore, about insuring their own anonymity (assured to all participants to every extent possible). For instance, the three who recounted having engaged in sexual relations with their former wives subsequent to divorcing requested that the specifics shared in the interviews be concealed. They did not want to inadvertently stigmatize their former wives in some way by making these disclosures public.[4] In contrast, eight of the other nine men who voluntarily recounted such experiences urged that the details be publicized: "Maybe *this* will get me on *Donahue,*" was one man's explanation. And numerous participants engaging in traditionalist actions insisted that the protection of their identities was of no concern to them; several urged that their names, and especially that of the former wife, and sometimes that of her attorney, be publicized.

Only one of the men engaged in innovative lines of action had remarried. He and his former wife, who was also remarried, had a de facto shared custody arrangement. Another person's former wife had remarried and subsequently divorced, and a third's was intending to remarry within the year. One of the eight unmarried fathers was considering marriage. Other researchers have found that cooperation between divorced parents is highest when neither has remarried; for example, Ahrons and Wallisch (1987a) concluded that "the number and frequency of childrearing activities shared between the former spouses (the 'co-parental sharing scale') was highest when neither partner had remarried and lowest when only the husband had remarried. The amount of support in co-parental interaction was highest and conflict lowest when neither partner had remarried, while conflict was highest and support lowest when only the husband had remarried. If neither former spouse had remarried, they were also most likely to spend time together with each other and their children; they were least likely to do so if only the husband had remarried" (p. 235-36).

In addition to being atypical in their low rates of remarriage, this group varied from the others also in the number of men who had considered marital reconciliation after separation. Before actually divorcing, four men and their estranged spouses separated, reunited, and again separated. Two others had hoped for a marital reunion after separation and even divorce, and another respondent was actively seeking a reconciliation after having initiated the divorce more than 2 years before. Another allowed that his former wife still hoped for a reconciliation even though he did not, believing that "too much water was over the dam." Eight of the nine men and/or their former spouses, then, had considered reconciliation. Doubt about divorcing was related to their commitment to involved parenting as well as to uncertainties about the quality of the marital relationship. The latter is not unusual. For instance, Kelly and associates (1988) found in their study of divorcing couples who participated in mediation that parents who were able to cooperate about their children were often ambivalent about the pending divorce: "It may well be that, as a result of communicating directly and effectively enough with each other to be able to reach a series of agreements, the mediation respondents became more ambivalent about their pending divorces" (p. 465). And Friedman (1982) observed that the lack of best case scenarios of divorce in the psychiatric literature, in part, may be because the same characteristics that are likely to encourage people to construct a positive outcome in divorce also would encourage them to continue or repair their marriages. In commenting on the extensiveness and complexity of their relations with the former wife, each of these nine indicated that, as several put it, "we might as well have stayed married." One noted, "It's crazy, really. Don't ask me why we divorced. Our attorney finally asked us that one day: 'Just why are you getting a divorce, anyway?' To be honest, I'm even less certain now than I was then. It was a mutual decision too."

Physical violence or its threat had occurred between only two of this subset and their former spouses. In both cases, the violence had consisted of an isolated, brief event in the immediate postseparation phase and was regretted. Each said both he and his estranged wife were responsible for the incident. The action had only deepened the distrust that had to be overcome as they sought to establish a workable, joint parenting arrangement.

None of the nine had initiated court action against the former wife with regard to child custody or access although two, both having de facto shared custody, had sought to change the levels of child support. Two men, one a sole and the other a co-custodial father, had been "pulled into court" in attempts, which proved unsuccessful, by their former wives to obtain full custody. Their relationship with the former spouse "had taken a nosedive" but "had improved considerably" since then, and both men hoped and expected that they would not be "sideswiped," as one put it, by a future custody fight. Another of these nine participants had been brought before the court for noncompliance with child support, and one other about a property settlement dispute.

Predivorce family dynamics and patterns, including the marital division of labor, were not at the root of their own or, they reported, the former wife's expectations that they be integrally involved with their children (see also Wallerstein and Blakeslee 1989). Although over half reported having been "unusually active," compared to other fathers especially, only two of the nine had shared childrearing and child care more or less fully with their wives while married. One, who was employed in his family's business and able to establish a flexible work schedule, explained:

> She worked part-time all of our marriage and I stayed home with the kids. I stayed home generally Friday, Saturday, Sunday, and Monday mornings and took care of the kids while she worked. I didn't care how long I worked in the day or at night, I always made sure I was at home at 4 o'clock with my kids, had dinner with them, did things with them, washed them up, and got them to bed. Then I'd go back to work. But they knew I was around with them. I took them to the doctor's. I changed their diapers. I fed them. I cared for them. I enrolled them in school. Signed them up for music lessons and sports. Got them rec cards, library cards. You know, I did all those things too. They were *our* kids. Not *hers*. Not *mine*. *Ours*.

When the children became older teenagers, he observed, they would probably choose to have less involvement with both parents. "But, in the meantime," he said, "I didn't want their lives altered. At this point they didn't need to have their lives changed." Somewhat ironically, even though his postdivorce parental involvement was an extension of his earlier efforts, he alone among those involved in parenting partnerships subsequent to divorce had a tense relationship with his former wife, whom he described as being "less than fully cooperative. . . . She can be difficult when she chooses. It's a guessing game. I never know what she'll do."[5]

With only one exception, these men and their estranged spouses had negotiated their parenting arrangements privately and then presented them to attorneys for official acceptance. One person described the process: "So the divorce, when you come down to it, didn't involve any true battles or fights or anything. We both worked to keep it on an even keel even though we were upset. It was basically a moderate process, based on agreements and an equal division of everything, although it took longer than it probably needed to because of the slowness of the lawyer who had to approve it. We just had the house, the cars, some furniture, and a few monetary assets." Circumvention of the legal system and its "family experts," such as therapists and social workers, was deliberate: Engaging wholeheartedly in the formal divorce system could only undermine the possibilities of a positive postdivorce outcome, each insisted. But avoiding legal engagement was indicative of the relationship between them and their wives, and the choices made as they entered divorce. It was not a causal factor in the attainment of relatively harmonious postdivorce associations, as various other men, engaged in more conventional lines of action, tried to argue.

All nine men, in concert with most respondents, believed that men are, or can become, victims of divorce, primarily because the legal system favors mothers: Their rights to remain fathers after divorce could be jeopardized if the legal or judicial systems intruded into their private lives. But, and especially in contrast to the majority, these men were minimally concerned about protecting their rights; they made relatively little use of the rhetoric of rights to frame their experiences, relations, and feelings. Active in a fathers' rights group (as was another, with two more having attended meetings for a brief period), this person shared the majority viewpoint that divorce is inherently gender biased. He credited the avoidance of legal entanglement to both his former wife and himself.

> I compromised on a lot of things that maybe some people in my position would not have. But, in turn, I'm sure she compromised on a lot of things too. Now I don't want it to seem like I have nothing but positive views for the legal system. I do not. But I think it's, I think from the beginning, it's in your control. And it's a fight to keep in it in your control, and if you can keep it in your control, I think you come out all right. I could easily have gone out and gotten my own lawyer and she could easily have gone out and gotten her own lawyer and we could easily have fought about the house and the money. We had savings accounts. We could easily have fought about all of that. We both had received inheritance from different relatives. We could have fought about that. We could have fought about, you know, anything, custody. We both were hurt. We both were scared. But we both cared *first* about our child.

Agreeing that women are favored in divorce, these men nevertheless held more complex views than the majority of respondents. They viewed the former wife's authority in the postdivorce situation as a logical outcome of her usually greater parental activity and responsibility. Moreover, it was her willingness to negotiate a shared parenting arrangement and her support for his extensive involvement that made it possible to be an active, nurturing divorced father, not only his own desires, actions, or traits. Thus the workable and satisfactory joint parenting arrangements were not a result of successful maneuvering through the legal system, securing of individual rights, or devaluing of the former wife as a mother and the boosting, consequently, of their own credibility or significance as practicing fathers. This person, a father of three, offered this account:

> We had that commitment all along. We said to each other that, "When we go through this process, one thing that we don't want to have happen, we don't want the nightmare visited on the kids. At all costs, within reason, we need to keep their needs as a primary concern." We just kept talking and talking. I have to give my former wife some credit for this because she really didn't try to sabotage this. . . . The irony is that while staying together in a marriage that wasn't working for the sake of the kids was not, for me, the right decision to make, in maintaining whatever peripheral relationship I have with my former wife now, it's for the sake of the kids. I think my former wife has done a terrific job in keeping the emotional focus on the kids.

Fathers involved in shared custodial arrangements, of whatever sort in terms of allocation of time, depended most on the cooperation and support of the children's mother. This respondent had initiated the divorce. A father of two young children, he attributed their successful parenting partnership to his former wife's willingness to collaborate, which, in turn, was based on her respect for and trust in him.

> She has a strong commitment to the children's interests. I thank God that she can do that and she is not, and I am not, using the children, you know, to hurt the other. She has never used the children as leverage, thank God, that's all I can say. We both could. But we still can see that the children are separate people. I attribute some of it to my background. My background is in education, it is working with kids, and not only their educational needs but their emotional needs as well. She once said, "If you didn't have your background in early education that you do, you probably wouldn't have the kids as much as you do."

Even the two sole custodial fathers, whose former wives "visited" their children without assuming specific and continuous parental responsibilities, relied on their former spouses not to divert their energies with a custody fight or interfere with the residential and parenting situations. As one said, "She valued my parenting. Otherwise, she'd drag me into court." Furthermore, each believed that his former spouse had left the children with him when she quit the marriage out of her concern for the children. "She left without them because she loved them and thought I was better equipped to care for them then. I've told the kids that too: 'She left you here with me because she loved you. We both love you.'"

Collaborations With Former Wives

Recognized, fostered, and endorsed by both parents, according to the men, was a parental interdependence. Family was represented as a network of relationships, and the notion of a broken family was only partial to these men's understandings of family after divorce. Although divorce so far only had altered their living arrangements and modified their conceptions of how family life occurred, they could yet become marginalized, they feared, and the family thus broken. What existed for the time being, however, was a family consisting of "us" and "them," the children and him and the children and their mother, respectively, rather than "me and them," as characterized by the majority of participants. Two men reformed the conventional definition of family to fit the situation of divorce: They, the former wife, and children constituted a single unit that had dual residences. For example, explaining his argument for a continuation of their parenting arrangement in spite of divorce, this informant observed: "Dad [I] was no longer living at home but the care situation could remain the same, we were still one family. The only thing that has changed is that now mom and dad don't live together. That's all. I'm still here for them. So is she. We're their parents. Not *one* of us, *both* of us."

The contours of the parenting partnerships differed somewhat among the nine. The variations depended especially on the particulars of the custody arrangement. But each of the parenting partnerships was consistent with the "cooperative" pattern identified by Maccoby and associates (1990) from among families in which both parents were seeing their children. (The other three of the four discerned patterns included "disengaged," "conflicted," and "mixed.") Moreover, in terms of shared activities, the parenting partnerships fit the interactions characterized by Ahrons and Wallisch (1987b, p. 278) as "co-parental": sharing major and day-to-day decisions, childrearing problems, and co-parenting problems; discussing children's personal problems; sharing children's school and medical problems; planning special events in children's lives; discussing children's adjustments to divorce, progress, and accomplishments; and examining and planning child-related finances.

The two custodial fathers, having somewhat limited relationships with their former wives, did not feel especially supported in the logistics or activities of day-to-day parenting. Each insisted that he and the former spouse had gradually become more interdependent with respect to parenting and that he actively supported the mother-child relationship. The character of the parenting collaborations was more varied among the seven who shared parenting with their former spouses. Two men, for example, adhered to relatively fixed time schedules and parenting routines and were committed, along with the former wife, to a stance of emotional detachment, except with regard to their children. Another had a less formal and more flexible association with his former spouse regarding scheduling and responsibility sharing. But beyond their mutual parenting they held to a limited interpersonal relationship. Two men's former spousal relations entailed a broad sharing of parenting along with a high degree of flexibility and openness to changes and negotiations in schedules, activities, and care arrangements. They were friends, although not intimate ones, as this person explained:

> Our relationship is amicable, if that's the proper word. I would describe it that way, an amicable relationship. I don't particularly go out of my way to talk to her. I have my moments and sometimes I really want to talk to her. Other times I don't want to talk to her at all and I just leave, I don't want to be there. We're both very concerned about the children. We went together to see the principal. We also went to see the school counselor. Or if my son has a soccer game, we'll be together. We had one last week and we have one this week. We're both committed to going, it's our kids and we're both committed to be there to see them, to support them by being there.

The other two men maintained active friendships as well as parenting partnerships with their former spouses. This father of one described, at length, the emotional depth of his relationship with his former wife and their reliance on each other. He said, in part:

> My relationship with my ex-wife is fine, we are friends, good friends. I think there was a period of the marriage bond between us fading and the friendship bond between us becoming. I don't think that we went to the lawyer's to sign the papers and walked away friends. We didn't do that. There was the hurting time until the divorce was finally settled. Then there was the time in getting resettled and I think we're still doing that [3 years later]. You know, her life has gone on, mine has gone on. And we're both growing in different

situations now. But we're bonded by our daughter. After the divorce we continued to do things as a family. When I lived there, up until I moved here a year and a half ago, I saw our daughter probably three times a week, which included her coming and staying at my place. Probably one of those times a week included my ex-wife. We did something, whether it was go to dinner or whatever, be at her house, or go to a school activity. We shared a lot, you know. Recently, we had a talk about my sister, she died just last August. That brought back a lot of memories because they had become like sisters. They were that close, so it was a loss for all of us. So she was there with me at the funeral. We don't act like we're married, but we don't act like we're just friends. She's a support for me and I'm a support for her. And you know, like I said, she takes care of my daughter and I will always have respect for her, I always have, and I always will because she's the mother of my child. That's the way I look at it. I talk to them probably three times a week, or they call me.

Parenting partnerships that included friendships with the former spouses shifted somewhat as circumstances changed. For instance, a high degree of emotional intimacy had prevailed between one respondent and his former wife until she learned of his remarriage considerations. She then pared back their relationship to one focused predominantly on their parenting and attempted to exclude the sharing of other intimate matters. And another person and his former spouse were beginning to confide in and depend on each other, "like very close friends," more frequently than previously. His explanation for the shift was that she had ended her relationship with a boyfriend, a decision she had discussed with him in advance. Almost all of these men believed that a serious, romantic involvement with another, on the part of either themselves or the former wife, posed threats, or would, to their carefully cultivated, postdivorce relationships.

MINIMIZING CONFLICT

In the relational context in which the goal was "to hold the children at the center," little overt antagonism or tension with the former wife was allowed to erupt. Precluding or limiting conflict was the essence of fostering and protecting a positive, stable, and sustained father-child relationship, regardless of the specific residential arrangements or feelings about the former spouse. Differences were either openly confronted in an effort to resolve them or "deliberately sidelined—KO'd, kicked out." Simmering tensions and repeated conflicts were the bane of parenting partnerships and could lead only to their decreased parental involvement and participation. Of this, they were certain.

Former wives also were given credit for minimizing conflict. "I said earlier that she has no desire to change the time-sharing arrangement. What she has a desire to change right now is child support and the status of the house. She's not threatening me with either of those though. She tries not to rock the boat either." Dissension could not be avoided or contained without the former spouse's cooperation. Nevertheless, these men viewed themselves as having a particular and greater burden for preventing or reducing conflict because the "legal system's biases operate against us, against men, not women." This next father, for instance, concluded that preserving his parental access was more important than stressing the unfairness, as he saw it, of his child support arrangement. Taking on the issue, he feared, would incite further conflict that, in turn, could lead to a decline in his parental access.

> At the point she took me to court, I requested the time that I spent with the kids be increased. They bounced it [my request] out. . . . But I basically thought the judge was upset with me for back child support. They alluded that I was playing games since I was self-employed [in computer sales]. But I wasn't. I was a victim of association [being a divorced father] versus what actually was going on. I was behind about $3,300. It was about 6 months behind. Therefore, I went out and found some additional jobs: delivering pizzas and being a relief taxi driver. I tried to increase my work in sales. So I found more jobs. I pay my child support on time and got it caught up. Then I asked for more time [and got it].

Related to conflict management and integral to these men's accounts and generally absent in the others' was the notion of parental obligation. Child support, for example, a contentious issue brought up repeatedly by most of the others, was discussed by these nine men in terms of children's needs rather than in terms of antagonisms with the former wife. Child support orders were not viewed as violations of their rights. That they were a part of the formal divorce proceedings and so constituted state intervention into their private lives did not disturb them. Although some were concerned about competing financial obligations, none of these nine men was resentful about child support. (Only four others, all neo-traditionalist fathers, were in their company.) Child support was a parental responsibility, "whether married or not." One said, "They're my children. Of course I would never deny them economic support." Or "I've never considered not paying. They're my responsibility too." This next father, whose child was with him about one-third of the time, explained his position:

I'm paying $250 a month. Actually, I pay out a lot more than that. I take care of my daughter's clothes throughout the year. I keep her in play and school clothes. And since I moved here, I pay for her airfare back and forth. And I cover her expenses while she's here. I cover the health care, that was in my divorce agreement which is fine with me. If I was to average it for the year, it more likely comes out that I spend over $400 per month. But whatever the amount of money is, it's been hard sometimes paying that out once a month or whatever. But I don't think it's ever been an issue. Because I look at it again as I look at other things. Whether I was there or whether I'm here, whether I was married or divorced, I'm still going to be spending money on my daughter, either way. So for a court to tell me that I have to spend $250 a month, well, I wish it was that easy. I wish that's all I had to spend—$250 a month! I'm sure her mother feels the same way about all the expenses she has. I wish it was that easy. But I hate to tell people, raising kids is expensive.

He later said, "I guess it's all a matter of attitude."

Being integrally involved in parenting was financially costly, and fathers sharing custody, whether arranged informally or legally, were concerned about the seeming failure of the law or judiciary to take their other expenses and contributions into account when child support levels were set.[6] In contrast to the majority of men complaining about their extra expenses, co-custodial fathers' expenditures were regular and substantial; only one co-custodial father paid no child support, and he was violating a legal agreement. Not recognized within the system, these men pointed out, were their direct child-related costs: housing and food, transportation, recreation, and clothing. This person explained his financial situation: "The court order is $400 a month per child: $1,200 per month after taxes plus roughly about 115 a month for their medical insurance. That equals about 29% of my gross, which is in line with New York standards [see New York Child Support Standards Act 1988]. But after taxes, it's about 60% of my income. There are no hidden pockets of money." He and his former wife had worked out an arrangement in which the children lived with him about one-third of the year.

So they're here a lot, which is wonderful. It's the way I want it. But it's a financial strain when they are here because they eat like adults. It's to the point now where I can't afford to take them out to a movie or out to dinner. When she [the former wife] asks me for extra money, like for camp expenses or something, I have to say I don't have it. There's just no extra money. Essentially she's getting paid child support for what amounts to $13,000 prorated over an 8-month period for what amounts to be $9,000 worth of expenses.

Like the others, these men had some ambivalence about the relationship between child support payments and the former wife as the direct recipient. This father of two, for example, discussed his mixed feelings: "There was this small financial issue because I felt like 'I'm giving her a lot of money per year.' I had this tendency to think, 'Why should I pay her all this money when she's probably just going to go out and marry another guy who's making money?' Like, 'Where do I get my income when I'm paying for the child support?' I have no other worldly manner in my life to get additional money to cover that. But it wasn't that she didn't deserve it or anything like that. They need the money. It was that 'I'll have to pay even when she remarries.' " The assumption that the former spouse would remarry, if she had not already, and be economically supported by another man (even though all of the former spouses were employed) was held by most participants in the study, irrespective of their predominant strategies of action. A related assumption was that their children would benefit financially by the former wife's remarriage.[7] The innovative men's ambivalence pointed to the ways in which the definitions of family and family obligations were challenged by divorce. In contrast to the majority of other participants, however, these men sided, despite divorce, with family persistence rather than disintegration.

Not allowing financial matters, especially child support, to become major points of contention and thus to interfere with their workable postdivorce relations with the former spouse took cognitive and emotional effort: "It's kind of tough dealing with the money. I put the check in the same place every week, same place in the bag so she doesn't need to ask me, 'Where is the check?' but she does, every week. But I don't say anything, why would I confront her? What would I say? And what could it lead to? I usually just say, 'Well, it's in the bag.' " And a father of three who was seriously strapped financially had chosen so far not to seek a reduction in his child support obligation even though he had assumed many childrearing costs since the time the agreement was written. He was reluctant to risk "upsetting the cart."

Conciliatory acts regarding monetary matters were not one sided. Actions aimed at minimizing conflict over finances were taken also by their former wives, according to the men. One father, for instance, had not paid child support for over 6 months. He and his former wife had equal salaries and fully shared childrearing, including child care, costs. She had neither threatened nor initiated legal action for his support noncompliance although she disagreed with his logic as to why he should not resume paying.

Integral also to the maintenance of parenting partnerships was the men's position that communicating about their children was a shared responsibility, not primarily the former wife's. And when one or the other parent was characterized as carrying more of the "communication work," it was attributed to personality, not to gender identity or role. This father described his part in the afterdivorce family communication system:

> I would say that with regard to issues surrounding the kids, easily three quarters of the time, I'm probably the one who initiates the communication, does the communication work. We talk a little bit about where the kids are. We agreed [after she moved out of the area] to meet every few months or so to kind of talk face-to-face about our issues and concerns about the kids. You know: "What do you see?" "What do we see?" "Is there a consistency of concerns that we see? How are you dealing with it? How are we dealing with it?" "Do we need to be a little bit more consistent, if it's at all possible?" We're never really talking about major issues, we haven't had any. But those kind of face-to-face, in-person contacts have usually been initiated by me. I'll write letters to her, and I think I've become a better writer and communicator not only with my former wife and children but with my friends as a result of this.

Differences in assessments of children's well-being, styles of parenting, and views of parental obligations, for example, had to be confronted. The respondent cited above continued, touching on some of the ambiguities involved in co-parenting after divorce. "I think we agreed on the need and desire to love our children and to give to them things of ourselves as well as material things. But I think how we got there differed, in some instances more significantly than others. And, in some ways, that may have reflected how we were brought up. And some of those things are still present, and we just have to keep working with them." This custodial father, who had a de facto joint custody situation in which he cared for their young child about two-thirds of the time, pointed to some of his concerns about parenting differences.

> I do think she undermines me to some extent, such as with the bedtime issue—him not getting enough sleep when he stays there and then sleeping in the car when he comes home—or the succession of boyfriends, and too much TV. I bring these up to her, and then she doesn't do anything. But that's fine. She doesn't have to agree. But it can be difficult because we need a joint attitude with regard to our son. We need to provide him a consistent environment. But I have no control over this. I can grit my teeth if I want to but I have to let it go. She loves him too. Maybe she thinks she's doing the best for him. I think she probably is doing the best she can. Who knows? Maybe she does know better. We try to cooperate. We get along. We both want to protect our son. We try to keep talking.

Such levels of communication required a level of trust between the former spouses that was not only rare in divorce for the majority of participants but apparently was absent from many, perhaps most, of their ended marriages. Protecting the parental partnership by minimizing conflict necessitated a management of feelings, especially about the former wife and ended marriage. This father, for example, who became a co-parent almost 2 years after divorcing, unlike the others who successfully established parenting partnerships during the separation and early divorce period, referred to the need to come to grips with his feelings: "My former wife wasn't really into it from the vindictive side. If anything there was the guilt thing: If we'd have worked at the marriage, the divorce would never have happened, and she knew that too. But as a result we both probably came out of it as better people. We both grew up over the years. We had to. There never was much friction. I got over it pretty quickly. The problem was me, really. I had to get over those feelings [of resentment for her leaving the marriage]. I did. And this [arrangement] works for us, for both of us."

Maintaining an emotional equilibrium was the most challenging aspect of the postdivorce parenting partnership, and an achieved balance occasionally proved to be tenuous. Critical incidents typically demonstrated divergent ideas about parenting and family life and, as well, potential threats to the established collaborative enterprise. Having a relationship with his former wife that was focused solely on their shared parenting arrangements, this father sought professional counseling over his confusion about how to handle the presence in their children's lives of his former wife's new boyfriend. His remarks covered a complex array of issues:

I just recently found out he [the boyfriend] has a key to the house. I was there to pick up the kids but with a different car, and this guy walked up and unlocked the door and walked in. I said, "Oh, I didn't realize that we had this situation going on." At first, when he walked in, I had a strong reaction inside of me. But then I thought about it: In this day and age, I see guys living with girls. I keep trying to put it in the context of what's going on today. But I just don't understand it. I can't have someone come live in my house. Here's a stable family neighborhood and here's this woman giving a man a key to her house where she lives with children. Okay, so he's well-educated. But there's a lot of crazy, well-educated people out there too. It's not that, I mean, I don't know who he is. In my mind, I'm thinking, "It's so acceptable." But I feel real funny about having anybody just come live with me. I don't think I could do it really. It's at my kids' expense, their psychological well-being. I try to think how it would affect them if I had somebody come and live with me, and I know that it would affect them. That's why I called the child psychologist. . . . I don't want to put my kids in the middle, between their parents. I think the ones really being abused through all of this divorce stuff, psycho-

logically, is the kids: They're being told, "You either go with mommy or dad."
I don't want my kids told that, ever. I wouldn't care if my wife [*sic*] was the
worst person in the world, she's still their mother. What I might think of her
or what she does should have nothing to do with her relationship with the
children. She's their mother.

And this custodial father was concerned about the possible effects of his
former wife's "lifestyle" on their children. He felt stymied because although he wanted to protect his children, he also wanted them to have more
than "the typical visiting relationship kids have with the other [noncusto-
dial] parent."

She sees the kids now 2 days a week. I'm trying to get down her visitation
only to Sunday right now because she's going through a process of love
problems, love deceptions. She's of the age, well, she's saying she's never
going to remarry again and she's desperate, and desperately looking for a
husband. So she's going through this process of "should I marry this guy, or
that guy, or that guy?" She's having men stay overnight while the kids are
there. My daughters told me about it, and I told them I didn't think it was
good for them to stay and sleep over at their mother's house while these
things are happening. And they agree with me. The only way I can cut down
to just Sundays is to have her agreement or file a petition through the court—a
Revision of Visitation—and I won't go back to court. We talk sometimes. But
she tells me it's none of my business.

BEING "DEVIANTS"

The innovative men viewed their postdivorce association with the former wife as being so atypical as to be "abnormal"; in acting as they did,
they defied the mythical and contemporary portrayals of divorced couples.
Each of these nine asked during the interview how divorced parents "are
supposed to" interact and associate and for an "objective" assessment of
their situations. Researchers Ahrons and Wallisch (1987b) encountered a
similar experience: "The respondents themselves noted that they were very
unsure of 'appropriate' ways to relate, often asking the interviewer how
they were 'supposed' to relate" (p. 294). And seven of the nine innovative
men explicitly qualified their positive assessments. For example, in describing the bond of friendship and mutual support that existed between
him and his former wife, this person, divorced nearly 4 years, insisted
several times that their postdivorce relationships was "not just a bed of
roses": "Believe me, you know, is that thing [tape recorder] going? I
hope so, so it won't be unbelievable that I said this [after having described

extraordinary levels of parental cooperation]. It has not been all peaches and cream with us, not just a bed of roses. We disagree with things. Believe me, we've had our disagreements. We had one about 2 weeks ago about something, by phone. There are still feelings there, hurt feelings. There are still things. You don't uproot your life like that and walk away the next day and act like nothing happened. It stays with you. And we talk about it, just recently we had another talk about it." This next respondent, who attributed his successful shared custody situation to his co-parenting status prior to divorce and his insistence that his children's care situation not be altered, said:

> I am upset, I don't want you to think I'm not. I don't want to create the impression I'm not. I am upset because of the way it happened [she became involved with someone at work]. But when the light went off in my head: "I can lead the life I want because, married or not, I have my three children," then it all became okay. Besides, I realize that if I had to live with her I'd be probably more upset than with the situation I'm in. I should send her a thank-you note. I guess that's uncalled for since I'm the only of the two of us here to give my side of the story. I'm not angry. But I don't want you to think it's all been easy either. She could be more cooperative. She could [be].

Their relationships with their former spouses were equivocal. That they were parents together and committed to supporting each other in their childrearing was clear. But the parameters to their emotional relationships beyond parenting posed dilemmas. This person, for example, had a relationship with his former wife that was unusually cooperative and friendly, and they routinely pursued activities together with their children. Yet emotional matters, ones "close to the heart," as he said his former wife had described them, were especially awkward and sometimes off-limits. For instance, discussing his fears that if she remarried, he would be displaced from his children's lives by the new stepfather, he noted: "We talk about it, she and I, sometimes. She tries to reassure me, which is what I want from her, I guess. But then, how can she, really, on this?" After discussing how they had gone to visit their oldest child's school principal together, and considering aloud how he might consult with a therapist, he continued: "She won't go in with me to counseling, no way. She wants to deny there's any problem. She wouldn't go to joint counseling when we had problems. Let me restate that. I would not want to be with her, put it that way. I don't think she would go but nor would I want to be in that situation with her. I would feel very uncomfortable being in that setting with her. It would be counterproductive. So they'd have to see us separately, rather than the two of us together."

Having a shared-custody arrangement in which caring and financial responsibilities were equally divided, this next person was "working on" a marital reconciliation with his former wife who, he reported, was less optimistic about its prospects than was he. Recognizing relational constraints and dilemmas, he described feelings of defensiveness they had with each other about their parenting. "I've only a couple of times seen an emotional outbreak from the kids where they've said they don't want to go, or they want to go back to mommy's. I don't know what mom has experienced because I know that's something that she wouldn't share with me: If at any time the kids said they wished they were with daddy or, 'When is daddy coming over to pick us up, because we want to be with him?' She wouldn't share those type of things with me, which I understand." Although the shared commitments to their children and continued communication helped parry feelings of distrust, discord was not entirely precluded. Shared parenting after divorce was not "a piece of cake," accomplished with ease. Guidelines were few. As Maccoby and associates (1990) observed in their discussion of the initial findings from the Stanford Custody Project: "There is still relatively little information concerning the details of interparental cooperation—that is, the logistics of managing visitation and alternation, the division of responsibilities, the frequency and nature of communication, the amount of mutual undermining versus mutual backup—that prevails under different custodial arrangements" (p. 142).

The Logistics of Shared Parenting

"Time sharing," as several of the men involved in parenting partnerships referred to their parenting arrangements, took various forms and ranged in allocations of roughly one-quarter and three-quarters to equally half-time. Scheduling was the "key to success." For instance, this next father's children lived primarily with their mother, although they spent about one-third of each year with him and his wife, who was an active third member of the parenting partnership. The remainder of the time they lived with their mother and stepfather. Reviewing his children's scheduling and commuting between homes, this person said,

> We have a very set schedule. They come every other weekend: every other weekend, a week in March, five weeks in the summer, a week at Christmas, or 10 days really. Since they're in private school, they have a lot of vacation. They come for Thanksgiving for almost a week. We meet halfway on [Highway] 95. I think the kids have benefited from parents and stepmother setting priorities which sets their needs, particularly during the periods of

transitions, as the highest priority. I think they've benefited from that. That's included negotiating. It gets absurd after a while how far each one goes from Philadelphia to here on 95; so going down to pick them up, it's one exit and dropping them off is another exit. It's worked out. It's been basically pretty painless, to some degree. When they get older [and are able to drive], it will become less of an issue.

His present wife not only participated with him in handling arrangements concerning his children but also with his former wife directly. Together, the biological parents and stepmother had a *parenting coalition* (Visher and Visher 1988, p. 28). (The children's stepfather reportedly remained only on the periphery of the children's lives.) Rare among divorced parents and their subsequent spouses, such coalitions are beneficial, "providing the most healthy family environment for raising both children and step-children" (Giles-Sims 1987, pp. 147-48; see also Ahrons and Wallisch 1987a). The only father in the study having such an arrangement, he described his family life and parenting activities with rich details and was clearly the most satisfied and optimistic respondent.

Flexibility was crucial to continued harmonious and workable relations. Having sole custody officially, this father shared custody in practice. "She has relatively free access. I try to give her full access. We exchange times occasionally. For example, last Thanksgiving was to be my holiday, but her favorite uncle was dying so I said she could take him with her to see him. She's flexible too, but this is recent. On her weekends, she has him from Friday night to Monday morning, but she works Friday nights. She's finally agreed that he can stay with me now on Fridays. I was so enthusi-astic about that; it's just great." And this father of a preteen described the arrangement with his former wife: "He also comes for an extended session during the summer plus the usual long holiday kind of thing. She gets him for the first half of the holiday, and I get him for the second. But it's all open for what's convenient. She called me a month ago and said she had a chance to take a week off and go out of town, could I take him that week? I said, 'Well, yeah, sure, I can take him. I have to do a bit of rearranging with work but it's fine. So okay, fine, let's do it.' So it's a very flexible arrangement."

Older children were participants in the management of the shared par-enting situation. But they were excluded from parental disputes. The father of the preteen son continued: "A lot of what happens with him is arranged directly with him. He's nearly 13 years old. You know, 'You're going to stay Tuesday again, right?' 'Yeah, right.' 'What time are you coming over?' So it's been Tuesday nights or one night midweek and then at least every other weekend, usually part of every weekend. He comes, we arrange it ourselves, things are arranged through him. We're [My former wife and I are] careful to not involve him in any way in our discussions about money or anything else that might become tense."

The allocation and assumption of particular parental responsibilities varied among the men and their former spouses, depending primarily on their respective work and custody schedules. For instance, the several men whose children were quite young and whose former wives had part-time employment typically did not arrange or handle such matters as doctors' appointments. They did regularly attend, often jointly with the former wife, school or church functions involving their children. Men whose children were in the elementary or middle school grades and whose former wives had full-time employment tended to share parenting tasks more equitably. For instance, although they met regularly to plan the following week's schedule, this person and his former spouse had developed a routine division of labor. Her mother was instrumental in the continuing success of their arrangements.

> As far as how we split the care, I would say the maternal grandmother has 30%, her mother has 30%, and I have 40%. My daughter's mother primarily handles the pediatrician, although it's not always that way. If I was available, I'd take her to the pediatrician. I try to attend as many school functions as I can. But when it comes right down to the decision making, I handle the ophthalmologist, dentist, and some of the outside activities. It works nice that way. Somebody's going to be working and someone has to have free time, so you have to find it. You'd like to say that both parents would be at everything and, hopefully, if she gets married someday, we'll both be at her wedding! But, you know, in the meantime, we can't both be at everything. It works fine, we've worked it out.

Four of the nine men and their former wives managed the bulk of child care by holding different work schedules. This next person worked a regular day shift and his former wife evenings; she cared for their young child during the day and on alternate weekends. They too depended on assistance from their child's grandparents. Referring to his former wife, he said,

> She lives about 10 or 15 minutes away but works only a few blocks from where we live. So she picks him up and brings him back each day. It's more practical. He doesn't have to be up as early as if I had to take him there. Besides, while she's reliable—she's never missed a day—she's not punctual, and it was a real problem before we moved here [next door to his parents']. When she was late picking him up, then I was late to work and we were all

stressed out. Now he can stay with my parents until she arrives, if she's late. Once when he was sick, she came to my place to care for him. The other time he was sick, I took time off from work and I stayed with him.

Four other sets of parents also relied on one or more of their children's grandparents for additional child care assistance. Thus two-thirds of the men engaging in innovative lines of action after divorce and their former wives had additional family assistance in managing their children's care: Five were able to depend on children's grandparents and one on his wife, his children's stepmother.

Two other men and their former spouses collaborated in managing afterschool supervision for their children even though both parents were at work. This father's child lived primarily with his mother:

> Because I work and his mother works and we're not happy with a 12-year-old going to an empty house [usually the mother's] and also with the unsupervised or unstructured time that he spends, I want him to call. He can reach me but often can't get through to her, so this is the way we do it. I want to make sure that he's okay, and that he's working on his homework, and that he's not getting himself into a situation where he's going to get himself into any problems. "Just call me and let me know you're all right. Just check in with me." He does. He's really good about it. And if there's any problem, then I try to reach her to keep her posted too.

HOUSEHOLD TRANSITIONS

Also deemed to be critical to their children's well-being were the transitions between the parents' households. The ease of these transfers served as a measure of the overall success of collaborative parenting. Accordingly, both parents were obligated to facilitate the shifts, to keep them smooth and without trauma or upset. Maintaining routines and preventing conflict during their contacts were the predominant strategies for effective management of children's movements between parents.

> Their mother and I help them make the transitions between households by starting a schedule and keeping to it. We have helped them do that by discussing ahead of time changes that are going to occur. One way that I've done it concretely is through a calendar. We have a calendar in the apartment, and we have d's for dad's and m's for mom's. The kids sit down at the calendar and I go through the calendar with them. I don't go more than a week with them but they know exactly where they're going to be and when. Before my youngest gets into school, she knows what a calendar is and how to keep the

records! So I guess it's schedules that makes it work: We've remained faithful
to the schedule. We don't change it because of our desires or frustrations or
angers with one another. If time is missed, it is missed as a result of another
obligation that one of us has that's not related to family but to work. If I miss
time with the kids, I always make sure that somewhere in the very near future
I would make that up. I still do. Say there's a day I miss or, maybe because
of my job, I would be out of town for Wednesday and Thursday. I would ask
her if it would be okay if the girls and I spend an extra weekend together, or
I'd make it up on a couple of Sunday nights. Unless they had something
planned, she always agrees. We keep the kids totally out of the picture when
it comes to issues between us. They know that we keep to the schedule.

Three other fathers of younger children also maintained calendars to
provide children a visual representation of their living arrangements and
movements.

Each of the men involved in parenting partnerships had homes that
included bedrooms and play or study space for their children, as did some
of the other participants. Unlike in most of the others' circumstances,
however, their children kept an array of personal belongings at their homes
as well as those of their mothers'. And most carried some items, such as
homework and favorite toys or select books, and sometimes clothing, with
them as they moved between their parents' residences.

We're totally self-sufficient. The things that we do share are the larger
clothing items, like coats and boots and snowpants in winter. Both girls have
a backpack that they carry their daily things in, their things for school and
the baby-sitter's. So they're both self-sufficient. They have their own ward-
robe at daddy's and at mommy's. When they're with me, I buy them clothes.
When they're with mom, she buys them clothes. There's a free exchange of
clothing; they wear whatever they have on. It has just begun to happen when
one of them wanted something at the other house. I think it's a certain
maturity beginning where they're more willing to take things back and forth
now. I've always been supportive of it.

Among the six men living in relatively close proximity to the former wife,
they and, according to them, their children's mother made trips with
varying frequency between the two homes to pick up or deliver needed or
forgotten items. Generally, children, particularly those over about age 5,
telephoned freely between the residences. Accommodations to the exigen-
cies of family life were common and frequent, viewed as necessary for
easing children's lives in the postdivorce circumstance.

In sum, the nine men engaged in innovative action had distinctly different relations with the former spouse than did the majority of other men.

Not only was conflict kept to a minimum and inconsequential, and feelings of resentment and anger moderated, but cooperation and flexibility, based on a deliberate prioritizing, were kept paramount: "It's best for the kids." The well-being of their children took precedence over interpersonal differences with the former spouse. The objective was to view and relate to the her primarily as the other parent of their children, not as the former wife, an opponent, or antagonist. The relationships and roles of former spouse and parent were disaggregated. This deliberately orchestrated separation was both a consequence of and contributing factor to the gradual declining of strains specific to the ending of their marriage. As one man noted: "We declared a truce. I guess we even formed a new alliance. You've heard of global warming? I'm responsible for it! I quit fighting with her, *we* quit fighting, and the universe began to warm up."

Notes

1. "Too much of the literature on men overlooks the importance of their opportunities, thus implying that what (little) men do in the family reflects their choices and preferences. Microstructural theory reminds us that people's actions are circumscribed by the social organization of experiences available by particular types of action" (Cohen 1989, p. 222).

2. Theorist Weedon (1987) set the perception of choices by individuals within an broad discourse analysis: "Knowledge of more than one discourse and the recognition that meaning is plural allows for a measure of choice on the part of the individual and even where choice is not available, resistance is still possible" (p. 105).

3. Although no answer is available through this study as to why these men differed from the others and why these men and their former wives found successful ways to parent jointly despite divorce, one obvious research need is to study the character of specific marriages and, for those which terminate, divorces. Cuber and Harroff's (1965) typology of five marriages and Blumstein and Schwartz's (1983) study of American couples suggest several marital types to explore in relation to divorce and postdivorce relationships. So too, much more specific research needs to be undertaken exploring gender role attitudes and activities and the perceived quality of marriages and divorces.

4. Researchers Ahrons and Wallisch (1987b) commented on the significance of maintaining secrecy about postdivorce sexual liaisons: "Margaret Mead's interpretation of the source of our discomfort in acknowledging a continuing relationship between former spouses may indeed still be valid: 'Any contact between divorced people to some smacks of incest; once divorced, they have declared by law that they are sexually inaccessible to each other, and the aura of past sexual relations make further relationship incriminating' (Mead 1971, p. 111)" (p. 273).

5. The findings in the present study about the relatively low level of conflict between parents sharing parenting in some fashion after divorce—only one of the nine innovative fathers, as well as the other five primary-parent fathers, had continuing antagonisms with their former wives and the former relatively little compared with most men in the study—differ from other studies (e.g., Maccoby et al. 1990; Bowman and Ahrons 1985; Luepnitz 1982). The probable explanation for this divergence is the variation by states in divorce law. In New York state, the location of the present study, parents typically share custody and childrearing only when both parents agree to do

so; thus shared parenting is a self-selected circumstance. In other states, such as California, for example, conflicted parents sometimes reach agreement by entering into shared custody arrangements (Mnookin et al. 1990). For instance, drawing from the findings of the California-based Stanford Custody Project, Maccoby et al. (1990) concluded: "Dual-residence parents talked to each other somewhat more frequently and in general maintained a higher level of cooperative communication. However, they did not experience less discord, and the prevalence of the conflicted pattern was as great in the dual-residence families as in the primary-residence ones. Within each residential group, there was great variability in how much cooperation or conflict the divorced couple maintained when both continued to be involved in parenting. These results would appear to indicate that sharing the residential custody of children after divorce does not systematically exacerbate conflict between the parents, nor does it systematically moderate such conflict" (pp. 152-53). Comparative research examining states' patterns and variations needs to be undertaken.

6. For discussions of the complexity of calculating child support, see Cassetty and Douthitt (1984), Cassetty (1983), Leehy (1991); with respect to this and co-custodial parents sharing financial responsibility, see Garfinkel (1992).

7. Chambers (1988) argued that the only clear role recognized socially for stepfathers, while married to the children's mother, is that of economic provision. See also Pasley and Ihinger-Tallman (1987a).

9

INNOVATIVE, NURTURING FATHERS

Only 9 of the 75 participants were nurturing divorced fathers, according to the multiple criteria of caring for and caring about their children and having a parental commitment central to their self-concepts (May and Strikwerda 1992a). Parenting for them was primary, unlike for the majority for whom other matters and relationships took precedence. These nine, engaged in innovative strategies of action, which encompassed parenting partnerships with their former wives, had qualitatively different relations with their children than did the majority of other respondents. Their approaches to parenting were distinctive also. Integrally involved in all facets of parenting, their predominant concerns were their children's welfare, happiness, and development and the character of the father-child relationship. One co-custodial father, who had declined several desirable promotions to remain in close proximity to his children, said, "I'm here to help them grow up, to see what life is about, to experience what they are supposed to experience, go to the right schools and to see that they have enough money to do what they need, to have what they want, and have the values that they're supposed to have. I'm very concerned that all happens. It's going to be the values that I believe in; I'm going to help instill those in them. I want to make sure that they have those values. I'm going to be with them as often as I can."

Largely irrespective of the particular topic of discussion, caring for and about their children punctuated the nurturing fathers' narratives, and they talked extensively and with detailed specifics about their children. When discussing their children, these particular men seldom shifted to various other issues, as did most other participants. They were focused on parenting activities and challenges, and their meanings. These fathers were neither alienated from their offspring nor disenfranchised from parenting. Being divorced was only one factor in their parenting, not the essential or overarching one. The primary significance of the former spouse was as the mother of their children and the parenting partner. For the most part, the numerous other aspects of postdivorce life given precedence by other participants—rights and fairness and their counterpoints, grievances about the unjustness of the divorcing process and its outcome, and resentments about access and support—were relatively unimportant. Being highly involved parents by choice and with the former wife's cooperation and support, these nine men largely circumvented or were spared the general cultural ambiguity surrounding the role and status of divorced father (see Risman 1989; Frey 1986; Greif 1979; Hanson 1985, 1986a, 1986b; Seltzer 1991b).

Only two of these nine fathers had been a primary parent during marriage. The other seven fathers had made "major changes" to become, as one said, "really involved and caring" (see also Risman 1989; Frey 1986; Fassinger 1989; Coltrane 1989; Greif 1982). He continued, "If it wasn't for the divorce, I wouldn't have changed my priorities. I might have just as well have forgotten I was a parent otherwise. And I did [make the changes]. It has been the pivotal point of my life, my divorce. I took a job that paid considerably less and didn't require travel just so that I would now have time to spend with my child and really become a parent." In contrast, only 6 of the other 66 fathers described having made significant adjustments or alterations to accommodate the changed family and parenting situation. Describing the crisis that threw him into the primary parent role, in which he cared for the children alone for some months, this next father characterized his adjustments in terms of gender roles in marriage and family.

It was terrifying at first, just terrifying. I remember the night she walked out the door. And I cried at the thought of it: I said to myself, "How in the hell am I going to do this?" I was raised in a stereotypical way, stereotypically male. I did not cook. I did not particularly clean. I was working a lot, so it was "come home and play with the baby." The youngest was just a year and a half, the other one was going towards 3. So it was like playtime. I didn't have any responsibility for their daily care. I'd hardly changed a diaper before. I didn't know what parenting was about, really. I mean, who teaches us how to parent? I really didn't know how to ask for help. I don't truly remember the first year. It was day by day by day. After about a year, I managed to figure out that I had my act together. But it goes deeper than all of that. I had to learn to relate to them, relate to them as people.

Further reflecting on the changes made, he speculated about his likely family participation had his wife not left: "I would have probably, I'm forecasting here, I think I would have fallen into the stereotyped dad: I would have come home from work, I wouldn't have worried about what they were doing from morning to night. My ex would've run their daily social life and where they went and what they did. I would have been called upon to be *dad* in the family. It's what we both knew how to do. To think what I would have missed is staggering." What he might have added, as well, is that conformity to the conventional role would have been met with general social support.

Women served as these men's parenting models. Three of the nurturing fathers observed that their parenting exemplar was their mothers, three noted that theirs was the former wife, and another credited his sister. The turn to women for parenting role models reinforced the perception that, in seeking to be an "alternative divorced father," he was appropriating women's activities and characteristics. The one person who credited his father as being his principal parental role model believed, nevertheless, that he had adopted parental approaches common to women, not men: *Both* he and his father were atypical. Each of these men, as did many of the participants, lamented that he had few or no male role models for parenting. Most neither personally knew other men who were integrally involved in childrearing nor had viable cultural images of such men.

These nurturing fathers then very clearly saw their parenting approaches and actions as being "feminine": They had become primary parents by appropriating skills and characteristics typical of mothers and atypical of fathers. That is, in seeking to be alternative fathers they drew on mothering as a model for parenting and adopted behaviors and postures usually associated with the feminine or female. Two described themselves as "closet mothers." Sharing parenting equally with his former wife, this father characterized his objectives as he sought to adjust to the divorce circumstance: "I have tried to be a mother, tried to be the image of what a mother should be, do with them in given times what a mother would do, provide a lot of the emotions she would give them, etcetera. You know, do what a *good* mother does."

More was involved in the nurturing fathers' accommodations than an expansion of roles—combining employment with primary parenting and abandoning the conventional division of family labor based on gender. Interactional and communication styles had to be modified. This custodial father indicated as much when he said, "I had to learn to relate to them as people." This next person became a co-custodial parent subsequent to divorce: "One thing, my college or high school friends would never believe that I'm doing this. They would probably say I was the least likely person to be a single parent [in a de facto shared custody arrangement]. I have a sarcastic, dry humor that isn't always conducive for emotional relationships. I was a heavy drinker and partyer at college. They just wouldn't have expected me to be a single parent, let alone to want it." Most of these fathers observed that they had to learn to listen, "learn to listen to my children *and* to my wife, my former wife," said a co-custodial father who added: "Strange, isn't it, the timing?"

Parenting was enhanced and not diminished by divorce. Uniformly, the nurturing fathers believed that they had become more conscientious parents following divorce, both by choice and necessity: They could not rely as extensively on the children's mother to keep them attuned to family dynamics or "to cover the gaps or gaffes." One person, whose children spent about one-third of their time with him, explained: "I think I'm actually a better father to my children now than maybe I was back then [when married]. I'm certainly much more conscious now with how I communicate with them as their father, making certain that we're still staying connected. This is kind of like virgin territory; no one in my family was very concerned with communication or feelings."

This next father believed he was a "better and more capable parent" since divorcing because he was able to parent more autonomously, not because he had to make more of an effort to be involved, as was the case for the others. Divorce had empowered him to break out of the traditional mode of fathering, that is, being the disciplinarian and exercising an authoritarian approach.

They see a level-headed dad now, they don't see someone who is the ruler or master-type over them. It seemed like in the marriage the role I had to play, she would tell them not to do this or to do that, whatever, scold them and hit them, whatever, and tell them I would take care of it when I got home. I said, "I'm just not a good guy-bad guy relationship." I didn't like having to come home and get mad at one or all of them because [I had to] "take care of things as they come." My parenting has changed. I'm now the parent I want to be rather than the parent that was developing. I do enjoy them 100%, 100%.

These fathers were confident about their integral roles in their children's development. They knew their children as individuals, distinct from their mothers and siblings. Moreover, they were overwhelmingly proud of their children. Discussing his oldest child's early problems in adjusting to her parents' divorce, this father explained:

> She's fine now. She's happy and she's always on the honor roll. She's so talented in so many areas. It amazes me. She just did a term paper at school. She and her friends wrote a term paper on Mexico, and she discovered a lot of things that she didn't know about her family background. She was very impressed. She came home with this really good paper: "Daddy, I want you to keep this for yourself." I was so touched. The youngest had no problems at all. She does things so well with little emphasis. It's as if she is in a second life already and she's just having to comply with this life. It's very comical. She comes home from school, "Got to do my homework, dad." She's there for an hour. Comes out, "Got to watch TV for 30 minutes." Stands up after 30 minutes. Shuts it off. Calls a friend. Checks her clothes for tomorrow. Everything is methodical and under control. Somehow you get the feeling she already knows about tomorrow and will do it well. She has all this confidence.

Recognition of children's uniqueness included acknowledgments that their perspectives and experiences might vary: "I'll tell you, if you ask my kids what life is like with me, if you can get it out of them, it's a 100% different version [than mine], I'm sure—just being children, just being people. My favorite is always the time when *they* thought you were absolutely just horrible when *you* thought you were doing something really great for them [laughing]." None of these fathers expressed concern about his role as an adult male figure in his children's lives, and none remarked about a son's potential sexual orientation. (Nor, in common with the other fathers, did any one of the nurturing fathers express a concern about a daughter's possible sexual inclination.)

Generally absent in the accounts of these fathers was the language of power and control, whether with regard to their overall situation, the former wife, or their children. Parental authority was based on their caring, knowledge, and experience as adults in relation to and interaction with their children. Their parenting style was *authoritative,* which, as described by Hetherington (1987, citing Baumrind 1971), on the basis of research with divorced parents, involves high levels of warmth, involvement, monitoring, and maturity demands, moderately high but responsive control, and relatively low conflict. Hetherington (1987, p. 197) concluded that a majority of divorced mothers use the authoritative style, whereas divorced fathers vary across the four styles identified: permissive, disengaged, authoritarian, and authoritative. These fathers, then, as they recognized, were similar to divorced mothers in their parenting styles.

Parenting was intensely meaningful to these fathers, "the most significant thing I've ever done or will ever do," as one said. This father tried to explain:

> I can't give an answer to what it means to be a father to me, but I can tell you when I know I'm a father. When it's 3 o'clock in the morning, when he's awakened, and he reaches up and touches me. Then all the bullshit in between, the worries, the negativity, the anxieties—they're all washed away. It's the moments of the really positive contacts that clean out and make it all seem so worthwhile. Or he'll walk up behind me while I'm doing something and just pat me; it's the small unexpected touches and moments. I'm getting all teary trying to talk about this. . . . Maybe 20 years from now, if he's all screwed up—I don't know. I hope to be able to say I did everything I could, but of course I won't be able to say that. But I want to be able to. I take this all very seriously. It's important to me to be a good person, I want him to be and become a good person. So far, so good, I think.

Any vestiges or hints of sentimentality about parenting as a divorced father were quickly offset by efforts to deromanticize it. This custodial father of two children, for example, after expounding on the delights of his children, then issued a few cautionary remarks by comparing parenting with its portrayals in movies.

> [The movie] *Kramer vs. Kramer* was bullshit for me, it really was. Both sides of it were total bullshit. It was a movie about this subject for people who have no idea what the subject is about. They tried to do very emotional things with him and his son and everything, and that's just not how it happens. You know, there are very beautiful, precious moments, but you usually only discover them when they're already over with and they have a life span of about 5 seconds! You know, there's no scene and by the time you set it up, it's gone. And it's really true. On a daily basis, it's a crummy job but I wouldn't have it any other way. It's probably the most rewarding job you could ever do. . . . What happened by being single is that I was forced into all of this. I've benefited so greatly, I can't even begin to tell you how much.

Assertions of confidence and mastery of parenting were typically qualified with doubts: "I wasn't made for this, you know? I was raised to be man, not a mother or like a mother." Yet prevalent throughout these nine men's accounts was evidence of competent, committed parenting.

Parenting Strategies

Being responsive to children and their needs, establishing routines and sharing the dailiness of family life, and maintaining open communication were at the core of the nurturing fathers' efforts to parent successfully—effectively and meaningfully.[1] This custodial father, for example, discussed his children and his parenting:

> You don't preoccupy their lives trying to find out what the hell is wrong with mom and dad, so instead they can live their lives. All along that's what I've tried to do, to focus their life and mine in terms of what is most important to them. I'm sure when they grow up, there's going to be some sort of good that has rubbed off on them! . . . I want them to do and be, first of all and most of all, decent human beings. I have not impressed into them that they have to make a lot of money or have a big home. But they must be just good human beings who appreciate other people, have cultural and spiritual values, that sort of thing. The rest, as long as they know what is right and wrong, the rest falls into place. That's basically what I want to give them. The rest is easy! I'm so relaxed, aren't I? They need constant looking after. They are children. They need lots of supervision, lots of attention. Watching them, what are they doing? What did they say? Is that what they really mean? A lot of, *a lot of,* support and supervision, that's what they need. They need a lot from me, *a lot.*

This next father of three had not pressed his former wife to sell the family home and divide the equity as mandated by the divorce agreement. That choice cost him, however, because without that money, he found it necessary to supplement his income and so worked a second job during the 50% time that the children were with their mother.

> I don't want their lives disrupted if it's not necessary. I want them to be able to stay in the house. I took my portion of our savings and I bought a townhouse with it. Now I have a place for them, okay? I have their bedrooms sets and everything set up, and have clothes and everything. This weekend we're building a playroom in the basement, painting the walls and stuff like that. We've got a swimming pool, basketball courts, and so on. I don't live in what you'd call luxury, but it's home. They've got a large park right next door, baseball and football fields over there, and an ongoing recreational program all summer long. . . . They have woods all around and it's more of an environment like what they were used to. And we're just three miles from their mother's home. They have sleepovers and everything. I know all the families that they play with, all the friends that they're with. I keep in contact with them too.

The securing of routines was partly situational; spending regular and large blocks of time together with their children both allowed and required the establishing of set patterns and practices. Creating workable and satisfying situations, deemed necessary to children's healthy development, took forethought and effort. Although this person's children lived primarily with their mother, about 3 hours' driving time away, they spent roughly one third of their time with him and his wife. Parenting, he argued, required deliberation regardless of marital status. But the parents' divorce and their remarriages increased the complexity of family experiences and arrangements so that parenting required even greater vigilance.

> I think that in addition to our commitment to regular communication with them by the telephone, we've tried to identify things that they enjoy doing, things that they're good at, and when they're with us, try to nurture those kinds of activities, promote those kinds of skills and abilities. Trying to stress, to some degree, their individual abilities and qualities as being different from each other, and to build their individual levels of confidence. That tends to be much more of a challenge on weekends than when they're here for longer periods of time. We do whatever activities they want to do. We do three different things a lot of times. They're all pretty athletic, they're all good at different things. . . . We also try to reinforce that, even though they're with us for only a fairly short period of time, that this is really a family unit. We talk. We do what needs to be done. Say if one has problems with homework, we sit down and try to work it out. If the house has to be cleaned, they each have jobs and responsibilities, and they know what they are. We always have a big dinner on Saturday. We all sit down together, and there's a lot of conversation. It's always their favorite foods and we have a good time. Breakfasts are also good times when we all sit together. Summers and vacation times are similar, only, of course, there's a bigger sense of routine, we all just settle into it. There's no transition [between the homes]. They just come in and there's no adjustment time. There's no need to figure out what the situation is. They're very different households, but they understand their roles, their place, in each of them. It's as if they've just walked in from school on Friday nights [during the school year]. We're a regular family.

Shared participation in recreational activities was one part of shared family life, not the center as it was for many visiting fathers whose association with their children occurred primarily during fixed and limited periods. This person's children lived with him about 40% of the time. He contrasted the early postdivorce months, when he lived in his parents' home and recreational activities dominated their time together, with their present situation:

It always seems that there's something to do [now]. When I first left, every minute of the day was planned. But now because of our living situation—our own home—the kids and I have dead time involved too, and that's real important. We didn't have that the first 6 months we were out. We didn't have the space to have that time. We had an 8 by 10 bedroom where I had a set of bunk beds and a single bed. That was it. We did a lot of traveling, parks and things, play, fun. Now we lead a normal family life, you know: fun activities mixed in with regular home life—school, work, chores, you name it, play, laundry, meals.

"Absolutely" essential to their parenting, according to these exceptional fathers, was open dialogue, the continuance of which they saw as their responsibility, not their children's or the former wife's. Although communication was direct, not channeled through the children's mother, the family communication system was triadic: When it came to parenting, father, child(ren), and mother were inextricably linked regardless of the divorce. The communication matrix was deliberately developed, nurtured, and sustained.

When children lived some distance away when they were with their mothers, as was the circumstance for three of the nine men, special efforts at maintaining contacts were needed. "Checking in" and "touching base" was part of these fathers' parenting repertoires. "We always talk three or four times a week, I call her every couple of days. Sometimes she calls me. The regular phone contacts help. I mean, you know, when I first moved here, I thought I had to send a letter every day and call the next day. I still send letters and we still send cards back and forth but it's not every day. I think we've become more comfortable with this. But I never let more than a couple of days go by without calling her. I need it. She needs it." The frequent contacts worked, he noted as he continued: "I don't think that we have to reconnect when she comes. The relationship is always there, it has always been there, and continues to be there. The language, I guess, is that we're bonded; that lasts. I'm the one who has to adjust though, it's so hard when she leaves. I just feel lost for a few days. It's a tough adjustment for me. It happens every time, still."

On rare occasions, when an issue was deemed to be potentially explosive, the former wife was "left out of the [communication] loop." This co-custodial father, whose collaboration with the children's mother was the most constricted of these nine, discussed a recent situation in which one child after the other had not come to his home as scheduled. He decided to talk directly with his oldest son without first conferring with his former wife because she was a party to the behaviors in question, at least to the extent that she knew the children were not following the established arrangements.

> So we were out to dinner. I asked him, "What's going on here?" He said, "Well, we're feeling like we're being ping-ponged." "Oh, ping-ponged." "Yeah," he said, "we have to go to mom's house, come to your house, and back and forth, like a ping pong ball." So I said, "Hmmm. Well, when you go over to your friend's house, like after school and then have to go home, that's not being ping-ponged?" So I used those kinds of experiences and he recognized it. I asked him where he got the term. He said, "Well, I don't know, Dad." Their mom's standard answer when I ask her something is, "Well, I don't know." I said, "Well okay, but consider this: I'm your father and we have a divorce situation and so we have two households. There's mine, where you're at home with your father; when you come with me you're not being ping-ponged. Then you're at your mother's, that's not being ping-ponged either. We are a family." I said, "So next week you're all three coming to your father's." So they all three came. We stopped playing that game. I'm not sure what it was about, but I don't want to press them on it. Everything seems normal.

The father whose former wife's boyfriend had begun to stay overnight in the home with the children present described a conversation with them and his efforts not to convey his negative and turbulent feelings.

> I asked my kids what they thought. My youngest thinks he's a pretty nice guy, he plays with them. I think my middle one is the one having more of the effects. My oldest one, who's a little more verbal, expressed rather calmly that he's having difficulty but he's going to come around. I said, "You're having difficulty, but you're going to come around?" [laughing] I'm not that calm by nature, but I was trying to be calm so they wouldn't see my initial reaction. If I sit there and tell them how I really feel, because I don't like it, then I create a situation in which they feel they can't talk to me because this is the way I feel. So if I tell the child psychologist, she helps me. Plus the fact that when I know what's going on in their own minds, then I'll know better how to treat them. If I tell the teachers, they're aware of what's going on and can help the kids and tell me if the kids have some needs or some problems. At least I can do these things, and it seems to work so much better [than confronting my former wife].

Circumventing the former spouse was a precarious move. The parenting partnership worked out between them required a level of basic trust that, in turn, necessitated joint decision making and continuing dialogue about their children. Talking to their children about a serious matter without consulting with the former wife was done only when the potential risks were deemed less costly than those in addressing her.

Assessments of Children's
Development and Well-Being

The nine nurturing fathers were overwhelmingly positive in their assessments of their children: They had adjusted well to divorce and the postdivorce situation and their relationships with both parents were affectionate and appropriate.[2] These evaluations, like the men's descriptions of their parental relationships and roles, were supported with particular and numerous examples. For instance: "You know, their behavior around me is fine, we have a good time. They are relaxed. They're familiar with all of this. They fight with each other, misbehave. Not the whole time, of course, but they act normal. They don't behave any differently here or there [with their mother] apparently." Another co-custodial father said, "My kids are happy. My kids don't have any real adjustment issues. They never did seem to. They're totally comfortable with this arrangement." Having a de facto custody situation in which his children lived primarily with their mother, this father asserted that "they are all really blossoming, and they've never shown any lasting adjustment problems. And they openly care about each other. It's wonderful to watch, these kids." He continued, describing an incident involving his youngest son.

> This is the only kind of relationship he really knows or remembers so this is kind of what it's like for him.[3] It's really interesting because his kindergarten teacher said, when we went to his parent conference and asked how he was doing, the teacher said, "He really is a terrific little guy." They'd asked the class to draw pictures. Oh, they were making something for Father's Day or something like that, one of those days. One of his little friends got all upset and started to cry. The teacher asked why he was crying. The little boy said, "I have two fathers and one mother." And the teacher was kind of flabbergasted and my son put his around him and said, "Oh, I have two fathers too, why don't you just make two pictures? That's what I'm doing." It was a message that it's okay, this is the way things are.

Although noting that they could support only their own viewpoints, these men insisted that their former wives shared their positive evaluations. Because jointly assessing their children's development and emotional states was one of the pillars of the parenting partnerships, they frequently discussed their children with each other. A close link between divorced men's cooperative and friendly relationships with their former wives and affirmative assessments of their children has been discerned in other research. Koch and Lowery (1984), for example, noted that "men who reported a satisfactory relationship with their former spouse were also more likely to have positive and enjoyable relationships with their children. The parent-child relationship was not related to visitation when the influence of the former spousal relationship was held constant. This suggests that, after divorce, parental cooperation facilitates the quality of the father-child relationship" (p. 63). And in her exploratory study of 85 divorced couples, Ambert (1988) found that "both men and women in friendly ex-couples showed a very high level of satisfaction with their children: on a 5-point scale, they scored 4.6 while, in the dislike ex-couples, men's satisfaction was 3.7 and women's 3.3" (p. 341; see also Ahrons and Wallisch 1987a, 1987b).

When asserting that their children were developing "normally," the nurturing fathers typically demonstrated some understanding of the stages of child development and growth, and range of "normal" behaviors. Most attributed this knowledge to their intentional efforts to become informed. All but two of these fathers had sought personal counseling or parenting education courses subsequent to separation and divorce. Five, including this next father, had pursued both.

> My two children are great kids, wonderful people. They're both very smart. They listen to me, not that listening to me is the measure of them being great kids. But they're very responsive and social. How to put this? I have read lots. Supposedly young kids from divorce are very serious and sober, distanced. But they're very touchable, affectionate, funny. They have great senses of humor, especially the younger one. They do and say wonderful things. I guess it's the luck of the draw, they're just great kids. I worry all of the time. Do I give them too much or too little? I took a parenting class. I read a lot, and I'm in therapy. And my parents try to encourage me all they can. They say, "Does it feel like the right thing to do? Then do it!"

Not only were the nurturing fathers' assessments of their children far more positive but their evaluations were more complex and multifaceted than those offered by most participants. Children's adjustments involved more than the actual marital separation and divorce. Moving and changing schools had involved major transitions for some of their offspring. Being introduced to his new woman friend too soon after the separation had delayed his children's adjustments, explained a father of two. Two other men noted that their offspring had to cope with their mothers' shifting to full-time from part-time employment just before or right after separating; another child's mother had gone from no employment to part-time work. And over half of these fathers believed that their own impatience, which they attributed to the stresses associated with the divorcing process and related emotional conundrum, contributed to their children's initial anxiousness.

These fathers were emotionally invested in their positive evaluations of their children: Intimately involved in the rearing of their children, their assessments reflected on them as parents. Problems or concerns could not be disowned by being laid at the mothers' doorsteps. Moreover, they wanted to believe that all of them—children, themselves, and the former wife (the children's mother)—were getting on with their lives and doing well. Nonetheless, these men's assessments of their children were not sanguine and categorical, and each carried residual concerns that divorce-related problems could emerge for their children at any point and potentially be long term. But the problems, or possible ones, facing their children differed from those identified by most other fathers. For example, rather than having to learn to cope with continuing tension and conflict between the parents, as was commonly the case, this father's child had to learn to accept the divorce despite the parents' amicable relationship.

There was one period where she finally, I think she reached the age of 6 or 7, that she started—I think because there was so much of my presence there—wanting to know why I didn't stay and was still leaving. We went through that period for a very brief time. It was just a matter of my and her mother's consistency, I think, that paid off. We explained to her each time she got upset, she cried, we explained the same way each time that I did not live there. It had no reflection on any of our relationships, just I did not live there. "I had my own place. You have your place and that's the way it is. The way it's going to be." And, "No, I was not going to just stay one night." A couple of times she would say, "Well, just stay tonight." She would cry. And I would say, "No, I'm not going to." Now I can go back and stay with them. . . . I'm not saying that when she's 15, she won't have a problem with it again. Or she may have other questions that she didn't have when she was 6 or 7 or 8.

Not having both parents readily available for conversation or consultation, the consequence of the parents living in separate homes, was a challenge confronting their children, according to each of these nine men. As a co-custodial parent stated: "They're not able to share their daily experiences with mom and dad at the same time. They don't have a mommy and a daddy who they can sit down on the couch together and share with. They have to tell their news twice and I think lots of time it gets lost. I think I lose a lot. Mom loses a lot."

Circumspection about their affirmative assessments was coupled with cautiousness about the possibility of being overly sensitive to the reputed adverse effects of divorce on children. This person had initiated his divorce and accepted less than equal parenting time to spare his children the potential trauma of a custody struggle.

> One thing we do get into, maybe my former wife more than me, is over-psychologizing about the impact that divorce and separation is having on the kids. "Well, the reason they're doing this or that is because they're acting out." And while to some degree that might be true, I never think of that as the first issue. I think they've been extremely fortunate in terms of a relatively smooth, nonanxiety-filled separation and divorce of their parents. While we have our disagreements, I think we certainly try to keep those disagreements, and there aren't many of them really, we do keep them out of the listening range of the kids, just as we tried when we were together. But I think there is a tendency to read too much into probably what is just normal child development process.

Referring to a recent book on the effects of divorce on children, he continued: "Will *my* daughters have 'a difficult time in developing relationships with men of a lasting and meaningful nature because their mother and father got divorced'? That begins to read a little too much into dysfunctions with male and female relationships. Anyway, most [men and women] are having difficulties; many are clueless about how to develop meaningful relationships today, period. We all can see that relationship problems aren't limited to families with divorce. Is this just a self-interested interpretation? I don't know. It's something I keep having to ask myself."

This next father, having a de facto shared parenting circumstance in which everything—childrearing, caring time, economic providing—was divided equally, was uncharacteristic in his assessments of his children. He felt split, torn in two directions. On the one hand, he "had to conclude" that his children were well-adjusted and relatively unaffected by the divorce. He believed they were benefited by no longer being exposed to their parents' arguing and unhappiness. On the other hand, he was convinced that children are invariably harmed by divorce and that his children could be no exception. To believe otherwise, he insisted, "was pure foolhardiness."

I want to make sure that they understand that they're not out there all by themselves even though this is a horrible time in their lives. . . . On the outside, they're two very happy, compliant kids. They love to please. But it frightens me with the oldest sometimes because I don't see it as a normal 6-year-old who wants to be so compliant or pleasing as she does. They're happy from what I can see. . . . As they get older, maybe they'll begin to understand why they feel the way they do and become able to verbalize that. I hope that I'm a parent and that their mom is a parent who is able to sit down and get them to talk about living in two separate homes and being different.

He was seeking a marital reconciliation despite the past marital strife with his former wife and his affection for another woman, from whom he had parted, in order to minimize the long-term damaging effects of the parents' divorce: "It's hard to make a blanket statement that it's not the best thing for kids for a couple to stay together. I haven't been convinced of that in my situation yet. And I doubt if I ever will be." Furthermore, marital reconciliation would insure his involvement in his children's upbringing: "I'm doing it because of my overwhelming fear that I'm going to lose these kids [because of divorce]."

The men's lingering concerns that their children were adversely affected by divorce, or "must be," was reinforced by the responses of others. Children of divorce were, at least according to the judgments of some, inevitably damaged and stigmatized by divorce. They complained, as did custodial mothers in an earlier study (Arendell 1986), that their efforts to minimize the trauma of the family disruptions were undermined by the social climate. For instance, this father, who had not wanted to divorce, had subsequently formed a highly collaborative parenting partnership with his former wife. "Our son [at 6 years of age] had some problems in school at the beginning of the year, which we talked to the principal about, problems like not being able to sit still, not finishing his work, having difficulty concentrating. The first thing the principal said was, 'It may be because of the *dysfunctionality* of the family.' That's what he said." Despite these parents' many efforts to maintain a loving and stable environment for their children, their family was stigmatized by the parents' divorce, labeled for its arrangements, not its functioning.

This next father was "furious" because his children were discriminated against because their parents were divorced and they were Latino. After struggling with the local school district to have them taken out of the English as a Second Language program—where they were placed, he argued, only because he was an immigrant and a divorced parent—he enrolled them in a parochial school where they were mainstreamed immediately into regular classes. Both were consistently high achievers who regularly earned places on the school's honor roll.

> I always make sure that if anybody is going to tell me anything or look down at me for being a single parent, I immediately jump all over them. I hate that kind of an attitude from anybody. I don't care who they are—lawyers, neighbors, teachers. I've had some pretty serious arguments with people who tried to depict me in a particular way because I'm a single parent. I remember at the registration of my kids, one of the teachers, "Oh, you're a single parent." "Well, is there something wrong with it?" Right away she apologized for about 30 minutes. But I'm very defensive when it comes to that. I want my children treated for who they are, not for who is in their home. My opinion is that they go to the school to learn, that is their job. If they aren't learning or there is some problem, tell me. Don't give me some stupid explanation that because the mother isn't there, that the children are learning disabled. It's completely wrong, whether it's the father or mother who is not in the home.

PERSONAL LIFE COURSE
DEVELOPMENTAL ISSUES

Unlike many of the other men in the study, the primary-parent fathers did not eagerly anticipate the time at which their youngest (or only) child would reach age 18 and thus "emancipate" them, "freeing" them of economic responsibility and, "finally," of the former wife. Rather, they lamented the inevitable changes that would come as their children became more mature and autonomous. "I realize that when they're in high school, they will want to do other things on weekends [than spend the time entirely with me], and I know I will have to go through the pain of adjusting. I thought I had this parenting thing all figured out, but I'm realizing that I have to make major adjustments now that they're getting older. Now I have to figure out how to let go of them." Talking about the challenges in maintaining his close relationships with his children as they became older, especially because they lived several hundred miles away much of the year with their mother, this next father expressed particular concerns about his relationship with his oldest daughter who was now a young teenager:

> I want to make sure that she realizes that it's okay to talk about some of these things, and the only way that I know how to do it is by dealing with the issue head-on. Saying, "I haven't seen you in 3 or 4 weeks and I have to tell you that I miss you, but I also want to let you know that it's okay for you to lead your own life. What are we going to do to stay close? What are we going to

do? I'm worried that emotionally you're going to be going in a different direction." I understand when she doesn't come. The reasons she has are legitimate. There are things going on in her life and that's okay. We're making some adjustments. But it still worries me.

Being divorced and having their children live between two parents' homes accelerated developmental issues associated with children's growing up. These issues were entwined with the residual fears that divorce would lead to the "loss of my kids." The "normal" family life cycle, in which children grow and mature over the course of the years and gradually become more autonomous and independent, separating more steadily from dependence on the parents, was disrupted and separation was occurring "prematurely." These fathers feared that both they and their former wives were kept outside of whole segments of their children's lives given the amount of time children were away from them when with the other parent. Integral involvement in their children's upbringing and close collaboration with the other parent did not offset these concerns.

A Price Exacted

Contented with although not complacent about their postdivorce situations, and particularly their children's general well-being and development, these fathers confronted unique dilemmas. Role and identity conflicts were ever present and far more significant than those experienced by most of the other participants. In defying conventional expectations and behaviors, and in spite of their high levels of parental satisfaction, they received little social or institutional support in being caring fathers.

Tensions and conflicts between work and family were standard experiences for these fathers, as they are for many American parents (e.g., Cohen 1989; Coltrane 1989; Pleck 1985; Hochschild 1989; Thompson and Walker 1989; Schorr 1989; Martin 1991; Hayes, Palmer, and Zaslow 1990; Presser 1988). Rather than helping to dislodge the notion of the separation of spheres—family or private and work or public (e.g., Bernard 1981; Cancian 1987), parenting after divorce reinforced it. The institutionalized context remained unchanged even in the midst of dramatic family and individual changes. Moreover, the coordination of the multiple demands of employment and family assumed some unique dimensions given their alternative family arrangements. This custodial father, who while married had worked numerous jobs "in pursuit of the American dream" and whose former wife was unavailable to assist in child care or rearing during the initial year or so following divorce, described his adjustments.

I've had jobs: construction, office, insurance companies, investment company. I used to work for Metropolitan, I was what you call an "upper manager." Finally, the only way that I could watch my kids and keep my sanity, so to speak, and having the problem you can't find anybody decent to look after your kids—somebody who really cares for them as much as you do, there's nobody but yourself—I quit my job and started my own business. I gave up the idea of becoming a CEO somewhere. I started my own carpentry business. This way when my kids were in school, I could be working. I could go for an hour, be back an hour, leave for another hour, and not have to punch a clock or answer to anybody. I can set up my own hours, do what I want, and make as much as I want. And I can do some furniture refinishing and building here when they're at home. I could make much more [money] but I keep time for them. And I made enough so that I bought a house, my own. I have a house. I have a business. I have the kids. How happy can you be! But still I would like more time with them. It's my constant refrain.

The others, who retained paid salaried or wage work rather than turning to self-employment, were expected by managers and bosses to make private arrangements for family needs: Parenting was not to interfere with work. When employers did recognize conflicts between work and family, insisted the men, accommodations were aimed at mothers, not fathers. As men, if they sought or took temporary relief from employment for family matters, they were "eyed with suspicion." Certain that coworkers and supervisors watched them to see if the managing of parenting impacted their productivity, they were sensitive to others' attitudes and responses. Secretiveness was necessary, concluded this father: "At work, sometimes they look at me as if there's something wrong with me for this. For instance, when I took off to go to the nursery school open house last week, I had the day coming. I wasn't cheating them. But they acted like it was a strange thing for me to do. You know, I have pictures on my desk of my son and people seem to get turned off by it. But women have pictures of their children and everyone seems to accept that. Female employees at my work don't get treated the same way. Now I just won't tell them when I take off for him. If he's sick or something, I'll just tell them I'm sick."

Particularly eroded after divorce was adherence to the conventional definitions of masculine success through occupational or career advancement. This manager of a major national chain store, for example, discussed his deliberate move to shared parenting nearly 2 years after divorce. "Since the divorce I have had to change priorities. I went from a more than 65-hour-a-week job to just 40 hours and took a major cut in pay. I was constantly moving up to more challenging stores, ones that were in a mess and I was to straighten out. So I went initially from more than $60,000 a year to just $18,000. . . . I have to admit that sometimes I wonder if I've just bombed out. I mean, look at my [low] salary." And workplace flexibility held this custodial father in a job which paid less than others he might have secured.

> What happened is a lot of absences with the kids being sick and one thing and another. Fortunately, I worked for a guy who was fairly good about it. I would get pressured from time to time. But I kept my job. My job has never paid well, but it gave me 12 personal days a year and I'm at the point, where I've been for years, that I have 4 weeks' vacation every year. So the personal time, whatever you'd call it, is usually gone by September. The vacation time—it's not one of those places you have to take it in weeks or something— you could take a day here and there, that worked well in the summer. I've always taken the last week or so of August off, usually because that's when day camp and whatever ended, usually in the middle of August. So it [vacation time] was usually just about enough to finish off the year and take care of the summer.

Others declined offers of promotion that would have required relocation.

Concerns about having too little time for parenting and supervising their children were common. Most at issue was the family-work nexus, not the former wife. Discussing these worries, this father confided: "I'm not always satisfied with the amount of time I have with him. . . . I worry about all of this, how to make a living and how to be available at the same time. But I have to make a living and I have to have a life. So does his mother. I would like much more time with him. Maybe if I win the Lotto, then I can give him a full-time father. Short of that, I don't see it happening. I worry about it though. But I need to work, of course, and so do the best I can." Empathy for the former wife with respect to work-family conflicts was common among this group. She, too, experienced obvious conflicts between work and children. For example: "During the summer I was worn out, worn out, by the time she, my daughter, left. But I realized what her mother goes through. We'd get up, we'd get ready. Rush, rush. I'd take her to day camp. I go do my work, you're here, you're there, you're there, you pick her up, you go home and do this and do that, wash clothes, and so on and on. I enjoyed it, really enjoyed it, don't get me wrong. But it did wear me out. I needed to be able to take more time off but couldn't. I realize this is what her mother goes through most of the year. It's tough, really tough."

The most overextended fathers were the several who received little or no assistance from the former spouse or the children's grandparents. This particular father was most similar to a majority of custodial mothers in other studies in that he was raising his children basically unaided (see

Arendell 1986; Hetherington et al. 1978, 1982; Weitzman 1985; Wallerstein and Kelly 1980; Wallerstein and Blakeslee 1989).

> I know a fella who has four children, single, and people refer to him the same
> way I've heard them refer to me: how wonderful he is, as if these were
> someone else's kids he was raising. And every morning he takes all four kids
> to his mother's house, drops them off, and then either goes there after work
> for dinner, or goes home and cleans up and goes out and gets his kids later
> when he's finished his date. He and I were comparing notes and he thinks he
> has it just as hard as I do. I kept on trying to say, very tactfully, "How would
> you like to do this without your mom?" And I really didn't get any
> response. I guess it's all where you're coming from. Probably not too easy
> for him either. But I think some people have no idea how it is when you have
> nobody around to help. This guy irked me a little bit with his complaining
> about how tough he's had it. I wish to God I had somebody occasionally to
> leave them with for a few hours, somebody who cares about them.

Support from parents, which was extensive for five fathers, included
emotional, child care, financial, and other logistical. Help ranged from
occasional and supplementary to regular and essential. This father of three
elementary school-aged children credited his mother with his successful
managing of co-parenting and the holding of two jobs: "She's a jewel, she's
helped out a lot. See, a lot of guys don't have the situation of all the help
from their parents. Where would I be without my mother?" And this next
person observed,

> A lot of it [managing successfully] is my parents: They create an environment
> in which it's possible to be loving and supportive. They're there when I'm
> feeling down and alone. They support me in every way. They paid for the
> divorce. I'm now paying them back. They take only $300 a month for the
> apartment, which is nothing in this county. Stable is the word to describe my
> family. They make it possible for me to give my children stability; actually,
> for both their mother and me to give them stability. I'm not fully alone, or I
> would be in serious trouble.

Two other men turned regularly to their parents for financial assistance. "I
mean, I go shopping the day before the kids come, so the refrigerator is
full. The cereal boxes are all there. They walk in and just take the food out,
but before that I've been at my mother's house eating. My parents know
my situation. I've borrowed more money from my mother and father. They
have been fantastic people. They've been my major support, even more. I
can't describe the support they've been." Relying on support from parents

was justified and rationalized even as it was appreciated: Depending on parental assistance as an adult was a previously unforeseen development, unique to the divorce situation. Such dependence significantly countered basic assumptions of successful adult manhood: "Who would have thought this could happen? I'm a grown guy who depends on his parents."[4] Several noted, however, that they received special treatment because they were men actively participating in the rearing of their children. Such support came almost always from women (see Arendell 1986).

Although relatively better off financially than the vast majority of divorced custodial mothers, as is the case nationally (Holden and Smock 1991; U.S. Bureau of the Census 1990, 1991, 1992; Burkhauser and Duncan 1989; Furstenberg and Cherlin 1991; Duncan and Hoffman 1985),[5] none of the nine fathers was affluent, and three faced continuing challenges in meeting their basic living and child-rearing expenses. With the exception of one father who had stopped paying support some 6 months previously, these men both paid child support and covered numerous childrearing costs directly as their children lived with them a sizable proportion of time. Two-thirds of these fathers had little or no discretionary income. For instance, this father was left with little money for covering recreational activities with his youngest child. Covering the costs of the divorce, establishing a second home, paying child support, contributing to an older child's college expenses, and adjusting to a decrease in earnings depleted his resources. "It's a little hard for him now with all the things I'm going through with the economic problems. I can't say, you know, 'You're staying with me this week. What are we going to do? Go to the movies, go ice-skating, go fishing?' I don't have the money to spend on him and he knows that and it bothers him a little bit. It bothers me a lot."

Being a primary parent carried opportunity costs as well as immediate financial ones. Each of the nine believed his career or occupational advancement had been restrained by his family situation. Offered as evidence were the achievements of brothers or male friends and coworkers who had proceeded more rapidly through the ranks than had they. None of the six who discussed the need to pursue further formal education in order to better secure his and his children's economic futures had been able to do so. Time and money shortages interfered with implementing plans with an eye on the future: "There's so much going on here that it's almost impossible to juggle school responsibilities with family responsibilities with work responsibilities. And where would I find the money? So going back to school remains on the back burner; I need to if I'm going to advance in this work and I would love to have some adult intellectual conversation, but I just can't do it now." Gilbert's (1985) observation that limits on career development are not solely voluntary (although they are largely voluntary) has particular resonance with respect to these men who were actively engaged in both parenting and employment after divorce.

Social Lives and Isolation

Restricted by the dual demands of primary parenting and employment was an independent social life, especially dating. The eight unmarried nurturing fathers were constrained in courtship activities by the competing demands on their time, energy, emotions, and finances. They were not kept from more potent social lives principally by the overflow of negative feelings about their former marriages and spouses, as were some other participants. Even when somewhat hesitant about entering an intimate relationship, these men were not distrustful or disdainful of women generally. Rather, their limited involvement with women had to do with the need to make pragmatic choices, as this person indicated: "What social life? Usually I play handball on Monday nights, though sometimes I have the kids on Mondays. Tuesday I see the kids. So that leaves Wednesday and Thursday open because Friday, Saturday, and Sunday I'm with the kids. So anything I want to do has to be on Wednesday or Thursday, and sometimes I work those nights. And sometimes I'm just tired or have things to do: bills, taxes, groceries, and such. It rolls by, time goes by."

Working a second job to supplement his income and "stay up with the child support," this next co-custodial father's normal state by the end of each week was fatigue. He managed to hold two jobs and be an active parent only because his mother stayed with his children in the early morning hours when they were still sleeping and he had to be at work. His social life was limited to activities with his children: "There's just no room for any woman. By Fridays I'm really pooped, okay. So when my kids are there, I put in a movie, and we call it junk night. We have pizza and popcorn and any kind of junk they want. I fall into the chair and fall asleep while they watch the movie. But by Saturday I'm okay and we're up and out." And this custodial father "coveted" his rare moments of "spare time": "I get my free time now, people think I'm crazy, but I get my free time sitting in the car outside the places I take them. Saturday mornings is the highlight: While they're at their gymnastics lessons, I go and get breakfast in this little diner and I have a paper and I have an entire hour, which is outright solitude. It's all to myself, and I know where they are and what they're doing."

Like many of the other men in the study, and despite their limited dating, seven of the eight unmarried men engaged in innovative actions (the other was seeking a marital reconciliation) proclaimed, "for the record," as one said, his heterosexuality: "It's not that I have any problems 'that way,' I'm just too busy to meet someone," said one co-custodial father. A father of two talked about the evolution of his attitudes in which he came to identify more with being a parent than an unmarried, "available male."

> Not dating hasn't been a problem. As far as dating, I think the last time I was into sort of dating, oh, I guess, was 3 years ago. That was the last time I was really into going out. I mean, I could date anybody who had two legs. But now I'm in a different place. I'm going through a different process right now. My kids need more attention. The days of drinking and coming home with a girl for several days is all gone. I did that some when the kids would be at their mother's. It has nothing to do with my kids—the change, well, maybe it does. It's the process of life; it's not that important anymore. I know I can walk into a bar and pick someone up. It used to be a challenge. It's not anymore. I don't know what it is. Not that there's anything wrong with me. I'm perfectly capable! I don't show any stress when I meet a woman. I think I'm growing up. I think I'm more mature and coming to ask myself questions before I do things. I'm more sensitive to other people too, their needs, women's, which I wasn't before. Now I want to know someone, no more of the "just picking some girl up." I have more respect now, I think, maybe as a result of this parenting. I'm changed.

Tensions about their sexuality were heightened by the labeling of their parenting involvement as "feminine," "female-like," or "womanly." Further, they were subject to two standards. If they were not involved sexually with someone, they argued, then others suspected their sexual identity. On the other hand, if they were openly active sexually, they were subject to the criticism of being an irresponsible parent. This father's complaint about the negative images surrounding the "stereotypical divorced male" was common even though the particulars of his situation were unique:

> There's only one mother who has taken the attitude, she's taken a side [in the divorce], and she's uncomfortable with my kids. But my kids were good friends with her children, and I don't understand why she's taken the attitude that her kids can't come over here. I have nobody staying at my house or anything. I'm not serious and even if I was, I've always expressed to anybody I've dated, and that's been very few girls, that, "Past 8 o'clock, you can't stay." As my kids begin to get ready for bed, then she has to go and that's just the way it is. But again, it's the myths out there, the images about divorced fathers, that make people suspicious about me and my kids.

The bigger concern overall, however, was the social isolation related to parenting. It was particularly keen for the sole custodial fathers because their associations with their former spouses were not as intense as those of the men sharing custody. This custodial father said, for example:

> I think it's the biggest drawback, the terrible loneliness of being a single parent. Terribly lonely. You're not only physically by yourself, but you feel isolated, you feel like you're in a cement box sometimes. There's no one, you know, I mean, whoever taught us how to raise kids? It's got to be tough enough with two parents. But, at least, then you have somebody, at least creative debate, you know: "Well, that was stupid and you should try this." Instead, it's been making every decision. So there was none of that, and that really, really is tough.

Although a problem identified by divorced custodial mothers as well (Arendell 1986; Kurz 1995), the problem of isolation may have been somewhat greater for these divorced fathers, given basic gender differences: Men tend to be less self-disclosing, to seek less support or assistance, and to be more emotionally dependent on their spouses than women (Sattel 1976; Pleck 1992b; Rubin 1983; Tannen 1990). Only the one remarried father, and to lesser extents, the two men having especially close friendships with their former wives, did not feel as if they "were quarantined," isolated from whole segments of adult life in the carrying of parental responsibilities. The drama of engaged parenting as a divorced father occurred largely behind closed doors, opened only partially to the former wife and, for five men, to one or both parents. But parents were not peers. This father, whose child lived with him about two-thirds of the time, characterized his quandary:

> Lots of people question me, or imply that they're suspicious. I have four groups, ways, people relate to this situation. One, they think there's an ulterior motive, like I don't want to ever pay her any money. Two, they think I'm just such a good person, a wonder, really. But no one ever thinks that about a mother who raises her child after divorcing. Three, they suspect that my ex-wife is incompetent, that she's mentally ill or something else is the matter with her and I'm just keeping it a secret. Four, they think I'm just crazy!

A major element in their perceptions of isolation was the separation from other men and nonfamilial activities. "A couple of the guys I've known—I don't have very many male friends, I didn't have any to start with and this, raising my children, just sort of killed it; I was never around anymore—but a couple of the guys I would know would say, 'Come on and do so and so,' and I'd say, 'No, I can't do that, my daughters' dance class is in an hour' or something. They'd look at you like 'So?' They really don't understand. What could we talk about? We have nothing in common, nothing, really." He continued later, describing his efforts to locate "male camaraderie."

> I really was all excited and everything about going to these men's things because I'd heard they were so successful. And I put myself through all kinds of hell to go there, because I'm not that kind of social animal and because it meant arranging for someone to watch my kids. So I get there and we sat in a huge circle and there were about 25 people, men, I mean, and we were supposed to share our thoughts and feelings. And when it's over, they give you their literature and I found it proselytizing; it becomes a kind of new religion. I can't deal with it. And I couldn't believe what kinds of things were being said. Men were talking about the minimum frequency it was okay to see your kids and what was a reasonable amount to pay for a cleaning woman. Most of the time was spent talking about ways they were getting back at their ex-wives. To tell you the truth, I never found any support in the few times I tried different groups for fathers either, for divorced fathers. They just seemed to live in a totally different world than I do. So it's tough that way. I don't relate much to men, and most women view me, maybe any involved father, with some suspicion.

The one remarried father also experienced feelings of isolation:

> I sometimes feel emotionally isolated from my male peers. And that may be my own problem. I don't like to go bowling on Wednesday evening, you know. I'd much rather do this kind of stuff [sit and talk]. There are times when it's pretty lonely and maybe that's my own choice because apparently there are other male groups where if you want to get some kind of emotional support for what's going on, it's out there. I have to push myself sometimes to go out and do "men's things." But I haven't felt a real strong need for that because things have seemed okay. There's even some groups for parents who only have their kids part of the time. I don't know other fathers with shared custody like this. I did go to one of those single-parents' groups once but found it depressing and grim. It didn't work out like I'd hoped it would.

Several men, in contrast, felt their participation in groups somewhat moderated their isolation; two belonged to fathers' rights groups and another to a single-parents' group comprised of both mothers and fathers. Even so, and despite the shared experiences that led them to participate in the groups, relations with other members were constricted. The person working on a marital reconciliation, for example, had told no one in his fathers' rights group about his actions or hopes even though he met with some members weekly and had been exploring reconciliation for nearly 8 months. Furthermore, both men who belonged to a fathers' rights organization noted that their affiliations often felt conditional: Their particular perspectives and experiences were not shared by the other members in their groups nor, they argued, was their commitment to cooperating with the former wife understood. One had walked out of a recent meeting because of the group's "woman bashing": "I'm going back, I've decided, but next time it starts up, I'm stating my opposition to this kind of regression."

Distanced from other men, the nine primary parent fathers found they held much in common with women, especially mothers of dependent children with whom they more typically shared a child- and parenting-centeredness (see Risman 1989; Risman and Schwartz 1989; Schwenger 1989). Generally, those few persons who were consistently supportive of their efforts as divorced fathers were women—the former wife; mother; sisters; in several cases, friends; and in one situation, a present wife. But, consistent with gender relations generally (Franklin 1988; Kimmel and Messner 1992), other men's assessments carried substantial weight, and the impact of their indifference or censure was not offset by women's support. This father, for example, received extensive emotional and logistical support in his parenting efforts from his former wife and his mother, and friendly encouragement from a coworker, also a woman. Nonetheless, to his regret, he was estranged from the significant men in his life. "Even my father and brother told me to get on with my life, to start acting 'like a man' and let these kids go, that my involvement with them would just interfere with my work and future relationships with women. They told me that other people were going to think I was a wimp, you know, unmanly, for not standing up to my former wife."

Identity Management

These nurturing fathers, men engaged in innovative lines of action, varied from the other respondents in their definitions and management of self (Goffman 1959; Hochschild 1983, 1989; Perinbanayagam 1990, 1985) as well as in their behavioral styles and objectives. Unlike the majority, who presented themselves as overwhelmingly confident and certain, the primary-parent fathers were openly ambivalent and questioning.[6] On the one hand, they were far more satisfied with their postdivorce circumstances, and especially their parenting and parental relationships, than the others. On the other hand, their "deviancy" exacted a price. Identity questions persistently confronted them. They and others around them defined their actions and perspectives as being appropriations of "women's activities and experiences" or "mothers' lives." In explaining that he had "tried to be a mother, I have tried to be a mother, to . . . do with them in given times what a mother would do," this co-custodial father followed his characterization with the question: "So who, what, does that make me?" And this co-custodial father of a young child, for example, commented: "I just have to keep asking myself: 'Why are you doing this?' I need to constantly ask myself if I'm doing this for my child or for some other reason. Am I trying to prove something? Who am I hurting in the process?"

Rejecting the constraints and consequences of conventional expectations and seeking alternative lines of action, these men nonetheless used the norms of masculinity as the measure of self (Lyman 1987; Pleck 1992a, 1989b; Hantover 1978; Kimmel and Messner 1992; Arendell 1992b). The person least beset with identity questions was the one remarried father who had established, together with his former as well as present wife, a parenting coalition. His "deviancy" as a nurturing father engaged in collaboration with his former spouse was actively offset by other phenomena: a successful and satisfying profession, a stable and happy marriage and family life, and a wife who actively encouraged him and validated his efforts.

These divorced fathers live in a society stratified, ideologically and institutionally, by gender. Particular performances of gender carried more status and power than others, and, accordingly, these men found themselves wanting. Self-doubt and reprisals were reinforced by past inexperience, isolation, and the extensive interdependency with the former wife that countered the cultural paradigm of divorce. Adopted strategies and attitudes—cooperation and nurturing, for instance—were contrary to the major themes of the gendered divorce discourse. Fathering was not a recognized primary component of adult men's definitions of self (Chodorow 1978, 1989; Hearn 1987). Identity—the masculine self, battered by the "failure of the marriage"—was not unequivocally shored up by the success of postdivorce parenting. Although workable, successful, and pleasurable, the primary focus on parenting, despite their pride in it, and the interdependency with the former wife were aberrant.

These men encountered both a lack of institutional support for alternative postdivorce behaviors and fathering and a broad failure of the culture. Social arrangements and cultural scripts conveyed a body of expectations that, as men, their ultimate obligation, when all of the other niceties about modern men were stripped away, was personal autonomy intertwined with interpersonal dominance, even if benign. The one expected ongoing postdivorce family obligation was economic support. Yet, because the obligation to provide financial resources countered autonomy and the divorce situation undermined the authority typically related to provision, even that responsibility was subject to dispute. Not called for and largely unsupported was their steadfast caring for and emotional nurturance of their children. These men's search for a parental discourse was personal, privately negotiated with the former wife and their children and, in one case, also with a present wife. But a postdivorce child-centeredness was a poor match for the power and pervasiveness of the system of gender stratification and beliefs. It was the masculine discourse of divorce that was socially assumed and supported: Divorce was war and they were supposed to be victorious or, at least, ever-persistent warriors, not compromising caregivers. Having actively sought and forged satisfying and workable parental relations and involvement, in conjunction with the former wife as their children's other parent, these men saw themselves and were treated as cultural eccentrics. In sum, whereas the majority of fathers in the study were at odds with the divorce outcome, the former wife, and often, if sometimes only by extension, their children, it was the nurturing fathers, engaged in innovative lines of action, who were at odds with the cultural norms and expectations of masculinity.

Notes

1. In his more narrow phenomenological study of 10 divorced custodial fathers as primary parents (which only a minority of the 75 participants in the present study were) and independent of any gender analysis, Frey (1986) discerned 10 themes: "The structure [to the experience of being a divorced father as primary parent] was comprised of a multitude of constituents. These constituents were: primary parenthood is a role that is actively pursued; for the primary parent, there is lessened free time; for the primary parent, a closeness and an identification with one's children develops; being a primary parent is a continuous job; the primary parent develops a sense of commitment to maintaining the role; being a primary parent can simultaneously be experienced in terms of opposites; the role of the primary parent is filled with uncertainty which causes one to question one's parenting abilities; as a primary parent, one develops new realizations about oneself and one's children; as a primary parent, one becomes more aware of the effects divorce can have; as a primary parent, the establishment of a family is actively sought; as a primary parent, one becomes more aware of others' reactions to single parenthood" (p. 7).

2. See Aquilino (1993) for a comprehensive overview of the findings on young adult children of parents who divorced; children raised by fathers have continuing close relationships with them, unlike children whose fathers were noncustodial parents.

3. Regarding the relationship between children's adjustment to divorce and their ages, see, for example, Chase-Lansdale and Hetherington (1990), Emery (1988), Furstenberg and Cherlin (1991), Wallerstein and Blakeslee (1989), and Zaslow (1988).

4. The fathers involved extensively in parenting, whether as co- or sole custodial parents after divorce, had kin relations that more closely fit Gerstel's description of the kin relations for custodial mothers than for fathers; not the parent's gender but the parenting situation is the central factor. As observed by Gerstel (1988): "Children serve as integrators with kin for both mothers

and fathers, but in very different ways. For men, they provide access to kin as emotional providers; for women, as instrumental ones. This gender difference is perhaps best explained by the patterns of custody characteristic of our sample and the nation as a whole. Women, who typically provide the daily care of children, turn to kin for practical help. In contrast, men typically have only weekend care (if that) of children. As other studies show, one of the major problems of such 'visiting' fathers is keeping the children entertained, finding them social and leisure activities to enjoy. . . . Consequently, as our study suggests, these fathers turn to and receive help from kin in ways that ease their 'special burden' " (p. 217).

5. Myer and Garasky (1992) reported that according to analyses of the Current Population Survey, in 1989, mothers in mother-only families had a mean personal income of $12,959 compared to a mean personal income for fathers in father-only families of $24,178, or 187% of the mothers'. A comparison among divorced parents specifically indicates that the incomes of fathers are 1.5 times as high as the incomes of mothers. Nonetheless, significant numbers of father-only families also live in poverty: 18.2% of father-only families with children under age 18 are poor, compared with 7.3% of married couple families with children and 42.6% of mother-only families. "Even though they are not as poor as custodial-mother families, a significant percentage of custodial-father families are very poor, and many more are near-poor" (pp. 17-18).

6. The options perceived available in divorce by the participants were not of equivalent value. "How we live our lives as conscious thinking subjects, and how we give meaning to the material social relations under which we live and which structure our everyday lives, depends on the range and social power of existing discourses, our access to them and the political strength of the interests which they represent. . . . Having grown up within a particular system of meanings and values, which may well be contradictory, we may find ourselves resisting alternatives. Or, as we move out of familiar circles, through education or politics, for example, we may be exposed to alternative ways of constituting the meaning of our experience which seem to address our interests more directly" (Weedon 1987, pp. 26, 33).

10

MAKING PROGRESS,
MAKING POLICIES

Being an American divorced father in the early and mid-1990s meant being caught in the hiatus precipitated by changing family and gender. Divorced fathers were situated in a culture that offered them few guidelines about their places and activities as parents (Seltzer 1991b; Tepp 1983). Furthermore, the context facing these men was one in which conformity to the conventions of masculinity, together with the related individualistic ethic, often opposed the demands of engaged, nurturing parenting. The dictates of masculinity ran contrary to the interpersonal demands induced by divorce from their children's mother. Two distinctive and poignant paradoxes stand out in this study. On the one side, men responding to divorce in conventional ways, both traditionalist and neo-traditionalist fathers, had little empathy for their children and scant self-reflectiveness even as they were frustrated and discontented with their parenting circumstances. Confident that their perspectives were the appropriate and correct ones and that their preoccupation with the former wife inescapable, these participants made little connection between their actions and unsatisfactory relationships with their children. These men did not see how they contributed, in attitude and action, to the estrangement from or limited emotional connections with their offspring. They failed to recognize that it was their children who were the actual losers, subjected unwittingly to the continuing antagonisms between their parents and hindered from having a closer and more expressive relationship with their fathers. Parenting and relations with their children were treated as a byproduct of a range of issues (see also Koch and Lowery 1984), a bottleneck of uneasy interpersonal associations, structural restraints, conflicted emotions, and thwarted hopes. Handicapped by their prior family experiences, especially their reliance during marriage on their wives for facilitating the father-child relationship and managing the routines of daily caregiving and nurturing, most did little to extend their parenting repertoire. Most of these fathers did not even imagine alternative parental relations; they basically wanted more of the limited kinds of association they already had.

Similarly, at least some, perhaps most, of these gender conformists turned to traditional definitions and behaviors. This was not only a backlash response to unfamiliar and often unwanted marital changes. They perceived no other options, or none that were relatively cost free in that they would not have called for voluntary relinquishment of some power and control. Their vision was stunted by the discourse of masculinity and, in turn, the masculinist discourse of divorce (Arendell 1992a, 1992b). Despite the extensiveness of such claims in many of the participants' accounts, men's claims of oppression, in general, are found wanting: Men's or fathers' rights discourse, appropriated from various discourses, including "liberal legal feminist equality rhetoric" (Fineman 1991, p. 5), frames issues in the terms of formal or symbolic equality. It ignores, denies, or obscures persistent gender inequities experienced by women even though gender disadvantage remains overwhelming women's (Rhode 1989). The arguments that men are oppressed as men, at best, "rely on a philosophically inadequate theory of social oppression; at worst they are disingenuous and self-serving" (Clatterbaugh 1992, p. 188).[1] As used by the participants, rights-talk was overwhelmingly self-serving, although shortsighted (even if unrecognized), and obscured family relationships and children's interests (see also LaFollette 1992; Seidler 1992).

Cultural ambiguity surrounding men's family roles, especially in the context of divorce, also clouded their views and reinforced their claims of legitimacy about their chosen paths. And, as counterproductive as conventional responses proved to be with respect to parenting involvement and quality of the parental relationship, they were socially endorsed. Society remained stratified by gender, continued to promote the gender belief system that perpetuated sexism and inequality, and supported a lack of reflectiveness about the source and basis of entitlements. The division of labor, particularly in the family and with respect to parenting, continued to be, for the most part, gender based.

On the other side of the paradox, the nine men engaging in innovative strategies of action and involved, nurturing parenting felt isolated and deviant. Gender subversives (Bem 1993), they gave priority to their children's well-being and were dependent on a small nucleus of people—especially the former wife, but also, for some, their parents and, for one, a present wife. Often deemed to be unmanly by others for their cooperative actions with the former spouse and childrearing involvement, they partitioned their paid work lives from parenting as best they could. Their career and income advancements were impeded. Few supports were available, and role conflicts were common, as they are for divorced mothers engaged in primary parenting (e.g., Arendell 1986; Kurz 1995).

That these exceptional men were able to negotiate the current cultural maze surrounding divorced fatherhood, as well as the emotional turmoil surrounding marital dissolution and changed living arrangements, and locate and construct alternatives to typical behaviors was, in one sense, remarkable. Pressures to conform came from nearly every direction. In another sense, these men's abilities to act in innovative ways testifies to the creative, fluid, and emergent character of social life: Gender roles and identities and family relationships are dynamic and unfolding, continuously open to renegotiation, redefinition, and adjustment (e.g., Cohen 1989; Risman 1989).

How these men both subscribed to and participated in the themes of the masculinist discourse of divorce and forged unique courses of action warrant much greater research attention. "Best case scenarios" in divorce can direct our attention and acceptance away from the more standard prototype in which conflict and tension reign and in which children in divorce often either basically lose one parent or become the pawns in their parents' interpersonal struggles. Moreover, understanding how such men maneuver in creative ways and cope with the personal implications and effects of the "crises in masculinity" can abet the efforts to enrich fathers' parenting participation and move us collectively toward gender justice. On a more abstract level, examining the trajectories particular individuals travel during times of significant social and personal change can enhance our understanding of what it is to be a social being, a character in the human community.

The predominant strategies of action evidenced by the participants in this study—traditionalization and innovation—and the related types of divorced fathering—traditionalist and neo-traditionalist, and nurturing, respectively—point us to several perplexing problems. How can we help better direct their attentions to their children? How can we protect and secure parental rights *together* with parental obligations, irrespective of marital status? How can we achieve gender fairness, in the here and now?

More specifically, with respect to the participants in this study, the traditionalist fathers offer the most dismal and bleak picture in terms of proposing successful intervention. Given their behaviors and perspectives, it is unlikely that these fathers will move toward best case scenarios in divorce. At the same time, these men should not be written off; parent education about children's needs and developmental processes would likely help some to better understand their children and improve their parenting involvement and relationships. Personal counseling can assist them to move beyond their anger and bitterness, to let go emotionally of the ended marriage and preoccupation with the former wife. Counseling intervention can help foster greater empathy for their children and recognition that they are distinctive persons.

The neo-traditionalist fathers offer a more viable opening for divorce intervention and positive movement. Through education and consciousness-raising processes, focusing on family, parenting, and the gender system and its consequent sexism, with its costs and constraints, these fathers can be encouraged to examine more critically their basic assumptions. By investigating their taken-for-granted notions about men and women and their relationships, and about marriage, family, and divorce, some may discern a wider array of options and choices. By emphasizing and reinforcing these men's concerns about their children and helping them to better separate their former spousal from parental roles, these men can be further empowered as caring parents. Development of various problem-solving and conflict resolution strategies and emphasis on parental obligations as inseparable from parental rights can assist them in devising alternative definitions of their situations and courses of action. Counseling or mediation intervention is particularly promising for this group because, as the nurturing fathers' situations demonstrate, highly involved, satisfying parenting after divorce is enhanced by parental collaboration and cooperation (see also Parkinson 1987).

The nurturing, primary-parent fathers, engaged in innovative lines of action, offer a model of what is possible in divorce and fathering. What these men need, as do divorced mothers who face similar circumstances in terms of role overload, work-family conflicts, and economic hardships, is to have their situations lightened. Why should it be so difficult to be a nurturing, engaged father? Where are the institutional and ideological supports for parenting? Needed also is a more vocal and widespread critique of the conventions of masculinity: that caring fathers are subject to criticism and stigmatization points to a seriously flawed ideological system.

Policy Issues

Divorce is not only a personal trouble but a public issue (Mills 1959), more generally, and this study directs us to an array of policy issues. Policy needs and ramifications are broader than the interests of particular individuals or a single constituency. Thus, although this exploratory study focused on a small number of divorced fathers living in New York, the policy proposals I suggest here extend to children, mothers, and fathers, and society, more generally. Although the processes and outcomes of divorce and every participant's experiences and perspectives need examining, significant change will come about only with the continued evaluation and transformation of marriage and family and the related ideological and stratification systems. The policy areas addressed, then, pertain to a variety of family issues.

Almost inevitably, family members hold competing interests in divorce. Children's interests are not necessarily synonymous with their father's (see also Fineman 1991), contrary to some participants' insistence. Indeed, evidence of having disparate interests was demonstrated by the lack of empathy for their children that was shown by more than a few of the men who responded in conventional ways to divorce. Obviously, children's interests are not necessarily synonymous with their mother's, either. Just as the concerns of family members are not always the same, neither are the coping strategies of particular individuals equally beneficial to all. Hetherington (1987) indicated, for instance, that "coping strategies that lead to positive outcomes for one family member may adversely affect the adjustment of another member of the family during divorce" (p. 204).

Children's interests are inextricably linked to changing family arrangements and ideals and changing gender roles. Family policy scholars recognize that changing cultural definitions and social roles and statuses can contribute to competing concerns. For example, Kamerman and Kahn (1978) observed that "whatever the rationalizations, it is evident that what was viewed as best for father in the past was not always best for mother or child; from the perspective of traditional roles, what is now best for mother may not be best for father or child; what is best for the child may not be best for father and mother, and so forth. Here, one goal of family policy could be to ease the tensions that may emerge as a consequence of the changing roles of men and women" (p. 480; see also Thorne 1993). Policy innovations and reforms must acknowledge these complexities. The task is not an insurmountable one. Swedish family policy, for example, explicitly recognizes that in some instances choices *between* family members and *among* family roles may need to made (Kamerman and Kahn 1978, p. 480).

Numerous social science and legal scholars and researchers have delineated family and divorce-related policy suggestions.[2] For example, Ferreiro (1990) summarized strategic goals in divorce: "Based upon the preponderance of research available about factors affecting children's well-being in divorced families, it is reasonable to take the position that public policy for divorcing families should be directed toward three objectives. It should (a) protect the ties between parents and children, (b) minimize parental conflict, and (c) ensure adequate child support. A fourth objective, that custody laws be gender neutral is grounded in ethical and political values about equity" (pp. 423-25). Divorce-related policy issues, despite the previous attention given them, warrant restating: Although now a common occurrence, divorce often results in dismal family outcomes and emotional, interpersonal, and economic turmoil.

Each of the following policy domains is a necessary component of a comprehensive national family policy. Of the 14, the first 6 are relatively more specific to divorce than the others, which apply to family more broadly. The last three areas—ending sexism, valuing unpaid caring labor, and redefining our collective responsibility to children—come full circle, bringing together the findings of this study with the larger sociopolitical context in which these participants experienced divorce. Gender, family, and child-rearing, more specifically, are at the crux of these recommendations.

Divorce policy, ultimately, must keep the well-being of dependent children the central concern. This priority is consistent with family policy more generally (Zimmerman 1988), of which family law is a component (Kamerman and Kahn 1978). For too long, the welfare of children in divorce has been given short shrift in the United States (Riley 1991; Glendon 1987). Parents' interests are not to be neglected, of course, "so long as they are kept subordinated to the interests of children" (Chambers 1984, p. 499).[3] Addressing the needs of contemporary children in divorce can contribute to an advancement in children's situations in American society, generally.

DIVORCE LAW AND LEGAL PROCEDURES

The recent "divorce revolution" in family law is incomplete (e.g., Riley 1991; Sugarman and Kay 1990). Legal scholar Kay (1990), for instance, argued that the project begun with no-fault divorce reforms remains unfinished. The goal is "to create a legal framework for family dissolution that is perceived by all parties as fair and that will facilitate a healthy emotional transition between marriage and divorce. Such a framework should enable all family members to be as free as possible of anger, bitterness, and anxiety stemming from the dissolution process itself, and to help them rebuild postdivorce lives that are relatively unscarred, if not unaffected, by the earlier family breakdown" (p. 11). Legal reforms must move "toward a nonpunitive, nonsexist, and nonpaternalistic framework for marital dissolution" (Kay 1990, p. 28). Among other things, such movement will help promote a nonpathological view of divorce. Reviewing the divorce research, Raschke (1987) concluded: "By reconceptualizing divorce as one of the normal consequences of marriage and hence removing it from the socially created and socially defined deviance milieu of our society, concerned professionals will be taking a step out of the 'dark ages of sick deviance' into the 'sunlight of healthy normalcy.' The millions of men, women, and children whom divorce has already touched and will touch in the future will be the true beneficiaries" (p. 620; see also Kurz 1995). And, in his summary discussion of treatment for divorced fathers, Friedman (1982) noted: "It is not only men, in their role as separating fathers, who lack a 'best case' model for divorcing fathers, it is also the psychiatrists and social workers who treat them, their wives, and children, and the lawyers who provide services to both or all three groups involved" (pp. 566-67).

Fault grounds for divorce need to be abolished entirely in the states where they still exist, including New York. All states need to further eliminate practices and procedures that contribute to adversarial relations. The various legal weapons of the "divorce war arsenal" must be abolished. One area that must be closed off is the readily available option in many states for repeat and spurious custody challenges and court hearings. Continued comparative evaluation of the various states' divorce laws, processes, and bureaucratic arrangements is also imperative. For instance, the dual court system—the state supreme court and family court—involved in New York divorce and related determinations needs evaluation. How prevalent, for example, is the strategy, described by some respondents, of playing one court system against the other to delay the divorce and/or gain ground while transacting a settlement? What are the benefits and costs of the dual court system? Does it meet the objectives for which it was established?

Although the no-fault principles for marital dissolution can be uniform and applied systematically within respective states, policies regarding other facets of divorce settlements, such as property division, child custody, and economic support, must be more flexible: "The facts [about who divorces and what families are affected] mean that there is no stereotypical couple (if there ever was) around which one can structure marriage, divorce, and remarriage policy. The law must serve this diversity of families with different needs" (Sugarman 1990, p. 2). At the same time, legal statutes must ensure key protections, which requires establishing baselines and precluding broad judicial discretion in some areas. The biases of juridical practitioners should have no place in divorce. Whether the evaluation of individual family situations is best accomplished within the legal system, even if only on the periphery, or outside it, with the use of trained mediators, for instance, remains a debated topic.[4] Further study and evaluation are needed, and informal as well as formal decision-making processes must be explored. "The overwhelming majority of divorce disputes, over 90 percent by some estimates, are settled by the parties. Therefore, reform must be directed at improving the informal processes rather than at substituting a more formal, and probably less desirable, one. . . . There are no easy answers in the reform of divorce any more than in criminal justice or other legal processes. But it is clear that we cannot reform the divorce process until we observe the actual dynamics of the procedure by which it is accomplished" (Erlanger et al. 1987, p. 603).

A PRIMARY-CARETAKER RULE

Child custody requires constant policy evaluation and continued reform. Numerous scholars have called for a rejection of the standard of the best interests of the child because of its conceptual ambiguity and broad judicial latitude (e.g., Weitzman 1985; Fineman 1991; Emery and Wyer 1987a, 1987b; Mnookin 1975; Furstenberg and Cherlin 1991; Polikoff 1983). For example, legal scholar Chambers (1984) stated: "The current approach states use for resolving custody disputes in divorce—a case-by-case inquiry into the best interests of the child—has many flaws. One has been that neither legislatures nor custom has provided judges with a coherent framework for thinking about what children's interests are. A second, equally serious, has been the inability of judges to make accurate determinations, under the circumstances prevailing in the context of litigation, of the quality of most individual children's relationships with their parents or of parents' skills at childrearing" (p. 568). Another problem with the present standard is its utility in the argument, increasingly put forth by some fathers' rights groups and argued by some participants in the present study, that a child's best interests are economic. In this view, the parent with the higher income should be granted custody; not surprisingly, given the principal promoters of this perspective, the higher earning parent is usually the father. Claims based on superior economic resources are unjust, as Chambers (1984, p. 541) concluded: Men benefit from institutional discrimination in the gender-stratified society, which they collectively maintain, only then to claim its privileges and demand further ones as earned entitlements (see Franklin 1988).

Called for by various scholars criticizing the best-interests standard is the development and implementation of some version of a primary-care-taker rule.[5] The primary caretaker is defined simply: the parent who "has typically spent far more time giving care to the child than the other parent" (Chambers 1984, p. 501).[6] In his call for a primary-caretaker rule, Chambers (1984), drew on child psychology's attachment theory, arguing the importance for children to remain with the parent who has provided the bulk of the nurturance and care (see also Goldstein et al. 1979).[7] "Three arguments can be advanced for preferring placement with parents who have been the primary caretaker: they know more about the particular child; they have demonstrated a dedication to meeting the child's needs; and they have built an emotional bond with the child that may be more important for the child to sustain on a daily basis than whatever bond the child has with the other parent" (Chambers 1984, p. 527).

Similarly emphasizing the well-being of children as the overriding concern in divorce and custody assignments, Furstenberg and Cherlin (1991) noted that "the primary caretaker standard for physical custody would help some parents function effectively (since fewer mothers would be pressured into accepting unfavorable financial settlements) and would reduce continuing conflict by decreasing the possibility of custody dis-putes" (p. 116). And, after thorough and systematic analysis of the effects of recent divorce law reform and practice, Fineman (1991) was unequivo-cal in her advocacy of the primary-caretaker rule. She anticipated, and rebutted, likely criticism of the recommendation: "If fathers are left out [by the use of the primary-caretaker rule for deciding custody], they can change their behavior and begin making sacrifices in their careers and devoting their time during the marriage to the primary care and nurturing of children. Men can exercise the same 'free' choice that women tradition-ally have in these matters, adjusting their outside activities to care for their children. Men who choose not to devote their time and attention to the children during the marriage but wish to care for them after the marriage ends can bargain against the mother's entitlement as primary caretaker by making financial or emotional concessions at divorce" (p. 183).[8] Acknow-ledging that not all couples adhere to the conventional division of parent-ing labor, she maintained, "In cases in which both parents acted as true primary caretakers, I predict that few custody battles would ensue and the cooperative patterns concerning the children established during the mar-riage would continue" (Fineman 1991, p. 183).

A further advantage to moving to a primary-caretaker standard is that the proclivity to define custody as a symbol of victory or defeat would be dislodged or, at least, shaken loose. Parents would know the basis on which custody determinations are made (Chambers 1984). Moreover, the rights to be secured would be explicitly and first children's: the *right to the stability and security* of the primary-parent/child relationship. That maternal custody would predominate, at least in the near term as the conventional parenting division of labor persists, would not in itself be evidence of gender injustice against men. It would be, however, a pronouncement and cautionary tale regarding the consequences of traditional family arrangements in contemporary times: A mother's primary caretaking may be conducive for men during marriage (e.g., Polatnick 1973),[9] but becomes problematic on divorce. Just as women need to recognize the risks in being economically dependent in marriage should divorce occur,[10] men need to appreciate the potential consequences of not participating fully, from the time of a child's birth, in parenting and child caregiving. Furthermore, within the primary-caretaker rule, the promotion of increased paternal involvement would be placed primarily on the predivorce and not the postdivorce family (Fineman 1991). Biological claims and the vestiges of patriarchal prerogative would be subordinated to social ties and emotional bonds.

Shared or Joint Residential Custody

Certainly when both parents are interested in sharing childrearing after the dissolution of their marriage, they should be supported in developing and carrying out parenting partnerships or, in lieu of that level of cooperation, workable and satisfactory parallel parenting arrangements (Furstenberg and Cherlin 1991), with high levels of involvement for both. Empowering parents to explore shared physical custody requires that attorneys and others abandon adversarial approaches, implicit as well as explicit, to custody and other determinations.

But, as desirable as it might seem in the abstract, shared or joint residential custody cannot be a standard imposed on parents irrespective of their desires, situations, or family histories and relationships. To uniformly mandate joint custody under the auspices of equal treatment of parents, as numerous fathers insisted should be the objective of divorce law reform, is to subordinate children's interests and needs by disregarding their primary emotional connections and to perpetuate marital inequities (Fineman 1988, 1991).[11] Moreover, opportunities for former spousal dissension and disagreement are tremendous in joint custody situations.[12] Research findings are unequivocal that children are adversely affected by high levels of parental conflict; the jury is still out on the consequences for children of joint residential custody (Furstenberg and Cherlin 1991; Kline et al. 1989; Maccoby, Depner, and Mnookin 1988; Block et al. 1986, 1988; Hetherington et al. 1985; Emery 1988; Chase-Lansdale and Hetherington 1990). Shared custody and its outcomes warrant much more extensive study.

Joint Legal Custody

Continued investigation of joint legal custody is needed also. On the one hand, shared legal custody may be appropriate, perhaps even in a majority of cases, given the objective of better ensuring the participation of noncustodial parents in decision making regarding their offspring. Furstenberg and Cherlin (1991), exploring the issue and noting that it affords opportunities for former spousal conflict, nevertheless ultimately recommended it: "A preference for joint legal custody would reaffirm fathers' continued right to maintain an important role in the child's upbringing and would send a signal that fathers are expected to be responsible for their children even after a divorce. To be sure, the gesture would be largely symbolic—fathers with joint legal custody don't seem to act differently from those who don't have it. But it would provide a moral foundation for efforts to involve fathers in continued child care and increase the amount of child support they pay. . . . [It is] a high risk/high payoff strategy" (p. 113; see also Maccoby et al. 1988, 1990; Mnookin et al. 1990).

Because joint legal custody can be problematic, especially in that it creates a context in which the noncustodial parent can exercise undue power and control over the custodial parent, finely tuned, affordable, and unbiased mediation services must be available. Avenues for prompt discussion and conflict resolution must be ensured to minimize the possibilities for one parent to exploit or misuse the other. Caution is in order: Even if supports are available, joint legal custody may be an inherently flawed arrangement. Custodial parents must have the ultimate authority to safeguard their children, which may mean, in some situations, making decisions and taking actions without the noncustodial parent's involvement or consent.

PARENTAL ACCESS

The visitation system needs to be reconsidered concurrent with the establishment of the primary-caretaker standard. To be meaningful parent participants and to nourish satisfying and deep connections with their children, noncustodial parents need access to them (Arditti 1990). Although in this study, for example, having limited access under the standard visitation arrangement was not unsatisfactory in and of itself to all respondents—indeed, numerous fathers chose to have even less involvement with their children than that offered by the agreement—for others, the level of visitation assigned and allowed was woefully inadequate.[13] The possibilities for meaningful parenting were undermined further for men wanting more involvement. The constricted parental access only served to reinforce their sense of being marginalized, increase the emotional distance from their children, and exacerbate feelings of anger and frustration that, in turn, heightened the potential and rationale for former spousal conflict.

Equality in time allocations is not the overarching issue with respect to access. As one of the fathers desiring more parenting involvement indicated, the division of time might be as disproportionate as "40-60, 30-70, 25-75, or 20-80." No single formula will fit all families. The point is that the standard visitation arrangement, as assigned to a majority of these New York participants, afforded far too little time and involvement for those wanting to be active parents.

Implementation of more flexible access guidelines can be facilitated by assisting custodial parents to recognize that an increase in the other parent's involvement is not indicative of a diminished parental commitment or an evasion of responsibility. Nor is it a personal defeat (see also Emery 1988). Even though these qualifications are in order, a custodial mother is not usually the major barrier to father involvement: Various studies indicate that many custodial mothers desire greater paternal involvement with their children (e.g., Arendell 1986; Wallerstein and Kelly 1980; Wallerstein and Blakeslee 1989; Furstenberg and Nord 1985; Kurz 1995). More custodial mothers would likely encourage increased father involvement if conflict were kept to a minimum and services for handling dissension and disagreement readily available. Already divorced persons acting toward each other with parental goodwill and cooperation alter their arrangements as their situations evolve, needs demand, and children desire.

Where a nonresidential parent's motivations for greater parental involvement are suspect, for instance, believed to be aimed primarily at harassment of the former spouse, preventive measures can be incorporated into a visitation agreement. For example, arrangements can be made whereby children are transferred between parents through an intermediary, thus enabling former spouses to avoid direct contact. A schedule for the nonresidential parent's telephoning of children can be established so that the parent and children are assured of regular and frequent contact with each other, without needing to directly engage the other parent. Similarly, such arrangements can be established for children's telephoning of the custodial parent when with the other. And, as is already being put into place across the nation, determination of the level of support and manner of distribution can be removed from private negotiations and exchange. By minimizing the possibilities for confrontations between antagonistic parents and providing mediation services for prompt intervention when trouble occurs, the emphasis is placed on dependent children and their relationships with their parents. Presumably, then, those nonresidential parents whose primary interests are other than the children's well-being will fade away when denied opportunities for continued engagement and conflict with the former spouse (Furstenberg and Cherlin 1991; Furstenberg 1988).

CHILD SUPPORT AND A CHILD
SUPPORT ASSURANCE PROGRAM

The mandates of the Family Support Act of 1988 go a major distance toward insuring that a nonresidential parent's obligations of economic support are appropriate and met (Garfinkel and McLanahan 1990; Garfinkel, McLanahan, and Robins 1992; Corbett 1992). Extending the Child Support Enforcement Act of 1984, the Family Support Act directed states (by 1992) to establish uniform formulas for determining the level of child support awards. Additionally, the act required states to devise and incrementally institute an administrative collection and dispersal system for payments, removing them from the private exchange between parents (Martin 1990). Both the child support award and payment compliance are enhanced greatly by the act (Garfinkel, McLanahan, and Robins 1992) even though loopholes remain, implementation and enforcement are uneven. And a primary flashpoint for conflict between former spouses is eliminated within the revised system.

The recent reforms in the child support system are not a panacea for all of the economic problems confronting children and their custodial parents. For instance, little attention is given to nonresidential parents who choose unemployment or underemployment to avoid making or to significantly lower child support payments. Nonresidential parents still can enter the underground economy, to better circumvent the enforcement mechanisms of the child support system, and/or relocate to another state, although the federal government is seeking to close these options. Importantly, the economic circumstances of children whose parents are poor or near-poor are not addressed in the recent reforms of the child support system (e.g.,

Sidel 1992; Martin 1990; Garfinkel and McLanahan 1990; Krause 1988, 1990).

Needed now are the development and implementation of a child support assurance program, such as that existing in various European countries (Kahn and Kamerman 1988; Garfinkel 1988; 1992), through which a residential parent would receive support even if the other parent delayed or defaulted on payment. A leading proponent of a child support assurance system in the United States, Garfinkel (1992) argued: "All parents living apart from their children would be obligated to share their income with them. The sharing rate, or percentage of the nonresident parent's income to be shared, would be specified by law and would depend only upon the number of children owed support. The resulting child support obligation would be collected through payroll withholding, as are income taxes and Social Security taxes. A child with a living, nonresidential parent would be entitled to benefits equal to either the child support paid by the nonresident parent or a socially assured minimum benefit, whichever was higher. Should the nonresident parent pay less than the assured benefit, the government would make up the difference" (p. 8). Such a program would give "promise of reinforcing parental responsibility, increasing equity, and reducing poverty and welfare dependence" (Garfinkel 1988, p. 334).

Broad public as well as scholarly discussion of the child system must continue. Despite recent attention to the glaring inadequacies of the system and attempts to better enforce private obligations of support to dependents, fundamental gaps within and divergent perspectives on the system remain largely unaddressed (see Chambers 1979, 1988; Krause 1988, 1990; Haskins 1988; Ollerich, Garfinkel, and Robins 1991). Arditti (1991), for example, criticized the general approach to child support enforcement: "While receiving support among some researchers and policymakers, [it] ignores social, emotional, and interpersonal factors that may contribute to men's resistance to pay child support" (p. 108; see also Krause 1988, 1990). Also neglected are situations of competing interests. For example, most Americans believe that divorced persons should be free to enter subsequent marriages, taking on additional family responsibilities, irrespective of their obligations to children of prior marriages. How are competing financial obligations to be resolved in circumstances, experienced by perhaps a majority of divorced wage earners, in which resources simply are not sufficient for contributing adequately to two (and sometimes more) families' economies? Some parents simply are too poor to contribute in any significant measure to their children's support. Some will refuse to pay no matter what the sanctions (see Chambers 1982, 1988; Rhode and Minow 1990; Krause 1990).

A privatized child support system, as presently exists, and a support assurance program are not the only possibilities for dealing with the economic needs of children and, although indirectly, their residential parents. Other possibilities, which could be implemented singly or in various combinations with the present or a reformed child support system, include, for example, a divorce insurance system and/or a universal family or children's allowance.[14] On marrying, for example, couples could be assessed a premium toward a national divorce insurance fund. Or married couples could be levied a small annual tax. A universal family or children's allowance is preferable, given the overarching goal to protect all children from the ravages of poverty and low-income conditions. But, realistically, such an allowance system is unlikely to be implemented any time soon in the United States because of the nation's ideological commitments, especially to the ethics of individualism, self-reliance, and self-sufficiency. Either option—divorce insurance or a family or children's allowance— will require reform of the tax system.

Revisions or alternatives to the child support system alone are not adequate for situations in which a spouse, most typically the wife, was a full-time parent and homemaker during marriage and thus was economically dependent. As various researchers have demonstrated (e.g., Weitzman 1985; Seltzer and Garfinkel 1990; Rhode and Minow 1990; Burkhauser and Duncan 1989; Holden and Smock 1991), the present system of spousal maintenance or alimony, which in most cases aims at limited and short-term support, is deficient. Special economic protections for the full-time homemaker-mother or, less commonly, the full-time homemaker-father, need to be instituted. The divorce-related impoverishment of midlife and older women urgently demands policy attention (Arendell and Estes 1991; Kitson and Morgan 1990; Morgan 1991).

MEDIATION AND COUNSELING SERVICES

Families undergoing transitions or experiencing difficulties living with divorce need readily available and affordable mediation and counseling services.[15] Further, mediation and/or family counseling should be mandated for all divorcing couples with minor offspring. Scholars and proponents of mediation in divorce, Milne and Folberg (1988) argued: "Mediation reduces hostility by encouraging direct communication between the participants. This facilitates the permanence of a settlement agreement and reduces the likelihood of future conflict. Mediation tends to defuse hostilities by promoting cooperation through a structured process. . . . Mediation presumes that parents have the authority and responsibility to determine and do what is best for their children as well as what is best for their entire family constellation, regardless of how it might be rearranged following divorce" (p. 9). Mediation is not the ultimate panacea, however. Patrician (1984) cautioned that mediation, although often preferable and more successful in divorce resolution than the traditional adversarial-based approach, offers no easy remedy: "All factors that may contribute to custody dissatisfaction or conflict need to be explored and understood in order to design responsible intervention and prevention strategies" (p. 55).

The objectives of expanded mediation services and/or divorce counseling include helping men and women to recognize and deal with their feelings, to disaggregate spousal from parental roles, and to develop conflict resolution and problem-solving skills, all toward less acrimonious divorce and more satisfactory outcomes, especially with respect to their children. Mediators need to be aware of and sensitive to the processes of uncoupling and the range of possible emotional responses (Vaughan 1986; Riessman 1990). Significantly, they need to be cognizant of the effects of gender on perspectives and interactional dynamics and strategies—communication, disclosure, intimacy, problem-solving strategies, and attributions (Tannen 1990; Riessman 1990; Cancian 1987; Hochschild 1989; Pleck 1985; Magaña and Taylor 1993). A well-trained mediation team, consisting of both a woman and a man, can help diminish the possibilities for replicating marital power inequities in mediation sessions. Mediators also must be sensitive to the influences and complex interactions of social influences on family experiences and perspectives such as ethnicity and race, religion, and socioeconomic class status, as well as gender.

PARENT EDUCATION COURSES

Divorce appears "here to stay," like family (Bane 1976). Marital dissolution, in all likelihood, will continue at high rates among couples with minor children (Bumpass and Sweet 1989). Society has a stake in and responsibility for how divorce occurs and affects children (see also Glendon 1987; Chambers 1984). Called for is not a reversal of reforms that have made divorce more accessible and affordable but a closer regulation of divorce with respect to dependent children (e.g., Riley 1991). Parents wanting to dissolve their marriages should be required, in addition to participating in divorce mediation, to complete a parent education course. Child developmental processes and stages, the effects of both divorce and parental conflict on children, and communication and problem-solving processes and strategies would be among the issues covered as would be thorough and informed discussion of custody and visitation options: "As for physical custody, education about options is perhaps the major policy tool available" (Emery 1988, p. 142). Parents would not have to attend the class meetings together but, instead, could be encouraged to attend different sessions in order to exchange child care. Concern for children would be the paramount consideration, dictating social policy even as adults are allowed to terminate their marriages at will.

OUTLAW CORPORAL PUNISHMENT

The use of physical force by any family member against any other must be stopped. Although increasing public outrage and policy attention has been directed at wife abuse (e.g., Harlow 1991; Dobash and Dobash 1992; Chapman 1990),[16] the use of corporal punishment against children "within certain bounds" remains mostly an acceptable family practice in American society (e.g., Straus 1991; Sigler 1989; Gelles and Conte 1990; Gelles and Straus 1990). The line between "reasonable" and "excessive" punishment is, however, at best, ambiguous and subject to widely differing definitions and inconsistencies (Straus, Gelles, and Steinmetz 1980; Straus 1991). Abundant research evidence indicates that physical punishment has dubious value as a teaching or disciplining strategy, promotes distrust and fear, and teaches children to engage in aggressive and violent behaviors. And Straus (1991), among others, argues that childhood physical punishment promotes adult violence and deviance. *Only* in families (and in some school districts, using the justification of *parens patriae;* see Grubb and Lazerson 1988) is the use of force by a bigger and more powerful person against a smaller, dependent, and more vulnerable person allowed. Corporal punishment is a regressive practice that is inconsistent with the child-rearing goals of fostering cooperation and trust. Moreover, the use of physical punishment against children is a carryover of an outdated system of patriarchy (Therborn 1992).

The divorce situation and complexity of modern family arrangements only adds greater urgency to the need to end these practices. After divorce, the issue of the physical punishment of children can become a quagmire. For example, which adults have the right to physically punish children after the family transitions attendant to marital termination: only residential parents? nonresidential parents? stepparents? a parent's boyfriend(s) or girlfriend(s)? maternal grandparents? paternal grandparents? paid caregivers? What constitutes discipline and what constitutes excessive force, and who is to decide?

Changing attitudes in this area will be a lengthy process because many Americans believe parents have almost unlimited authority with respect to the discipline of their children. Thus the use of physical force against minors needs to be ended by legal fiat; simultaneously, a public education program about alternative childrearing practices and disciplinary methods must be developed and implemented. Parenting courses could be instituted at the workplace, for example, for greater expediency and efficiency in reaching the general public. So too, an extensive and systematic media campaign could be aimed at ending all corporal punishment of children and promoting alternatives. It is high time that professionals and caring adults speak out against physical punishment and end their general stance of public timidity on this issue. Just because a majority of Americans, according to national surveys, support corporal punishment does not mean that it is an appropriate or just form of child discipline. As history testifies with regard to various parental practices (e.g., Aries 1962; Levine and White 1993), what is deemed acceptable at one point in time, even if by a large majority, is not necessarily judged acceptable at a later time.

With regard to custody and visitation-related allegations of child sexual or physical abuse, a comprehensive system aimed at protecting children is essential. Children's safety must be the overarching concern. Professionals must be trained in the areas of detecting, responding to, and preventing child neglect and abuse—sexual, physical, and both. At the same time, those who knowingly make false allegations must be prosecuted, and attorneys encouraging or constructing false claims sanctioned. By significantly limiting the possibilities for initiating custody contests, a primary-caretaker rule will help reduce the filing of fabricated charges.

PROFESSIONAL EDUCATION AND LEGAL SANCTIONING OF ILLEGAL ACTS

It is imperative that all persons having professional involvement with families be educated thoroughly in the processes and consequences of former spousal conflict, domestic violence, stalking, and child snatching. Finkelhor and associates (1990), for example, argued that the problem of child snatching can be redressed. An increased focus on deterrence, mediation, and emergency hotlines; more expedient judicial and legal processes; a publicizing of penalties and laws; and enforcement are needed. These apply, as well, to all other forms of harassment, intimidation, and violence. All activities that endanger or potentially endanger the safety and well-being of children or an estranged or former spouse must be met with prompt and appropriate official action. The surprising ease with which numerous men in this study discussed acts of violence or its threats, fantasies of killing or otherwise harming the former wife, and child snatching points to the current cultural acceptability of such practices (see also Kurz 1995). Such acceptability, whether overt or tacit, must be reversed: Every person has a fundamental *human right* to safety irrespective of the nature of interpersonal or familial relationships.

FULL EMPLOYMENT: DECENT MINIMUM EARNINGS AND ECONOMIC EQUITY

All parents must be able to earn incomes sufficient to support their families at a decent level. Even more significant than redressing the inequities and inconsistencies in the child support system is insuring parents' access to adequate wages. An increase in the minimum-wage level and expansion of the earned-income tax program are two significant and available strategies for lifting families out of and above poverty (e.g., Martin 1990). Minimizing economic hardship by insuring decent levels of earned incomes has particular salience for divorced parents. Further, enabling women to achieve economic parity will help to liberate men from the burdens of the good-provider role and loosen the bonds of conventional masculinity, necessary to enable men to participate more fully in parenting before and after divorce. Sociologist Bernard's (1981) question, posed in early analysis of changing gender roles—"What will replace the good provider role?"—may well have been premature. Although long in decline (Bernard 1981; Weiss 1987; Goode 1982; and Furstenberg and Cherlin 1991), the good-provider role, as demonstrated in this study of divorce, remains vibrant and powerful. As it presently stands, divorce often pushes men more fixedly into the good-provider role even though the level of support expected is typically low, offering or expecting from them little else in the way of parenting. Indeed, in marital dissolutions involving minor children, the role is subject to rejuvenation, even if met with resistance by individual players.

The devaluing and denigrating of women and their family activities are inevitable possibilities as long as society remains stratified by gender. Without access to fair wages and occupational opportunities, women cannot achieve social or economic equality with men and will remain in the subordinate stratum. Husbands and former husbands choosing to do so will be able to misuse their power while disclaiming their actions: "As long as economic inequalities still exist between the sexes (and we do not expect these problems to disappear soon), there will remain sex inequalities in marital power, in remarriage probabilities and 'needs,' and in the division of labor within marriage. Thus, as long as men have greater resources as well as alternatives to egalitarian exchange relations within marriage, there is no reason to expect that they will voluntarily move in that direction in great numbers" (Finlay et al. 1985, p. 652).

WORKPLACE REFORMS

The American workplace is not family-friendly (e.g., Hayes et al. 1990; O'Connell and Bloom 1987; Presser 1988). To enable parents—divorced, never married, or married—to better coordinate the multiple demands of family and employment, it is imperative to institute such workplace options as flexible work schedules, part-time employment with benefits, and comprehensive, paid family leave (e.g., Sidel 1992; Martin 1990; Garfinkel and McLanahan 1990).

HOUSING, HEALTH CARE,
EQUITABLE EDUCATION, AND CHILD CARE

Housing, health care, and equitable education are basic rights of citizenship and should be available irrespective of family composition, transitions, or income status. They are components of social policy in all other social welfare states (Martin 1990; Zimmerman 1988; Kahn and Kamerman 1988; Kamerman and Kahn 1978). And all families, without regard to income source or level, need access to decent, affordable, and regulated child care for children of varying ages and needs (Hayes et al. 1990).

ENDING INSTITUTIONAL SEXISM:
DISMANTLING THE GENDER BELIEF SYSTEM

The gender-based inequities of divorce are inevitable in a society organized and stratified by gender: To reform divorce requires transformation of marriage and family. Kay (1990) made the point: "If we have learned anything from the work of Weitzman, Marcus, and others, it is that we cannot expect to remedy the defects of marriage at the point of divorce" (p. 29). Only continued probing and eroding of gender prescriptions and structural arrangements will further undo the shackles of tradition. Risman and Schwartz (1989) asserted that "if we are right, that gender is created by everyday life and everyday institutions, then escaping gender constraints is a matter of redesigning the social structure" (p. 8). More realistic portrayals of and education about marriage, family, and gender can help reduce stereotypes and unrealistic romantic notions that complicate and undermine relationships. Through education, both women and men can come to appreciate how all persons will benefit from the erosion of gender stratification and the conventional gender belief system. Additionally, ending gender stratification, although necessary, is not sufficient: A just and equitable society requires an end to all systems of stratification—class, race and ethnic, and age.

VALUING UNPAID
DOMESTIC AND CARING LABOR

Related to gender and economic equity, and thus to divorce reform, is a transformation of our attitudes and approaches to unpaid family work. The activities of caring for children and dependent adults (who increasingly will be elderly seniors) need to be recognized as the socially necessary and valuable labor that they are (Arendell and Estes 1991; Finch and Groves 1983). We can value and support caregivers, to begin with, by implementing a comprehensive parental and family leave act that applies to all employees, irrespective of size of firm or scope of work week; reforming the public assistance program to insure families a decent minimal standard of living or, preferably, supplanting it with a universal family allowance system; and reforming the tax and Social Security systems so as to not penalize either families with children or caretakers who opt out of the labor force for periods of time to provide care (Arendell and Estes 1991). Significantly, until caring activities are genuinely valued, many men will be reluctant to assume the responsibilities of primary or shared caregiving. And until men participate more fully in child-rearing, the system of gender stratification will persist. Until men share parenting, custody in divorce will be a contentious issue, for many. "We should foster the nonsexist practice of shared parenting for infants and children. If we are successful in doing so, the parents who have experienced this behavior during marriage are more likely to wish to continue that practice after divorce, and to do so voluntarily" (Kay 1990, p. 35).

REDEFINING SOCIETY'S
OBLIGATION TO ITS CHILDREN

The nation is responsible for its children, for all of its children (see Kamerman 1991). The lack of child-centeredness shown by some respondents in this study of divorced fathers was, unfortunately, not unique to them. Rather, it is frequently demonstrated by society at large. Complaints thrown at particular parents or groups about their inadequate parenting care or assumption of responsibility are too often hypocritical, occurring as they do in a society that tolerates a poverty rate among children of over 20%; allows children to live, play, and be schooled in unsafe conditions; fails to provide preventive health care and needed medical treatment; and promotes consumerism and individualism to the neglect and exclusion of primary relationships, family, and community. An examination and reformulation of our dominant values is needed urgently if families are to be places where children can be successfully nurtured and reared, guided into becoming fully functioning, psychologically and physically healthy persons who are competent in interpersonal relationships and able to engage as full members of a participatory democracy. Further erosion of the vestiges of patriarchy and consistent resistance to the systematic efforts to reinstitute male dominance are necessary. And although efforts are exerted to resist the backlash occurring in response to gender and family changes, committed and caring parents must be supported, recognized, and honored as exemplars.

In conclusion, divorce-related policy must seek to insure children's overall well-being, assure fairness for men and women alike, and ease family transitions. Given the difficult emotional character of divorce for most, the persistence and power of the gender belief system, societal ambivalence about facilitating family life and parenting, cultural resistance to gender equity, and continued gender socialization of children along largely conventional lines, it will neither be easy nor quick to transform society. Divorced fathers choosing to be nurturing, actively engaged parents are likely to remain a minority until major social changes are implemented. The times ahead are not likely to be smooth. We must commit ourselves to the goal of fostering a society that empowers families of all arrangements and in every developmental stage to more ably nurture and care for its members. Only a broad-based quest to improve the quality of life for all Americans will move us toward a truly just and decent society. The possibilities for improving American divorce outcomes, and family life more generally, are innumerable. What we have shown to date is a lack of will.

Notes

1. Clatterbaugh (1992) rejects the three conceptual arguments that try to make the case that men are oppressed: the socialization argument, reversal argument, and expendability argument. Only the dehumanization theory "meets the minimal criteria of adequacy" (p. 81), and accordingly, men are not oppressed as men. Summing up an analysis of the organized men's rights movement that has contributed to rights-talk in divorce, Clatterbaugh (1988) noted: "The great

weakness of the men's right perspective, then, is not that it points to masculine burdens but that few are able to accept its elaborate caricature of reality" (p. 82).

2. According to the feminist and poststructuralist theorist Weedon (1987): "As we acquire language, we learn to give voice—meaning—to our experience and to understand it according to particular ways of thinking, particular discourses, which pre-date our entry into language. These ways of thinking constitute our consciousness, and the positions with which we identify structure and our sense of ourselves, our subjectivity. Having grown up within a particular system of meanings and values, which may well be contradictory, we may find ourselves resisting alternatives. Or, as we move out of familiar circles, through education or politics, for example, we may be exposed to alternative ways of constituting the meaning of our experience which seem to address our interests more directly" (p. 33).

3. For recent divorce-related policy discussions, see, for example, Fineman (1991); Chambers (1979, 1982, 1984, 1988, 1990); Furstenberg and Cherlin (1991); Emery (1988); Emery, Hetherington, and Dilalla (1984); Kay (1990); Kahn and Kamerman (1988); Ferreiro (1990); Glendon (1987); Sugarman and Kay (1990); Jacob (1988); and Garfinkel and McLanahan (1990). As is the case with family policy more generally, models for divorce-related policy are available, especially from the Scandinavian countries; see Kamerman and Kahn (1978), Kahn and Kamerman (1988), Zimmerman (1988, 1992), Saldeen (1992), Kamerman (1991), Bradley (1990), Trost and Hultaker (1986), and Sidel (1992).

4. Scholars addressing the debate about whether divorcing persons are best served by attorneys and the conventional legal system or mediators or proposing a rationale for one approach over the other include Fineman (1991), Furstenberg and Cherlin (1991), Kay (1990), Folberg and Milne (1988), Milne (1988), Kelly et al. (1988), Emery and Wyer (1987a, 1987b), and Erlanger et al. (1987).

5. For a profeminist position by a men's group advocating a primary-caretaker rule and rejecting mandatory joint custody, see "Policy Statement on Child Custody Laws," by the National Organization for Changing Men (1989). The statement concludes: "This policy statement has detailed the ways in which child custody laws that have been instituted by men have caused women and children fear, violence, and privation. Men within the National Organization for Changing Men understand that loyalty to other men cannot come at such a cost to women and children. Because silence implies consent, it is time for men who abhor violence against women and children to speak out against this injustice and get these laws changed. Men can no longer hide behind complacency and male privilege, allowing the bitterness and the manipulative, coercive, and controlling behavior of their peers to be the foundation of public policy" (1989, p. 3).

6. Chambers (1984) urged that we take a "child's experience" perspective, drawing from Wald who "has tried to identify such elemental qualities [constituting "primary goods"—essential qualities of a parent or a parent-child relationship— within a family] from the writings in child psychology, child development, and child placement in divorce. The list includes the following: the need to sustain a secure relationship with a parent figure, to feel valued by the parent figure, to enjoy his [sic] childhood day by day, and to develop a range of capacities to function as an adult, most particularly, to be able to love, to have a sense of self-worth, and to have a sense of control over his [sic] life. The child of divorce who has known both parents will also want the opportunity for regular contact with both parents in a conflict-free setting. The writers upon whom he draws are not self-consciously building a theory of 'primary goods,' but the qualities are remarkably consistent with the child's eye perspective argued for in this article" (Chambers 1984, p. 498, foonote 60).

7. For a recent review and synthesis of attachment theory, see Bretherton (1993). Chambers (1984) rejected the argument that the primary caretaker's parent deserves custody as compensation for years of providing care, an argument put forth later by Fineman (1988, 1991). He stated: "It is an argument with strong initial appeal— taking care of children requires great effort, persistence,

and the subordination of personal needs—but it is, in the end, unpersuasive. As a broad moral principle, we should be reluctant to use children as 'rewards' under any circumstances" (Chambers 1984, p. 501). He noted, as did many of the respondents in the study, that rewarding a parent for being a primary caretaker ignores the reality that the division of labor within the family, although gendered, involved a partnership in which both parents contributed. A few participants in the present study extended the argument and concluded that logically, fathers, having been the family breadwinner, deserve custody. Chambers also rejected this argument.

8. Fineman repudiated the arguments that a primary-caretaker standard would be contrary to the objective of reducing conflict in the divorcing process and that parents can informally reach a satisfactory and healthy custody outcome: "Surely we need not resort to the adversary system to perform the fact-finding function of identifying the parent primarily responsible for the day-to-day care of children. Nor should we be optimistic about the ability of parents who are recent adversaries to 'work out arrangements concerning their children' " (1988, p. 774). See Kay (1990) for a discussion of Fineman's position and an urging, instead, of a strategy that encourages active participation by both parents irrespective of divorce: "Contemporary social, cultural, and economic factors all tend to inhibit fathers from any realistic commitment to qualifying as the primary caretaker of children. . . . As I have suggested elsewhere, the legal system should not facilitate the continuance of the conventional practice of designating a single primary caretaker for children" (p. 35).

9. In a still widely cited article, Polatnick (1973) argued that women retain primary responsibility for childrearing and childcare because the gender-based division of labor reinforces the status quo: "The allocation of child-rearing responsibility to women, I have argued, is no sacred fiat of nature, but a social policy which supports male domination in the society and in the family. Whatever the 'intrinsic desirability' of rearing children, the conditions of the job as it's now constituted—no salary, low status, long hours, domestic isolation—mark it as a job for women only. Men, as the superordinate group, don't want child-rearing responsibility, so they assign it to women. Women's functioning as child-rearers reinforces, in turn, their subordinate position" (p. 79).

10. For discussions of the economic consequences of divorce for women, see, for example, Burkhauser and Duncan (1989), Holden and Smock (1991), Arendell (1986), Weitzman (1985), Hoffman and Duncan (1988), Arendell (1987), Morgan (1991), and Kitson and Morgan (1990).

11. Ferreiro (1990) reflected on the dilemma of equity in custody matters: "The issue of equity is different from the other issues in the debate about joint custody. The other questions can be studied by social scientists and answered with empirical data. Equity, however, is a question of values, which belongs in the political arena, and while it is generally agreed that public laws should be equitable, the question is, What is fair? Little is known about how a couple's perception about the equity or inequity of their divorce agreement affects their ongoing parenting negotiations or their level of conflict. Equity theory predicts that perceived inequity will increase the likelihood of conflict: the greater the inequity, the greater the attempts to restore equity; . . . however, equity issues in divorce have not been studied. Under laws which preclude joint custody unless both parents agree, the mother is given inequitable power . . . since women are more likely than men to oppose joint custody and maternal presumption still prevails in fact, if not in law. . . . On the other hand, when presumption/ preference statutes increase the pressure for judges to order joint custody for disputing parents, the parents affected are most precisely those who are the most hostile and least able to resolve their conflicts. . . . This issue constitutes the central dilemma for policy-makers" (p. 423).

12. Views vary in the joint custody debate with regard to how significant a factor parental conflict is. For example: "Probably the best conclusion that can be drawn from existing research is that joint custody appears to be preferable when both parents elect this option but that joint custody should not be *imposed* on unwilling parents in mediation or in a court hearing" (Emery

and Wyer 1987b, p. 478; see also Scott and Emery 1987). In contrast: "Our presumption is that *joint custody* should be considered first in the form of rebuttable presumption, and then ruled out only where appropriate in the child's best interest. . . . Our experience is that the *minimal cooperation* necessary for parents to become *able to do it* can be achieved if we structure joint custody plans to minimize negotiations and maximize clarity" (Williams 1988, p. 4, italics in original).

13. The standard visitation arrangement typically granted parental access every other weekend, with an overnight stay, and one evening a week. Additional time was granted usually for certain holidays and during the summer months.

14. "Tougher enforcement of court-ordered child support and alimony payments is a first step toward making the post-divorce well-being outcomes of men and women more equal. But government support and child-care insurance against nonpayment would provide even greater protection. . . . This would treat at least certain types of marital dissolution as a 'socially insurable' risk that could be financed in a manner similar to other socially insurable market risks" (Burkhauser and Duncan 1989, p. 21).

15. Pearson and Thoennes (1988) suggested that "the low participation in mediation [to date] in divorce is tied to the attitudes of the legal community and public ignorance about the mediation alternative" (p. 431; see also Emery 1988; Emery and Wyer 1987a).

16. For example, hearings have been held recently before Congress regarding domestic violence, specifically wife abuse, and a Violence Against Women Act has been proposed (U.S. Congress 1990, 1991).

REFERENCES

Abramovitz, Mimi. 1988. *Regulating the Lives of Women.* Boston: South End Press.

Adams, David. 1988. "Treatment Models of Men Who Batter." Pp. 176-99 in *Feminist Perspectives on Wife Abuse,* edited by Kersti Yllö and Michele Bograd. Newbury Park, CA: Sage.

Ahrons, Constance. 1983. "Predictors of Parental Involvement Postdivorce: Mothers' and Fathers' Perceptions." *Journal of Divorce* 6(3):55-59.

Ahrons, Constance R. and Lynn Wallisch. 1987a. "Parenting in the Binuclear Family: Relationships Between Biological and Stepparents." Pp. 225-56 in *Remarriage and Stepparenting: Current Research and Theory,* edited by Kay Pasley and Marilyn Ihinger-Tallman. New York: Guilford.

———. 1987b. "The Relationship Between Former Spouses." Pp. 269-96 in *Intimate Relationships: Development, Dynamics, and Deterioration,* edited by Daniel Perlman and Steve Duck. Newbury Park, CA: Sage.

Alder, Christine. 1992. "Violence, Gender, and Social Change" (Part of a symposium titled Thinking About Violence). *International Social Science Journal* 44:267-78.

Ambert, Anne-Marie. 1988. "Relationship Between Ex-Spouses: Individual and Dyadic Perspectives." *Journal of Social and Personal Relationships* 5:327-46.

Andersen, Margaret L. 1993. *Thinking About Women: Sociological Perspectives on Sex and Gender.* New York: Macmillan.

Aquilino, William S. 1993. "Impact of Childhood Family Structure and Later-Life Parental Divorce on Young Adults' Relationships With Parents." Unpublished manuscript, University of Wisconsin–Madison, Department of Child and Family Studies.

Arditti, Joyce A. 1990. "Noncustodial Fathers: An Overview of Policy and Resources." *Family Relations* 39:460-65.

Arendell, Terry. 1986. *Mothers and Divorce: Legal, Economic, and Social Dilemmas.* Berkeley: University of California Press.

———. 1987. "Women and the Economics of Divorce in the Contemporary United States." *Signs: Journal of Women in Culture and Society* (Fall):121-35.

———. 1992a. "Father Absence: Investigations Into Divorce." *Gender & Society* 6:562-86.

———. 1992b. "Social Self as Gendered: A Masculinist Discourse of Divorce." *Symbolic Interaction* 5(2):151-81.

———. 1994a. "Divorce: It's a Gender Issue." *Family Advocate* 17(1):30-34.

———. 1994b. "Taking Gender Seriously: A Proposal for a Feminist-Interactionism." Presentation at the American Sociological Association, Los Angeles, California, August.

Arendell, Terry and Carroll Estes. 1991. "Older Women in the Post-Reagan Era." Pp. 221-37 in *Critical Perspectives on Aging: The Political and Moral Economy of Growing Old,* edited by Meredith Minkler and Carroll L. Estes. New York: Baywood.

Aries, Philip. 1962. *Centuries of Childhood: A Social History of Family Life.* New York: Vintage.

Arliss, Laurie P. 1991. *Gender Communication.* Englewood Cliffs, NJ: Prentice Hall.

"As Far Away as You Can Get." 1990. *Time* 135(March 5):20.

Astrachan, Anthony. 1985. *How Men Feel.* New York: Doubleday.

"Attitudes of College Freshmen." 1993. *Chronicle of Higher Education.* 39(January 13):A30-A33.

Babbee, Earl. 1992. *The Practice of Social Research.* 8th ed. Belmont, CA: Wadsworth.

Backett, Kathryn. 1982. *Mothers and Fathers: Studies of Negotiation of Parental Behavior.* New York: St. Martin's Press.

———. 1987. "The Negotiation of Fatherhood." Pp. 74-90 in *Reassessing Fatherhood,* edited by Charlie Lewis and Margaret O'Brien. Newbury Park, CA: Sage.

Bane, Mary Jo. 1976. *Here to Stay: American Families in the Twentieth Century.* New York: Basic Books.

Barrett, Michelle and Mary McIntosh. 1982. *The Anti-Social Family.* London: Verso.

Basow, Susan A. 1992. *Gender Stereotypes and Roles.* 3rd ed. Pacific Grove, CA: Brooks/Cole.

Bauer, Bob and Daphne Bauer. 1985. "Visitation Lawsuit." P. 167 in *Men Freeing Men,* edited by Francis Baumli. Jersey City, NJ: New Atlantis.

Baumrind, Diane. 1971. "Harmonius Parents and Their Preschool Children." *Developmental Psychology* 4(1): 99-102.

Bellah, Robert. 1992. *The Good Society.* New York: Alfred A. Knopf.

Bellah, Robert, Richard Madsen, William Sullivan, Ann Swidler, and Steven Tipton. 1985. *Habits of the Heart: Individualism and Commitment in American Life.* New York: Harper & Row.

Belle, Deborah. 1987. "Gender Differences in the Social Moderators of Stress." Pp. 257-277 in *Gender and Stress,* edited by Rosalind C. Barnet, Leigh Bienen, and Grace K. Baruch. New York: Free Press.

Bem, Sandra Lipsitz. 1993. *The Lenses of Gender: Transforming the Debate on Sexual Inequality.* New Haven, CT: Yale University Press.

Benedek, Elissa and Diane H. Schetky. 1985. "Allegations of Sexual Abuse in Child Custody and Visitation Disputes." Pp. 145-56 in *Emerging Issues in Child Psychiatry and the Law,* edited by Diane Schetky and Elissa Benedek. New York: Brunner/Mazel.

Berger, Beatrice and Peter Berger. 1983. *The War Over the Family.* Garden City, NJ: Doubleday.

Berger, Peter and Hansfried Kellner. 1964. "Marriage and the Social Construction of Reality." *Diogenes* 46:1-25.

Bernard, Jessie. 1981. "The Good-Provider Role: Its Rise and Fall." *American Psychologist* 36:1-12.

Bernardes, Jon. 1985. "'Family Ideology': Identification and Exploration." *Sociological Review* 33:275-97.

Beutler, Ivan, Wesley Burr, Kathleen Bahr, and Donald Herrin. 1989. "The Family Realm: Theoretical Contributions for Understanding Its Uniqueness." *Journal of Marriage and the Family* 51:805-16.

Blair, Sampson Lee and Daniel T. Lichter. 1991. "Measuring the Division of Household Labor." *Journal of Family Issues* 12(1):91-113.

Blankenhorn, David, Steven Bayme, and Jean Bethke Elshtain. 1992. *Rebuilding the Nest: A New Commitment to the American Family.* Milwaukee, WI: Family Service America.

Blauner, Bob. 1989. *Black Lives, White Lives: Three Decades of Race Relations in America.* Berkeley: University of California Press.

Block, Jack, Jeanne H. Block, and Per F. Gjerde. 1988. "Parental Functioning and the Home Environment in Families of Divorce: Prospective and Concurrent Analyses." *Journal of American Academy of Child and Adolescent Psychiatry* 27:207-13.

Block, Jeanne H., Jack Block, and Per F. Gjerde. 1986. "Personality of Children Prior to Divorce: A Prospective Study." *Child Development* 57:827-40.

Blumberg, Rae Lesser and Marion Tolbert Coleman. 1989. "A Theoretical Look at the Gender Balance of Power in the American Couple." *Journal of Family Issues* 10:225-50.

Blumer, Herbert. 1969. *Symbolic Interactionism: Perspective and Method.* Englewood Cliffs, NJ: Prentice Hall.

Blumstein, Phillip and Pepper Schwartz. 1983. *American Couples: Money, Work, Sex.* New York: William Morrow.

Bohannon, Paul. 1970. *Divorce and After.* Garden City, NY: Doubleday.

Bordo, Susan. 1990. "Feminism, Postmodernism, and Gender-Skepticism." Pp. 133-56 in *Feminism/Postmodernism,* edited by Linda J. Nicholson. New York: Routledge.

Bourdieu, Pierre. 1987. *Outline of a Theory of Practice.* Cambridge, UK: Cambridge University Press.

Bowman, Madonna E. and Constance R. Ahrons. 1985. "Impact of Legal Custody Status on Fathers' Parenting Postdivorce." *Journal of Marriage and the Family* 47:481-88.

Bradley, David. 1990. "Financial Support for Children: The Swedish Example." *Family Law* 20:349-51.

Bretherton, Inge. 1993. "Theoretical Contributions From Developmental Psychology." Pp. 275-301 in *Sourcebook of Family Theories and Methods: A Contextual Approach,* edited by Pauline Boss, Ralph LaRossa, W. Schumm, and Susan Steinmetz. New York: Plenum.

Brink, Pamela J. 1991. "Issues of Reliability and Validity." Pp. 163-64 in *Qualitative Nursing Research: A Contemporary Dialogue,* edited by Janice Morse. Newbury Park, CA: Sage.

Brod, Harry. 1987a. "Introduction: Themes and Theses of Men's Studies." Pp. 1-17 in *The Making of Masculinities,* edited by Harry Brod. Boston: Unwin Hyman.

———. 1987b. "The Case for Men's Studies." Pp. 39-62 in *The Making of Masculinities,* edited by Harry Brod. Boston: Unwin Hyman.

Brown, Carol. 1981. "Mothers, Fathers, and Children: From Private to Public Patriarchy." Pp. 239-68 in *Women and Revolution,* edited by Lydia Sargent. Boston: South End Press.

Bruch, Carol. 1983. "Developing Normative Standards for Child-Support Payments: A Critique of Current Practice." Pp. 119-32 in *The Parental Child-Support Obligation,* edited by Judith Cassetty. Lexington, MA: Lexington Books.

Bumpass, Larry and James A. Sweet. 1989. "Children's Experience in Single-Parent Families: Implications of Cohabitation and Marital Transitions." *Family Planning Perspectives* 21:256-60.

Burgess, Ernest. 1926. "The Family as a Unity of Interacting Personalities." *The Family* 7:3-9.

Burke, Kenneth. 1962. *A Grammar of Motives and a Rhetoric of Motives.* Cleveland, OH: World.

Burkhauser, Richard and Greg Duncan. 1989. "Economic Risks of Gender Roles: Income Loss and Life Events Over the Life Course." *Social Science Quarterly* 70(1):3-23.

Cahn, Naomi R. 1991. "Civil Images of Battered Women: The Impact of Domestic Violence on Child Custody Decisions." *Vanderbilt Law Review* 44:1041-97.

Cancian, Francesca. 1987. *Love in America: Gender and Self Development.* New York: Cambridge University Press.

Canter, R. J. and B. C. Meyerowitz. 1984. "Sex Role Stereotypes: Self-Reports of Behavior." *Sex Roles* 10:293-306.

Cassetty, Judith. 1983. *The Parental Child Support Obligation.* Lexington, MA: Lexington Books.

Cassetty, Judith and Robin Douthitt. 1984. "The Economics of Setting Adequate and Equitable Support Payment Awards." *Texas State Bar Secre. Rep.* Special Child Support and Visitation Issue.

Chambers, David. 1979. *Making Fathers Pay: The Enforcement of Child Support.* Chicago: University of Chicago Press.

———. 1982. "Comment—The Coming Curtailment of Compulsory Child Support." *Michigan Law Review* 80:1614-34.

———. 1984. "Rethinking the Substantive Rules for Custody Disputes in Divorce." *Michigan Law Review* 88:477-569.

———. 1988. "The Federal Government and a Program of 'Advance Maintenance' in the United States." Pp. 343-49 in *Child Support: From Debt Collection to Social Policy,* edited by Alfred Kahn and Sheila Kamerman. Newbury Park, CA: Sage.

———. 1990. "Stepparents, Biological Parents, and the Law's Perceptions of 'Family' After Divorce." Pp. 102-29 in *Divorce Reform at the Crossroads,* edited by Stephen D. Sugarman and Herma Hill Kay. New Haven, CT: Yale University Press.

Chapman, J. R. 1990. "Violence Against Women as a Violation of Human Rights." *Social Justice* 17(2):54-70.

Charmaz, Kathy. 1988. "The Grounded Theory Method: An Explication and Interpretation." Pp. 109-26 in *Contemporary Field Research: A Collection of Readings,* edited by Robert M. Emerson. Prospect Heights, IL: Waveland.

———. 1990. " 'Discovering' Chronic Illness: Using Grounded Theory." *Social Science and Medicine* 30:1161-72.

———. 1991. *Good Days, Bad Days: The Self in Chronic Illness and Time.* New Brunswick, NJ: Rutgers University Press.

Chase-Lansdale, P. Lindsay and E. Mavis Hetherington. 1990. "The Impact of Divorce on Life-Span Development: Short and Long Term Effects." Pp. 105-50 in *Life Span Development and Behavior.* Vol. 10, edited by David L. Featherman and Richard M. Lerner. Hillsdale, NJ: Lawrence Erlbaum.

Cheal, David. 1991. *Family and the State of Theory.* Toronto: University of Toronto Press.

Cherlin, Andrew. 1978. "Remarriage as an Incomplete Institution." *American Journal of Sociology* 84:634-50.

———. 1981. *Marriage, Divorce, Remarriage.* Cambridge, MA: Harvard University Press.

————, ed. 1988. *The Changing American Family and Public Policy.* Washington, DC: Urban Institute Press.

Chesler, Phyllis. 1991. *Mothers on Trial: The Battle for Children and Custody.* San Diego, CA: Harcourt Brace Jovanovich.

Chiriboga, David A. and Linda Catron. 1991. *Divorce: Crisis, Challenge, or Relief?* New York: New York University Press.

Chiriboga, David A., John Roberts, and Judith A. Stein. 1978. "Psychological Well-Being During Marital Separation." *Journal of Divorce* 2:91-96.

Chodorow, Nancy. 1978. *The Reproduction of Mothering: Psychoanalysis and the Sociology of Gender.* Berkeley: University of California Press.

————. 1989. *Feminism and Psychoanalytic Theory.* New Haven, CA: Yale University Press.

Chodorow, Nancy and Susan Contratto. 1982. "The Fantasy of the Perfect Mother." Pp. 54-75 in *Rethinking the Family: Some Feminist Questions,* edited by Barrie Thorne with Marilyn Yalom. New York: Longman.

Clatterbaugh, Kenneth. 1988. "Masculinist Perspectives." *Changing Men* 17(Winter):17-18.

————. 1990. *Contemporary Perspectives on Masculinity: Men, Women and Politics in Modern Society.* Boulder, CO: Westview.

————. 1992. "The Oppression Debate in Sexual Politics." Pp. 169-90 in *Rethinking Masculinity: Philosophical Explorations in Light of Feminism,* edited by Larry May and Robert Strikwerda. Lanham, MD: Rowman and Littlefield.

Cohen, Theodore. 1989. "Becoming and Being Husbands and Fathers: Work and Family Conflict for Men." Pp. 220-34 in *Gender in Intimate Relationships: A Microstructural Approach,* edited by Barbara J. Risman and Pepper Schwartz. Belmont, CA: Wadsworth.

Collins, Randall. 1985. *Three Sociological Traditions.* New York: Oxford University Press.

Coltrane, Scott. 1989. "Household Labor and the Routine Production of Gender." *Social Problems* 36:473-90.

————. 1990. "Birth Timing and the Division of Labor in Dual-Earner Families." *Journal of Family Issues* 11(2):157-81.

Coltrane, Scott and Neal Hickman. 1992. "The Rhetoric of Rights and Needs: Moral Discourse in the Reform of Child Custody and Child Support Laws." *Social Problems* 39:400-20.

Connell, Robert. 1987. *Gender and Power.* Palo Alto, CA: Stanford University Press.

————. 1992. "Masculinity, Violence, and War." Pp. 176-83 in *Men's Lives.* 2nd ed., edited by Michael Kimmel and Michael Messner. New York: Macmillan.

Cook, Judith A. and Mary Margaret Fonow. 1990. "Knowledge and Women's Interest: Issues of Epistemology and Methodology in Feminist Sociological Research." Pp. 58-58 in *Feminist Research Methods: Exemplary Readings in the Social Sciences,* edited by J. McCarl Nielsen. Boulder, CO: Westview.

Corbett, Thomas. 1992. "The Wisconsin Child Support Assurance System: From Plausible Proposals to Improvable Prospects." Pp. 27-52 in *Child Support Assurance,* edited by Irwin Garfinkel, Sara McLanahan, and Phillip K. Robins. Madison, WI: Institute for Research on Poverty.

Cowan, Carolyn and Philip Cowan. 1988. "Who Does What When Partners Become Parents: Implications for Men, Women and Marriage." *Marriage and Family Review* 12(3-4): 105-31.

Cuber, John F. and Peggy B. Harroff. 1965. "Five Types of Marriage." Pp. 43-65 in *The Significant American,* edited by John Cuber and Peggy B. Harroff. New York: Hawthorn.

Dahlstrom, Edmund. 1989. "Theories and Ideologies of Family Functions, Gender Relations, and Human Reproduction." Pp. 57-78 in *Changing Patterns of European Family Life,* edited by Maren Bak. New York: Routledge.

Daly, Kerry. 1992. "The Fit Between Qualitative Research and Characteristics of Families."
    Pp. 1-14 in *Qualitative Methods in Family Research,* edited by Jane Gilgun, Kerry Daly,
    and Gerald Handel. Newbury Park, CA: Sage.
Deaux, Kay and Mary E. Kite. 1987. "Thinking About Gender." Pp. 92-117 in *Analyzing
    Gender: A Handbook of Social Science Research,* edited by Beth B. Hess and Myra Marx
    Ferree. Newbury Park, CA: Sage.
Deaux, Kay and Brenda Major. 1990. "A Social-Psychological Model of Gender." Pp. 89-99
    in *Theoretical Perspectives on Sexual Difference,* edited by Deborah L. Rhode. New
    Haven, CT: Yale University Press.
Denzin, Norman. 1992. *Symbolic Interactionism and Cultural Studies.* Cambridge, UK: Basil
    Blackwell.
Denzin, Norman K. and Yvonna S. Lincoln, eds. 1994. *Handbook of Qualitative Research.*
    Thousand Oaks, CA: Sage.
DeVault, Marjorie. 1991. *Feeding the Family: The Social Organization of Caring as Gen-
    dered Work.* Chicago: University of Chicago Press.
Dill, Bonnie Thornton. 1988. "Our Mother's Grief: Racial Ethnic Women and the Mainte-
    nance of Families." *Journal of Family History* 13:415-31.
Dingwall, Robert and David Greatbatch. 1991. "Behind Closed Doors: A Preliminary Report
    on Mediator/Client Interaction in England." *Family and Conciliation Courts Review*
    29:291-303.
Dizard, Jan and Howard Gadlin. 1990. *The Minimal Family.* Amherst: University of Massa-
    chusetts Press.
Dobash, Russell and R. Emerson Dobash. 1992. *Women, Violence, and Social Change.*
    London: Routledge.
Donnelly, Denise and David Finkelhor. 1992. "Does Equality in Custody Arrangement
    Improve the Parent-Child Relationship?" *Journal of Marriage and the Family* 54:837-45.
Douthitt, Robin. 1988. "The Division of Labor Within the Home: Have Gender Roles
    Changed?" *Sex Roles* 20:693-704.
———. 1990. "An Evaluation of the Relationship Between the Percentage-of-Income Stand-
    ard and Family Expenditures for Children." Institute for Research on Poverty, Discussion
    Paper No. 921-90 (September), University of Wisconsin–Madison.
Doyle, Richard. 1976. *The Rape of the Male.* St. Paul, MN: Poor Richard's Press.
———. 1985. "Divorce." P. 166 in *Men Freeing Men,* edited by Francis Baumli. Jersey City,
    NJ: New Atlantis.
Dudley, James R. 1991. "Increasing Our Understanding of Divorced Fathers Who Have
    Infrequent Contact With Their Children." *Family Relations* 40:279-85.
Duncan, Greg D. and Saul D. Hoffman. 1985. "A Reconsideration of the Economic Conse-
    quences of Marital Disruption." *Demography* 22:485-98.
Eagley, A. H. and A. Mladinic. 1989. "Gender Stereotypes and Attitudes Toward Women and
    Men." *Personality and Social Psychology Bulletin* 15:543-58.
Ehrenreich, Barbara. 1983. *The Hearts of Men: American Dreams and the Flight From
    Commitment.* New York: Oxford University Press.
Ehrensaft, Diane. 1987. *Parenting Together: Men and Women Sharing the Care of Their
    Children.* New York: Free Press.
Ely, Margot with Margaret Anzul, Teri Friedman, Diane Garner, and Ann McCormack Stein-
    metz. 1991. *Doing Qualitative Research: Circles Within Circles.* New York: Falmer.
Emerson, Robert M. 1988. *Contemporary Field Research: A Collection of Readings.* Prospect
    Heights, IL: Waveland.
Emery, Robert. 1988. *Marriage, Divorce, and Children's Adjustment.* Newbury Park, CA:
    Sage.

Emery, Robert E., E. Mavis Hetherington, and Lisabeth F. Dilalla. 1984. "Divorce, Children, and Social Policy." Pp. 189-266 in *Child Development Research and Social Policy*. Vol. 1, edited by Harold Stevenson and Alberta Siegal. Chicago: University of Chicago Press.

Emery, Robert E. and Melissa M. Wyer. 1987a. "Child Custody Mediation and Litigation: An Experimental Evaluation of the Experience of Parents." *Journal of Consulting and Clinical Psychology* 55(2):179-86.

———. 1987b. "Divorce Mediation." *American Psychologist* 42(2):472-80.

Encyclopaedia Judicia. Vol 7. 1971. Jerusalem, Israel: Macmillan.

Epstein, Cynthia Fuchs. 1988. *Deceptive Deceptions*. New York: Russell Sage.

Epstein, Steven. 1991. "Sexuality and Identity: The Contribution of Object Relations Theory to a Constructionist Sociology." *Theory and Society* 20:825-73.

Erlanger, Howard S., Elizabeth Chambliss, and Marygold Melli. 1987. "Participation and Flexibility in Informal Processes: Cautions From the Divorce Contest. *Law and Society Review* 21:585-604.

Faller, Kathleen Coulborn. 1991. "Possible Explanations for Child Sexual Abuse Allegations in Divorce." *American Journal of Orthopsychiatry* 61(1):86-91.

Faludi, Susan. 1991. *Backlash: The Undeclared War Against American Women*. New York: Crown.

Family Law of the State of New York. 1990. Flushing, NY: Looseleaf Law Publications.

Fassinger, Polly A. 1989. "The Impact of Gender and Past Marital Experiences on Heading a Household Alone." Pp. 165-80 in *Gender in Intimate Relationships: A Microstructural Approach,* edited by Barbara J. Risman and Pepper Schwartz. Belmont, CA: Wadsworth.

Ferguson, Ann. 1989. *Blood at the Root: Motherhood, Sexuality and Male Dominance*. London: Pandora.

Ferree, Myra Marx. 1990. "Beyond Separate Spheres: Feminism and Family Research." *Journal of Marriage and the Family* 52:866-84.

Ferree, Myra Marx and Beth B. Hess. 1987. "Introduction." Pp. 9-30 in *Analyzing Gender: A Handbook of Social Science Research,* edited by Beth B. Hess and Myra Marx Ferree. Newbury Park, CA: Sage.

Ferreiro, Beverly Webster. 1990. "Presumption of Joint Custody: A Family Policy Dilemma." *Family Relations* 39:420-26.

Filene, Peter. 1986. *Him-her-self: Sex Roles in Modern America*. Baltimore: Johns Hopkins University Press.

Finch, Janet and Dulcie Groves. 1983. *A Labour of Love: Women, Work and Caring*. London: Routledge & Kegan Paul.

Fineman, Martha Albertson. 1988. "Dominant Discourse, Professional Language, and Legal Change in Child Custody Decision-Making." *Harvard Law Review* 101:727-74.

———. 1991. *The Illusion of Equality: The Rhetoric and Reality of Divorce Reform*. Chicago: University of Chicago Press.

Finkelhor, David. 1984. *Child Sexual Abuse: New Theory and Research*. New York: Free Press.

Finkelhor, David, Richard J. Gelles, Gerald T. Hotaling, and Murray A. Straus, eds. 1983. *The Dark Side of Families: Current Family Violence Research*. Beverly Hills, CA: Sage.

Finkelhor, David, Gerald Hotaling, and Andrea Sedlak. 1990. *Missing, Abducted, Runaway, and Thrownaway Children in America*. Washington, DC: U.S. Department of Justice.

Finlay, Barbara, Charles E. Starnes, and Fausto B. Alvarez. 1985. "Recent Changes in Sex-Role Ideology Among Divorced Men and Women: Some Possible Causes and Implications." *Sex Roles* 12:637-53.

Flax, Jane. 1987. "The Family in Contemporary Feminist Thought: A Critical Review." Pp. 223-53 in *The Family in Political Thought,* edited by Jean Elshtain. Amherst: University of Massachusetts Press.

———. 1989. "Postmodernism and Gender Relations in Feminist Theory." Pp. 51-74 in *Feminist Theory in Practice and Process,* edited by Micheline Maslon, Jean O'Barr, Sarah Westphal-Wihl, and Mary Wyer. Chicago: University of Chicago Press.

Folberg, Jay H. and M. Graham. 1979. "Joint Custody of Children Following Divorce." *Davis Law Review* 12:523-81.

Folberg, Jay and Ann Milne. 1988. *Divorce Mediation: Theory and Practice.* New York: Guilford.

Fontana, Andrea and James H. Frey. 1994. "Interviewing: The Art of Science." Pp. 361-76 in *Handbook of Qualitative Research,* edited by Norman K. Denzin and Yvonna S. Lincoln. Thousand Oaks, CA: Sage.

Foote, Nelson. 1981. "Identification as the Basis for a Theory of Motivation." Pp. 333-42 in *Social Psychology Through Symbolic Interaction.* 2nd ed., edited by Gregory Stone and Harvey Farberman. New York: John Wiley.

Foster, Henry and Doris Freed. 1973. "Divorce Reform: Brakes on Breakdown?" *Journal of Family Law* 13:443-93.

Fox, Greer Litton. 1985. "Noncustodial Fathers." Pp. 393-415 in *Dimensions of Fatherhood,* edited by Shirley M. Hanson and Frederick W. Bozett. Beverly Hills, CA: Sage.

Franklin, Clyde W., II. 1988. *Men and Society.* Chicago: Nelson-Hall.

Fraser, Nancy. 1989. *Unruly Practices: Power, Discourse, and Gender in Contemporary Social Theory.* Minneapolis: University of Minnesota Press.

Fraser, Nancy and Linda Gordon. 1994. "A Genealogy of Dependency: Tracing a Keyword of the U.S. Welfare State." *Signs: Journal of Women in Culture and Society* 19:309-36.

Freed, Donna and Timothy Walker. 1989. "Family Law in the Fifty States." *Family Law Quarterly* 22:408-29.

Frey, Richard G. 1986. "Being a Divorced Father as Primary Parent: A Phenomenological Investigation." *Family and Conciliation Courts Review* 24:71-78.

Friedman, Henry J. 1982. "The Challenge of Divorce to Adequate Fathering: The Peripheral Father in Marriage and Divorce." *Psychiatric Clinics of North America* 5:565-81.

Frye, Marilyn. 1993. "Oppression." Pp. 7-9 in *Feminist Frontiers III,* edited by Laurel Richardson and Verta Taylor. Englewood Ciffs, NJ: Prentice Hall.

Furio, Joanne. 1993. "Can New State Laws Stop the Stalker?" *Ms.* January/February, pp. 91-92.

Furstenberg, Frank. 1987. "The New Extended Family: The Experience of Parents and Children After Remarriage." Pp. 42-61 in *Remarriage and Stepparenting: Current Research and Theory,* edited by Kay Pasley and Marilyn Ihinger-Tallman. New York: Guilford.

———. 1988. "Good Dads—Bad Dads: Two Faces of Fatherhood." Pp. 193-209 in *The Changing American Family and Public Policy,* edited by Andrew Cherlin. Washington, DC: Urban Institute.

Furstenberg, Frank and Andrew Cherlin. 1991. *Divided Families: What Happens to Children When Parents Part.* Cambridge, MA: Harvard University Press.

Furstenberg, Frank, S. Philip Morgan, and Paul Allison. 1987. "Parental Participation and Children's Well-Being After Marital Dissolution." *American Sociological Review* 52: 695-701.

Furstenberg, Frank and Christine Nord. 1985. "Parenting Apart: Patterns of Childrearing After Marital Disruption." *Journal of Marriage and the Family* 47:893-904.

Furstenberg, Frank and Graham B. Spanier. 1984. *Recycling the Family: Remarriage After Divorce.* Beverly Hills, CA: Sage.

Garfinkel, Irwin. 1986. "Utilization and Effects of Immediate Income Withholding and the Percentage-of-Income Standard." Special Report 42, Institute for Research on Poverty, University of Wisconsin–Madison.

———. 1988. "Child Support Assurance: A New Tool for Achieving Social Security." Pp. 328-42 in *Child Support: From Debt Collection to Social Policy,* edited by Alfred Kahn and Sheila Kamerman. Newbury Park, CA: Sage.

———. 1992. *Assuring Child Support: An Extension of Social Security.* New York: Russell Sage.

Garfinkel, Irwin and Marieka Klawitter. 1990. "The Effects of Routine Income Withholding of Child Support on AFDC Participation and Costs." *Journal of Policy Analysis and Management* 9(2):155-77.

Garfinkel, Irwin and Sara McLanahan. 1990. "The Effects of the Child Support Provisions of the Family Support Act of 1988 on Child Well-Being." *Population Research and Policy Review* 9(3):205-34.

Garfinkel, Irwin, Sara McLanahan, and Phillip K. Robins. 1992. "Findings of the Child Support Reform Project: Introduction and Summary." Pp. 3-26 in *Child Support Assurance,* edited by Irwin Garkfinkel, Sara McLanahan, and Phillip K. Robins. Madison, WI: Institute for Research on Poverty.

Garrison, Marsha. 1990. "The Economics of Divorce: Changing Rules, Changing Results." Pp. 75-101 in *Divorce Reform at the Crossroads,* edited by Stephen D. Sugarman and Herma Hill Kay. New Haven, CT: Yale University Press.

Gelles, Richard and Jon R. Conte. 1990. "Domestic Violence and Sexual Abuse of Children: A Review of Research in the 80s." *Journal of Marriage and the Family* 52:1045-58.

Gelles, Richard and Murray Straus. 1990. *Intimate Violence: The Causes and Consequences of Abuse in American Families.* 2nd ed. New York: Touchstone.

Gerson, Kathy. 1993. *No Man's Land: Men's Changing Commitments to Family and Work.* New York: Basic Books.

Gerstel, Naomi. 1988. "Divorce and Kin Ties: The Importance of Gender." *Journal of Marriage and the Family* 50:209-19.

Gerzon, Mark. 1982. *Choice of Heroes: The Changing Face of American Manhood.* Boston: Houghton Mifflin.

Giddens, Anthony. 1987. *Social Theory and Modern Society.* Stanford, CA: Stanford University Press.

Gilbert, Lucia A. 1985. *Men in Dual-Career Families: Current Realities and Future Prospects.* Hillsdale, NJ: Lawrence Erlbaum.

Giles-Sims, Jean. 1987. "Parental Role Sharing Between Remarrieds and Ex-Spouses." *Youth & Society* 19(2):134-150.

Gilligan, Carol. 1982. *In a Different Voice: Psychological Theory and Women's Development.* Cambridge, MA: Harvard University Press.

———. 1983. "Do the Social Sciences Have an Adequate Theory of Moral Development?" Pp. 33-51 in *Social Science as Moral Inquiry* edited by Norma Haan. New York: Columbia University Press.

Girdner, Linda K. 1988. "How People Process Disputes." Pp. 45-57 in *Divorce Mediation: Theory and Practice,* edited by Jay Folberg and Ann Milne. New York: Guilford.

Glaser, Barney. 1978. *Theoretical Sensitivity.* Mill Valley, CA: Sociology Press.

Glaser, Barney and Anselm Strauss. 1967. *The Discovery of Grounded Theory.* New York: Aldine.

Glendon, Mary Ann. 1987. *Abortion and Divorce in Western Law: American Failures, European Challenges.* Cambridge, MA: Harvard University Press.

Glenn, Evelyn Nakano. 1987. "Gender and the Family." Pp. 348-80 in *Analyzing Gender: A Handbook of Social Science Research,* edited by Beth B. Hess and Myra Marx Ferree. Newbury Park, CA: Sage.

Goffman, Erving. 1959. *Presentation of Self in Everyday Life.* New York: Doubleday.

———. 1971. *Relations in Public.* New York: Harper Colophon.

———. 1975. *Gender Advertisements.* New York: Harper & Row.

Goldstein, Joseph, Anna Freud, and Albert Solnit. 1979. *Beyond the Best Interests of the Child.* New York: Free Press.

Gomes-Schwartz, Beverly, Jonathan M. Horowitz, and Albert P. Cardarelli. 1990. *Child Sexual Abuse: The Initial Effects.* Newbury Park, CA: Sage.

Goode, William. 1982. "Why Men Resist." Pp. 131-50 in *Rethinking the Family: Some Feminist Questions,* edited by Barrie Thorne with Marilyn Yalom. New York: Longman.

Gordon, Linda, ed. 1988. *Heroes of Their Own Lives: The History and Politics of Family Violence: Boston 1880-1960.* New York: Viking/Penguin.

———. 1990a. "Family Violence, Feminism, and Social Control." Pp. 178-98 in *Women, the State, and Welfare,* edited by Linda Gordon. Madison: University of Wisconsin Press.

———. 1990b. *Women, the State, and Welfare.* Madison: University of Wisconsin Press.

Gore, Susan and Mary Ellen Colten. 1991. "Gender, Stress, and Distress: Social Relational Influences." Pp. 139-64 in *The Social Context of Coping,* edited by John Eckenrode. New York: Plenum.

Gove, Walter R. and Hee-Choon Shin. 1989. "The Psychological Well-Being of Divorced and Widowed Men and Women: An Empirical Analysis." *Journal of Family Issues* 10(1):122-44.

Greif, Judith Brown. 1979. "Fathers, Children, and Joint Custody. *American Journal of Orthopsychiatry* 49:311-19.

———. 1982. "The Father-Child Relationship Subsequent to Divorce." Pp. 49-57 in *Therapy With Remarriage Families,* edited by James Hansen. New York: Allyn and Bacon.

Griswold, Robert L. 1993. *Fatherhood in America: A History.* New York: Basic Books.

Grubb, W. Norton and Marvin Lazerson. 1988. *Broken Promises: How Americans Fail Their Children.* Chicago: University of Chicago Press.

Guba, Egon G. and Yvonna S. Lincoln. 1994. "Competing Paradigms in Qualitative Research." Pp. 105-17 in *Handbook of Qualitative Research,* edited by Norman K. Denzin and Yvonna S. Lincoln. Thousand Oaks, CA: Sage.

Gubrium, Jaber and James Holstein. 1990. *What Is Family?* Mountain View, CA: Mayfield.

Gusinger, Shan, Philip A. Cowan, and David Schuldberg. 1989. "Changing Parent and Spouse Relations in the First Years of Remarriage of Divorced Fathers." *Journal of Marriage and the Family* 51:445-56.

Halem, Lynn. 1980. *Divorce Reform: Changed Legal and Social Perspectives.* New York: Free Press.

Halle, David. 1987. *America's Working Man: Work, Home, and Politics Among Blue Collar Property Owners.* Chicago: University of Chicago Press.

Hanson, Shirley M. H. 1985. "Single Custodial Fathers." Pp. 369-92 in *Dimensions of Fatherhood,* edited by Shirley M. Hanson and Frederick W. Bozett. Beverly Hills, CA: Sage.

———. 1986a. "Father/Child Relationships: Beyond *Kraemer vs. Kraemer.*" Pp. 135-61 in *Men's Changing Roles in the Family,* edited by Robert A. Lewis and Marvin B. Sussman. New York: Haworth.

———. 1986b. "Parent-Child Relationships in Single-Father Families." Pp. 181-96 in *Men in Families,* edited by Robert A. Lewis and Robert E. Salt. Newbury Park, CA: Sage.

Hantover, Jeffrey P. 1978. "The Boy Scouts and the Validation of Masculinity." *Journal of Social Issues* 34:184-95.

Harding, Sandra. 1991. *Whose Science? Whose Knowledge? Thinking About Women's Lives.* Ithaca, NY: Cornell University Press.

Hare-Mustin, Rachel T. 1988. "Family Change and Gender Differences: Implications for Theory and Practice." *Family Relations* 37:36-41.

Harlow, Caroline Wolf. 1991. *Female Victims of Violent Crime.* Washington, DC: U.S. Department of Justice.

Hartmann, Heidi. 1981a. "The Family as Locus of Gender, Class, and Political Struggle: The Example of Housework." *Signs: The Journal of Women in Culture and Society* 6(3): 143-69.

————. 1981b. "The Unhappy Marriage of Marxism and Feminism: Toward a More Progressive Union." Pp. 1-42 in *Women and Revolution,* edited by Lynda Sargent. Boston: South End Press.

Haskins, Ron. 1988. "Child Support: A Father's View." Pp. 306-27 in *Child Support: From Debt Collection to Social Policy,* edited by Alfred Kahn and Sheila Kamerman. Newbury Park, CA: Sage.

Hayes, Cheryl D., John Palmer, and Martha J. Zaslow, eds. 1990. *Who Cares for America's Children? Child Care Policy for the 1990s.* Washington, DC: National Academy Press.

Hearn, Jeff. 1987. *The Gender of Oppression: Men, Masculinity, and the Critique of Marxism.* New York: St Martin's.

Herman, Judith with Lisa Hirschman. 1981. *Father-Daughter Incest.* Cambridge, MA: Harvard University Press.

Hess, Beth B. and Myra Marx Ferree, eds. 1987. *Analyzing Gender: A Handbook of Social Science Research.* Newbury Park, CA: Sage.

Hess, R. D. and K. A. Camara. 1979. "Post-Divorce Family Relationships as Mediating Factors in the Consequences of Divorce for Children." *Journal of Social Issues* 35:79-96.

Hetherington, Elizabeth Mavis. 1987. "Family Relations Six Years After Divorce." Pp. 185-205 in *Remarriage and Stepparenting: Current Research and Theory,* edited by Kay Pasley and Marilyn Ihinger-Tallman. New York: Guilford.

Hetherington, Elizabeth, Mavis Cox, and Richard Cox. 1976. "Divorced Fathers." *Family Coordinator* 25:417-28.

————. 1978. "The Aftermath of Divorce." Pp. 149-76 in *Mother-Child, Father-Child Relations,* edited by J. H. Stevens, Jr. and M. Matthews. Washington, DC: National Association for the Education of Young Children.

————. 1982. "Effects of Divorce on Parents and Children." Pp. 233-88 in *Nontraditional Families: Parenting and Child Development,* edited by Michael E. Lamb. Hillsdale, NJ: Lawrence Erlbaum.

————. 1985. "Long-Term Effects of Divorce and Remarriage on the Adjustment of Children." *Journal of the American Academy of Child Psychiatry* 24:518-30.

Hetherington, Elizabeth, Mavis Cox, and M. S. Hagan. 1986. "Divorced Fathers: Stress, Coping, and Adjustment." Pp. 103-34 in *The Father's Role: Applied Perspectives,* edited by Michael E. Lamb. New York: John Wiley.

Hiller, Dana and William W. Philliber. 1986. "The Division of Labor in Contemporary Marriage: Expectations, Perceptions, and Performance." *Social Problems* 33(February): 191-201.

Hochschild, Arlie. 1990. *Ideology and Emotion Management: A Perspective and Path for Future Research.* University of California, Berkeley, Department of Sociology.

Hochschild, Arlie with Anne Machung. 1983. *The Managed Heart: Commercialization of Human Feeling.* Berkeley: University of California Press.

————. 1989. *The Second Shift.* New York: Viking.

Hoffman, Samuel and Greg Duncan. 1988. "What Are the Economic Consequences of Divorce?" *Demography* 25:415-27.

Holden, Karen and Pamela J. Smock. 1991. "The Economic Costs of Marital Dissolution: Why Do Women Bear a Disproportionate Cost?" *Annual Review of Sociology* 17:51-78.

hooks, bell. 1984. *Feminist Theory: From Margin to Center.* Boston: South End Press.

Hopkins, Patrick D. 1992. "Gender Treachery: Homophobia, Masculinity, and Threatened Identities." Pp. 111-30 in *Rethinking Masculinity: Philosophical Explorations in Light of Feminism,* edited by Larry May and Robert Strikwerda. Lanham, MD: Rowman and Littlefield.

Hughes, Everett C. 1945. "Dilemmas and Contradictions of Status." *American Journal of Sociology* 50:353-59.

Hunter, James Davison. 1991. *Culture Wars: The Struggle to Define America.* New York: Basic Books.

Ilfeld, F. W., H. Ilfeld, and J. Alexander. 1982. "Does Joint Custody Work? A First Look at Outcome Data of Relitigation." *American Journal of Psychiatry* 139:62-66.

Jacob, Herbert. 1988. *Silent Revolution: The Transformation of Divorce Law in the United States.* Chicago: University of Chicago Press.

Jacobs, John W. 1982. "The Effect of Divorce on Fathers: An Overview of the Literature." *American Journal of Orthopsychiatry* 139:1235-41.

————. 1983. "Treatment of Divorcing Fathers: Social and Psychotherapeutic Considerations." *American Journal of Psychiatry* 140:1294-99.

Jaggar, Allison. 1983. *Feminist Politics and Human Nature.* Totowa, NJ: Rowman and Allenheld.

Johnston, Janet R., Marsha Kline, Jeanne M. Tschann. 1989. "On-Going Postdivorce Conflict in Families Contesting Custody: Do Joint Custody and Frequent Access Help?" *American Journal of Orthopsychiatry* 59:576-92.

Jones, D. and A. Seig. 1988. "Child Sexual Abuse Allegations in Custody or Visitation Cases: A Report of 20 Cases." Pp. 22-36 in *Sexual Abuse Allegations in Custody and Visitation Cases,* edited by E. Bruce Nicholson with Josephine Bulkley. Washington, DC: American Bar Association.

Kahn, Alfred J. and Sheila A. Kamerman. 1988. "Child Support in the United States: The Problem." Pp. 10-19 in *Child Support: From Debt Collection to Social Policy,* edited by Alfred Kahn and Sheila Kamerman. Newbury Park, CA: Sage.

Kamerman, Sheila B. 1991. "Doing Better By Children." *Journal of Law and Politics* 8:75-88.

Kamerman, Sheila B. and Alfred J. Kahn, eds. 1978. *Family Policy: Government and Families in Fourteen Countries.* New York: Columbia University Press.

Kasper, Anne. 1986. "Consciousness Re-Evaluated: Interpretive Theory and Feminist Scholarship." *Sociological Inquiry* 56(1):30-49.

Kaufman, Michael. 1987. *Beyond Patriarchy: Essays on Pleasure, Power, and Change.* Toronto: Oxford University Press.

Kay, Herma. 1990. "Beyond No-Fault: New Directions in Divorce Reform." Pp. 6-36 in *Divorce Reform at the Crossroads,* edited by Stephen D. Sugarman and Herma Hill Kay. New Haven, CT: Yale University Press.

Kelly, Joan B., Lynn Gigy, and Sheryl Hausman. 1988. "Mediated and Adversarial Divorce: Initial Findings From a Longitudinal Study." Pp. 453-74 in *Divorce Mediation: Theory and Practice,* edited by Jay Folberg and Ann Milne. New York: Guilford.

Kimmel, Michael. 1987. "The Contemporary Crisis of Masculinity in Historical Perspective." Pp. 121-54 in *The Making of Masculinities: The New Men's Studies,* edited by Harry Brod. Boston: Allen and Unwin.

Kimmel, Michael and Michael Messner, eds. 1989. "Introduction." Pp. 1-9 in *Men's Lives.* 1st ed., edited by Michael Kimmel and Michael Messner. New York: Macmillan.

———. 1992. *Men's Lives.* 2nd ed. New York: Macmillan.

Kitson, Gay and William M. Holmes. 1992. *Portrait of Divorce: Adjustment to Marital Breakdown.* New York: Guilford.

Kitson, Gay and Leslie Morgan. 1990. "The Multiple Consequences of Divorce: A Decade Review." *Journal of Marriage and the Family* 52(November):913-24.

Kline, Marsha, Jeanne M. Tschann, Janet R. Johnston, and Judith S. Wallerstein. 1989. "Children's Adjustment in Joint and Sole Physical Custody Families." *Developmental Psychology* 25(3):430-38.

Koch, Mary Ann P. and Carol R. Lowery. 1984. "Visitation and the Noncustodial Father." *Journal of Divorce* 8(2):47-65.

Kollock, Peter and Jodi O'Brien. 1994. *The Production of Reality: Essays and Readings in Social Psychology.* Thousand Oaks, CA: Pine Forge.

Komter, Aafke. 1989. "Hidden Power in Marriage." *Gender & Society* 3:187-216.

Krause, Harry D. 1988. "Reflections on Child Support." Pp. 227-50 in *Child Support: From Debt Collection to Social Policy,* edited by Alfred Kahn and Sheila Kamerman. Newbury Park, CA: Sage.

———. 1990. "Child Support Reassessed: Limits of Private Responsibility and the Public Interest." Pp. 166-90 in *Divorce Reform at the Crossroads,* edited by Stephen D. Sugarman and Herma Hill Kay. New Haven, CT: Yale University Press.

Kressel, K., N. Jaffee, B. Tuchman, C. Watson, and M. Deutsch. 1980. "A Typology of Divorcing Couples: Implications for Mediation and the Divorce Process." *Family Process* 19: 101-16.

Kruk, Edward. 1991. "Discontinuity Between Pre- and Post-Divorce Father-Child Relationships: New Evidence Regarding Paternal Disengagement." Pp. 195-227 in *The Consequences of Divorce,* edited by Craig A. Everett. New York: Haworth.

Kurdeck, Lawrence. 1986. "Custodial Mothers' Perceptions of Visitation and Payment of Child Support by Noncustodial Fathers in Families With Low and High Levels of Preseparation Interparent Conflict." *Journal of Applied "Developmental Psychology* 7:307-23.

Kurz, Demie. 1995. *For Richer, For Poorer: Mothers Confront Divorce.* New York: Routledge.

LaFollette, Hugh. 1992. "Real Men." Pp. 59-74 in *Rethinking Masculinity: Philosophical Explorations in Light of Feminism,* edited by Larry May and Robert Strikwerda. Lanham, MD: Rowman and Littlefield.

Lamb, Michael E., ed. 1981. *The Role of the Father in Child Development.* New York: John Wiley.

———. 1986. "The Changing Roles of Fathers." Pp. 3-28 in *The Father's Role: Applied Perspectives,* edited by Michael E. Lamb. New York: John Wiley.

———. 1987. "Introduction: The Emergent American Father." Pp. 3-25 in *The Father's Role: Cross-Cultural Perspectives,* edited by Michael E. Lamb. Hillsdale, NJ: Lawrence Erlbaum.

Lamb, Michael, Joseph Pleck, and James Levine. 1986. "Effects of Increased Paternal Involvement on Children in Two-Parent Families." Pp. 141-58 in *Men in Families,* edited by Robert A. Lewis and Robert E. Salt. Newbury Park, CA: Sage.

Laqueur, Thomas W. 1993. "The Facts of Fatherhood." Pp. 155-75 in *Rethinking the Family: Some Feminist Questions,* edited by Barrie Thorne with Marilyn Yalom. Boston: Northeastern University Press.

LaRossa, Ralph. 1988. "Fatherhood and Social Change." *Family Relations* 37: 451-57.

LaRossa, Ralph, Linda A. Bennett, and Richard J. Gelles. 1981. "Ethical Dilemmas in Qualitative Family Research." Pp. 95-111 in *The Psychosocial Interior of the Family.* 3rd ed., edited by Gerald Handel. New York: Aldine.

LaRossa, Ralph and Maureen Mulligan LaRossa. 1989. "Baby Care: Fathers vs. Mothers." Pp. 138-54 in *Gender in Intimate Relationships: A Microstructural Approach,* edited by Barbara J. Risman and Pepper Schwartz. Belmont, CA: Wadsworth.

LaRossa, Ralph and Jane H. Wolf. 1985. "On Qualitative Family Research." *Journal of Marriage and the Family* (August):531-40.

Lauer, Robert H. and Warren H. Handel. 1977. *Social Psychology: The Theory and Application of Symbolic Interactionism.* Boston: Houghton Mifflin.

Leehy, Peter. 1991. "The Child Support Standards Act and the New York Judiciary: Fortifying the 17 Percent Solution." *Brooklyn Law Review* 56:1299-1351.

Levine, Robert and Merry White. 1993. "The Social Transformation of Childhood." Pp. 273-93 in *Families in Transition: Rethinking Marriage, Sexuality, Child Rearing, and Family Organization,* edited by Arlene Skolnick and Jerome Skolnick. New York: HarperCollins.

Lewin, Miriam and Lilli M. Tragos. 1987. "Has the Feminist Movement Influenced Adolescent Sex Role Attitudes? A Reassessment After a Quarter Century." *Sex Roles* 16:125-35.

Lewis, Robert A. 1986. "Introduction: What Men Get Out of Marriage and Parenthood." Pp. 11-25 in *Men in Families,* edited by Robert A. Lewis and Robert E. Salt. Newbury Park, CA: Sage.

Lewis, Robert A. and Robert E. Salt, eds. 1986. *Men in Families.* Newbury Park, CA: Sage.

Liljestrom, Rita. 1986. "Gender Systems and the Family." Pp. 132-49 in *Sociology: From Crisis to Science?* Vol. 2, edited by Ulf Himmelstrand. London: Sage.

Lincoln, Yvonna and Egon Guba. 1985. *Naturalistic Inquiry.* Beverly Hills, CA: Sage.

Loewen, J. W. 1986. "A Comparison of Maternal, Paternal, and Joint Custody: Understanding the Varieties of Postdivorce Family Life." *Journal of Divorce* 9:1-12.

———. 1988. "Visitation Fatherhood." Pp. 195-213 in *Fatherhood Today: Men's Changing Role the Family,* edited by Phyllis Bronstein and Carolyn P. Cowan. New York: John Wiley.

Lofland, John. 1978. *Interaction in Everyday Life.* Beverly Hills, CA: Sage.

Luepnitz, Deborah. 1982. *Child Custody: A Study of Families After Divorce.* Lexington, MA: D. C. Heath.

Lyman, Peter. 1987. "The Fraternal Bond as a Joking Relationship: A Case Study of the Role of Sexist Jokes in Male Group Bonding." Pp. 148-64 in *Changing Men: New Directions in Research on Men and Masculinity,* edited by Michael Kimmel. Newbury Park, CA: Sage.

Maccoby, Eleanor E., Charlene E. Depner, and Robert H. Mnookin. 1988. "Custody of Children Following Divorce." Pp. 91-114 in *Impact of Divorce, Single Parenting, and Stepparenting on Children,* edited by E. Mavis Hetherington and Joseph Arasteh. Hillsdale, NJ: Lawrence Erlbaum.

———. 1990. "Coparenting in the Second Year After Divorce." *Journal of Marriage and the Family* 52:141-55.

Magaña, Holly A. and Nancy Taylor. 1993. "Child Custody Mediation and Spouse Abuse: A Descriptive Study of a Protocol." *Family and Conciliation Courts Review* 31:50-64.

Mahoney, Martha R. 1991. "Legal Images of Battered Women: Redefining the Issue of Separation." *Michigan Law Review* 90(1):1-89.

Marcus, Isabel. 1988/89. "Locked In and Locked Out: Reflections on the History of Divorce Law Reform in New York State." *Buffalo Law Review* 37:374-95.

Marotz-Baden, Ramona, G. R. Adams, N. Bueche, R. Munro, and G. Munro. 1979. "Family Form or Family Process? Reconsidering the Deficit Family Model Approach." *Family Coordinator* 28:5-14.

Marsiglio, William. 1991. "Paternal Engagement Activities With Minor Children." *Journal of Marriage and the Family* 53:973-86.

Martin, George. 1990. *Social Policy in the Welfare State.* Englewood Cliffs, NJ: Prentice Hall.

————. 1991. "Family, Gender, and Social Policy." Pp. 323-45 in *The Sociology of Gender: A Text-Reader,* edited by Laura Kraemer. New York: St. Martin's Press.

Martin, Teresa Castro and Larry L. Bumpass. 1989. "Recent Trends in Marital Disruption." *Demography* 26(1):37-51.

May, Larry and Robert Strikwerda. 1992a. "Fatherhood and Nurturance." Pp. 75-92 in *Rethinking Masculinity: Philosophical Explorations in Light of Feminism,* edited by Larry May and Robert Strikwerda. Lanham, MD: Rowman and Littlefield.

————, eds. 1992b. *Rethinking Masculinity: Philosophical Explorations in Light of Feminism.* Lanham, MD: Rowman and Littlefield.

McCracken, Grant. 1988. *The Long Interview.* Newbury Park, CA: Sage.

McIsaac, Hugh. 1981. "Mandatory Conciliation Custory/Visitation Matters: California's Bold Stroke." *Conciliation Courts Review* 19(2):73-77.

McKee, Lorna and Margaret O'Brien. 1983. "Interviewing Men: 'Taking Gender Seriously.' " Pp. 147-59 in *The Public and the Private,* edited by E. Garmarnikow, David Morgan, J. Purvis, and Daphne Taylorson. London: Heinemann.

McLanahan, Sara and Julia Adams. 1987. "Parenthood and Psychological Well-Being." *Annual Review of Immunology* 5:237-57.

McLindon, J. B. 1987. "Separate but Unequal: The Economic Disaster of Divorce for Women and Children." *Family Law Quarterly* 94:130-52.

Mead, George H. 1934. *Mind, Self, and Society.* Chicago: University of Chicago Press.

Mead, Margaret. 1971. "Marriage in Two Steps." *Redbook* (July), 28-33.

Men's Rights Incorporated. 1985. *Are Men's Problems Serious?* [Mimeograph].

Messner, Michael. 1992. "Boyhood, Sports, and the Construction of Masculinities." Pp. 161-75 in *Men's Lives.* 2nd ed., edited by Michael Kimmel and Michael Messner. New York: Macmillan.

Mills, C. Wright. 1959. *The Sociological Imagination.* New York: Oxford University Press.

Milne, Ann. 1988. "The Nature of Divorce Disputes." Pp. 27-44 in *Divorce Mediation: Theory and Practice,* edited by Jay Folberg and Ann Milne. New York: Guilford.

Milne, Ann and Jay Folberg. 1988. "The Theory and Practice of Divorce Mediation: An Overview." Pp. 3-26 in *Divorce Mediation: Theory and Practice,* edited by Jay Folberg and Ann Milne. New York: Guilford.

Milne, Ann, Peter Salem, and Kristin Koeffler. 1993. "When Domestic Abuse Is an Issue." *Family Advocate* (Spring):34-39.

Mnookin, Robert. 1975. "Child Custody Adjudication: Judicial Functions in the Face of Indeterminacy." *Law and Contemporary Problems* 39(3):226-93.

Mnookin, Robert and L. Kornhauser. 1979. "Bargaining in the Shadow of the Law." *Yale Law Journal* 88(950):952-58.

Mnookin, Robert, Eleanor E. Maccoby, Catherine R. Albiston, and Charlene E. Depner. 1990. "Private Ordering Revisited: What Custodial Arrangements Are Parents Negotiating?" Pp. 37-74 in *Divorce Reform at the Crossroads,* edited by Stephen D. Sugarman and Herma Hill Kay. New Haven, CT: Yale University Press.

"The Morgan Case: The Child Is Found." 1990. *Newsweek* (March 5)115:23.

Morgan, David. 1975. *Social Theory and the Family.* London: Routledge & Kegan Paul.

———. 1981. "Men, Masculinity, and the Process of Sociological Inquiry." Pp. 83-113 in *Doing Feminist Research,* edited by Helen Roberts. London: Routledge & Kegan Paul.

———. 1985. *The Family, Politics, and Social Theory.* London: Routledge and Kegan Paul.

———. 1990. "Issues in Critical Sociological Theory: Men in Families." Pp. 67-106 in *Fashioning Family Theory,* edited by Jetze Sprey. Newbury Park, CA: Sage.

Morgan, Leslie. 1991. *After Marriage Ends: Economic Consequences for Mid-Life Women.* Newbury Park, CA: Sage.

Morgan, S. Philip, Diane N. Lye, and Gretchen A. Condran. 1988. "Sons, Daughters, and the Risk of Marital Disruption." *American Journal of Sociology* 94(1):110-29.

Morse, Janice M. 1992. "Strategies for Sampling." Pp. 127-45 in *Qualitative Nursing Research,* edited by Janice M. Morse. Newbury Park, CA: Sage.

Myer, Daniel R. and Steven Garasky. 1992. "Custodial Fathers: Myths, Realities, and Child Support Policy." Discussion Paper, University of Wisconsin–Madison, Institute for Research on Poverty.

National Center for Health Statistics. 1992. *Monthly Vital Statistics Report.* Washington, DC: U.S. Department of Health and Human Services.

National Organization for Changing Men. 1989. "Policy Statement on Child Custody Laws." January 22, Pittsburgh, PA.

New York Child Support Standards Act. 1989. Albany, NY.

Nordstrom, Bruce. 1986. "Why Men Get Married: More and Less Traditional Men Compared." Pp. 31-54 in *Men in Families,* edited by Robert A. Lewis and Robert E. Salt. Newbury Park, CA: Sage.

Norton, Arthur J. and J. E. Moorman. 1987. "Current Trends in Marriage and Divorce Among American Women." *Journal of Marriage and the Family* 49:3-14.

Novinson, Steven. 1983. "Post-Divorce Visitation: Untying the Triangular Knot." *University of Illinois Law Review* 1:121-200.

Oakley, Ann. 1981. "Interviewing Women: A Contradiction in Terms." Pp. 30-61 in *Doing Feminist Research,* edited by Helen Roberts. London: Routledge & Kegan Paul.

O'Connell, Martin and D. E. Bloom. 1987. "Juggling Jobs and Babies: America's Child Care Challenge." *Population Trends and Public Policy Series, No. 12.* Washington, DC: Population Reference Bureau.

Okin, Susan Moller. 1989. *Justice, Gender, and the Family.* New York: Basic Books.

Olesen, Virginia. 1994. "Feminisms and Models of Qualitative Research." Pp. 158-74 in *Handbook of Qualitative Research,* edited by Norman K. Denzin and Yvonna S. Lincoln. Thousand Oaks, CA: Sage.

Ollerich, D., Irwin Garfinkel, and Phillip K. Robins. 1991. "Private Child Support: Current and Potential Impacts." *Journal of Sociology and Social Welfare* 18: 3-23.

Olsen, L. 1983. "The Family and the Market: A Study of Ideology and Legal Reform." *Harvard Law Review* 1495-1562.

Paradise, J., A. Rostain, and M. Nathanson. 1988. "Substantiation of Sexual Abuse Charges When Parents Dispute Custody or Visitation." *Pediatrics* 81:835-39.

Parke, Ross D. 1985. "Foreword." Pp. 9-12 in *Dimensions of Fatherhood,* edited by Shirley M. Hanson and Frederick W. Bozett. Beverly Hills, CA: Sage.

Parkinson, Lisa. 1987. "Fathers and Conciliation Services." Pp. 246-60 in *Reassessing Fatherhood,* edited by Charlie Lewis and Margaret O'Brien. Newbury Park, CA: Sage.

Pasley, Kay and Marilyn Ihinger-Tallman. 1987a. "The Evolution of a Field of Investigation: Issues and Concerns." Pp. 303-14 in *Remarriage and Stepparenting: Current Research and Theory,* edited by Kay Pasley and Marilyn Ihinger-Tallman. New York: Guilford.

———. eds. 1987b. *Remarriage and Stepparenting: Current Research and Theory.* New York: Guilford.

Pateman, Carol. 1989. *The Disorder of Women: Democracy, Feminism, and Political Theory.* Stanford, CA: Stanford University Press.

Patrician, Marty. 1984. "Child Custody Terms: Potential Contributors to Custody Dissatisfaction and Conflict." *Mediation Quarterly* 1(3):41-57.

Pearson, Jessica. 1982. "Mediation: Assumptions, Approaches, and Outcomes." Panel 513 at the 59th annual meeting of the Orthopsychiatric Association, San Francisco, March.

Pearson, Jessica and Nancy Thoennes. 1988. "Divorce Mediation Research Results." Pp. 429-42 in *Divorce Mediation: Theory and Practice,* edited by Jay Folberg and Ann Milne. New York: Guilford.

Perinbanayagam, Robert. 1985. *Signifying Acts: Structure and Meaning in Everyday Life.* Carbondale: Southern Illinois University Press.

———. 1988. "The Meaning of Uncertainty and the Uncertainty of Meaning." *Symbolic Interaction* 9:105-26.

———. 1990. "How to Do Self With Things." Pp. 315-40 in *Beyond Goffman: Studies on Communication, Institutions, and Social Interaction,* edited by Stephen Riggins. Berlin: Mouton-de Grueyer.

Pestello, Frances G. and Patricia Voydanoff. 1991. "In Search of Mesostructure in the Family: An Interactionist Approach to Division of Labor." *Symbolic Interaction* 14(2):105-28.

Pleck, Joseph. 1985. *Working Wives, Working Husbands.* Beverly Hills, CA: Sage.

———. 1987. "American Fathering in Historical Perspective." Pp. 83-97 in *Changing Men: New Directions in Research on Men and Masculinity,* edited by Michael Kimmel. Newbury Park, CA: Sage.

———. 1992a. "Men's Power With Women, Other Men, and Society: A Men's Movement Analysis." Pp. 19-27 in *Men's Lives.* 2nd ed., edited by Michael Kimmel and Michael Messner. New York: Macmillan.

———. 1992b. "Prisoners of Masculinity." Pp. 98-107 in *Men's Lives.* 2nd ed., edited by Michael Kimmel and Michael Messner. New York: Macmillan.

Polatnick, Margaret. 1973. "Why Men Don't Rear Children: A Power Analysis." *Berkeley Journal of Sociology* 18:45-86.

Polikoff, Nancy. 1983. "Gender and Child-Custody Determinations: Exploding the Myths." Pp. 183-202 in *Families, Politics, and Public Policy,* edited by Irene Diamond. New York: Longman.

Polkinghorne, David E. 1988. *Narrative Knowing and the Human Sciences.* Albany: State University of New York Press.

Popenoe, David. 1988. *Disturbing the Nest: Family Change and Decline in Modern Societies.* New York: Aldine de Gruyter.

Presser, Harriet B. 1988. "Shift Work and Child Care Among Young Dual-Earner American Parents." *Journal of Marriage and the Family* 46:551-63.

Raschke, Helen J. 1987. "Divorce." Pp. 597-624 in *Handbook of Marriage and the Family,* edited by Marvin Sussman and Suzanne Steinmetz. New York: Plenum.

Rawls, John. 1971. *A Theory of Justice.* Cambridge, MA: Harvard University Press.

Reinharz, Shulamit with Lynn Davidman. 1992. *Feminist Methods in Social Research.* New York: Oxford University Press.

Rhode, Deborah L., ed. 1990. *Theoretical Perspectives on Sexual Difference.* New Haven, CT: Yale University Press.

Rhode, Deborah L. and Martha Minow. 1990. "Reforming the Questions, Questioning the Reforms: Feminist Perspectives on Divorce Law." Pp. 191-206 in *Divorce Reform at the*

Crossroads, edited by Stephen D. Sugarman and Herma Hill Kay. New Haven, CT: Yale University Press.

Richards, David A. J. 1980. "The Individual, the Family, and the Constitution: A Jurisprudential Perspective." *New York Law Review* 55(1):1-62.

Richardson, Laurel. 1994. "Writing: A Method of Inquiry." Pp. 516-29 in *Handbook of Qualitative Research,* edited by Norman K. Denzin and Yvonna S. Lincoln. Thousand Oaks, CA: Sage.

Richardson, Laurel and Verta Taylor. 1993. *Feminist Frontiers III.* Englewood Cliffs, NJ: Prentice Hall.

Riessman, Catherine Kohler. 1990. *Divorce Talk: Women and Men Make Sense of Personal Relationships.* New Brunswick, NJ: Rutgers University Press.

Riessman, Catherine and Naomi Gerstel. 1985. "Marital Dissolution and Health: Do Males or Females Have Greater Risk?" *Social Science and Medicine* 20: 627-35.

Riley, Glenda. 1991. *Divorce: An American Tradition.* New York: Oxford University Press.

Risman, Barbara. 1989. "Can Men 'Mother'? Life as a Single Father." Pp. 155-64 in *Gender in Intimate Relationships: A Microstructural Approach,* edited by Barbara J. Risman and Pepper Schwartz. Belmont, CA: Wadsworth.

Risman, Barbara and Pepper Schwartz. 1989. "Being Gendered: A Microstructural View of Intimate Relations." Pp. 1-9 in *Gender in Intimate Relationships: A Microstructural Approach,* edited by Barbara J. Risman and Pepper Schwartz. Belmont, CA: Wadsworth.

Robins, Phillip K. 1989. "Why Are Child Support Award Amounts Declining?" Discussion Paper 885-59, Institute for Research on Poverty, University of Wisconsin–Madison.

Roman, Mel and William Haddad. 1978. *The Disposable Parent: The Case for Joint Custody.* New York: Holt, Rinehart, and Winston.

Rosenblum, Karen. 1990. "The Conflict Between and Within Genders: An Appraisal of Contemporary American Femininity and Masculinity." *Sociological Inquiry* 56(1):46-61.

Rossi, Alice and Peter Rossi. 1990. *Of Human Bonding: Parent-Child Relations Across the Life Course.* New York: Aldine de Gruyter.

Rotundo, E. Anthony. 1985. "American Fatherhood: A Historical Perspective." *American Behavioral Scientist* 29:7-25.

Rubin, Gayle. 1975. "The Traffic in Women: Notes on the 'Political Economy of Sex' " Pp. 157-210 in *Toward an Anthropology of Women,* edited by Rayna Reiter. New York: Monthly Review Press.

Rubin, Lillian. 1976. *Worlds of Pain: Life in the Working-Class Family.* New York: Basic Books.

———. 1983. *Intimate Strangers: Men and Women Together.* New York: Harper & Row.

Ruddick, Sara. 1983. "Preservative Love and Military Destruction: Some Reflections on Mothering and Peace." In *Mothering: Essays in Feminist Theory,* edited by Joyce Trebilcot. Totowa, NJ: Rowan and Allanheld.

———. 1993. "Thinking About Fathers." Pp. 176-90 in *Rethinking the Family: Some Feminist Questions,* edited by Barrie Thorne with Marilyn Yalom. Boston: Northeastern University Press.

Russell, Diana E. H. 1986. *The Secret Trauma: Incest in the Lives of Girls and Women.* New York: Basic Books.

Saldeen, David. 1992. "Sweden: Property, Maintenance and State Support." *Journal of Family Law* 30:409-15.

Sandelowski, Margarete, Diane Holditch-Davis, and Betty Glenn Harris. 1992. "Using Qualitative and Quantitative Methods: The Transition to Parenthood of Infertile Couples." Pp. 301-11 in *Qualitative Methods in Family Research,* edited by Jane Gilgun, Kerry Daly, and Gerald Handel. Newbury Park, CA: Sage.

Sattel, Jack. 1976. "The Inexpressive Male: Tragedy or Sexual Politics." *Social Problems* 23(4):469-77.

Scanzoni, John. 1982. *Sexual Bargaining: Power Politics in the American Marriage.* 2nd ed. Chicago: University of Chicago Press.

Schatzman, Leonard and Anselm Strauss. 1973. *Field Research: Strategies for a Natural Sociology.* Englewood Cliffs, NJ: Prentice Hall.

Schneider, Elizabeth M. 1990. "The Dialectic of Rights and Politics: Perspectives From the Women's Movement." Pp. 226-49 in *Women, the State, and Welfare,* edited by Linda Gordon. Madison: University of Wisconsin Press.

———. 1991. "The Dialectic of Rights and Politics: Perspectives From the Women's Movement [1986]." Pp. 318-22 in *Feminist Legal Theory: Readings in Law and Gender,* edited by Katharine T. Bartlett and Roseanne Kennedy. Boulder, CO: Westview.

Schor, Juliet B. 1992. *The Overworked American: The Unexpected Decline of Leisure.* New York: Basic Books.

Schorr, Lisbeth B. with Daniel Schorr. 1989. *Within Our Reach: Breaking the Cycle of Disadvantage.* New York: Doubleday.

Schuman, D. 1986. "False Allegations of Physical and Sexual Abuse." *Bulletin of the American Academy of Psychiatry and Law* 14:5-21.

Schwandt, Thomas. 1994. "Constructivist, Interpretivist Approaches to Human Inquiry." Pp. 118-37 in *Handbook of Qualitative Research,* edited by Norman K. Denzin and Yvonna S. Lincoln. Thousand Oaks, CA: Sage.

Schwenger, Peter. 1989. "The Masculine Mode in Speaking of Gender." Pp. 101-12 in *Speaking of Gender,* edited by Elaine Showalter. New York: Routledge.

Scott, Elizabeth S. and Robert Emery. 1987. "Child Custody Dispute Resolution: The Adversarial System and Divorce Mediation." Pp. 23-56 in *Psychology and Child Custody Determinations,* edited by Lois Weithorn. Lincoln: University of Nebraska Press.

Scott, Joan. 1988. *Gender and the Politics of History.* New York: Columbia University Press.

Seidler, Victor J. 1989. *Recreating Masculinity: Reason, Language, and Sexuality.* London: Routledge.

———. 1991. *Recreating Sexual Politics: Men, Feminism and Politics.* London: Routledge.

———. 1992. "Men, Feminism, and Power." Pp. 209-20 in *Rethinking Masculinity: Philosophical Explorations in Light of Feminism,* edited by Larry May and Robert Strikwerda. Lanham, MD: Rowman and Littlefield.

Seltzer, Judith A. 1991a. "Legal Custody Arrangements and Children's Economic Welfare." *American Journal of Sociology* 94(4):898-929.

———. 1991b. "Relationships Between Fathers and Children Who Live Apart: The Father's Role After Separation." *Journal of Marriage and the Family* 53(1):79-101.

Seltzer, Judith A. and Suzanne M. Bianchi. 1988. "Children's Contact With Absent Parents." *Journal of Marriage and the Family* 50:663-77.

Seltzer, Judith A. and Yvonne Brandreth. 1994. "What Fathers Say About Involvement With Children After Separation." *Journal of Family Issues* 15:49-77.

Seltzer, Judith A. and Irwin Garfinkel. 1990. "Inequality in Divorce Settlements: An Investigation of Property Settlements and Child Support Awards." *Social Science Research* 19:82-111.

Seltzer, Judith A., Nora Cate Schaeffer, and Hong-Wen Charng. 1989. "Family Ties After Divorce: The Relationship Between Visiting and Paying Child Support." *Journal of Marriage and the Family* 51:1013-32.

Sheffield, Carole J. 1987. "Sexual Terrorism: The Social Control of Women." Pp. 154-70 in *Analyzing Gender: A Handbook of Social Science Research,* edited by Beth B. Hess and Myra Marx Ferree. Newbury Park, CA: Sage.

Sherman, Robert and Rodman Webb. 1988. *Qualitative Research in Education: Focus and Methods.* London: Falmer Press.

Sidel, Ruth. 1990. *On Her Own: Growing Up in the Shadow of the American Dream.* New York: Viking.

————. 1992. *Women and Children Last.* 2nd ed. New York: Penguin.

Sigler, Robert T. 1989. *Domestic Violence in Context: An Assessment of Community Attitudes.* Toronto: Lexington Books.

Skolnick, Arlene. 1991. *Embattled Paradise: The American Family in an Age of Uncertainty.* New York: Basic Books.

Skolnick, Arlene and Jerome Skolnick. 1994. "Introduction: Family in Transition." Pp. 1-18 in *Families in Transition: Rethinking Marriage, Sexuality, Child Rearing, and Family Organization.* 8th ed., edited by Arlene Skolnick and Jerome Skolnick. New York: HarperCollins.

Smelser, Neil. 1963. *Theory of Collective Behavior.* New York: Free Press.

Spanier, Graham and Linda Thompson. 1984. *Parting: The Aftermath of Separation and Divorce.* Beverly Hills, CA: Sage.

Sprey, Jetze. 1990. "Theoretical Practice in Family Studies." Pp. 9-33 in *Fashioning Family Theory,* edited by Jetze Sprey. Newbury Park, CA: Sage.

Stanley, Liz and Sue Wise. 1983. *Breaking Out: Feminist Consciousness and Feminist Research.* Boston: Routledge and Kegan Paul.

Stoltenberg, John. 1989. *Refusing to Be a Man.* Portland, OR: Breitenbush.

Stone, Gregory. 1962. "Appearance and Self: A Slightly Revised Version." Pp. 86-118 in *Human Nature and Social Process,* edited by Arnold M. Rose. Boston: Houghton Mifflin.

Straus, Murray. 1991. "Discipline and Deviance: Physical Punishment of Children and Violence and Other Crime in Adulthood." *Social Problems* 38(2):133-55.

Straus, Murray, Richard Gelles, and Suzanne Steinmetz. 1980. *Behind Closed Doors: Violence in the American Family.* Garden City, NY: Anchor.

Strauss, Anselm. 1978. *Negotiations.* San Francisco: Jossey-Bass.

————. 1987. *Qualitative Analysis in the Social Sciences.* Cambridge, UK: Cambridge University Press.

Strauss, Anselm and Juliet Corbin. 1990. *Basics of Grounded Theory: Grounded Theory Procedures and Techniques.* Newbury Park, CA: Sage.

————. 1994. "Grounded Theory Methodology: An Overview." Pp. 273-85 in *Handbook of Qualitative Research,* edited by Norman K. Denzin and Yvonna S. Lincoln. Thousand Oaks, CA: Sage.

Sugarman, Stephen D. 1990. "Introduction." Pp. 1-5 in *Divorce Reform at the Crossroads,* edited by Stephen D. Sugarman and Herma Hill Kay. New Haven, CT: Yale University Press.

Sugarman, Stephen D. and Herma Hill Kay, eds. 1990. *Divorce Reform at the Crossroads.* New Haven, CT: Yale University Press.

Swidler, Ann. 1980. "Love and Adulthood in American Culture." Pp. 120-50 in *Themes of Work and Love in Adulthood,* edited by Neil J. Smelser and Erik Erikson. Cambridge, MA: Harvard University Press.

————. 1986. "Culture in Action—Symbols and Strategies." *American Sociological Review* 51:273-86.

Tannen, Deborah. 1990. *You Just Don't Understand: Men and Women in Conversation.* New York: Ballantine Books.

Taylor, Steven J. and Robert Bogdan. 1984. *Introduction to Qualitative Research Methods: The Search for Meanings.* New York: John Wiley.

Teachman, Jay. 1991a. "Contributions to Children by Divorced Fathers." *Social Problems* 38:358-71.

———. 1991b. "Who Pays? Receipt of Child Support in the United States." *Journal of Marriage and the Family* 53:759-72.

Tepp, Alan. 1983. "Divorced Fathers: Predictors of Continued Paternal Involvement." *American Journal of Psychiatry* 140:1445-60.

Terkel, Studs. 1992. *Race: How Blacks and Whites Think and Feel About the American Obsession.* New York: New Press.

Therborn, Goran. 1992. "Children's Rights and Patriarchy." Public Lecture, November, University of Wisconsin–Madison.

Thoennes, Nancy and Jessica Pearson. 1988. "Summary of Findings From the Sexual Abuse Allegations Project." Pp. 1-22 in *Sexual Abuse Allegations,* edited by E. Bruce Nicholson. Washington, DC: American Bar Association.

Thomas, Darwin and Jean E. Wilcox. 1987. "The Rise of Family Theory: A Historical and Critical Analysis." Pp. 81-102 in *Handbook of Marriage and the Family,* edited by Murray Sussman and Suzanne Steinmetz. New York: Plenum.

Thomas, W. I. and Dorothy Thomas. 1928. *The Child in America.* New York: Alfred A. Knopf.

Thompson, Linda. 1992. "Conceptualizing Gender in Marriage: The Case of Marital Care." *Journal of Marriage and the Family* 54:3-18.

———. 1993. "Feminist Methodology for Family Studies." *Journal of Marriage and the Family* 55:557-69.

Thompson, Linda and Alexis Walker. 1989. "Gender in Families: Women and Men in Marriage, Work, and Parenthood." *Journal of Marriage and the Family* 51:845-71.

Thompson, Ross A. 1986. "The Father's Case in Child Custody Disputes: The Contributions of Psychological Research." Pp. 53-87 in *Men in Families,* edited by Robert A. Lewis and Robert E. Salt. Newbury Park, CA: Sage.

Thorne, Barrie. 1982. "Feminist Rethinking of the Family." Pp. 1-24 in *Rethinking the Family: Some Feminist Questions.* 1st ed., edited by Barrie Thorne and Marilyn Yalom. New York: Longman.

———. 1993. "Feminism and the Family: Two Decades of Thought." Pp. 3-30 in *Rethinking the Family: Some Feminist Questions.* 2nd ed., edited by Barrie Thorne and Marilyn Yalom. New York: Longman.

Thornton, Arland. 1989. "Changing Attitudes Toward Family Issues in the United States." *Journal of Marriage and the Family* 51:873-93.

Tronto, Joan. 1989. "Women and Caring: What Can Feminists Learn About Morality From Caring?" Pp. 172-87 in *Gender/Body/Knowledge: Feminist Reconstructions of Being and Knowing,* edited by Alison M. Jaggar and Susan R. Bordo. New Brunswick, NJ: Rutgers University Press.

Trost, Jan E. and Orjan Hultaker. 1986. "Legal Changes and the Role of Fathers: Swedish Experiences." Pp. 85-97 in *Men's Changing Roles in the Family,* edited by Robert A. Lewis and Marvin B. Sussman. New York: Haworth.

Tushnet, Mark. 1984. "An Essay on Rights." *Texas Law Review* 62(8):1363-1403.

Uchitelle, Louis. 1993. "Three Decades of Dwindling Hope for Prosperity." *New York Times,* May 9: 1A.

Uhlenberg, Peter, Teresa Cooney, and Robert Boyd. 1990. "Divorce for Women After Midlife." *Journal of Gerontology: Social Sciences* 45:S3-S11.

U.S. Bureau of the Census. 1990. *Current Population Reports, 1987.* Series P-23, No. 167, "Child Support and Alimony: 1987." Washington, DC: Government Printing Office.

————. 1991. *Current Population Reports, 1989.* Series P-60, No. 173, "Child Support and Alimony: 1989." Washington, DC: Government Printing Office.

————. 1992. *Statistical Abstracts of the United States, 1988.* "National Data Book and Guide to Sources." Washington, DC: Government Printing Office.

U.S. Congress. 1990. *The Violence Against Women Act of 1990.* Report No. 101-545. Washington, DC: Government Printing Office.

————. 1991. *The Violence Against Women Act of 1991.* Report No. 102-197. Washington, DC: Government Printing Office.

————. 1992. *Senate Bill* 1002. Washington, DC: Government Printing Office.

U.S. Department of Labor, Bureau of Labor Statistics. 1991. *Employment and Earnings.* January. Washington, DC: Government Printing Office.

Vaughan, Diane. 1986. *Uncoupling: Turning Points in Relationships.* New York: Oxford University Press.

Velicer, Wayne F., Lorraine H. Huckel, and Catherine E. Hansen. 1989. "A Measurement Model for Measuring Attitudes Toward Violence." *Personality and Social Psychology Bulletin* 15:349-84.

————. 1989. "Parenting Coalitions After Remarriage: Dynamics and Therapeutic Guidelines." *Family Relations* 38:65-70.

Wadlington, Walter. 1990. *Cases and Other Materials on Domestic Relations.* 2nd ed. Westbury, NY: Foundation Press.

Wallerstein, Judith and Sandra Blakeslee. 1989. *Second Chances: Men, Women, and Children a Decade After Divorce.* New York: Ticknor and Fields.

Wallerstein, Judith and Shauna B. Corbin. 1986. "Father-Child Relationships After Divorce: Child Support and Educational Opportunity." *Family Law Quarterly* 20(2):109-28.

Wallerstein, Judith and Joan Kelly. 1980. *Surviving the Break-Up: How Children and Parents Cope With Divorce.* New York: Basic Books.

Walzer, Michael. 1983. *Spheres of Justice.* New York: Basic Books.

Warren, Carol. 1989. *Gender Issues in Field Research.* Newbury Park, CA: Sage.

Watzlawick, P., ed. 1984. *The Invented Reality: Contributions to Constructivism.* New York: Norton.

Weber, Max, 1947. *The Methodology of the Social Sciences*, trans. Edward A. Shils and Henry A. Finch. Glencoe, IL: Free Press.

Weedon, Chris. 1987. *Feminist Practice and Poststructuralist Theory.* New York: Basil Blackwell

Weisel, Martha S., ed. 1989. "Divorce Litigation: Custody, Property, Support." *Divorce Litigation* 1(7):1-8.

Weiss, Robert S. 1987. "Men and Their Wives' Work." Pp. 109-24 in *Spouse, Parent, Worker: On Gender and Multiple Roles,* edited by Faye Crosby. New Haven, CT: Yale University Press.

————. 1990. *Staying the Course: The Emotional and Social Lives of Men Who Do Well at Work.* New York: Free Press.

Weitzman, Lenore. 1985. *The Divorce Revolution: The Unexpected Social and Economic Consequences for Women and Children in America.* New York: Free Press.

————. 1988. "Child Support Myths and Reality." Pp. 251-76 in *Child Support: From Debt Collection to Social Policy,* edited by Alfred Kahn and Sheila Kamerman. Newbury Park, CA: Sage.

West, Candace and Don H. Zimmerman. 1987. "Doing Gender." *Gender & Society* 1:125-51.

Wharton, Amy. 1991. "Structure and Agency in Socialist-Feminist Theory." *Gender & Society* 5:373-89.

Whitehead, Barbara DaFoe. 1993. "Dan Quayle Was Right." *Atlantic Monthly* 271(4):47-84.

Williams, Frank S. 1988. "Child Custody and Parental Cooperation." *Joint Custodian* (January):1-6.

Wiseman, Jacquelyn. 1979. *Stations of the Lost: The Treatment of Skid Row Alcoholics.* Chicago: University of Chicago Press.

Wolchik, Sharlene A., Sanford L. Braver, and Irwin N. Sandler. 1985. "Maternal Versus Joint Custody: Children's Postseparation Experiences and Adjustment." *Journal of Clinical Child Psychology* 14(1):5-10.

Wolfe, Alan. 1989. *Whose Keeper? Social Science and Moral Obligation.* Berkeley: University of California Press.

Zald, Mayer N. and John D. McCarthy, eds. 1979. *The Dynamics of Social Movements.* Cambridge, MA: Winthrop.

Zaretsky, Eli. 1976. *Capitalism, the Family, and Personal Life.* New York: Harper & Row.

Zaslow, Martha. 1988. "Sex Differences in Children's Response to Parental Divorce. Part 1: Research Methodology and Postdivorce Family Forms." *American Journal of Orthopsychiatry* 58(3):355-78.

Zill, Nicholas. 1988. "Behavior, Achievement, and Health Problems Among Children in Stepfamilies: Findings From a National Survey of Child Health." Pp. 325-68 in *Impact of Divorce, Single Parenting, and Stepparenting on Children,* edited by E. Mavis Hetherington and Joseph D. Arasteh. Hillsdale, NJ: Lawrence Erlbaum.

Zimmerman, Shirley. 1988. *Understanding Family Policy: Theoretical Approaches.* Newbury Park, CA: Sage.

———. 1992. *Family Policies and Family Well-Being: The Role of Political Culture.* Newbury Park, CA: Sage.

Zimring, Franklin. 1990. "Foreword." Pp. vi-viii in *Divorce Reform at the Crossroads,* edited by Stephen D. Sugarman and Herma Hill Kay. New Haven, CT: Yale University Press.

Zinn, Maxine Baca. 1989. "Family, Feminism, and Race in America." *Gender & Society* 4:68-82.

INDEX

ABOUT THE AUTHOR

Terry Arendell is Associate Professor and Chair of the Department of Sociology and Anthropology at Colby College. Between 1989 and 1994 she was on the faculty at Hunter College, Department of Sociology. Her interests include interpretive sociology, family, gender, feminist theory, and qualitative research methods. She is the author of *Mothers and Divorce: Legal, Economic, and Social Dilemmas* and has published recently in the journals *Symbolic Interaction, Gender & Society,* and *Family Advocate*. Her work in progress includes an edited volume on contemporary parenting, using a social constructionist perspective.